The Economics
of Corporate Finance

THE ECONOMICS
OF CORPORATE FINANCE

SEYMOUR FRIEDLAND

Joel Dean Associates, Inc.,
Professor of Economics and Business
Claremont Graduate School

PRENTICE-HALL, INC., Englewood Cliffs, New Jersey

[1966]

Library of Congress Catalog Card No. 65-18497

Printed in the United States of America C-22988

Current Printing (last digit):
10 9 8 7 6 5 4 3 2 1

PRENTICE-HALL INTERNATIONAL, INC., *London*
PRENTICE-HALL OF AUSTRALIA, PTY. LTD., *Sydney*
PRENTICE-HALL OF CANADA, LTD., *Toronto*
PRENTICE-HALL OF INDIA (PRIVATE) LTD., *New Delhi*
PRENTICE-HALL OF JAPAN, INC., *Tokyo*

TO GLORIA WITH LOVE

Preface

Since World War II, the contents of the first course in corporate finance has gradually shifted from legal and institutional description, to an emphasis on analytic techniques for financial management. The shift has been desirable in that it has made finance appear relevant for others than those involved in the Wall Street variety of high finance. The apparent irrelevance of the descriptive approach to finance was only one and, perhaps, a minor criticism of the older approach. More important is the near-aimlessness of a series of legal and institutional descriptions. The analytic approach to finance has not met this criticism. There exists today an impressive array of analytic techniques ranging from straightforward analysis of accounting ratios through the rarified environment of operations research. A course oriented toward techniques of analysis runs the danger of becoming simply a series of technique descriptions—as aimless intellectually as the institutional approach appeared to be. This is a real danger and is illustrated by the theme of many finance course texts, roughly describable as "What every financial manager should know."

The objection is not necessarily to the "how-to-do-it" aspects of the modern finance course. Students respond to what appear to be practical approaches, although many of the techniques included in a modern finance course are as yet rarely found in business practice. The objection is not to what the course contains, but to what is omitted.

The omission is a framework for analysis on which can be hung the various analytic approaches *and* the more traditional institutional materials. What are the advantages of this framework? For students planning to take only the first course in finance, the framework is a key to general understanding, and general understanding is the aim of a survey course. For finance majors, the development of an over-all analytic framework is a device which can be used to integrate the more specialized advanced courses to be taken later, hopefully resulting in a comprehensive knowledge of finance, rather than a miscellaneous collection of snippets of knowledge.

To be fair, it should be admitted that most authors of finance texts and many teachers have an implicit framework of analysis. But the student rarely gets this, particularly in the first course when it is most important. The purpose in writing this book, then, is the explicit development of such a framework for financial analysis.

The framework consists of treating the firm as if it were trying to choose an optimal balance sheet. If risk were ignored, this would be virtually identical to the problem posed in micro-economic theory, that is, the optimal balance sheet in a certain world would be one which maximized the present value of the firm's profit stream. Without risk, however, most of the interesting financial problems disappear.

With the addition of risk, the relationships among individual assets, the asset portfolio, and the capital structure become very complex, even with the very simple basic asset decision models used in the text. Nonetheless, students with background in elementary statistics and economics should have no difficulty at a technical level. For the basic asset models, no mathematical competence is required beyond what is normally given in high school algebra. It should be noted, however, that the individual asset models can be replaced with much more sophisticated models and yet retain the general framework.

The contents of Part I develop for each of the major assets—fixed assets, inventory, accounts receivable, cash, and marketable securities—the use of a decision model which involves a simple go-no go decision device. If the expected addition to the value of the ownership interest resulting from the decision is positive, the decision is to invest (or disinvest if that is the problem posed). Proposals involving negative increments to net worth are rejected. Risk is introduced by considering the variance of the probability distribution of increments to the ownership interest. The asset portfolio, or combination of assets, is determined by comparing the over-all risk and return of the asset mix to the preference function of the firm with respect to risk and return.

In part II the effect of the various kinds of capital structure decisions (debt vs. equity, long- vs. short-term debt, etc.) on the expected income stream generated by the asset portfolio are analyzed. The combination of the characteristics of the asset portfolio and the requirements of different kinds of capital structures with firm preferences between risk and return generate the optimal balance sheet.

Part III contains material which is unusual in a corporate finance text, namely, the development of the social accounting system used by the Federal Reserve called the flow-of-funds. The accounting system is related to a theoretical model of an economy without financial institutions. Then, the effect of financial institutions are considered. This is followed by three chapters describing the major financial institutions of the United States economy and their relationship to the corporation. Finally, the growth pattern of the corporate nonfinancial sector of the economy is analyzed during the post-war period.

The materials of part III have been included for two reasons. Clearly, one's understanding of corporate finance is incomplete without some knowledge of the over-all economic environment in which firms make financial decisions. Traditionally, discussions of financial markets and institutions have been reserved for courses in money and banking. My own experience has been that students fail to carry this knowledge into the corporate finance class. Partly, perhaps, this is because money and banking courses mainly deal with problems of monetary and fiscal policy, although there has been a recent renewal of interest in the role of financial institutions. Further, many undergraduate business schools have moved to replace the traditional money and banking course with courses in the new disciplines, such as behavioral sciences, that have become so important in business school curricula. Most graduate business programs do not require separate courses in money and banking or financial institutions. Thus, more and more students come into the first corporate finance course with virtually no knowledge of either the money or capital markets and, for those who have had some exposure, the exposure doesn't really "take." If my experience is typical, most instructors are already spending a substantial portion of the course discussing financial institutions, the determination of interest rates, etc.

I have tried, however, to do something more than just add six chapters dealing with macro-financial problems to a corporate finance text. If it is possible to gain understanding of corporate finance by treating the corporation as an entity seeking an optimal balance sheet, why not treat other entities, such as households, commercial banks, life insurance companies, etc., in the same way? More specifically, the knowledge of corporate finance developed in Parts I and II can be applied to other economic units with surprisingly little modification. In effect, Part III is an attempt to demonstrate the breadth of generality of the framework developed in detail in Parts I and II.

Inevitably, a textbook reflects the author's needs and tastes, even though no two instructors have the same needs and tastes. It is, therefore, prudent to make the book as flexible as possible. To a large extent, the three sections are independent. There is, however, little flexibility within a section. It is difficult to understand Chapter 3 without understanding Chapter 2. One exception is in Part III, which has been written so that Chapter 11, which describes the flow-of-funds accounting system, and Chapter 12, which presents a sectoral model of the flow-of-funds, can both be omitted without affecting the ability of the student to understand the remainder of the section. It is even possible to omit Chapter 12 alone.

Various versions of this book have been multilithed and used in undergraduate and graduate classes in the Claremont Colleges. It may be useful to pass on some of the better experiences that the instructors in Claremont have had. Going right through the book from Chapter 1 through Chapter 16 makes for a busy semester, although life would be less hectic if the book were used over two quarters. Written problems, cases, and term papers were assigned and completed very satisfactorily even though there was no time for extensive class room discussion. Despite the pace in the introductory course, the students did quite well later in advanced courses.

The first ten chapters were also used in combination with one of the better-known case books. Because the course combined lectures with case discussion, only eight cases were covered, but these were the more difficult cases and went easy well. Graduate and undergraduate students have had good responses to the book, but, in all fairness, at least part of this was probably due to the fact that I was either teaching the course, or the students knew that the material had been written by a member of their faculty.

Like any author, I am, if only unintentionally, something of an intellectual thief. To the best of my ability, I have tried to acknowledge my debts in the readings list that follows each chapter. The suggestions and criticisms of Professor Richard S. Bower, The Amos Tuck School of Business Administration, Dartmouth College; Professor James K. Kindahl, Amherst College; Professor Richard Lesher, Ohio State University; Professor Ezra Solomon, Stanford University who carefully read various versions of this manuscript were extremely helpful. The remaining faults are the result of my own stubborness.

Although readers will undoubtedly note some errors in the arithmetic examples, they will fail to note the number of times I have managed to get one and one to add up to two. Credit for the correct answers goes to the many students who, regardless of their motives, were kind enough to work through the arithmetic examples and correct my errors. Much thanks must also go to (Mrs.) Terry Wagner who carefully typed the "final" version and then retyped the revisions. As any family man who has tried to write a book or article at home knows, there is one large debt as yet unacknowledged. But it is too large an obligation for the preface and so I have saved it for the dedication page.

SEYMOUR FRIEDLAND
Claremont, California

Table of Contents

Part III: The Financial Economy

THE ASSET PORTFOLIO

PART

I

Introduction

1

Financial management is the study of economic units, such as firms or households, from a particular point of view. We see economic units as decision makers, concerned with the kinds and quantities of assets (things of value) that they will hold and the means by which they will finance (raise the money for) the acquisition of these assets. The means of finance may involve a change in asset composition, such as reducing the asset cash by $5,000 in order to buy a machine costing $5,000. Or the total of assets may be increased by either borrowing money, which results in a liability, or increasing the ownership investment, i.e., an increase in net worth, or equity.

For example, imagine a household with a $20,000 checking account as its only asset and with no liabilities, making net worth $20,000. If the household purchases a $20,000 house, it can finance the purchase by using the checking account only, by borrowing part of the purchase price of the house and using the checking account to finance the remainder of the price, or by borrowing the entire $20,000, if a willing lender can be found, and leaving the checking account intact.

The three alternatives and the original situation, which is also an alternative, are shown in Table 1-1 in the form of balance sheets. The problem of financial management is to try to explain the process by which the economic unit decides which of the four balance sheets is best, or optimal, for it. Why might an increase in liabilities be undesirable? Or why might the household prefer not to exhaust its cash balance completely?

This example of balance sheet choice is much simpler than the problems of choice facing most economic units. The household in the example has

Table 1-1

1(a)

ORIGINAL BALANCE SHEET FOR HOUSEHOLD

Cash $20,000	Liabilities $0
Total assets 20,000	Net worth 20,000
	Total liabilities and net worth.. 20,000

1(b)

AFTER NO BORROWING

Cash $0	Liabilities $0
House 20,000	Net worth 20,000
Total assets 20,000	Total liabilities and net worth.. 20,000

1(c)

AFTER BORROWING $15,000

Cash $15,000	Liabilities $15,000
House 20,000	Net worth 20,000
Total assets 35,000	Total liabilities and net worth.. 35,000

1(d)

AFTER BORROWING $20,000

Cash $20,000	Liabilities $20,000
House 20,000	Net worth 20,000
Total assets 40,000	Total liabilities and net worth.. 40,000

---

only to choose, on the asset side, between holding cash, a house, or some combination of cash and house. In reality, choices would extend over a host of other asset types and combinations of assets. On the liability side of the balance sheet, the household can only choose between equity or a combination of debt and equity financing, whereas there may be different kinds of debt available, such as short-term debt, maturing within a year, all the way to very long-term mortage financing that might not mature for 30 years. Other kinds of economic units, such as business firms, have additional alternatives to financing, as by adding to net worth in a variety of ways.

Thus the problem of explaining how economic units choose balance sheets is difficult. To ease the task somewhat, certain economic units will be excluded from consideration. If households, governments, and nonprofit institutions, such as churches, colleges, and foundations, are omitted, the number of units to be treated is reduced by literally millions. Not only is the problem simplified quantitatively, but we have also reduced the kinds of behavior that must be explained. The motivations of households or colleges are presumably quite different from the motivations of business firms, which last are all that remain. Eliminating nonbusinesses leaves us a much more homogeneous group of economic units to analyze.

The problem, however, is still formidable. There are over eleven million business organizations in the United States. More than ten million of these are unincorporated, either sole proprietorships or partnerships. Unlike corporations, such organizations are not legally distinct from their owners. The single proprietor and the members of a partnership must include their net income from business, whether the net income is distributed to the owners or reinvested in the business, as personal income for tax purposes. A corporation can issue fractional shares of ownership called *common stock*. The purchaser of these shares normally cannot lose more than he paid for the shares, whereas an owner investor in a partnership or a sole proprietorship may forfeit his personal assets to satisfy business creditors under certain conditions. This will not normally occur in a corporation because the corporation is a legal entity apart from its owners. Because of the various legal limitations of the partnership and sole proprietorship, these forms of organization find it difficult to raise large amounts of capital, and it is also not easy for them to delegate managerial authority within the organization. As a result, they are usually small. Although over 90 per cent of all business organizations are partnerships and sole proprietorships, these organizations account for only 25 per cent of the total receipts of all business firms. The elimination from consideration of unincorporated enterprises means that we shall be primarily concerned with medium and large firms.

Financial corporations will not be considered. Such corporations include banks, insurance companies, and investment banking firms. Their assets are almost completely the liabilities of other economic units. Also, many financial corporations have legal limits both on the types of assets they may hold and on the means by which they finance the acquisition of assets. Although it is awkward to discuss the inventory and equipment decisions of nonfinancial corporations and simultaneously consider the securities purchases of life insurance companies, many of the principles discussed for nonfinancial corporations will be applicable to financial corporations as well. The financial corporation will reenter the study later when the sources of funds available to the nonfinancial business corporation are treated.

Finally, the almost sixteen thousand corporations whose major activities involve farming, fishing, or forestry will be omitted. This omission is more for the sake of statistical convenience than for substantive reasons. Most of the data used to illustrate and support the analysis separate farms from nonfinancial, nonfarm, corporate businesses but do not differentiate between noncorporate and corporate farms. Of course, most of the farming enterprises have been eliminated already since over 36 million unincorporated businesses are engaged in farming, fishing, or forestry.

THE SIGNIFICANCE OF BUSINESS
CORPORATIONS: CAPITAL EXPENDITURES

Having eliminated some fifty-three million households, more than ten million unincorporated businesses, over one hundred and two thousand governmental units, about ninety-four thousand financial corporations, and sixteen thousand farm corporations, to say nothing of the nonprofit institutions, there are only somewhat more than nine hundred and fifty thousand nonfinancial, nonfarm business corporations remaining. But this remaining group is very important. As shown in Table 1-2, the over 950,000 nonfinancial, nonfarm business corporations spent almost $40 billion in 1961 on investment goods, placing this sector of the economy second only to the consumer sector, almost three times more significant in capital expenditures than the noncorporate business group, which was the next most important business sector.

Table 1-2

PRIVATE CAPITAL EXPENDITURES
BY TYPE OF EXPENDITURE AND SECTOR, 1963
(In Billions of Dollars)

Sector	Consumer Durable Goods	Nonfarm Residential Construction	Plant and Equipment	Changes in Inventories	Totals
Consumer and nonprofit	51.5	17.9	3.9	—	73.3
Nonfinancial business					
Farm	—	—	5.1	0.3	5.4
Noncorporate	—	—	14.1	0.4	14.5
Corporate	—	3.6	32.4	3.9	39.9
Government	—	—	—	—	—
Financial					
Commercial banking	—	—	0.4	—	0.4
Insurance	—	—	0.3	—	0.3
Other financial institutions..	—	—	—	—	—
Rest of world	—	—	—	—	—
Totals..................	51.5	21.5	56.2	4.6	133.8

Source: *Federal Reserve Bulletin*, Board of Governors of the Federal Reserve System, Apr., 1964.

Why are these expenditures important? Capital expenditures affect gross national product (GNP), the final value of all goods and services produced annually in the United States. There is a complex interaction between GNP and capital expenditures. Generally, as capital expenditures increase, GNP rises.

A simple example may make the point. Assume that each economic unit in the country spends 90 cents out of each dollar increment to the income of the economic unit. Each dollar of capital expenditure made by corporations is income to whomever the corporations pay it. If corporations spend an additional $10 for capital goods, and the recipients of the $10 spend 90 per cent of the $10 increment to their incomes, they will spend $9. However, those who receive the $9 as increments to income will also spend 90 per cent of the increment, or $8.10. Ninety per cent of the $8.10 will be spent by whomever receives it, and, as a result, they will add $7.29 to their spending. And so it will go with each successive recipient spending 90 per cent of the diminishing increment to income. The total effect on spending and GNP will approach 10 times the original increment to spending, or $100. This is a simplified illustration of what is known as the *multiplier effect*. The value of the multiplier in the example is 10, but it depends upon the actual proportion spent of an increment to income, and this has been the center of considerable controversy among economists.

The reaction just described shows the effect of increased capital expenditures on GNP. Changes in GNP also may have an effect upon capital expenditures. Suppose that a firm requires $3 of capital goods in order to produce $1 of output. A $10 increase in output demanded will generate a $30 increase in capital expenditures as the firm expands productive facilities to meet the increase in demand. In reality, this relationship, which is called the *acceleration principle* or *derived demand*, is much more complex. If the firm has excess productive capacity before the increase in demand, there may be no impact on investment. Further, the relationship between the firm's stock of capital and output is apparently not constant. A given stock of capital may produce a wide range of outputs, although perhaps at varying per unit out-of-pocket costs. The latter point suggests that only in the long run would investment in capital goods be related to changes in GNP, or demand for output. Empirical studies of the behavior of business investment verify this suggestion. Table 1-3 shows GNP and the capital expenditures of nonfinancial, nonfarm business corporations from 1948 through 1963.

No value judgment can be made generally on whether a rise in the capital expenditures of business corporations is good or bad. When the economy suffers from unemployment of labor and capital, a rise in capital expenditures is desirable. When the economy is fully employed, however, an increase in capital expenditures can result in price and wage inflation.

To an individual firm, the choice of composition and quantity of capital expenditures can mean the difference between success and failure. The conservative decision not to expand plant or inventories can turn out to be wise under some conditions, but can result in lost sales if demand is strong. Of course, deciding to invest is no guarantee of success either. Even with the best forecasting and control devices, the firm can find itself with excess inventories, subject to obsolescence, or with unnecessary and expensive plant facilities. The firm must make important investment decisions facing an

Table 1-3

GROSS NATIONAL PRODUCTS* AND PRIVATE CAPITAL EXPENDITURES
OF NONFINANCIAL, NONFARM BUSINESS CORPORATIONS†

Year	GNP (In Billions of Dollars)	Private Capital Expenditures (In Billions of Dollars)
1948	259.4	19.6
1949	258.1	13.8
1950	284.6	21.7
1951	329.0	28.7
1952	347.0	23.6
1953	365.4	23.7
1954	363.1	20.2
1955	397.5	29.0
1956	419.2	34.4
1957	442.8	33.1
1958	444.2	23.9
1959	482.7	34.1
1960	503.4	33.6
1961	518.7	31.1
1962	556.2	37.5
1963	583.9	39.9

*From *Survey of Current Business*, Department of Commerce.
†From *Flow of Funds Accounts*, 1945–'62, 1963 *Supplement*, Board of Governors of the Federal Reserve System, pp. 56–57; and Federal Reserve Bulletin, April, 1964.

uncertain and perilous future. In this study, the problems of forecasting will receive little attention. Emphasis will be on means of utilizing forecasts so that, in the light of the best information available, the firm can make rational decisions.

INVESTMENT AND FINANCIAL ACTIVITIES

Capital expenditures involve just what the name implies, i.e., spending for capital goods such as plant, equipment, and inventories. The financial aspect of capital expenditures involves, in part, simply acquiring the money needed for the capital expenditures. Table 1-4 summarizes the means used by nonfinancial business corporations to finance capital expenditures for the period 1948 through 1963.

The most important source of financing is gross savings, shown in column (3), which consists of two parts: current profits reinvested in the firm, shown as retained earnings in column (1); and that portion of operating expenses representing the value of plant and equipment which, it is estimated, was used up in current production. The estimate is known as depreciation and will be discussed in detail later. For now, it is sufficient to note that the estimate of depreciated plant and equipment is deducted from revenues in

Table 1-4

THE FINANCING OF CAPITAL EXPENDITURES FOR NONFINANCIAL BUSINESS CORPORATIONS, 1948-1963
(In Billions of Dollars)

Year	Retained Earnings (1)	Capital Consumption (2)	Gross Savings (3) = (1) + (2)	Capital Expenditures (4)	Other Sources (5) = (4) − (3)	Other Uses (6) = (3) − (4)
1948	11.4	7.4	18.8	19.6	0.8	−0.8
1949	7.5	8.2	15.7	13.8	1.9	1.9
1950	15.4	9.1	24.5	21.7	2.8	2.8
1951	13.9	10.5	24.5	28.7	4.2	−4.2
1952	4.9	11.9	16.8	23.6	6.8	−6.8
1953	7.4	13.6	21.0	23.7	2.7	−2.7
1954	2.7	15.2	17.9	20.2	2.3	−2.3
1955	11.8	17.7	29.5	29.0	−0.5	0.5
1956	5.5	19.3	24.9	34.4	9.5	−9.5
1957	5.2	21.2	26.3	33.1	6.8	−6.8
1958	3.1	22.1	25.2	23.9	−1.3	1.3
1959	11.6	23.6	35.2	34.1		
1960	5.0	24.8	29.7	33.6	3.9	−3.9
1961	6.0	26.1	32.1	31.1	−1.1	1.1
1962	6.5	30.1	36.6	37.5	0.9	−0.9
1963	8.6	31.8	40.3	39.9	−0.4	0.4

Source: *Flow of Funds Accounts*, 1945–62, 1963 Supplement, Board of Governors of the Federal Reserve System; and *Federal Reserve Bulletin*, April, 1964.

determining income and net savings for firms. Thus, net savings are reduced by the amount of depreciation. However, depreciation does not reduce the cash resulting from sales. It is just a bookkeeping charge. Therefore, net savings understates the cash from normal operations, which firms can use to finance capital expenditures by the amount of depreciation charged. In addition to depreciation, capital consumption also includes the value of plant and equipment destroyed by fire or accident during the period. Again, this deduction does not reflect cash actually spent during the period. If the firm does replace destroyed equipment, this appears in the capital expenditures accounts. Thus, the total of net savings and capital consumption allowances constitutes the funds available for investment purposes that have been generated internally, i.e., from the operations of the firm. The total of net savings and capital consumption allowances is called *gross savings*.

In column (4), private capital expenditures (copied from Table 1-3) are shown. The most striking point is that internally generated funds almost equal capital expenditures for every year. Only a very small portion of capital expenditures of nonfinancial business corporations are financed by funds other than those generated internally. It must be remembered whenever we speak of the "nonfinancial corporate sector," the sector does not represent any given or average firm. Some firms undoubtedly have financed a substantial portion of capital expenditures from other than internally generated funds. Further, the *sector* is a consolidation of all the firms within the sector. This means that all transactions between firms are eliminated from the data, including the elimination of all interfirm financial transactions in which one firm borrows from or sells ownership shares to another firm.

Column (5) shows the annual amount of financing undertaken from sources other than those resulting from gross savings. These *external* sources do not necessarily represent increased indebtedness or sale of ownership securities. A firm can finance the difference between what it needs for capital goods and what it has saved by reducing cash balances or by selling other financial assets, such as government notes. The firm has a variety of alternatives available for financing the excess of capital expenditures over savings.

In several years, capital expenditures were less than gross savings, as indicated by the minus sign preceding the number in column (5). These surpluses of savings over expenditures occur because the firm does not have attractive investment opportunities in capital goods available at the time. The surpluses can be used to reduce indebtedness, to purchase securities, or to increase the firm's cash balance. The last two alternatives involve investment in financial assets as opposed to capital expenditures. A financial asset is a claim on some economic unit other than the investing firm. Cash, for example, is a claim on some bank, if held in the form of checking accounts, or on the national government, if held as currency.

Column (6) is identical to column (5), except that the signs preceding the numbers have been reversed. Instead of subtracting gross savings from capital expenditures in order to determine how much of the financing of capital expenditures must be raised from sources other than savings, we subtract capital expenditures from gross savings to determine the amount of savings used to finance things other than capital expenditures. This particular intepretation of the difference between capital expenditures and gross savings is used by the Federal Reserve Board in preparing flow-of-funds estimates published in the *Federal Reserve Bulletin.* The firm may be viewed as deciding how to distribute its savings. The alternatives are to change the level or composition of real assets, such as inventory or plant and equipment; to change the level or composition of financial assets, i.e., claims on others such as cash, accounts receivable (the money owed to the firm by other firms, usually resulting from a sale of merchandise on credit), or securities issued by other economic units; to change the level or composition of the firm's financial liabilities and ownership; or to achieve some combination of the three preceding alternatives.

Column (6) may be interpreted not only as gross savings — capital expenditures, but also as change in financial assets — (change in liabilities + change in net worth other than retained earnings). This difference, shown in column (6), is called *net financial investment.* When net financial investment is positive, the firm has not only financed all of its capital expenditures through gross savings, but has also either increased holdings of financial assets or reduced liabilities, or both. The algebraic sum of investment in capital goods and net financial investment must logically equal gross savings. Thus, Table 1-4 reflects in broad terms the aggregate balance sheet decisions made by corporate businesses over a 16-year period.

BALANCE SHEETS

Normal accounting balance sheets value assets on the basis of the original cost of the asset. An asset which costs $1,000 is valued at $1,000. The liabilities and net worth record the portions of the costs of the assets that were purchased using respectively creditors' money and owners' money. This method of measuring the variables that make up the balance sheet is extremely useful for a variety of purposes. It is inadequate, however, in one important respect. It provides no information about why a particular balance sheet has been chosen.

When a firm spends $1,000 to acquire an asset, there is only one thing we know about the real value of that asset to the firm. The asset must be worth more to the firm than $1,000. If the asset generates large earnings, its value can be much more than $1,000. The firm would not spend $1,000 on an asset which is worth less as used by the firm. At this point, let us ignore the problems of measuring the earnings value of assets and concentrate on the difference between balance sheets which value assets on a cost basis and those which value assets on an earnings basis.

The earnings value of assets will be equal to, or larger than, the cost value. Suppose that the house discussed in Table 1-1 has an earnings value of $25,000. On an earnings basis, the balance sheet shown in Table 1-1(c), in which $15,000 is borrowed, would be rewritten as follows:

Cash	$15,000	Liabilities	$15,000
House	25,000	Net worth	25,000
Total assets	$40,000	Total liabilities and net worth..	$40,000

Since the claims of creditors are fixed in money terms by lending agreements made between the household and the lender, the difference between the cost value and the earnings value of the house is credited to the owner.

Thus, the bookkeeping rules for the two kinds of balance sheets are the same. The only difference is the method of asset valuation. Under normal accounting rules, the earnings of an asset are not added to net worth until the earnings are realized. With the valuation based on earnings, the earnings are anticipated in the valuation.

The justification for using two different valuation methods will become obvious in later chapters. Essentially, the earnings valuation provides us with the framework of a balance sheet in which complex investment and financing decision rules can be developed more conveniently and with greater clarity than otherwise.

WHAT LIES AHEAD

A review of the ex-post record of the balance sheet decisions is interesting and can be informative. However, it does not yield direct information on how the individual firm makes such decisions. This study will attempt to answer the following questions among others:

How does the firm decide on the division of investment between capital expenditures and financial assets?

How does the firm decide more specifically, on the composition of its assets, i.e., should it invest in inventory, plant and equipment, accounts receivable, cash, the securities of other economic units, or what?

What are the determinants of gross savings for the firm, i.e., what determines the level of capital consumption, profits, and dividends?

How does the firm arrive at its capital structure, i.e., what makes the firm choose at different times to finance via ownership funds and debt, between retained earnings and stock issues, or between long-term and short-term debt?

What interrelationships, if any, are there between the capital structure, the cost of funds, and the level or composition of the firm's investment in assets?

Part 1 of this text will be concerned primarily with the determinants of the investment in assets. Four major asset groups will be studied separately: plant and equipment, inventory, accounts receivable, and cash. In order to be reasonably realistic in the discussion, the assets must be considered in terms not only of profitability, but of risk and impact on cash flow.

For example, a firm may face two investment alternatives. The first could involve expending immediately $1,000,000 with a 50/50 chance of receiving a $2,000,000 return or a $500,000 loss within a week. The rate of return on this investment would have an even chance of being either $+200$ per cent ($\$2,000,000/\$1,000,000$) or -50 per cent ($-\$500,000/\$1,000,000$). The expected return, which is the average of the two possible, or conditional, returns weighted by the probability of each occurring is 75 per cent, i.e.,

$$\frac{\$2,000,000 \times 0.5 + -\$500,000 \times 0.5}{\$1,000,000}.$$

The alternative might be an expenditure of $100,000 generating a possible return of $20,000 or of $10,000 with both returns being equally likely. The second investment might then return either 20 or 10 per cent, with the expected return of 15 per cent. Even though the first investment is more profitable than the second, there are at least two reasons for the firm's preferring the second. First, the more profitable investment may return a very large profit, but it may also return a very high loss. In other words, the first investment could be riskier, and the firm may prefer the assurance of at least a 10 per cent return on investment to a 50 per cent chance of losing $500,000. Second, the firm may be unable to raise the $1,000,000 required for the first investment. In order to study the three aspects of asset investment, it will be necessary to consider the over-all impact of investments on the balance sheet, as well as the individual assets.

Part 2 will focus attention on the choice of capital structure and the interrelationships between capital structure and asset investment. Again, we cannot assume that firm will always choose the cheapest kind of financing. The cheapest financing may be very risky or involve repayment with much greater rapidity than the firm can finance.

As an example of risk, consider the problem of debt financing vs. equity. Debt financing is borrowing. The firm is legally required to pay interest on the debt as required by the debt agreement, regardless of whether the firm has earned the interest through its operations. In addition, the firm is obligated to repay the debt at a specified time or, with demand notes, when the creditor requires repayment. Thus debt constitutes a fixed charge against earnings, regardless of the level of earnings, as well as a cash drain when it must be repaid. Equity financing is the sale of ownership shares. While a firm cannot long exist if it fails to pay something to equity holders, there is usually no legal requirement with the associated threat of involuntary liquidation of the firm. A firm with highly fluctuating earnings might well prefer expensive, but less risky, equity financing to cheap, but risky, debt financing.

To illustrate the cash drain problem that can be created by inappropriate financing decisions, the firm may be faced with two kinds of debt financing. The first might be very cheap, but have to be repaid within three months. The second might be more expensive, but not involve repayment for five years. Under these conditions, a firm may choose the more expensive, longer term financing because the amount of cash generated by the firm's operations is too small to finance the repayment of the shorter maturity debt.

Parts 1 and 2 can be thought of as the "microfinancial" elements of corporate finance, i.e., problems are viewed from the perspective of the individual firm. In Part 3 finance will be viewed from the perspective of the entire economy, i.e., the approach will be "macrofinancial." An aggregate approach permits us to analyze the results of the economy's savings-investment process not only on the corporate sector, but on the level and growth of GNP. To understand this process, we shall consider the structure and behavior of financial institutions, households, government, and international trade as well as the role of corporations.

Managing
Fixed Investments

2
Fixed investments represent assets that are expected to have a useful life of several years. Expenditures on fixed assets have averaged over 90 per cent of total capital expenditures by nonfinancial business corporations annually for the last decade. These expenditures include the acquisition of such assets as machinery, buildings, and land, but differ from capital expenditures, which include inventory investment as well as expenditures on fixed assets.

The relative importance of fixed assets varies from industry to industry. Generally, those firms involved in altering the physical characteristics of a good require a larger fixed asset investment per dollar of sales than do firms which produce services or are primarily engaged in the distribution of physical goods, as is indicated in Table 2-1. This table also shows that small firms typically have a smaller fixed asset investment per dollar of sales than do large firms.

Although it digresses from our main point, the inverse of the ratio used in Table 2-1, i.e., sales divided by fixed assets, can be interpreted as a measure of the effectiveness with which a firm utilizes its fixed capital. The table provides an implicit warning to the user of the *fixed asset turnover ratio* (as it is called): valid judgments on how fully a firm utilizes fixed capital depends upon the basis of comparison. It is meaningless to compare fixed asset turnover ratios between manufacturing firms and wholesalers, or between very large and very small firms. Indeed, it makes little sense to compare the ratio for the same firm at different points in time, if one point of time occurs

Table 2-1

FIXED ASSETS (NET OF DEPRECIATION) DIVIDED
BY BUSINESS RECEIPTS FOR BUSINESS CORPORATIONS,
BY SELECTED INDUSTRIES AND ASSET-SIZE CLASSES, 1960

	INDUSTRY				
Size Class of Assets	Mining	Con-struction	Manu-facturing	Public Utilities	Wholesale and Retail Trade
$1–25,000	0.44	0.05	0.09	0.13	0.05
$25,000–$50,000	0.30	0.06	0.12	0.24	0.06
$50,000–$100,000	0.48	0.07	0.12	0.28	0.06
$100,000–$250,000	0.46	0.09	0.12	0.38	0.06
$250,000–$500,000	0.56	0.09	0.12	0.43	0.05
$500,000–$1,000,000	0.63	0.08	0.12	0.45	0.05
$1,000,000–$2,500,000	0.69	0.09	0.14	0.49	0.05
$2,500,000–$5,000,000	0.78	0.09	0.16	0.57	0.05
$5,000,000–$10,000,000	0.83	0.08	0.19	0.70	0.06
$10,000,000–$25,000,000	0.99	0.16	0.22	1.23	0.06
$25,000,000–$50,000,000	1.02	0.14	0.27	1.44	0.06
$50,000,000–$100,000,000	1.16	0.20	0.28	1.65	0.08
$100,000,000–$250,000,000	0.87	0.30	0.28	2.16	0.10
$250,000,000–and up	0.98	—	0.37	2.33	0.08
Total, all sizes	0.86	0.09	0.26	1.83	0.06

Source: *Statistics of Income: Corporation Income Tax Returns*, 1960–1961, U. S. Gov.
Printing Office.

in a period of prosperity and the other in a recession. Sales fluctuate more sharply and rapidly than does the level of fixed assets.

The last point illustrates the major problem involved in fixed asset decisions. The firm must decide to invest or not today. Yet most of the useful life of the asset will occur in the future when business conditions can be much different than currently. To be sure, the firm can dispose of fixed assets which turn out to be unprofitable, but often only at a loss. Further, the decision not to invest, which can be as disastrous as a bad investment, is often impossible to correct. Only the future can judge the wisdom of any asset decision, especially a fixed asset decision.

Let it be admitted at the onset, we have no secrets to pass on about forecasting the future. As was said in the first chapter, this study is concerned with the means by which the future forecast is interpreted so as to make rational current decisions.

EVALUATING FIXED ASSET
INVESTMENT OPPORTUNITIES

A fixed asset opportunity may be viewed as a series of cash inflows and outflows over several accounting periods. Inflows represent such things as the increments to profit which it is hoped will be generated if the investment is undertaken. A more precise definition of cash inflows will be presented later in the chapter. Outflows represent the initial cost of purchasing and installing fixed assets, maintenance costs, and other expenditures which will result if the investment is made.

In this section, we are concerned with the technical problem of how to evaluate and compare these long-term investment opportunities. The reason for special concern with the technical problem can be illustrated as follows: If a firm were considering an asset which would cost $100 to acquire and would generate a cash inflow of $110 for a single period with no returns beyond the single period, the profitability can be calculated quite easily. A $10 gain over the $100 investment will be made and this can be called a 20 per cent return on the average amount invested. It is clear that another asset which also costs $100 but would generate $110 in the first period and $10 for a second period would be more desirable than the single-period investment. However, it is less clear how to measure the gain. Suppose that a third opportunity would cost $100 initially and would generate $60 per period for two periods. Which of these assets is most profitable? Calculating the profitability of assets which generate returns over several time periods is more difficult than it is to determine the profitability of single-period return assets.

THE AVERAGE RATE OF PROFIT

This is a relatively simple device for calculating the rate of return on fixed assets. The formula is

$$(2\text{-}1) \qquad r_a = \frac{S - D}{(1/2)C}$$

where S is the annual earnings expected from the asset before deducting the cost of that part of the asset which has been used up or depreciated during the year; D is an estimate of the depreciation and is the original cost of the asset divided by its expected life; and C is the original cost or cash outflow in order to acquire the fixed asset. Since part of S is the value of annual depreciation, the firm will receive back part of its original investment C each year and, over the life of the investment, will have invested $(1/2)C$. Thus Eq. (2-1) is simply the ratio of the net return from the asset divided by the average amount invested.

Using the three investment opportunities referred to above, the average rate of profit will be,
for the first opportunity,

$$0.20 = \frac{\$110 - \$100}{50};$$

for the second opportunity,

$$S = \frac{\$110 + \$10}{2} = \$60, \qquad D = \frac{\$100}{2} = \$50,$$

and

$$r_a = \frac{\$60 - \$50}{\$50} = 0.20;$$

for the third opportunity,

$$\frac{\$60 - \$50}{\$50} = 0.20.$$

The illustrations indicate a major drawback to the average rate of profit. It is not sensitive to the fact that the second opportunity is identical to the first, except that the second generates an added $10. Also, it did not differentiate between the second project and the third. Generally, the average rate of profit formula is insensitive to variations in the timing of inflows, or receipts.

Why is this important? Assume that the firm can earn 3 per cent per annum interest by depositing funds in a savings account. With the second investment opportunity, the firm could deposit $110 at the end of the first year and earn 3 per cent on it during the second year. At the end of the second year, the firm would have the $110 deposited at the end of the first year, $3.30 interest on the $110, plus $10 received from the investment during the second year, or a total of $123.30. With the third investment opportunity, the firm could deposit $60 in the savings account at the end of the first year, earn $1.80 on the deposit during the second year, which, added to the $60 generated by the investment during the second year, would give the firm a total of $121.80 at the end of the second year. Thus, as long as the firm can invest cash at a positive interest rate, when the asset generates returns is as important as the total amount of returns generated.

THE TIMING OF RETURNS

We have shown that, given the same original cost and total dollar return, as was the case with the second and third investment opportunities, the firm prefers to receive funds early rather than late. More generally, when all other things are equal, the firm prefers returns which are generated in the near future. Using this principle, it is obvious that the second opportunity is better than the third.

The phrase *all other things equal* is vital. Rarely are all other things equal. Compare investment opportunity 2 with an investment also costing $100, but generating a return of $55 at the end of the first year and $70 at the end of the second year. Assuming the firm can deposit the first year's return to earn 3 per cent the value of the second investment opportunity will be $123.30 at the end of the second year as calculated earlier. The value of the new opportunity will be $55 + 0.03($55) + $70 = $126.65 at the end of the second year. However, if the firm could find an opportunity to reinvest the returns generated by the fixed asset, that would yield 10 per cent instead of 3 per cent, the value of the investment which generates $110 the first year and $10 the second would be $110 + 0.10($110) + $10 = $131 at the end of the second year. The value of the funds generated by the new invest-ment would be only $130.50. In short, the relative desirability of a fixed asset will be determined not only by the relationships of the inflows S to cost C and the time distribution of the inflows, but also by the rate of return on the reinvestment of the inflows.

THE PAY-OFF PERIOD

This is an alternate criterion which firms may use in determining which fixed asset investments to undertake. It measures the length of time needed before the inflows from an investment equal the cost of the investment. Investments are ranked according to in-creasing payoff period and, the shorter the payoff period, the better the investment. When the annual inflows are constant, the payoff period may be calculated as follows:

$$(2\text{--}2) \qquad\qquad \frac{C}{S} = \frac{1}{r_p},$$

where the left-hand term is the payoff period, and r_p is the inverse of the payoff period, called the *payoff ratio*. The payoff ratio, because it is measured in the same units as a rate of return, is sometimes preferred to the payoff period, which is measured in fractions of time.

The three examples of investment possibilities used before were

1. $C = \$100$, $S_1 = \$110$ with no other returns;
2. $C = \$100$, $S_1 = \$110$, $S_2 = \$10$ with no other returns;
3. $C = \$100$, $S_1 = \$60$, $S_2 = \$60$ with no other returns.

The first investment returns inflows which equal cost in 0.909 year ($r_p = 1.10$). The second investment also has a payoff period of 0.909 year. The payoff period for the third investment is 1.67 years and the payoff ratio is 0.60. As with the average rate of return, the payoff period criterion does not discriminate between the first and second investments, despite the fact that investment 2 is superior to the first investment. Investment 3 is less desirable than investment 2, which is correct. But, as indicated in the previous section, investment 3 may be superior to investment 1 when the rate of return on reinvestment of inflows is low, but will be inferior when the rate is high. The short-comings of the payoff period criterion are that it fails to consider the over-all stream of returns, considering only returns to the point at which returns equal original cost; and that it does not consider the rate which the firm will earn on the reinvestment of the inflows.

THE INTERNAL RATE
OF RETURN

Objections which have been raised to the use of the average rate of profit and the payoff ratio are met by the internal rate of return. It con-siders the time distribution of the full range of forecast inflows and makes a specific assumption about the rate at which funds are reinvested.

To define the internal rate of return, it is useful to digress and discuss first the concept of present value. This digression will turn out to be very much to the point and not a digression at all.

Suppose you were offered the opportunity to buy a security which promised to pay $10 at the end of one year. Assuming you believed the promise, what is the maximum price you should be willing to pay for the security today in order to receive a return of 10 per cent on the amount invested?

First, define terms. The maximum amount you would be willing to pay will be called *gross present value* V'. The gross return from the investment, or $10, will be called S, as before. The 10 per cent rate of return, i, is the minimum rate of interest acceptable.

Given the symbols above, the price you would be willing to pay must be able to fulfill the conditions $S = V' + iV'$, i.e., the gross return must be large enough to include both the original investment and interest on the investment. This may be rewritten

$$S = V'(1 + i),$$

and by multiplying both sides of the equation by $1/(1 + i)$, we have

$$V' = S\frac{1}{1+i}.$$

Thus, the maximum price would be

$$\$9.09 = \$10(0.909).$$

Next, suppose you were offered a security which would pay $10 in two years' time. What would be the maximum price you would be willing to pay for this security to make no less than 10 per cent on the amount invested? Using the same symbols, except that the return will be called S_2, to indicate the two-year wait, $S_2 = V' + 2iV' + i(iV')$, i.e., the $10 must include the original investment V'; interest on the investment for two years, $2iV'$; and interest for the second year on the interest earned, but not paid, during the first year, $i(iV')$. This equation may be rewritten

$$S_2 = V' + 2iV' + i^2 V',$$

and, factoring V',

$$S_2 = V'(1 + 2i + i^2),$$

which is

$$S_2 = V'(1 + i)^2.$$

Multiplying both sides of the equation by $1/(1 + i)^2$, we have

$$V' = S_2\frac{1}{(1 + i)^2}.$$

The answer for the problem posed is then

$$\$8.26 = \$10(0.826)$$

The problem of determining the gross present value of a single future payment can be generalized as

(2-3)
$$V' = S_n \frac{1}{(1 + i)^n},$$

where n refers to the number of years before the payment is to be received.

To simplify the calculation, a table of $1/(1 + i)^n$ values is presented in Table 2-2. The column heads show the rates used, and the row captions indicate the number of years.

Now suppose you were offered a security promising to pay $10 at the end of one year and another $10 at the end of the second year. Still assuming that i is 10 per cent, what price would you be willing to pay? Obviously, the answer is $9.09 + $8.26 = $17.35. In other words, to find the gross present value of an investment providing returns for several periods, we simply set

(2-4)
$$V' = S_1 \frac{1}{1 + i} + S_2 \frac{1}{(1 + i)^2} + \cdots + S_n \frac{1}{(1 + i)^n}.$$

When all of the annual returns are equal, Eq. (2-4) becomes

(2-5)
$$V' = S \left[\frac{1}{1 + i} + \frac{1}{(1 + i)^2} + \cdots + \frac{1}{(1 + i)^n} \right],$$

i.e., the gross present value is nothing more than the sum of the $1/(1 + i)$ values for the relevant number of years, multiplied by the constant S value. To ease the calculations, the summation of the $1/(1 + i)$ terms is presented in Table 2-3 for different expected lives (n) and interest rates. At the intersection of $i = 0.10$ and $n = 2$, the summation of $1/(1 + i)$ is 1.736, so that the present value of a security promising $10 a year for two years is $1.736 \times \$10 = \$17.36$, where the 1-cent difference between the answer derived earlier, and this one is due to rounding.

To determine the internal rate of return for an asset, the question asked is somewhat different from that asked for present value. For present value, we know the future returns and the desired interest rate and would like to determine the value of the asset in present dollars. For the internal rate of return, we know the future returns S and the cost of the asset in current dollars C and want to determine the rate of return r. Replacing V' with C and i with r, Eq. (2-3) is rewritten

(2-6)
$$C = S_n \frac{1}{(1 + r)^n}$$

Table 2-2

$$\frac{1}{(1+i)^n} \quad \text{FOR VARIOUS VALUES OF } i \text{ AND } n$$

n	1%	2%	4%	6%	8%	10%	12%	14%	15%	16%	18%	20%	22%	24%	25%	26%	28%	30%	35%	40%	45%	50%
1	0.990	0.980	0.962	0.943	0.926	0.909	0.893	0.877	0.870	0.862	0.847	0.833	0.820	0.806	0.800	0.794	0.781	0.769	0.741	0.714	0.690	0.667
2	0.980	0.961	0.925	0.890	0.857	0.826	0.797	0.769	0.756	0.743	0.718	0.694	0.672	0.650	0.640	0.630	0.610	0.592	0.549	0.510	0.476	0.444
3	0.971	0.942	0.889	0.840	0.794	0.751	0.712	0.675	0.658	0.641	0.609	0.579	0.551	0.524	0.512	0.500	0.477	0.455	0.406	0.364	0.328	0.296
4	0.961	0.924	0.855	0.792	0.735	0.683	0.636	0.592	0.572	0.552	0.516	0.482	0.451	0.423	0.410	0.397	0.373	0.350	0.301	0.260	0.226	0.198
5	0.951	0.906	0.822	0.747	0.681	0.621	0.567	0.519	0.497	0.476	0.437	0.402	0.370	0.341	0.328	0.315	0.291	0.269	0.223	0.186	0.156	0.132
6	0.942	0.888	0.790	0.705	0.630	0.564	0.507	0.456	0.432	0.410	0.370	0.335	0.303	0.275	0.262	0.250	0.227	0.207	0.165	0.133	0.108	0.088
7	0.933	0.871	0.760	0.665	0.583	0.513	0.452	0.400	0.376	0.354	0.314	0.279	0.249	0.222	0.210	0.198	0.178	0.159	0.122	0.095	0.074	0.059
8	0.923	0.853	0.731	0.627	0.540	0.467	0.404	0.351	0.327	0.305	0.266	0.233	0.204	0.179	0.168	0.157	0.139	0.123	0.091	0.068	0.051	0.039
9	0.914	0.837	0.703	0.592	0.500	0.424	0.361	0.308	0.284	0.263	0.225	0.194	0.167	0.144	0.134	0.125	0.108	0.094	0.067	0.048	0.035	0.026
10	0.905	0.820	0.676	0.558	0.463	0.386	0.322	0.270	0.247	0.227	0.191	0.162	0.137	0.116	0.107	0.099	0.085	0.073	0.050	0.035	0.024	0.017
11	0.896	0.804	0.650	0.527	0.429	0.350	0.287	0.237	0.215	0.195	0.162	0.135	0.112	0.094	0.086	0.079	0.066	0.056	0.037	0.025	0.017	0.012
12	0.887	0.788	0.625	0.497	0.397	0.319	0.257	0.208	0.187	0.168	0.137	0.112	0.092	0.076	0.069	0.062	0.052	0.043	0.027	0.018	0.012	0.008
13	0.879	0.773	0.601	0.469	0.368	0.290	0.229	0.182	0.163	0.145	0.116	0.093	0.075	0.061	0.055	0.050	0.040	0.033	0.020	0.013	0.008	0.005
14	0.870	0.758	0.577	0.442	0.340	0.263	0.205	0.160	0.141	0.125	0.099	0.078	0.062	0.049	0.044	0.039	0.032	0.025	0.015	0.009	0.006	0.003
15	0.861	0.743	0.555	0.417	0.315	0.239	0.183	0.140	0.123	0.108	0.084	0.065	0.051	0.040	0.035	0.031	0.025	0.020	0.011	0.006	0.004	0.002
16	0.853	0.728	0.534	0.394	0.292	0.218	0.163	0.123	0.107	0.093	0.071	0.054	0.042	0.032	0.028	0.025	0.019	0.015	0.008	0.005	0.003	0.002
17	0.844	0.714	0.513	0.371	0.270	0.198	0.146	0.108	0.093	0.080	0.060	0.045	0.034	0.026	0.023	0.020	0.015	0.012	0.006	0.003	0.002	0.001
18	0.836	0.700	0.494	0.350	0.250	0.180	0.130	0.095	0.081	0.069	0.051	0.038	0.028	0.021	0.018	0.016	0.012	0.009	0.005	0.002	0.001	0.001
19	0.828	0.686	0.475	0.331	0.232	0.164	0.116	0.083	0.070	0.060	0.043	0.031	0.023	0.017	0.014	0.012	0.009	0.007	0.003	0.002	0.001	
20	0.820	0.673	0.456	0.312	0.215	0.149	0.104	0.073	0.061	0.051	0.037	0.026	0.019	0.014	0.012	0.010	0.007	0.005	0.002	0.001	0.001	
21	0.811	0.660	0.439	0.294	0.199	0.135	0.093	0.064	0.053	0.044	0.031	0.022	0.015	0.011	0.009	0.008	0.006	0.004	0.002	0.001		
22	0.803	0.647	0.422	0.278	0.184	0.123	0.083	0.056	0.046	0.038	0.026	0.018	0.013	0.009	0.007	0.006	0.004	0.003	0.001	0.001		
23	0.795	0.634	0.406	0.262	0.170	0.112	0.074	0.049	0.040	0.033	0.022	0.015	0.010	0.007	0.006	0.005	0.003	0.002	0.001			
24	0.788	0.622	0.390	0.247	0.158	0.102	0.066	0.043	0.035	0.028	0.019	0.013	0.008	0.006	0.005	0.004	0.003	0.002	0.001			
25	0.780	0.610	0.375	0.233	0.146	0.092	0.059	0.038	0.033	0.024	0.016	0.010	0.007	0.005	0.004	0.003	0.002	0.001	0.001			
26	0.772	0.598	0.361	0.220	0.135	0.084	0.053	0.033	0.026	0.021	0.014	0.009	0.006	0.004	0.003	0.002	0.002	0.001				
27	0.764	0.586	0.347	0.207	0.125	0.076	0.047	0.029	0.023	0.018	0.011	0.007	0.005	0.003	0.002	0.002	0.001	0.001				
28	0.757	0.574	0.333	0.196	0.116	0.069	0.042	0.026	0.020	0.016	0.010	0.006	0.004	0.002	0.002	0.002	0.001	0.001				
29	0.749	0.563	0.321	0.185	0.107	0.063	0.037	0.022	0.017	0.014	0.008	0.005	0.003	0.002	0.002	0.001	0.001	0.001				
30	0.742	0.552	0.308	0.174	0.099	0.057	0.033	0.020	0.015	0.012	0.007	0.004	0.003	0.002	0.001	0.001	0.001	0.001				
40	0.672	0.453	0.208	0.097	0.046	0.022	0.011	0.005	0.004	0.003	0.001	0.001										
50	0.608	0.372	0.141	0.054	0.021	0.009	0.003	0.001	0.001													

in order to determine the internal rate of return. Equations (2–4) and (2–5) can be rewritten in a similar fashion.

Turning to the three investment alternatives which were used in the discussion of the average rate of return and the payoff ratio, the internal rate of return for the first investment may be determined by solving the equation

$$\$100 = \$110 \frac{1}{1+r}.$$

Although a direct algebraic approach is possible, all investment proposals are not as simple as those used for illustrative purposes. Therefore, we shall utilize the same techniques that would be necessary for a more complex problem. Dividing both sides of the equation by $110,

$$\frac{\$100}{\$110} = \frac{1}{1+r}, \quad \text{or} \quad 0.909 = \frac{1}{1+r}.$$

Turning to Table 2-2 and moving along the row for $n = 1$, we find that $1/(1 + r) = 0.909$ in the 10 per cent column. Therefore $r = 0.10$.

Let us skip over the second investment for a moment and estimate the internal rate of return for the third investment. In Eq. (2–5), substitute C for V' and r for i. Using the data for the third investment, we have

$$\$100 = \$60 \left[\frac{1}{1+r} + \frac{1}{(1+r)^2} \right]$$

or

$$\frac{\$100}{\$60} = 1.667 = \frac{1}{1+r} + \frac{1}{(1+r)^2}.$$

In Table 2-3, in the $n = 2$ row, we find that the summations of $1/(1 + r)$ terms coming close to 1.667 occur for $r = 12$ per cent, where the summation is 1.690, and for $r = 14$ per cent, where the summation is 1.647. The internal rate of return then is approximately 13 per cent for the third investment proposal.

To determine the rate for the second investment, again C is substituted for V' and r for i in Eq. (2–4). Plugging in the data, the equation is

$$\$100 = \$110 \frac{1}{1+r} + \$10 \frac{1}{(1+r)^2}.$$

This equation may be solved algebraically. However, algebraic solutions become less accurate and finally almost impossible as n increases. More generally, r can be estimated for investment proposals where n is 2 or more and, where the annual inflows are unequal, by an iterative approach, i.e., by a search process in which we are looking for the value of r which, when

Table 2-3

$\dfrac{1}{(1+i)^n}$ FOR VARIOUS VALUES OF i AND n, CUMULATED FOR i

n	1%	2%	4%	6%	8%	10%	12%	14%	15%	16%	18%	20%	22%	24%	25%	26%	28%	30%	35%	40%	45%	50%
1	0.990	0.980	0.962	0.943	0.926	0.909	0.893	0.877	0.870	0.862	0.847	0.833	0.820	0.806	0.800	0.794	0.781	0.769	0.741	0.714	0.690	0.667
2	1.970	1.942	1.886	1.833	1.783	1.736	1.690	1.647	1.626	1.605	1.566	1.528	1.492	1.457	1.440	1.424	1.392	1.361	1.289	1.224	1.165	1.111
3	2.941	2.884	2.775	2.673	2.577	2.487	2.402	2.322	2.283	2.246	2.174	2.106	2.042	1.981	1.952	1.923	1.868	1.816	1.696	1.589	1.493	1.407
4	3.902	3.808	3.630	3.465	3.312	3.170	3.037	2.914	2.855	2.798	2.690	2.589	2.494	2.404	2.362	2.320	2.241	2.166	1.997	1.849	1.720	1.605
5	4.853	4.713	4.452	4.212	3.993	3.791	3.605	3.433	3.352	3.274	3.127	2.991	2.864	2.745	2.689	2.635	2.532	2.436	2.220	2.035	1.876	1.737
6	5.795	5.601	5.242	4.917	4.623	4.355	4.111	3.889	3.784	3.685	3.494	3.326	3.167	3.020	2.951	2.885	2.759	2.643	2.385	2.168	1.983	1.824
7	6.728	6.472	6.002	5.582	5.206	4.868	4.564	4.288	4.160	4.039	3.812	3.605	3.416	3.242	3.161	3.083	2.937	2.802	2.508	2.263	2.057	1.883
8	7.652	7.325	6.733	6.210	5.747	5.335	4.968	4.639	4.487	4.344	4.078	3.837	3.619	3.421	3.329	3.241	3.076	2.925	2.598	2.331	2.108	1.922
9	8.566	8.162	7.435	6.802	6.247	5.759	5.328	4.946	4.772	4.607	4.303	4.031	3.786	3.566	3.463	3.366	3.184	3.019	2.665	2.379	2.144	1.984
10	9.471	8.893	8.111	7.360	6.710	6.145	5.650	5.216	5.019	4.833	4.494	4.192	3.923	3.682	3.571	3.465	3.269	3.092	2.715	2.414	2.168	1.965
11	10.368	9.787	8.760	7.887	7.139	6.495	5.988	5.453	5.234	5.029	4.656	4.327	4.035	3.776	3.656	3.544	3.335	3.147	2.752	2.438	2.185	1.977
12	11.255	10.575	9.385	8.384	7.536	6.814	6.194	5.660	5.421	5.197	4.793	4.439	4.127	3.851	3.725	3.606	3.387	3.190	2.779	2.456	2.196	1.985
13	12.134	11.343	9.986	8.853	7.904	7.103	6.424	5.842	5.583	5.342	4.910	4.533	4.203	3.912	3.780	3.656	3.427	3.223	2.799	2.468	2.204	1.990
14	13.004	12.106	10.563	9.295	8.244	7.367	6.628	6.002	5.724	5.468	5.008	4.611	4.265	3.962	3.824	3.695	3.459	3.249	2.814	2.477	2.210	1.993
15	13.865	12.849	11.118	9.712	8.559	7.606	6.811	6.142	5.847	5.575	5.092	4.675	4.315	4.001	3.859	3.726	3.483	3.268	2.825	2.484	2.214	1.995
16	14.718	13.578	11.652	10.106	8.851	7.824	6.974	6.265	5.954	5.669	5.162	4.730	4.357	4.033	3.887	3.751	3.503	3.283	2.834	2.489	2.216	1.997
17	15.562	14.292	12.166	10.477	9.122	8.022	7.120	6.373	6.047	5.749	5.222	4.775	4.391	4.059	3.910	3.771	3.518	3.295	2.840	2.492	2.218	1.998
18	16.398	14.992	12.659	10.828	9.372	8.201	7.250	6.467	6.128	5.818	5.273	4.812	4.419	4.080	3.928	3.786	3.529	3.304	2.844	2.494	2.219	1.999
19	17.226	15.678	13.134	11.158	9.604	8.365	7.366	6.550	6.198	5.877	5.316	4.844	4.442	4.097	3.942	3.799	3.538	3.311	2.848	2.496	2.220	1.999
20	18.046	16.351	13.590	11.470	9.818	8.514	7.469	6.623	6.259	5.929	5.353	4.870	4.460	4.110	3.954	3.808	3.546	3.316	2.850	2.497	2.221	1.999
21	18.857	17.011	14.029	11.764	10.017	8.649	7.562	6.687	6.312	5.973	5.384	4.891	4.476	4.121	3.963	3.816	3.551	3.320	2.852	2.498	2.221	2.000
22	19.660	17.658	14.451	12.042	10.201	8.772	7.645	6.743	6.359	6.011	5.410	4.909	4.488	4.130	3.970	3.822	3.556	3.323	2.853	2.498	2.222	2.000
23	20.456	18.292	14.857	12.303	10.371	8.883	7.718	6.792	6.399	6.044	5.432	4.925	4.499	4.137	3.976	3.827	3.559	3.325	2.854	2.499	2.222	2.000
24	21.243	18.914	15.247	12.550	10.529	8.985	7.784	6.835	6.434	6.073	5.451	4.937	4.507	4.143	3.981	3.831	3.562	3.327	2.855	2.499	2.222	2.000
25	22.023	19.523	15.622	12.783	10.675	9.077	7.843	6.873	6.464	6.097	5.467	4.948	4.514	4.147	3.985	3.834	3.564	3.329	2.856	2.499	2.222	2.000
26	22.795	20.121	15.983	13.003	10.810	9.161	7.896	6.906	6.491	6.118	5.480	4.956	4.520	4.151	3.988	3.837	3.566	3.330	2.856	2.500	2.222	2.000
27	23.560	20.707	16.330	13.211	10.935	9.237	7.943	6.935	6.514	6.136	5.492	4.964	4.524	4.154	3.990	3.839	3.567	3.331	2.856	2.500	2.222	2.000
28	24.316	21.281	16.663	13.406	11.051	9.307	7.984	6.961	6.534	6.152	5.502	4.970	4.528	4.157	3.992	3.840	3.568	3.331	2.857	2.500	2.222	2.000
29	25.066	21.844	16.984	13.591	11.158	9.370	8.022	6.983	6.551	6.166	5.510	4.975	4.531	4.159	3.994	3.841	3.569	3.332	2.857	2.500	2.222	2.000
30	25.808	22.396	17.292	13.765	11.258	9.427	8.055	7.003	6.566	6.177	5.517	4.979	4.534	4.160	3.995	3.842	3.569	3.332	2.857	2.500	2.222	2.000
40	32.835	27.355	19.793	15.046	11.925	9.779	8.244	7.105	6.642	6.234	5.548	4.997	4.544	4.166	3.999	3.846	3.571	3.333	2.857	2.500	2.222	2.000
50	39.196	31.424	21.482	15.762	12.234	9.915	8.304	7.133	6.661	6.246	5.554	4.999	4.545	4.167	4.000	3.846	3.571	3.333	2.857	2.500	2.222	2.000

put in the equation, sets the present value of the S terms equal to C. Using 0.10 as an estimate of r and taking the $1/(1 + r)$ values from Table 2-2, the present value of the S terms is \$108.25. Since this is more than C, it follows that the $1/(1 + r)$ multipliers are too large, i.e., 0.10 is less than the true value of r. An estimated internal rate of return of 0.20 yields a present value of \$98.57, indicating that 0.20 is greater than the true internal rate of return. Interpolation between 0.10 and 0.20 indicates that 0.19 may be an accurate estimate for the internal rate of return. With 0.19, the present value of the S terms is \$100.35, which may be refined further, but would be sufficiently accurate for most practical purposes.

The results of using the three methods to evaluate the three illustrative fixed asset investments may be summarized as follows:

	Average Rate of Profit	Payoff Ratio	Internal Rate of Return
Investment 1	0.20	1.10	0.10
Investment 2	0.20	1.10	0.19
Investment 3	0.20	0.60	0.13

On the basis of reason, we know that investment 2 is superior to investment 1 because the second investment is identical to the first, except that it generates \$10 more in the second year. We also know that the second investment is superior to the third investment because, although both generate \$120 over the two years, the second investment generates more dollars in the first year. The internal rate of return is the only criterion of the three considered which indicates both that the second investment is superior to the first and that the second investment is superior to the third.

Despite the fact that the internal rate of return is more accurate in ranking investment proposals by relative profitability, many firms prefer the payoff ratio or the average rate of return because they are easier to calculate. How inaccurate are these two measures?

As is apparent from the three examples, the average rate of profit is closer to the internal rate of return than is the payoff ratio. However, the examples involved very short-lived investments. If the third investment proposal were to produce a cash inflow of \$60 a year for 40 years, instead of only 2 years, the payoff ratio would remain at 0.60. The average rate of profit would rise to $(\$60 - \$2.50)/\$50 = 1.15$. The internal rate of return would be, from Table 2-3, greater than 50 per cent, but less than 60 per cent, which rate would be the internal rate of return if the investment generated \$60 a year perpetually. Thus with long-lived investments, the payoff ratio is more accurate than the average rate of return. More generally, it can be shown that for investments with lives of less than twice the payoff period, $2(C/S)$, the average rate of return is more accurate than the payoff ratio, and the converse is true when expected life exceeds twice the payoff ratio.

Shortcomings of the Internal Rate of Return. A firm uses a pickup truck which must be either repaired or replaced. If repaired, the cost will be $500 and will generate inflows, net of maintenance, of approximately $392 a year for two years. A new truck will cost $2500 and will generate inflows, net of maintenance, of $1,076 a year for four years. Table 2-3 indicates that the sum of $1/(1 + i)$ terms for two years coming closest to 1.28($500/$392) occurs in the 35 per cent column, while the four-year summation coming closest to 2.32($2,500/$1,076) is in the 26 per cent column. According to the internal rate of return criterion, the firm should repair the existing truck.

But suppose that, in general, the firm can reinvest funds to yield only 10 per cent. If the funds generated by the repaired truck are reinvested at 10 per cent, the present value of the inflows is $680.51, or a surplus of $180.51 over the cost of the repairs. The present value of the inflows from the new truck at 10 per cent is $3,410,92, a surplus of $910.92 over the cost of the new truck. Even though the internal rate of return is larger for the repairs, the firm will make a larger surplus with the new truck. The reason for the different result is that, in using the present value, we considered the rate at which the firm expects to reinvest funds; whereas, with the internal rate of return, it is assumed that funds can be invested at the internal rate of return. This error, inherent in the internal rate of return, is only important when investment projects are, as in the example above, mutually exclusive, i.e., if one project is undertaken, the other project is ipso facto rejected.

Although not a shortcoming, it is worth noting that the internal rate of return in itself cannot tell us which investments are worth undertaking. All that emerges is a ranking of investment opportunities which, as has just been demonstrated, may not be accurate. In order to select the investments, it is necessary to know the lowest rate of return acceptable to the firm.

Next, a firm using a rented plant is considering the installation of some capital equipment with an initial cost of $60. The equipment is anticipated to generate inflows as follows: $S_1 = \$110$, $S_2 = \$20$, $S_3 = \$10$, and $S_4 = \$5$. However, the landlord insists that the rented facility be restored to its original condition when the equipment is removed at the end of four years. This will cost $95, which reduces S_4 to $-\$90$. What is the internal rate of return on the machine?

Confusing as it sounds, the rate is 7 per cent or 81 per cent! At the low rate, the $-\$90$ is only reduced by $1/(1.07)^4$, 0.764, and negative returns weigh heavily in the answer. At the higher rate, the effect of the negative return is reduced sharply by $1/(1.81)^4$, or 0.093, which makes the equipment appear to be very profitable. Such tricks can occur under conditions in which the S values fluctuate, and it is not really necessary for any S to be negative. Clearly, the usefulness of a criterion which capriciously produces more than one result is highly questionable.

Net Present Value.   Fortunately, there is a criterion of fixed asset investments which not only provides an unambiguous and accurate means of
ranking investments, but, unlike the internal rate of return, also indicates
whether or not investments should be undertaken. In the example of the
firm choosing between repairing an old truck or buying a new one, the internal rate of return was shown to be inaccurate. The surplus, i.e., the
difference between the present value of inflows and the cost, was larger for
the new truck, even though the internal rate of return was higher for repairing the old truck. The difference between V' and C will be called the *net
present value*, or simply *present value*, henceforth. It may be defined as

(2–7) $$V = V' - C.$$

Obviously, the value of i chosen will be critical in determining the results.
If i is very large, decisions will be biased against assets with a long life, and
the converse. The problems in estimating the appropriate value for i will
be discussed at length in a later chapter. For now, i will be defined as the
minimum acceptable rate of return at which the interests of the corporate
owners will not be damaged, and it will be called *the cost of capital.*

The decision rule for present value is that any investment with a positive
V should be undertaken. In the case of mutually exclusive investment proposals, as for the trucks, the asset with the higher present value should be
adopted.

By generally accepted accounting rules, fixed assets are valued at cost
C for balance sheet valuation. From what has been said, it is clear that,
unless the true value exceeds cost, the firm would have little interest in
acquiring the asset. It may help to understand the present value concept if
we momentarily assume that fixed assets are assigned the gross present value
of returns, V', on the balance sheet. Then, going back to the example of
the truck, if the firm decides, as it should according to the present value
criterion, to buy a new truck, the fixed asset truck would rise by $3,410.92,
V'. Assume the firm pays cash for the truck, which would reduce the asset
cash by $2,500, C. The logical way to handle the $910.92 difference, V, is to
increase net worth by this amount. This is the present value of the future
profits generated by the truck. In other words, net present value measures
the estimated increase in net worth resulting from the decision to acquire
an asset. Under normal accounting rules, the net present value would not
be shown on the balance sheet until it was actually realized, i.e., until the
future. Even then, since it would show up as operating profits, it could be
distributed to the owners as dividends and never actually increase net worth.
Nonetheless, we shall occasionally refer to the effect of acquiring an asset
with a positive net present value as being an increment to net worth.

Although the present value criterion has been used only to evaluate fixed
asset investments thus far, it has a much wider range of uses. Present value

should be used in dealing with inventory problems in which inventory may be stocked for several time periods. It is also used to help evaluate investment in accounts receivable and cash. Generally, regardless of the nature of the problem, present value should always be used for decisions involving dollars to be received or expended in future time periods.

ESTIMATING THE VALUE OF S

So far, little attention has been paid to the composition of the estimated gross inflows. In particular, the effects of taxes, depreciation, and any added investment in short-term assets resulting from the adoption of a fixed asset must be considered in order to achieve a logical evaluation of a fixed asset.

DEPRECIATION AND TAXES By law, the acquisition costs of assets with a useful life in excess of one year may not be charged to income in the year of acquisition. Instead, fixed assets with a limited physical life, such as plant and equipment, but not land, are subject to depreciation, or amortization, allowances. These allowances constitute the bulk of the capital consumption allowances for the corporate business sector, which were shown in the previous chapter as part of gross savings. Such allowances are treated as expenses and are deducted from income in determining taxable income.

The determination of the amount of the allowance depends on the original costs of the asset plus any improvements made during the asset's life, the number of years set for the depreciable life of the asset, and the rate of depreciation over the depreciable life. Depreciable life can be quite different from actual economic life. No one has certain knowledge of the economic life of the asset when it is acquired. The introduction of new techniques of production or changes in tastes can bring an end to the usefulness of a fixed asset long before it has reached what had been originally estimated as its economic life. However, even identical assets can have different estimated economic lives for different firms. Take an asset costing $100 with estimated returns, ignoring maintenance expenditures, of $50 a year. If maintenance expenditures are $10 a year, the asset is expected to last for five years; but the asset will last eight years if maintenance expenditures are $20 a year. Thus, the choice in a sense is between an asset with

$$C = \$100 \text{ and } S \text{ of } \$40 \text{ a year for five years}$$

and an asset with

$C = \$100$ and S of $30 a year for eight years.

If the cost of capital is 10 per cent, using Table 2-3, the net present value for the asset with a five-year maintenance schedule is $51.64, and for the asset with the eight-year schedule it is $60.05. The firm would prefer the eight-year schedule, which would set the expected economic life of the asset. However, another firm considering the same asset could arrive at a different conclusion if its cost of capital were higher. Suppose the cost of capital is 25 per cent. The net present value is $7.56 for the five-year schedule, but $-\$0.13$ for the eight-year schedule. With the higher cost of capital, the firm would prefer the shorter-lived alternative.

To complicate the picture further, it is quite conceivable that a firm with a 10 per cent cost of capital today may have a 25 per cent cost of capital in a few years. In this case, it may shift from a high maintenance schedule to low maintenance, reducing the expected life of the asset. The combination of obsolesence, variations in the cost of capital, and even differences among firms in forecast S values for similar assets makes the problem of setting an acceptable depreciable life confusing, to say the least. The Treasury Department issued a guideline schedule of depreciable lives for various assets in 1942, *Bulletin F*, which was modified in the direction of shortening depreciable lives in July, 1962. Depreciable lives used by firms turned out to be far shorter than the 1942 guidelines, but generally longer than the 1962 guidelines. To sum the situation, the depreciable life of an asset is a matter of negotiation between the firm and the Internal Revenue Service, with the IRS attempting to standardize depreciable lives by modifying guideline lives in the direction of business practice.

Firms may choose, for new assets, among three formulas in order to determine the rate at which depreciation will be charged. The methods are called *straight-line*, *double-declining-balance*, and *sum-of-the-years-digits*. Straight-line depreciation is determined by simply dividing the cost of the asset by its depreciable life, C/n, with the rate being $1/n$. The rate at which depreciation is charged under the double-declining-balance formula is $2(1/n)$, but it is charged on the book value of the asset, i.e., on the original cost less accumulated depreciation. The rate at which the sum-of-the-years-digits formula charges depreciation is somewhat more complicated. The denominator of the rate is the sum of the years of depreciable life. For an asset with a five-year depreciable life, the denominator would be $1 + 2 + 3 + 4 + 5 = 15$. The numerator varies, but will be n for the first year, $n - 1$ for the second, $n - 2$ for the third year, etc. Using the five-year asset, the rate for the first year would be 5/15, 4/15 for the second year, etc. When the rates are applied to original cost, the total depreciation charged over the depreciable life will be 15/15 original cost. Comparing the three formulas for an asset with a five-year depreciable life, the percentages of original cost charged off by each for each of the five years are:

Year	Straight-line, %	Double-declining, %	Reverse sum-of-digits, %
1	20	40.0	33.3
2	20	24.0	26.7
3	20	14.4	20.0
4	20	8.6	13.3
5	20	13.0	6.7
Totals	100	100.0	100.0

Under the double-declining-balance, it is arithmetically impossible to charge all the original cost as depreciation. Firms are allowed, however, to switch from either of the rapid amortization formulas to straight-line whenever they wish, although the reverse may be done only if the IRS concurs. Therefore, for the fifth-year charge under the double-declining-balance column, it is assumed that the firm has switched to straight-line depreciation.

Although depreciation, or amortization, is a true expense, it does not involve a cash expenditure, unlike most expenses. In effect, the cash expenditure occurred years before depreciation expense appears on the income statement, i.e., the cash expenditure occurred when the asset was purchased. To illustrate, take a firm with the following income statement:

```
Cash sales ........................... $1,000
Cash expenses ......................     700
Depreciation .......................      200
Net income before taxes ............. $  100
Taxes ..............................       30
Net income after taxes............... $   70
```

The cash account records an increase of $1,000 from the sales, a decline of $700 for expenses, and a decline of $30 as tax payment. Cash generated from operations during the period is $270, the sum of depreciation and after-tax income. Of course, depreciation does not always add to the cash account. If sales are less than cash expenses by the amount of depreciation, i.e., losses are $200, the cash account will increase not at all. But if the loss is less than the amount of depreciation, cash would still rise by the difference between depreciation and the loss. As an example, suppose that sales in the income statement above were $800. Cash would rise by $800 of sales and would fall by $700 of cash expenses. Ignoring the complexities of tax carry-backs, the effect of operations would be to raise cash by the amount of depreciation less the loss. In short, depreciation must be included with profits to state the cash inflow from operations accurately.

The adoption of rapid amortization formulas increases the net present value of fixed assets. Although the total amount of depreciation over the life of the asset is not affected by the formula used, the present value of the depreciation allowances is increased when the charges can be made earlier in the life of the asset.

A second effect of rapid amortization is to improve the cash position of the firm soon after investing in a fixed asset. However, the full effect of rapid amortization on cash will depend upon the growth rate of the firm. This is demonstrated in Table 2-4, in which the relationship between the effect of rapid amortization is compared for three different rates of expenditures on fixed assets. It is assumed that the capital expenditures are for assets with a depreciable life of three years. The rapid amortization formula used is the sum-of-the-years-digits. The first firm is assumed to have a zero rate of growth in fixed asset expenditures. The second grows by 100 per cent annually. And the third decreases capital expenditures 10 per cent per annum. By the third year, the relationship between annual depreciation and capital expenditures approaches a constant, although the dollar amount of depreciation varies except for the firm with the constant level of fixed asset expenditures.

Depreciation, as a percentage of fixed asset expenditures, measures the importance of depreciation as a means of financing fixed asset acquisitions. In the case of the constant level of expenditures, rapid amortization provides more funds for financing fixed asset purchases for the first two years. By the third year, and thereafter, both rapid and straight-line depreciation are equally important as a source of funds.

Table 2-4

COMPARATIVE IMPORTANCE OF STRAIGHT-LINE AND RAPID DEPRECIATION AS A SOURCE OF FUNDS FOR FINANCING FIXED ASSET EXPENDITURES, FOR ASSETS WITH A LIFE OF THREE YEARS, FOR DIFFERENT RATES OF GROWTH IN FIXED ASSET EXPENDITURES.

| | | DEPRECIATION | | | |
| | | STRAIGHT-LINE | | RAPID | |
Year	*Fixed Asset Expenditures*	*Dollars*	*% of Expenditures*	*Dollars*	*% of Expenditures*
		(a)			
		ZERO GROWTH			
1..........	$100	33	33	50	50
2..........	100	67	67	83	83
3..........	100	100	100	100	100
		(b)			
		GROWTH = 100% PER ANNUM			
1..........	$100	33	33	50	50
2..........	200	100	50	133	66
3..........	400	233	58	283	70
		(c)			
		GROWTH = −10% PER ANNUM			
1..........	$100	33	33	50	50
2..........	90	63	70	78	86
3..........	81	90	112	87	107

The importance of rapid amortization as a source of finance is shown in the case in which fixed asset expenditures increase at a rapid pace. By the third year, straight-line depreciation provides only 58 per cent of the funds needed for fixed asset expenditures. With rapid amortization, 70 per cent of the funds are provided through depreciation.

In the last case, annual expenditures on fixed assets decline. Unlike the rapid growth example, straight-line amortization provides a larger portion of annual fixed asset expenditures than does rapid amortization.

These examples indicate why rapid amortization is one of the policy tools used to stimulate investment. Firms can benefit from the cash effects of rapid amortization only if the level of annual capital expenditures are growing. At a constant level of expenditures, rapid amortization provides no liquidity advantages. It is a disadvantage if the level of capital expenditures falls. Rapid amortization may be viewed as a permanent loan from the Treasury Department to firms which are increasing the stock of fixed assets. It can also be shown that the cash advantage provided by rapid amortization is greater, the longer the life of the fixed asset, so that rapid amortization not only stimulates fixed asset investment, but encourages longer term investments.

The cash advantage would be unimportant if firms had ready access to other sources of funds with no greater risk or interest cost than the funds provided by depreciation. Generally, this is not so. If, as shall be discussed in more detail later, the firm usually can acquire external funds under conditions of a rising cost of capital, the real advantage of rapid amortization is that it increases the supply of relatively low cost funds. Thus, by lowering the cost of capital, rapid amortization increases the chances that a given investment will have a positive net present value. Again, this advantage goes only to the swift. It is an advantage to firms which face highly profitable fixed asset investment opportunities already, as witnessed by the increasing level of fixed asset expenditures.

All this discussion, it must be remembered, has significance only because of the existence of income taxation. Depreciation would be irrelevant as a source of cash if there were no income tax, and its importance as a source of funds varies directly with the tax rate. Its significance results from two facts: The Internal Revenue Service allows depreciation to be deducted from taxable income; and depreciation expense does not involve the payment of cash, which makes it unlike most expenses.

OTHER ASSETS
AND EXPENSES

Frequently, a proposed fixed asset will alter the levels of investment in other assets and other expenses. These changes may be the most important source of expected future returns from the fixed asset. A complete evaluation requires estimates of possible changes in inventory, accounts receivable, and cash investment, as well as in labor, materials, and other expenses.

It is important to distinguish between asset changes and expense changes. Suppose a new machine can produce at a far more rapid rate than an existing machine. Rapid production can make it necessary to hold larger stocks of raw materials and, if production rises but sales remain constant, in-process and finished inventories will also rise. No time period is involved. As long as the firm utilizes the new machine at a rapid production rate, the inventory will be larger than it was with the old machine. When the proposed new machine becomes an old machine, the added inventory will still exist—not the same physical units, but the same value. The physical units will have been sold, the funds reinvested to produce replacement inventory, and the replacements sold, etc., but the value of the firm's added inventory investment will remain. What has it cost the firm to add to its inventory investment? Essentially, the cost of the funds which have been tied up in inventory. The cost of the tied-up funds can be estimated by multiplying the increased inventory investment by the cost of capital. The product should be subtracted from S.

Unlike an investment in assets, an increase in expense will grow larger, the longer the period of time over which it is being measured. If the machine used in the example above required additional power costs estimated at $50 per month, the annual increment to power costs resulting from the adoption of the machine would be $600. At the end of the life of the machine, there would be no stock of electrical power remaining, as there was with the inventory. Therefore, it is correct to deduct the added power costs from the estimated returns.

It is as important to exclude irrelevant costs and investments as it is to include them when appropriate. An irrelevant cost might be floor space. A new asset, which will take up less floor space than its predecessor, should be credited with the savings only if the savings are real. If there is no alternative use for the released floor space, the savings are illusory. In short, physical differences between fixed assets are not always reflected in value differences.

Finally, the after-tax effects are what are significant. A tax rate of 48 per cent on taxable income means that the after-tax cost of a $1,000 expense is only $520. Changes in asset investments, as with the case of inventory cited above, are not deductible for tax purposes, but the interest cost of the tied-up, i.e., entailed, funds is.

SCRAP VALUE

Most assets will have a residual value when the firm decides to replace them. This residual value is often called *scrap value*. Scrap value may be either the net receipts from selling the asset, or the net present value of putting the asset to a different use within the firm.

Scrap value need not be positive. The receipts that are relevant from disposing of an asset include the actual sale price less any costs incurred in moving the old asset. In some cases, the costs of removal can exceed the sales price, making scrap value negative. What does the firm do with such assets? The answer may be given best by an example.

After a long and useful life, it is estimated that the maintenance costs of an old asset will exceed the net receipts. The firm calculates that keeping the machine will involve an after-tax negative cash inflow of $100 per annum. The firm does not believe that it can make forecasts into the infinite future and, as a matter of policy, does not plan beyond five years hence, i.e., it has a five-year planning period. Most firms do not forecast indefinitely into the future, and, sometimes, the limit of the planning period is referred to as the *firm's horizon*. At any rate, keeping the old machine means that the firm will have a negative S of $100 for the next five years. Estimated gross proceeds from the sale of the machine are $200, but, since the machine is in a concrete base and its removal will also involve making some special openings in the walls of the plant, the net proceeds of resale are − $600. The firm's options are either to keep the machine and incur an annual loss of $100 or to get rid of the machine and incur a lump-sum loss of $600. Since future dollars cannot be directly compared with current dollars, it is necessary to calculate the gross present value of the future losses. Assuming the cost of capital to be 10 per cent, the gross present value of the future losses is $379.10 (see Table 2-3). The firm will keep the machine because, according to the net present value decision rule, it is profitable to do so. The net present value of the machine is $V − C$, or − $379.10 − − $600 = $220.90, a positive net present value.

SCRAP VALUE AND ECONOMIC LIFE In the example, net scrap value was used to estimate C, the cost of an asset. When the asset was new, C was equal to the cash sacrifice of acquisition. What is the cash sacrifice of retaining an asset? Obviously, the net cash proceeds that would be received if the firm did not retain the asset. Thus, at any point after having acquired a fixed asset, the firm may reevaluate the original decision by substituting the net scrap value at that moment for C and recalculating the net present value on the basis of the current forecasts of S and the current value of the cost of capital. In short, the decision to acquire a fixed asset is not irreversible, although there may be a stiff price paid if the firm discovers that it made an error in the original decision.

In the original calculation of net present value, the expected scrap value of a fixed asset should be included as an increment to the final cash inflow S_n. It has already been shown, however, that scrap value can be of vital importance in determining the economic life of an asset. For many assets, the level of scrap value diminishes as the asset becomes older. If the asset is scrapped early in its life, the scrap value has a higher present value than if the firm decides to scrap later on. In such a case, the scrap value joins the expected cash inflows and the cost of capital as a factor determining the economic life of the asset. As an example, a firm is considering an asset with a cost of $100 and expected cash inflows, net of scrap value, of $20 per annum for the next five years. Scrap value diminshes as follows:

End of Year	Scrap Value
1	$95
2	90
3	80
4	70
5	50

The gross present values are:

If Held to End of Year	Gross Present Value @ 10%	Gross Present Value @ 15%
1	$104.54	$100.05
2	109.06	100.56
3	109.82	98.30
4	111.21	97.14
5	106.87	91.89

Since the present values of the asset at each possible life are mutually exclusive alternatives, the firm will choose the life which maximizes net present value. At a cost of capital of 10 per cent, the asset will be held for four years. At a cost of capital of 15 per cent, the firm will hold the asset for only two years.

SCRAP VALUE
AND BOOK VALUE

The book value of a fixed asset is the sum of original cost and improvements less accumulated depreciation. The net scrap value of a fixed asset can be greater than, less than, or equal to the book value. Since the determinants of the two values are quite different, there is no necessary coincidence between them. Scrap value is the net value of the asset to the firm if the asset is put to a different use or sold. Book value is determined by the original cost of the asset, any improvements made during the asset's life, the depreciable life of the asset, and the particular depreciation formula used. Looking at it another way, scrap value is an estimate of the current value of an asset used in an alternative way, or the opportunity cost of keeping the asset in its present use. Book value is a record of past decisions with no relationship to the present.

If the forecast values of S, the cost of capital, and the scrap value of an asset combine to generate a negative net present value for the asset in its current use, the asset should be scrapped regardless of book value. On occasion, however, the decision to sell an asset may be disputed if book value is greater than scrap value, because the sale will result in an accounting loss. When a firm decides that an asset should be scrapped, a loss may occur. But the source of the loss is that the original forecasts of S were overstated. Should the firm retain an asset with a negative net present value, losses will be increased, and the future will be charged with the errors of the past.

To see this more clearly, consider the following example. An asset has a book value of $300. With annual depreciation charges of $100, the remaining depreciable life is three years. Scrap value is zero, and estimated after-tax net cash inflow is −$30 a year for the next three years. The net present value is −$74.61 if the cost of capital is 10 per cent. If the firm scraps the asset, as it should, it not only rids itself of the $30 annual drain, but it can use the accounting loss of $300, the difference between book value and market value, as a deduction from taxable income. Assuming that income from other sources is positive, that the tax rate is 48 per cent, and that the $300 capital loss may be deducted in a single year, the accounting loss will increase after-tax cash inflow by $144 (0.48 times $300). In short, the firm not only gets rid of a losing asset, but realizes $156 in tax savings at the same time. Should the firm wait until book value is zero, it would realize no tax savings and would lose $30 a year in excess of the $100 annual depreciation charge. An old business maxim seems to cover this situation, "Don't throw good money after bad."

RISK

The firm makes a decision today on the basis of what it expects will happen in the future. These expectations have been summarized in this chapter into a value S for the future period. If the firm is absolutely certain that the expected S will be realized, the decision made by the firm may be called *riskless*, or *certain*. Few, if any, firms believe that the values forecast today will exactly equal the actual values that will be realized in the future. Risk is the difference between forecast values and actual values.

Two situations must be distinguished. In the first, the actual future value will be one of several possible values, and the firm knows each of the possible values. The forecast value is one of the possible values. This is analogous to a situation in which the firm is asked to draw one card from a pile of four, containing one ace, two kings, and one queen. The most likely card drawn will be a king. Assuming that the firm knows the composition of the pile of cards, it would expect to draw a king, although it might actually draw one of the other two. If the pile contained only kings, and the firm knew this, it would predict drawing a king, and the prediction would be certain.

Given the pile of three kinds of cards, the prediction is still king, but the prediction is risky.

To measure risk in a situation as described above, it is necessary to know not only all the possible outcomes, but also the value of each outcome. For example, if the firm were to receive $1 if it draws an ace, lose $1 if it draws a queen, and neither gain nor lose anything if it draws a king, it will still predict king, or $0. The risk is that it may lose $1 or gain $1. If, instead, the firm were to receive $1 million if it draws ace and lose $1 million if it draws queen, still receiving and losing nothing for a king, the prediction is still king, or $0, but the risk of playing the game is substantially greater.

In either game, we can measure the risk easily. In simplest form, the games can be described as follows:

		CONSEQUENCES	
Card	Chance of Drawing	$1 Game	$1 Million Game
Ace	One out of four	+ $1	+ $1 million
King............	One out of four	0	0
King............	One out of four	0	0
Queen	One out of four	− 1	− 1 million

A situation in which there are several possible consequences is a risky situation. If there is complete knowledge about the consequences, as in the illustrative card game, the situation can be measured precisely, and the risk can be called a *pure risk*. To be sure, the measurement shown above, though precise, is not very compact, but a more compact method of describing the degree of risk will be developed shortly.

At the opposite pole is complete uncertainty. Here the firm would have no knowledge whatsoever of the consequences of a decision. Forecasts in such cases become pure guesses, and there is no way of measuring uncertainty. Uncertainty, then, is a *pure gamble* with no knowledge of the consequences.

Most business forecasts involve both risk and uncertainty. On the basis of intuition, experience, and whatever insights are provided by market research and general business forecasts, the firm has some knowledge of the consequences or actual values that may arise in the future. However, in a dynamic economy, knowledge of the future is almost inevitably incomplete. In the analysis that follows, it will be assumed that the firm does have some knowledge about the possible future consequences of current decisions. Further, it will be assumed that the firm will use this incomplete knowledge as if the situation is one of pure risk. The effect of uncertainty will be to widen the range of possible consequences. For example, in a pure risk situation, the firm would know that a given business decision could result in a loss no greater than $1 million and a gain not exceeding $2 million. With uncertainty, the firm might well expand the range of possible consequences, say, to a loss of $3 million and a gain of $4 million. The term risk as used henceforth will refer to a condition in which pure risk and uncertainty are combined.

The distant future is more difficult to forecast than the near future because of more uncertainty. Therefore, assets which require a long economic life in which to generate a positive net present value tend to be riskier than assets which show profitability even with a short economic life. The returns of fixed assets which perform familiar functions presumably can be forecast more accurately than returns from assets which will be turning out a new unfamiliar product. Then, of course, some assets are inherently riskier than others. For example, the forecast returns of an investment in a jeep for mineral explorations probably are subject to more extreme variations between forecast and actual events than are the forecasts for an investment in a delivery truck.

Some firms attempt to adjust forecasts for risk either by reducing the expected inflows of the riskier assets or by using a higher cost of capital than would be used for a less risky investment. There are several objections to both of these methods. First, the adjustments simply reduce net present value, a so-called "conservative adjustment." Risk may result in actual events which are less favorable or *more* favorable than predicted. Understating the present value of risky assets is not a means of evaluating risk, but simply of shunning it. At a later point, we shall show that individual risky investments may not only be very profitable, but may work to reduce the over-all risk facing the firm.

Second, the adjustments are arbitrary and can become excessive. Discounting the future returns of a risky investment by 15 per cent instead of 10 per cent reduces the present value of the investment. Why not 20 per cent or 30 per cent or 11 per cent? When the risk adjustment involves reducing the values of S, an additional problem arises. A fixed asset proposal is apt to be initiated by the personnel closest to the area in which the asset will be used. Before the proposal can be adopted, it must pass through several layers of authority. Each of these may adjust for risk by reducing the estimated returns. By the time the proposal reaches the individual or committee responsible for making final decisions, the successive reductions will have whittled out most of the profitability of the asset.

The third objection to either of the methods described is that they provide no separate measure of risk. At this point, admittedly, the need for a separate measure, or index, of risk is not apparent. Later, however, such a measure will prove to be very valuable:

PROBABILITIES
AND FREQUENCIES

Suppose the firm were considering an asset with a forecast present value of $100, which was virtually identical to many other assets in which the firm had invested in the past. As a means of determining the accuracy of forecasts with this kind of asset, the firm has gone over its records and has determined that, if they had known the future perfectly, the present values calculated for the similar assets in which the firm had invested in the past would have been:

True Present Value	Relative Frequency
less than $70	0.05
$ 70–$ 80	0.25
80– 90	0.35
90– 100	0.20
100– 100	0.10
110 or more	0.05

i.e., 5 per cent of the past investments would have indicated a present value of less than $70 if the firm had been able to foresee the future perfectly, 25 per cent of the investments would have shown a net present value falling between $70 and $80, etc. Assuming that the economic and industrial conditions and expectations were no different for the current investment than for the similar ones of the past, the firm could treat the frequency distribution as if it were a probability distribution. As a probability distribution, the table would be interpreted to read, "There are 5 chances in 100 that the true present value of the proposed asset is less than $70. There are 25 chances out of 100 that the true value will fall between $70 and $80. There are 35 chances in 100 that the true value is from $80 to $90, etc."

This approach is similar to that used in a coin-tossing game. A balanced coin, fairly tossed, will yield either a head or a tail. Half the time, we should expect the result heads, and half the time, tails. On a single toss, it is impossible to tell the result. If you were lucky enough to find an honest gambler who would be willing to pay you $1 for each head, providing you would pay him $0.50 for each tail, your fortune and his bankruptcy would be assured. You would have a 0.5 probability of winning $1 and a 0.5 probability of losing $0.50 on each toss. The expected value of the toss is the money associated with each event multiplied by the probability that the event will occur. Thus, the expected value of the coin-tossing game would be $1(0.5) + (−$0.50)0.5 = $0.25. The expected value of a probability distribution is the weighted average of the possible events, where the weights are the probabilities.

Now suppose that the firm treats the investment as if it were a game of chance with the odds as stated in the frequency table above. For the sake of simplicity, the midpoint of each frequency class, e.g., 74.5 as the midpoint for the class $70–$80, will be treated as representative of the entire class. The midpoint for the lower open-end class will be 64.5, and for the upper open-end class, 114.5. The game is then as follows:

Possible or Conditional Value (1)	Probability (2)	Product (3) = (1) × (2)
$ 64.50	0.05	$ 3.225
74.50	0.25	18.625
84.50	0.35	29.575
94.50	0.20	18.900
104.50	0.10	10.450
114.50	0.05	5.725
Expected net present value		$86.500

What this means is that, assuming the frequency distribution is valid as a probability distribution, the firm can expect an average net present value of $86.50 for each investment. Some investments will be better, others worse.

STANDARD DEVIATION AND RISK

The expected net present value calculated above reflects the probability distribution and, to some extent, reflects the risk of this investment. However, compare this investment with a different investment having the following characteristics:

Conditional Value	Probability	Product
$85	0.1	$ 8.50
86	0.4	34.40
87	0.4	34.80
88	0.1	8.80
Expected net present value............................		$86.50

Although both investments have the same expected net present value, the first one is clearly riskier. Net present value may actually fall below $70 or rise above $110 for the initial investment, but will be within a much narrower range for the second investment.

Risk is described by the dispersion of probable outcomes. The wider the dispersion, the riskier the investment. The standard deviation is a generally accepted measure of dispersion. It is the square root of the sum of the squared difference between each conditional value and the expected value, then weighted by the probability associated with the conditional value. The standard deviation calculation for each of the assets discussed above is shown below:

FIRST INVESTMENT

Conditional Value	Expected Value	Difference	(Difference)²	Probability	Probability × (Difference)²
$ 64.50	$86.50	−22.00	484.00	0.05	24.20
74.50	86.50	−12.00	144.00	0.25	36.00
84.50	86.50	− 2.00	4.00	0.35	1.40
94.50	86.50	8.00	64.00	0.20	12.80
104.50	86.50	18.00	324.00	0.10	32.40
114.50	86.50	28.00	784.00	0.05	39.20
					146.00 = variance

$$\sqrt{146} = 12.1 = \text{standard deviation}$$

SECOND INVESTMENT

Conditional Value	Expected Value	Difference	(Difference)²	Probability	Probability × (Difference)²
$ 85	$86.50	−1.50	2.25	0.1	0.225
86	86.50	−0.50	0.25	0.4	1.000
87	86.50	0.50	0.25	0.4	1.000
88	86.50	1.50	2.25	0.1	0.225
					2.450 = variance

$$\sqrt{2.45} = 1.565 = \text{standard deviation}$$

The risk as measured by the standard deviation is almost eight times greater for the first investment than for the second. One warning: The standard deviation reflects the size of the units of the conditional values. If the first investment had been expressed in millions of dollars, its expected value would have been $86.5 million, and the standard deviation would have been $12.1 billion. Yet, the risk would be the same, regardless of the size of units. This problem can be solved by dividing the standard deviation by the expected value, and using the result as an index of relative risk. Thus, the first investment would have a relative index of $12.1/86.50 = 0.1399$ regardless of whether the conditional values are expressed in dollars or millions of dollars. The relative risk index for the second investment is $1.565/86.50 = 0.0181$.

There is some utility in being able to contrast the relative risk of various investments. We shall, however, use the absolute risk measure, i.e., the standard deviation, later to measure the risk of the total assets of the firm and shall not refer to the relative index again.

SELECTED REFERENCES

Bailey, M. "Formal Criteria for Investment Decisions," *Journal of Political Economy*, Oct., 1959.

Bodenhorn, D.: "On the Problem of Capital Budgeting," *Journal of Finance*, Dec., 1959.

Conard, J.: *An Introduction to the Theory of Interest*, Univ. of California, 1959.

Dean, J.: *Capital Budgeting*, U. of Columbia, New York, 1951.

————: "Measuring the Productivity of Capital," *Harvard Business Review*, Jan., 1954.

Domar, E.: "The Case for Accelerated Depreciation," *Quarterly Journal of Economics*, May, 1953.

Fisher, I.: *The Theory of Interest*, Kelley and Millman, NYC, 1954.

Friedland, S.: "How to Evaluate Investment Proposals," *California Management Review*, Winter, 1960.

Goode, R.: "Accelerated Depreciation Allowances as a Stimulus to Investment," *Quarterly Journal of Economics*, May, 1955.

Gordon, M.: *The Investment, Financing, and Valuation of The Corporation*, Irwin, Homewood, Ill., 1962.

————: "The Pay-off Period and The Rate of Profit," *Journal of Business*, Oct., 1955.

Gordon M., and E. Shapiro: "Capital Equipment Analysis: The Required Rate of Profit," *Management Science*, Oct., 1956.

Hirshleifer, J.: "On the Theory of Optimal Investment Decision," *Journal of Political Economy*, Aug., 1958.

————; "Risk, The Discount Rate, and Investment Decisions," *American Economic Review Papers and Proceedings*, May, 1961.

Jaszi, G. Wasson, R. and L. Grose: "Expansion of Fixed Business Capital in the United States," *Survey of Current Business*, Nov., 1962.

Lorie, J., and L. Savage: "Three Problems in Rationing Capital," *Journal of Business*, Oct., 1955.

Lutz, F.: *The Theory of Investment of the Firm*, Princeton Univ. Press, N. Y., 1951.

Markowitz, H.: *Portfolio Selection*, Wiley, New York, 1959.

Meyer, J. and E. Kuh: *The Investment Decision*, Harvard, Cambridge, Mass., 1959.

Schlaiffer, R.: *Probability and Statistics for Business Dicisions*, McGraw-Hill, New York, 1959.

Solomon, E.: "The Arithmetic of Capital Budgeting Decisions," *Journal of Business*, Apr., 1956.

————, ed.: *The Management of Corporate Capital*, Free Press Chicago, 1959.

Williams, J.: *The Theory of Investment Value*, North-Holland, Amsterdam, 1938.

APPENDIX

The Replacement Chain

The decision to invest in an asset is determined by whether or not the net present value of the asset is positive. All else given, the economic life of the asset is that number of years which will generate a higher net present value than will result from holding the asset for any other number of years. In effect, the firm makes the following set of calculations:

$$V_0^1 = -C_0 + \frac{1}{1+i}S + \frac{1}{1+i}C_1;$$

$$V_0^2 = -C_0 + \sum_1^2 \frac{1}{(1+i)^2}S + \frac{1}{(1+i)^2}C_2;$$

$$V_0^3 = -C_0 + \sum_1^3 \frac{1}{(1+i)^3}S + \frac{1}{(1+i)^3}C_3;$$

$$V_0^4 = -C_0 + \sum_1^4 \frac{1}{(1+i)^4} S + \frac{1}{(1+i)^4} C_4;$$

$$\cdot$$
$$\cdot$$
$$\cdot$$

$$V_0^n = -C_0 + \sum_1^n \frac{1}{(1+i)^n} S + \frac{1}{(1+i)^n} C_n,$$

where V_0^1 in the net present value from holding the asset for one year, V_0^2 is the net present value if the asset is held two years, etc.; C_0 is the initial cost of the asset;

$$\frac{1}{1+i}, \quad \sum_1^2 \frac{1}{(1+i)^2}, \quad \sum_1^3 \frac{1}{(1+i)^3}, \quad \sum_1^4 \frac{1}{(1+i)^4}, \quad \text{and} \quad \sum_1^n \frac{1}{(1+i)^n}$$

represent the present value factors for one, two ,three, four, and n years taken from Table 2-3, assuming S is constant and C_1, C_2, C_3, C_4, and C_n are the scrap values at the end of the first, second, third, fourth, and nth years, respectively. The number of years associated with the highest V will be the economic life of the asset.

At the end of one year, the net present value to be gained by holding the asset for the remainder of its economic life, which will be assumed to be four years, is

$$V_1^4 = -C_1 + \sum_2^4 \frac{1}{(1+i)^3} S + \frac{1}{(1+i)^3} C_4,$$

where the scrap value at the end of the first year is the cost of holding the asset. Since there are only three years of life remaining, the present value factors are adjusted accordingly. Even if we assume that the initial estimates of cash inflows, scrap values, and cost of capital are unchanged from those made in period 0, new assets may have become available and replacement may be desirable at the end of one year. What should be the criterion of replacement?

A possible criterion would be to replace an asset before it had reached the end of its economic life, if the new asset has a higher net present value than will be achieved by retaining the old asset. Though this criterion is relatively straightforward, it is not generally correct.

Suppose that, one year after having acquired an asset with an estimated economic life of four years, the firm compares its remaining net present value V_1^4 with the net present value of an *identical* but new asset. Using the criterion above, the firm will replace if $V_0^4 - V_1^4$ is positive. The difference between the two net present values is

$$V_0^4 - V_1^4 = -C_0 + C_1 + \sum_1^4 \frac{1}{(1+i)^4} S - \sum_2^4 \frac{1}{(1+i)^3} S$$
$$+ \frac{1}{(1+i)^4} C_4 - \frac{1}{(1+i)^3} C_3.$$

To simplify the problem, assume that the original cost of the new asset C_0 equals the scrap value of the asset after one year, C_1, and that C_3 and C_4 are zero. Then the firm will replace, if

$$\sum_1^4 \frac{1}{(1+i)^4} S > \sum_2^4 \frac{1}{(1+i)^3} S.$$

But, since the only difference between the two assets is that the new asset provides one more year of cash inflow than does the old, the firm will always replace after one year under these conditions. This will occur despite the fact that the maximum net present value of either the new or old asset is optimally four years. Using this replacement criterion, the firm will never realize the expected net present value.

To arrive at a correct solution to the replacement problem, the firm must consider the net present value associated with each of the possible replacement policies as applied to a chain of replacements. This can be done at the time the original asset is being considered. The formulation, assuming identical assets, is

$$V_1 = -C_0 + \frac{1}{1+i}(S + C_1 - C_0) + \frac{1}{(1+i)^2}(S + C_1 - C_0) + \cdots$$
$$+ \frac{1}{(1+i)^n}(S + C_1 - C_0);$$

$$V_2 = -C_0 + \frac{1}{1+i} S + \frac{1}{(1+i)^2}(S + C_2 - C_0) + \frac{1}{(1+i)^3} S$$
$$+ \frac{1}{(1+i)^4}(S + C_2 - C_0) + \cdots + \frac{1}{(1+i)^n}(S + C_2 - C_0);$$

$$V_3 = -C_0 + \frac{1}{1+i} S + \frac{1}{(1+i)^2} S + \frac{1}{(1+i)^3}(S + C_3 - C_0)$$
$$+ \frac{1}{(1+i)^4} S + \frac{1}{(1+i)^5} S + \frac{1}{(1+i)^6}(S + C_3 - C_0) + \cdots$$
$$+ \frac{1}{(1+i)^n}(S + C_3 - C_0);$$

$$\vdots$$

$$V_n = -C_0 + \sum_1^n \frac{1}{(1+i)^n} S + \frac{1}{(1+i)^n}(C_n - C_0).$$

V_1 is the net present value of a chain of replacements with replacement occurring every year. V_2 is the net present value of the chain when replacement is made in alternate years. V_3 shows the net present value with a three-year replacement period, etc. The firm would choose the replacement chain with the highest V. In the case of a chain of identical assets, the replacement period will equal the economic life estimated for a single asset.

ARITHMETIC EXAMPLE   Assume that the cost of capital is 0.1. The firm is considering an asset with the following characteristics:

Period	S	C at End of Period
0	$ 0	$20
1	10	10
2	10	10
3	10	0
4	10	0
5	0	0
6	0	0
.	.	.
.	.	.
.	.	.
n	0	0

Clearly, the economic life of this asset will not exceed four years if it can be replaced at that time by an identical asset. However, the economic life may be less than four years. The net present value for each possible life through four years is

$$V_0^1 = -\$1.82;$$
$$V_0^2 = +\$5.62;$$
$$V_0^3 = +\$4.87;$$
$$V_0^4 = +11.70.$$

The firm would adopt the asset with the expectation that it would have an economic life four years. After adoption, the net present value declines as the asset approaches the end of its economic life. The net present values remaining at the end of the first, second, third, and fourth years are

$$V_1^4 = \$14.87;$$
$$V_2^4 = \$7.36;$$
$$V_3^4 = -\$0.90;$$
$$V_4^4 = 0.$$

Using the criterion that an asset should be replaced when its net present value is less than the net present value of a new asset, the asset would be placed with an identical new asset at the end of year 2, since the net present value of the replacement asset would be $11.70 and the remaining net present value of the old asset would be only $7.36.

If, instead, the firm were to compare the present values associated with various replacement policies, it would calculate the present values associated with the chains shown in the table on the following page.

The net flows could be carried on for any number of years, but would retain the patterns shown above. If calculated for 20 years, the net present value associated with each replacement period is:

Replacement Period	V
1 year	− $20.00
2 years	24.59
3 years	15.60
4 years	28.42

It would be possible to calculate the present values associated with replacement periods of more than four years also. For example, the net present value of a five-year replacement period is $23.29, and the net present value will continue to decline as the replacement period is lengthened.

REPLACEMENT WITH NONIDENTICAL ASSETS

Comparing assets which are identical, except for age, is mainly useful as a pedagogic device to develop a correct replacement criterion in a simple fashion. The firm's problem is more apt to be concerned with assets that are not identical. However, the criterion for replacement developed with identical assets is the same when used to determine the point of replacement for assets that are dissimilar.

One-step Improvement. Suppose that the firm has an asset which was originally estimated to have a four-year life. One year has passed since the asset was adopted. A new asset is available, which is superior to the asset currently in use.

Superiority can occur in a combination of three ways: The new asset may be superior to the old in that the original cost of the new asset is less than the old. If this is the only way in which the new asset is superior and the assets are identical in all other respects, replacement will occur at the end of the old asset's original economic life.

The new asset may generate larger cash inflows. The source of the larger cash inflows could be lower labor requirements, reduced maintenance, larger productive capacity, etc. In this instance, the firm's problem is when to replace the old asset. The larger cash inflows may or may not be sufficiently

REPLACEMENT PERIOD

Year	1 YEAR			2 YEARS			3 YEARS			4 YEARS		
	S	$C_1 - C_0$	Net Flow	S	$C_2 - C_0$	Net Flow	S	$C_3 - C_0$	Net Flow	S	$C_4 - C_0$	Net Flow
0	—	—	-20	—	—	-20	—	—	-20	—	—	-20
1	10	-10	0	10	—	10	10	—	10	10	—	10
2	10	-10	0	10	-10	0	10	—	10	10	—	10
3	10	-10	0	10	—	10	10	-20	-10	10	—	10
4	10	-10	0	10	-10	0	10	—	10	10	-20	-10
5	10	-10	0	10	—	10	10	—	10	10	—	10
6	10	-10	0	10	-10	0	10	-20	-10	10	—	10
7	10	-10	0	10	—	10	10	—	10	10	—	10
8	10	-10	0	10	-10	0	10	—	10	10	-20	-10
9	10	-10	0	10	—	10	10	-20	-10	10	—	10
10	10	-10	0	10	-10	0	10	—	10	10	—	10
11	10	-10	0	10	—	10	10	—	10	10	—	10
12	10	-10	0	10	-10	0	10	-20	-10	10	-20	-10
13	10	-10	0	10	—	10	10	—	10	10	—	10
14	10	-10	0	10	-10	0	10	—	10	10	—	10
15	10	-10	0	10	—	10	10	-20	-10	10	—	10

large to justify the cash outflow that will be required for the firm to acquire the superior asset immediately. Should the firm replace immediately, next year, or the year after?

Finally, the new asset may be better than the old asset in that the scrap value of the new asset is larger. Superiority in scrap value could occur because the new asset has a greater range of alternate uses than the old asset. If scrap value is the only way in which the new asset is superior, replacement is not likely to occur until the old asset's originally estimated economic life is reached.

To simplify the discussion, assume that the superiority of the new asset is in the cash inflows. Assume that, if the old asset generated periodic cash inflows of S, the new asset will generate inflows of $(1 + m)S$. Again for simplification, assume that the cost, scrap values, and economic life of the new asset are the same as those for the old asset.

The firm's problem, then, is when to replace. An immediate replacement means foregoing the remaining three years of returns from the old asset and incurring the net cash outflow to acquire the new asset (i.e., the cost of the new asset less the scrap value of the old), and gaining the larger cash flows of the new asset. However, replacement can be postponed for one, two, or three years. We know already that the firm cannot rely on the simple criterion of replacement if the net present value of the new asset exceeds the net present value remaining in the old. Even if the new asset were not at all superior to the old, this criterion might lead to replacement simply because only three more years of inflow remain in the old asset.

It is necessary to consider the present value of a chain of replacements. The formulation of the calculations are shown below. V_0 is the present value of the decision to replace immediately. V_1 is the present value of the decision to replace next year. If the replacement is postponed two years, the net present value of the chain of replacements is V_2. And, if the firm waits until the end of the originally calculated life of the old asset before replacing, the present value is V_3. The firm will make the decision which is associated with the highest net present value.

$$V_0 = -C_0 + C_1 + \sum_1^n \frac{1}{(1 + i)^n}(1 + m)S + \frac{1}{(1 + i)^4}(C_4 - C_0)$$

$$+ \frac{1}{(1 + i)^8}(C_4 - C_0) + \cdots + \frac{1}{(1 + i)^n}(C_4 - C_0);$$

$$V_1 = \frac{1}{1 + i}(S + C_2 - C_0) + \sum_1^n \frac{1}{(1 + i)^n}(1 + m)S - \frac{1}{1 + i}(1 + m)S$$

$$+ \frac{1}{(1 + i)^5}(C_4 - C_0) + \frac{1}{(1 + i)^9}(C_4 - C_0) + \cdots$$

$$+ \frac{1}{(1 + i)^n}(C_4 - C_0);$$

$$V_2 = \frac{1}{1+i} S + \frac{1}{(1+i)^2} (S + C_3 - C_0) + \sum_1^n \frac{1}{(1+i)^n} (1+m) S$$

$$- \sum_1^2 \frac{1}{(1+i)^2} (1+m) S + \frac{1}{(1+i)^6} (C_4 - C_0)$$

$$+ \frac{1}{(1+i)^{10}} (C_4 - C_0) + \cdots + \frac{1}{(1+i)^n} (C_4 - C_0);$$

$$V_3 = \sum_1^2 \frac{1}{(1+i)^2} S + \frac{1}{(1+i)^3} (S + C_4 - C_0) + \sum_1^n \frac{1}{(1+i)^n} (1+m) S$$

$$- \sum_1^3 \frac{1}{(1+i)^3} (1+m) S + \frac{1}{(1+i)^7} (C_4 - C_0)$$

$$+ \frac{1}{(1+i)^{11}} (C_4 - C_0) + \cdots + \frac{1}{(1+i)^n} (C_4 - C_0).$$

Improvement Chains. The replacement problem involving a one-step improvement is applicable only in situations where technological change is relatively slow and uneven. Big technical breakthroughs occur occasionally, and the firm decides only when it must move to the new productive methods and machines. For certain kinds of fixed assets and certain industries, this is a reasonable approximation of reality.

But it is not an accurate description for all industries and all assets. New products, particularly, tend to have an unstable technology with improvements occurring very frequently. Even with older products, technological changes can be bunched in time, so that, for a few years, the established firm can be confronted with a series of technical improvements.

The problem raised by more or less continuous changes in technology is similar to the problem of replacement when the firm considers a one-step improvement, with an added twist. With a single improvement, the firm must decide whether to adopt the asset immediately or some time in the future. With a chain of improvements, the problem is essentially which asset to adopt: the one immediately available; an improved one that may be available in the near future; a still more improved asset that will not be available for several years; or should it wait many years for an enormously improved asset to be available.

Suppose the firm assumes that the cash inflows generated by assets that will be available in the future will grow at a compound rate equal to m, and that initial cost and scrap values will remain unchanged. Also, assume that any of the assets will have no value other than scrap value after four years. Thus, if the firm replaces an old asset generating annual inflows of S with an immediately available improvement, the new asset will generate inflows of $(1 + m) S$. However, if the firm waits a year to replace, it will be able to adopt an asset generating annual inflows of $(1 + m)^2 S$. In two years, the available replacement will generate annual inflows of $(1 + m)^3 S$, etc. If the asset which the firm has now was adopted last year, the firm can consider replacement immediately, after one year, after two years, or after three years at which time the old asset would have to be replaced in any event.

But if the replacement of the existing asset is the only matter considered, the firm may decide to replace immediately. Such a decision suggests that the firm will probably decide next year to replace the $(1 + m)S$ asset with the $(1 + m)^2 S$ asset available then. It will be setting out on a one-year replacement cycle, which may not be optimal if it considered the replacement alternatives available 10 or 20 years in the future. Thus, the firm is really engaged not only in determining when to replace an existing asset, but in determining the optimal replacement period, or economic life, for a particular kind of asset that will be subject to continuous technological change.

The formulation of the calculations for this decision are shown below. V_0 is not simply the net present value of the decision to replace immediately. It is the net present value of the decision to replace this kind of asset every year. V_1 is the net present value of a two-year replacement period. V_2 is the net present value of a three-year replacement period. And V_3 is the net present value of the decision to replace this kind of asset every four years. The firm will choose the replacement period associated with the largest net present value.

$$V_0 = C_1 - C_0 + \frac{1}{1 + i}[(1 + m)S + C_1 - C_0]$$

$$+ \frac{1}{(1 + i)^2}[(1 + m)^2 S + C_1 - C_0] + \frac{1}{(1 + i)^3}[(1 + m)^3 S + C_1 - C_0]$$

$$+ \cdots + \frac{1}{(1 + i)^n}[(1 + m)^n S + C_1 - C_0];$$

$$V_1 = \frac{1}{1 + i}(S + C_2 - C_0) + \frac{1}{(1 + i)^2}(1 + m)^2 S$$

$$+ \frac{1}{(1 + i)^3}[(1 + m)^2 S + C_2 - C_0] + \frac{1}{(1 + i)^4}(1 + m)^4 S$$

$$+ \frac{1}{(1 + i)^5}[(1 + m)^4 S - C_2 - C_0] + \cdots$$

$$+ \frac{1}{(1 + i)^n}[(1 + m)^{n-1} S + C_2 - C_0];$$

$$V_2 = \frac{1}{1 + i}S + \frac{1}{(1 + i)^2}(S + C_3 - C_0) + \frac{1}{(1 + i)^3}(1 + m)^3 S$$

$$+ \frac{1}{(1 + i)^4}(1 + m)^3 S + \frac{1}{(1 + i)^5}[(1 + m)^3 S + C_3 - C_0]$$

$$+ \frac{1}{(1 + i)^6}(1 + m)^6 S + \cdots + \frac{1}{(1 + i)^n}[(1 + m)^{n-2} S + C_3 - C_0];$$

$$V_3 = \frac{1}{1+i} S + \frac{1}{(1+i)^2} S + \frac{1}{(1+i)^3} (S + C_4 - C_0)$$
$$+ \frac{1}{(1+i)^4} (1+m)^4 S + \frac{1}{(1+i)^5} (1+m)^4 S + \frac{1}{(1+i)^6} (1+m)^4 S$$
$$+ \frac{1}{(1+i)^7} [(1+m)^4 S + C_4 - C_0] + \frac{1}{(1+i)^8} (1+m)^8 S + \cdots$$
$$+ \frac{1}{(1+i)^n} [(1+m)^{n-3} S + C_4 - C_0].$$

Both the one-step improvement and the continuous improvement cases are special cases drawn from a universe in which there are any number of patterns of technological change. The decision the firm makes right now is affected by the assumption made about the future pattern of technological change. One would suspect that most firms lack sufficient knowledge to make a precise estimate of future technological change. However, this does *not* mean that the firm can ignore future technological change. In effect, the firm makes a decision about future technological change even if it refuses to consider assets other than those currently available. If it only considers currently available assets, it is assuming the one-step improvement case. With rapid technological change, almost any assumption about future technology could lead to more profitable decisions than the assumption of no change. Thus, the firm must make some assumption about future technology. No matter how accurately it formulates the replacement criterion, the profitability of its decisions will depend on how well it can guess the future. Although the forecasting problem is less severe for most investment decisions in that the forecast period is closer to the present, forecasting is necessary for even the most short-lived investment. And good decision rules are not substitutes for good forecasts, but the combination leads to profitable operations. The point is that the enormous forecasting difficulties that may be associated with the replacement decision are not the result of the decision rule, but are part and parcel of the nature of business activities in a dynamic economy.

The Management
of Inventories

3

Almost $1 out of each $5 invested by non-financial business corporations is invested in inventories. There is considerable variation, however, in the relative importance of inventories among the various industry classifications. This is shown in Table 3-1. The data reflect the different production modes, with retail and wholesale trade carrying a large share of total assets in inventory investment, whereas public utilities hold almost no inventory.

The inventory data are balance sheet figures. The physical inventories represented by the values are in a state of more or less continual flux as sales are made, raw materials purchased, and finished goods produced. From the point of view of GNP and real investment, the *changes* that take place in inventory assets are more significant than the stock of inventory held at any one time. Net inventory investment for nonfinancial business corporations is shown in Table 3-2. For the 19 years shown in the table, inventories declined (negative inventory investment) for 3 years and rose by less than $1 billion for 3 years. On the other hand, inventories rose by more than $5 billion during 3 of the observed years. Thus, investment in inventories is highly volatile.

Inventory investment, be it positive or negative, may be planned or involuntary. Involuntary inventory investment occurs when past sales have been less than had been expected. When sales turn out to be more than expected, inventories are involuntarily depleted. Thus, an increase in inventory investment may reflect disappointing sales performance, or, if made in anticipation of good business, may be a harbinger of prosperous times.

Table 3-1

INVENTORIES FOR NONFINANCIAL BUSINESS CORPORATIONS IN DOLLARS AND AS A PERCENTAGE OF TOTAL ASSETS FOR SELECTED INDUSTRIES AND SIZE GROUPS, 1960

INDUSTRY

SIZE CLASS OF ASSETS	MINING		CONSTRUCTION		MANUFACTURING		PUBLIC UTILITIES		WHOLESALE AND RETAIL TRADE	
	$000	%	$000	%	$000	%	$000	%	$000	%
$1–$25,000	0.165	0.64	22.4	10.04	56.5	15.85	1.34	0.87	273	28.91
$25,000–$50,000	1.144	1.99	52.0	12.96	142.1	18.37	2.91	1.15	756	35.49
$50,000–$100,000	1.97	1.62	101.3	13.33	374.5	20.45	6.64	1.40	1,713	35.05
$100,000–$250,000	10.79	2.75	308.3	14.25	1,218.4	21.54	15.32	1.45	4,427	34.92
$250,000–$500,000	22.19	3.99	247.5	12.27	1,685.8	23.78	18.34	1.63	3,846	34.51
$500,000–$1,000,000	29.23	4.27	249.1	12.34	2,200.0	25.84	32.46	2.26	3,546	34.31
$1,000,000–$2,500,000	32.62	3.24	287.2	12.08	3,625.0	26.50	34.81	1.68	3,320	32.70
$2,500,000–$5,000,000	40.55	4.35	165.8	11.68	2,938.0	27.07	32.07	1.65	1,914	31.82
$5,000,000–$10,000,000	50.58	4.59	98.3	9.14	3,064.0	26.30	40.41	1.78	1,634	30.36
$10,000,000–$25,000,000	71.90	4.35	38.3	3.40	4,696.0	26.31	82.02	2.40	1,681	27.74
$25,000,000–$50,000,000	82.69	5.51	44.5	4.72	3,829.0	24.85	79.47	2.12	1,043	25.95
$50,000,000–$100,000,000	79.67	5.27	8.96	1.53	4,839.0	23.12	111.55	1.91	591	21.23
$100,000,000–$250,000,000	186.48	6.79	10.41	5.51	6,543.0	22.78	295.57	2.03	1,343	26.17
$250,000,000–and up	311.30	6.61	—	—	20,552.0	17.27	2,339.96	2.20	2,347	22.21
Total	921.3	5.44	1,643.0	10.69	55,763.0	21.26	3,093.0	2.13	28,434	30.83

Source: *Statistics of Income : Corporation Income Tax Returns,* 1960–1961, U.S. Gov. Printing Office.

Table 3-2

CHANGES IN INVENTORIES FOR NONFINANCIAL BUSINESS CORPORATIONS BY YEARS, 1946–1963
(Billions of Dollars)

Years	Change in Inventories	Years	Change in Inventories
1946	6.0	1955	4.9
1947	1.2	1956	4.9
1948	2.1	1957	0.6
1949	−1.7	1958	−2.6
		1959	6.1
1950	4.8		
1951	8.6	1960	2.7
1952	2.2	1961	0.7
1953	0.8	1962	4.0
1954	−1.9	1963	3.9

Source: *Flow of Fund Accounts, 1945–1962, 1963, Supplement*, Board of Governors of the Federal Reserve System, pp. 56–57; and *Federal Reserve Bulletin*, April, 1964.

Similarly, a decline in inventories may reflect either unexpected increases in sales or a curtailment of productive activity in anticipation of a decline in sales. The latter would be a planned reduction and the former involuntary.

Although the aggregate data on inventory investment do not in themselves reveal the nature of the change, other data can be used to aid in interpreting inventory changes. Data are available on backlogs, or unfilled orders. If an inventory accumulation coincides with a growth in a manufacturer's backlogs, the increase in inventory investment is likely to be voluntary, and the converse would also be true. Another indicator is shifts in the relative importance of inventories by stages of fabrication. These are shown for manufacturers in Table 3-3. When net inventory investment coincides with an increase in the relative importance of raw or purchased materials or goods in process of production, the inventory investment is apt to be planned. On the other hand, if the inventory accumulation reflects a growth in the relative importance of finished goods, inventory investment may have occurred because of a decline in demand.

Behind the aggregate figures lie a host of decisions as firms attempt to adjust inventory levels in the face of shifting demand and changing costs. In this chapter, we shall present some relatively simple models of the process of inventory decisions. Inventory models tend to be far more complex than are models for fixed asset decisions. One of the reasons for the added complexity and variety of inventory models is that the forecasting problem is simpler. Usually, the inventory forecast is for a year or less, and the shorter the forecast period, the more accurate the forecast. Also, the firm must consider only conditions of demand and competition in forecasting inventory. While this is no easy task, it is easier than the forecast for fixed assets, because changes in technology, i.e., the problem of obsolescence, must be

Table 3-3

**RELATIVE IMPORTANCE OF MANUFACTURING INVENTORIES,
BY STAGE OF FABRICATION END OF YEAR, 1948–1963**

Year	Purchased Materials, %	Goods in Process, %	Finished Goods, %
1948	42	24	34
1949	39	23	38
1950	43	24	33
1951	39	26	35
1952	37	29	34
1953	35	29	36
1954	34	28	38
1955	34	30	36
1956	33	30	37
1957	32	30	38
1958	33	29	38
1959	33	29	38
1960	31	28	41
1961[a].................	26	40	34
1962[a].................	25	40	34
1963[a].................	35	30	35

[a]Average of months.
Source: Office of Business Economics, *Survey of Current Business*, Department of Commerce.

included for fixed assets. In short, the forecasts for fixed assets are much more prone to error than the shorter and simpler forecasts for inventory. It follows that the virtues of a complex model for fixed assets are apt to be lost because of forecasting errors.

Despite the differences between the models used for the two assets, the decision variable is the same. Fixed assets are adopted if the present value of expected returns exceeds the cost of the asset, i.e., net present value is positive. The net present value measures the expected increase in net worth resulting from the decision. Inventory units are added when the expected value of the net profits from inventory sales is positive. Profits will, ignoring dividends, increase net worth.

Thus, inventory will be increased when the revenues expected from the sales exceed variable costs. Why variable costs only? Fixed costs, by definition, will remain the same regardless of a particular inventory decision and so should not be allowed to affect the decision. The variable costs will include the cost of producing or, in the case of trade firms, purchasing inventory, any losses resulting from failing to sell the quantity stocked, any losses resulting from failing to stock enough to meet actual demand, the costs of carrying inventory (i.e., warehousing, insurance, interest on invested funds), and the costs of ordering inventory. For firms involved in production, the costs of ordering inventory include such production expenses as setup costs for a production run, which will be less per unit of inventory as the size of the order increases, as well as the cost of placing an order with an outside supplier. For the models which shall be presented in this chapter, it is convenient to separate the costs of carrying and ordering inventory from other variable costs. With this division, inventory will be increased only when the following equation has a positive sign preceding it:

(3-1)   Sales — variable costs of sales other than carrying and ordering — carrying and ordering costs = expected value of inventory.

THE ECONOMIC ORDER QUANTITY

For the first case, assume a firm facing certain demand, i.e., it knows exactly what sales will be. Assume also that the variable costs of sales are known and constant per unit, i.e., the price of purchased or produced inventory does not change with quantity purchased. Under these conditions, the firm will invest in inventory if the difference between sales and variable costs of sales exceeds the costs of carrying and ordering inventory. Further, the only way in which the firm can increase the expected value of inventory is to reduce inventory costs, which is the sum of carrying and ordering costs.

The larger the inventory carried in the face of certain demand, the more funds will be invested in inventory, and the greater will be the warehouse and insurance charges, etc. In other words, carrying costs vary directly with the size of inventory. On the other hand, the larger the inventory, the fewer orders for inventory will have to be made in a given time period. Given demand, the fewer orders made, the larger will be the inventory at any one time. Thus, ordering costs will vary inversely with the size of inventory.

Viewed this way, the problem facing the firm under certain demand is to choose an order quantity which will minimize total inventory costs. At this point, it is useful to present the two components of total inventory costs in the form of equations.

ORDERING COSTS

Given the order quantity Q, the number of orders placed in a time period is the number of units the firm expects to sell, Y, divided by Q. The number of orders is multiplied by the cost per order, o, to determine the total ordering costs for the period. Thus, total ordering costs for a period are Yo/Q. If expected sales are 1,500 units for the time period and 40 units are ordered in each order, with each order costing $1, total ordering costs are

$$\frac{1,500(\$1)}{40} = \$37.50.$$

CARRYING COSTS

If a firm orders a quantity Q and sales are fairly constant during the period, on the average the firm will have an inventory of $Q/2$ on hand. The investment represented by an inventory of $Q/2$ is determined by multiplying the cost price per unit, I, by the inventory, i.e., $(Q/2)I =$ inventory investment. The cost of carrying inventory can then be determined by multiplying the average inventory investment by an index c, which includes the cost of capital, insurance costs, storage costs, etc., per dollar invested in inventory per period. Thus, total carrying costs are $QIc/2$. If c is 0.50 and I is \$1 per unit, the costs of carrying inventory when $Q = 40$ is $[40(0.5)\$1]/2 = \$10.00$.

DETERMINING THE OPTIMAL Q

Setting $Y = 1,500$ units, $o = \$1$ per order, $I = \$1$ per unit, and $c = 0.50$ per dollar invested in inventory, then total carrying costs, ordering costs, and the sum of these can be shown for various levels of Q:

Q	Total Ordering Costs		Total Carrying Costs		Total Inventory Cost
5	1,500($1)/5	= $300	[5($1)0.5]/2 =	$ 1.25	$301.25
25	1,500($1)/25	= 60	[25($1)0.5]/2 =	6.25	66.25
50	1,500($1)/50	= 30	[50($1)0.5]/2 =	12.50	42.50
75	1,500($1)/75	= 20	[75($1)0.5]/2 =	18.75	38.75
100	1,500($1)/100	= 15	[100($1)0.5]/2 =	25.00	40.00
125	1,500($1)/125	= 12	[125(1)0.5]/2 =	31.25	43.25

Inspection of this table indicates that the lowest total inventory cost occurs where $Q = 75$ units. However, there are some wide gaps between the order quantities shown in the table. Could there be a Q for which the inventory costs would be even less than \$38.75? As an aid in answering the question, note that for all order quantities below 75, ordering costs exceed carrying costs, and that carrying costs exceed ordering costs for the quantities above 75. At 75 units, ordering costs almost equal carrying costs. This suggests that the lowest total inventory costs might occur for the Q at which ordering costs equal carrying costs. The suggestion could be proven by differentiating the equation

$$\text{Inventory costs} = \frac{QIc}{2} + \frac{Yo}{Q}$$

and setting the derivative of inventory costs equal to zero. Rather than resort to calculus, let us determine the order quantity at which carrying costs equal ordering costs, which is

$$\frac{QIc}{2} = \frac{Yo}{Q}.$$

Multiplying both sides by Q and by 2, we have

$$Q^2 Ic = 2Yo.$$

Dividing both sides by Ic, we find

$$Q^2 = \frac{2Yo}{Ic},$$

which leaves

(3-2) $$Q = \sqrt{\frac{2Yo}{Ic}}.$$

Substituting the values used above in Eq. (3–2),

$$Q = \sqrt{\frac{2(1,500)\$1}{\$1(0.5)}} = 77 \text{ or } 78 \text{ units.}$$

At 77 units, carrying costs are $19.40, ordering costs are $19.25, and total inventory costs are $38.65.

Equation (3-2) is often referred to as the *economic-order-quantity formula*. It can easily be applied to conditions in which demand can be forecast with reasonable accuracy and sales are fairly constant from day to day. The square root relationship has some interesting effects. For example, suppose that expected sales moved from 1,500 units to 3,000 units. The economic order quantity would move from 77 units to 111. Thus, a doubling of sales increases the order quantity by only 44 per cent. The square root sign has a similar dampening effect on the relationships between changes in any of the variables under the square root sign and Q.

ORDERING DATES
AND SAFETY STOCKS

Next, assume that the expected sales of 1,500 units are to be spread evenly over a year consisting of 250 business days, or daily sales are to be 6. If inventory were delivered instantaneously, the firm would place an order for 77 units every 12.8 days. The number of days between orders does not change even when inventory is not delivered instantaneously. For example, if delivery occurs 5 days following the placement of order, orders would be placed every 12.8 days starting 7.8 days after the receipt of the previous order. If delivery takes 64 days, orders are still placed every 12.8 days, but the orders start 64 days prior to the receipt of the first order. In this instance, 5 orders would have been placed at intervals of 12.8 days between each order before the first order would be delivered.

When the time between order placement and delivery is certain, as in the examples above, no added inventory is required to tide the firm over. Suppose the firm discovers that, although delivery averages five days after order, the following frequency distribution of days between order placement and receipt of goods has taken place, after adjusting for weekends and holidays:

Number of Days Between Order and Delivery	Frequency Distribution
3	0.1
4	0.1
5	0.5
6	0.3

If the firm places an order 9.8 days following receipt of the previous order, there is only 1 chance in 10 that it will receive the order before it runs out of stock. There is 1 chance out of 10 that it will be out of stock for an entire day, i.e., delivery will take four days; 5 chances out of 10 that it will be out of stock for two days; and 6 chances out of 10 that it will have no merchandise for three days. If the firm decides to play it safely, and places its order six days before it expects to be out of stock, the order may arrive in three days, four days, or five days. The firm will not run out of stock, but will have increased average inventory, by receiving orders before they are needed 0.7 of the time. This will increase total carrying costs.

To solve this problem, the expected increase in carrying costs must be compared with the expected losses due to being out of stock. The excess inventories that occur because of early orders constitute a safety stock. The firm will increase the safety stock as long as the expected increase in carrying costs is less than the expected losses due to shortages of inventory. If the cost per average dollar invested in inventory is 0.5 on an annual basis, the cost is 0.002 on a daily basis. The carrying cost per day for 77 units, which cost $1 each, is $0.154. The expected increase in carrying costs if the firm places its orders six days before it expects to run out would be calculated as follows:

If Delivered in (days)	Extra Days	Cost per Day	Conditional Carrying Costs	Probability	Expected Added Carrying Costs
3	3	$0.154	$0.462	0.1	$0.0462
4	2	0.154	0.308	0.1	0.0308
5	1	0.154	0.154	0.5	0.0770
6	0	0.154	0.0	0.3	0.0
			Total expected increase in carrying costs		$0.1540

If the firm sells each unit for $2, purchases the unit for $1, and incurs a variable selling expense of $0.50 per unit sold, profit per unit sold is $0.50. The $0.50 per unit profit, or with six units sold per day the $3 per day profit, is lost when stock is out if we assume that the firm cannot backlog orders. In addition, the firm may incur added penalties because customers, who are disappointed because of a lack of stock, may permanently shift their business to another source of supply. Considering only the $3 per day as the cost of running out of stock, the firm will incur no out-of-stock costs if it orders six days before existing inventory will be depleted, but will incur carrying costs. If the firm orders five days before depletion, the expected cost of being out of stock will be:

If delivered in (days)	Days of No Stock	Out-of-Stock Cost per Day	Conditional Out-of-Stock Costs	Probability, %	Expected-Out-of Stock Costs
3	0	$3	$0	0.1	0.0
4	0	3	0	0.1	0.0
5	0	3	0	0.5	0.0
6	1	3	3	0.3	0.90

Since no-stock costs per day are much higher than added carrying costs, the firm would order about six days before the previous order is depleted. Added carrying costs would average $0.154 per inventory cycle, i.e., every 12.8 business days, or annual total carrying costs would average about $3.01. In the continuous case, safety stocks will be increased as long as the expected incremental carrying costs are less than the expected incremental no-stock costs. The expected no-stock costs for seven days is zero in the example. It is certain that stock ordered seven days prior to need will be carried as excess inventory for one day..

There is a 0.1 chance that for 3 of the 12.8 days in an inventory cycle inventory will increase by 77 units; a 0.1 chance that for 2 of the 12.8 days inventory will rise by 77 units; and a 0.5 chance that inventory will rise by 77 units for 1 of the 12.8 days. Thus,

$$77(3/12.8)0.1 + 77(2/12.8)0.1 + 77(1/12.8)0.5 = 6.017$$

average added units per inventory cycle. If there were no safety stocks, average inventory would be $77/2 = 37.5$ units. With the safety stocks, average inventory will be 37.5 + approximately 6 = 43.5 units.

Two points are worthy of special note. First, and obvious, even if demand is known, safety stocks may be held if delivery time is uncertain, and there is a penalty for running out of stocking. A manufacturing company faces the same problem and will have to hold safety stocks of finished goods if the time needed to produce goods is variable.

Second, the relationship between the optimal level of safety stocks and the variability of delivery time is complex. In the example, which involved relatively high out-of-stock, costs, the average level of safety stocks equaled about one day of sales, even though it could take as long as six days to replenish inventories. If a firm estimated safety stocks by simply averaging the time needed to replenish inventory, it might decide to hold an average of five-days' safety stock, increasing carrying costs well beyond the level justified by the consequences of having no stock.

VARIABLE DEMAND

The economic order quantity approach to inventory decisions can be used even when demand is not perfectly known and varies from day to day. Of course, as demand becomes increasingly variable, the economic order quantity is less likely to be a problem, and determining the quantity demanded takes on importance. With variable demand, it is better to determine first the number of units needed each day and then determine the economic order quantity.

UNSTORABLE INVENTORY

If demand is variable for a product which cannot be stored and sold at another time, as might be the case for newspapers, the problem confronting the firm has nothing to do with the economic order quantity. It is not feasible to have more than one order per day, nor to order more than one day's stock. Carrying costs and ordering costs are irrelevant. Instead, the firm wants to order each day that quantity which will maximize the difference between sales and cost of sales.

Each unit stocked and sold generates a return, which is the difference between the sales price and the sum of unit purchase cost and variable selling expenses per unit. Each unit stocked but not sold has to be scrapped, and the loss is the difference between the scrap value, if any, and the purchase cost per unit. On the basis of market research, past experience, etc., the firm predicts the variable demand in the form of a probability distribution. The firm will stock a unit of inventory if the expected value of the return, which is the return per unit multiplied by the probability that the unit will be sold, exceeds the expected value of the loss per unit, which is the loss per unit multiplied by the probability that it will not be sold.

As an example, assume that the firm forecasts the following probability distribution of demand:

Demand	Probability	Demand	Probability
0	0.01	6	0.15
1	0.02	7	0.11
2	0.09	8	0.06
3	0.14	9	0.05
4	0.19	10 or more	0.03
5	0.15		

From this, the probability that demand for one unit will occur is the probability that demand will equal 1 or more, which is the probability that demand will exceed zero, or 0.99. The probability that demand will be for less than one unit is the probability that demand will be equal to zero, or 0.01.

If the firm charges $2 for a unit which has a cost price of $1 and incurs $0.50 variable selling expenses per unit sold, the net return per unit is $0.50. Assume that the scrap value is zero, and the loss per unit not sold is the cost price, $1. The optimal inventory can then be found from the following:

Demand	Conditional Gain	Probability that Demand will be Equal or Greater	Expected Gain	Conditional Loss	Probability that Demand will be Less	Expected Loss
0	$0.00	1.00	$0.000	$0.00	0.00	$0.00
1	0.50	0.99	0.495	1.00	0.01	0.01
2	0.50	0.97	0.485	1.00	0.03	0.03
3	0.50	0.88	0.440	1.00	0.12	0.12
4	0.50	0.74	0.370	1.00	0.26	0.26
5	0.50	0.55	0.275	1.00	0.45	0.45
6	0.50	0.40	0.200	1.00	0.60	0.60
7	0.50	0.25	0.125	1.00	0.75	0.75
8	0.50	0.14	0.070	1.00	0.86	0.86
9	0.50	0.08	0.040	1.00	0.92	0.92
10 or more	0.50	0.03	0.015	1.00	0.97	0.97

If one unit is stocked, the expected value of the gain is $0.495, and expected value of the loss is $0.01, or the expected value of the first unit of inventory is $0.485. Since this is an increment to net worth, the unit will be stocked. Using the same reasoning, the firm will stock the first four units. If it stocks the fifth unit, the expected incremental value of return is $0.275 and the expected incremental value of the loss is $0.45. The firm expects a net loss from the fifth and all following units. Therefore the firm will stock an inventory of four units. The total expected increase to net worth is the sum of the incremental expected gains for the first four units less the sum of the incremental expected losses, or $1.37.

RISK

The standard deviation was used as an index of risk for fixed assets. So, too, for inventory. The expected value, or mean value, of the increment to net worth for four units in the example was $1.37. To determine the standard deviation, the differences between the expected and actual increments must be calculated. The actual events with four units stocked may be that demand will be zero, one unit, two units, three units, or four units or more. If demand is zero, the firm will lose $4, the purchase cost of the units. If demand is one unit, the firm will lose $3 on the unsold units and make $0.50 on the sold unit, or a net of −$2.50. If two units are sold, the firm loses $1. If three units are sold, the firm nets $0.50. And if four units are sold, the firm earns $2. The standard deviation can then be calculated by summing the probability-weighted squares of the product of the difference between the net return of each possible event and the expected value.

Demand (1)	Net Return (2)	Net Return-Expected Value (3)	(4) = (3)²	Probability (5)	(6) = (5) × (4)
0	−$4.00	−$5.37	28.84	0.01	0.2884
1	−$2.50	−$3.87	14.98	0.02	0.2996
2	−$1.00	−$2.37	5.62	0.09	0.5058
3	+$0.50	−$0.87	0.76	0.14	0.1064
4 or more	+$2.00	+$0.63	0.40	0.74	0.2960
				Variance =	1.4962

Standard deviation $- \sqrt{1.4962} = 1.22.$

Thus, the standard deviation of the asset inventory in the example is $1.22. This may be divided by the expected value to provide an index of risk independent of the units of measurement, as was done with fixed assets, yielding a risk index of 0.89.

SAFETY STOCKS

It has been shown that, even when demand is certain, the firm may find it profitable to hold safety stocks because the time between ordering replenishment stocks and the delivery of such stocks is variable. When demand is variable, the firm may find it profitable to hold safety stocks if there is a penalty for failing to meet demand. What is the penalty? It is not the profit the firm would have made on the sale of the item had it been in stock. That profit is part of the original calculation used to determine the optimal level of stock. If the item was not stocked, the decision was based on the fact that the profit times the probability that there would be a demand for the item was less than the loss if the item was not demanded multiplied by the probability that the item would not be demanded.

Despite this, a disappointed would-be customer could react to the firm's failure to meet his demand by taking away his future business and turning to other suppliers permanently. Suppose that, in the example of variable demand used before, the firm believed that, if it continued to stock four units, the probability of demands for more than four units would eventually become very small. The future probability distribution might then appear as

Demand	Probability
0	0.02
1	0.04
2	0.20
3	0.31
4 or more	0.43

using $0.50 as the profit per unit sold and $1 as the loss per unsold unit, the optimal inventory would become three units instead of four, and the total expected value of the inventory would drop from $1.37 to $0.97. Given these expectations, should the firm decide to stock four units now, it will find it optimal to stock only three units later. If demand shifts unfavorably again because of disappointed customers, the firm may find it optimal later to stock only two units. And so on, until the firm is out of business. Such a chain of events may seem improbable, but even the improbable occurs, as witness the reaction of many neighborhood grocery stores to the onslaught of the supermarket.

A simplified example of the decision problem can be built from the preceding illustration. Assume, in addition, that the cost of capital used to discount future returns is 10 per cent.

Should the firm stock 4 units today, demand will be for four or fewer units, or for more than four units. If the demand is for four or fewer units, the future expected value of inventory remains unchanged at $1.37, and the actual value of today's inventory has not been affected by safety stock con- siderations, i.e., there is no safety stock. However, if the demand is for five units and the firm stocks only four, the actual value of today's stock is still unaffected by safety stock, but the future value of inventory falls by $0.40 ($1.37 − $0.97). The present value of the loss at 1 per cent for one period is $0.396.

Next, consider what may happen if the firm has decided to stock the fifth unit. If demand is for less than five units, the firm loses $1 today because of the wasted unit, but the future expected value of inventory is unchanged. But if today's actual demand is five units, the firm gains $0.50 by selling an added unit today, and the future expected value of inventory is unaffected.

The two decisions, to stock four or five units, and the consequences of each of these decisions may be summarized in what can be called a payoff table:

| | ACTUAL CURRENT DEMAND | |
Decision	4 or Fewer Units	5 or More Units
Stock 4	0	− $0.396
Stock 5	− $1	+ 0.50

Regardless of the decision, the probability of demands being equal to four or fewer units is 0.45. The probability of demands being for five or more units is 0.55. Since the conditional values associated with each of the decisions have different probabilities, the probabilities must be included in the payoff table.

| | EXPECTED CURRENT DEMAND | | |
Decision	4 or Fewer Units	5 or More Units	Sum = Expected Loss
Stock 4..........	0.45($0)	0.55(− $0.396)	− $0.2178
Stock 5..........	0.45(− 1)	0.55(+0.50)	−0.1750

The decision to stock five units is expected to result in a smaller loss than the decision to stock four units, so the firm will stock at least five units.

To determine whether a sixth unit should be stocked, the calculation is repeated. The conditional values are unchanged, but the probabilities shift, since the concern now is whether demand will be for five or fewer units or for six or more units. The sixth unit will not be stocked since the expected incremental loss from stocking six units is $0.40, whereas the loss of staying at five units is only $0.1584.

This is identical with the problem of fixed assets: The reduction in expected value resulting from investment in a fifth unit is C, and the differences between future values if four units or five units are stocked today are equivalent to the S values for fixed assets. If the net present value of the investment is positive, the investment should be made, i.e., the fifth unit should be stocked. Should the investment be made, the same calculation would be made for stocking the sixth unit, seventh, etc., until the net present value of stocking an added unit is equal to, or less than, zero.

An alternative way of viewing the problem of safety stocks is to treat the safety stock as if it were insurance. The more units added to the safety stock, the smaller will be the losses from future adverse shifts in demand. The premiums for this kind of insurance are the declines in the expected value of today's inventory resulting from adding units. As more units are added to current inventory, the probability of selling the last unit declines, which means that the negative expected incremental value of each unit of safety stock will become successively larger. In effect, the premium, or cost, of each successive unit of insurance becomes larger. As the safety stock grows, the likelihood of having disappointed customers today becomes smaller, which reduces the future losses against which the safety stock is a protection. Thus, it becomes increasingly expensive to insure against losses that become increasingly smaller as the safety stock grows.

The following table taken from the previous example indicates the declines in expected value of current inventory which will occur as the safety stock grows. As indicated, these declines may be viewed alternatively as the costs of a series of investments or as the premiums paid for demand insurance.

Units Stocked	Decline in Total Expected Value of Inventory
5	$0.175
6	0.400
7	0.625
8	0.790
9	0.880
10	0.955

ECONOMIC ORDER QUANTITY AND VARIABLE DEMAND

When the firm faces a variable demand for a storable good, the optimal level of inventory may be determined by combining the incremental value approach with the economic order quantity. To illustrate this simply, let us use the example of variable demand presented earlier. We shall assume that the firm now has a storable type of inventory and has determined that the total expected value of inventory, not including carrying and ordering costs, is at a maximum when four units are available for sale each day. Further, the probability distribution facing the firm each day is the same for every business day, and there are 250 business days in the year.

On this basis, annual demand by the firm is 250 × 4, or 1,000 units yearly. If the firm places one order per day, annual ordering costs will be 250 × $1 (which is the cost per order) = $250. Carrying costs will be zero. If only one order is placed each year, ordering costs will be $1, but carrying costs will be the average inventory, 500, times the cost price per unit, $1, times the annual carrying costs per dollar invested in inventory, 0.5, = $250. From this, it should be clear that even in the case of variable demand, the firm can reduce inventory costs by using the economic order quantity. Using eq. (3–2), the economic order quantity is

$$\sqrt{\frac{2(1,000)\,\$1}{0.5(\$1)}} = 63 \text{ units.}$$

When the order quantity is 63 units, about 15.9 orders annually, annual order costs will be $15.90. The average inventory will be 31.5 units, so that the annual carrying costs will be about $15.75, making total inventory costs $31.65 for the year.

It is conceivable that the total inventory costs may exceed the expected value of inventory, excluding inventory costs. If so, the firm may decide to stock fewer units or, if it is impossible to bring inventory costs below the expected value of inventory, to stock no units at all. If we use the data from the variable-demand no-storage example, the firm expects each day's inventory to have a value of $1.37. The annual value of the inventory decision, still excluding inventory costs, would be 250 × $1.37, or $342.50. The net annual expected addition to net worth resulting from the decision to have four units available each day is $342.50 − $31.65 = $310.85. Since this is positive even after subtracting inventory costs, the firm will not alter its original decision.

LOSS CALCULATIONS

Given a storable good which can last over several demand periods, the calculation of the loss for an unsold unit can be very tedious. The loss may be defined as the difference between the expected value of the unit if sold today and the *present value* of the expected value if the unit is sold later. The unit may be sold tomorrow, the day after, or on any of several days thereafter. The conditional loss becomes the difference between the expected value if sold today and the sum of the following: the present value of the expected value if sold tomorrow × the probability that it won't be sold today + the present value of the expected value if sold in two days × the probability that it won't be sold tomorrow + the present value of the expected value if sold in three days × the probability that the unit will not be sold in two days + . . . + the present value of the loss when it is finally unsalable × the probability that it will not be sold in the day preceding its deterioration. The only practical way to solve this problem is to use an electronic computer.

It is quite possible to present a great variety of very complex approaches to determining inventory. The cases presented in this chapter are not meant to be exhaustive, but to illustrate the most general principles that underly the majority of inventory models. The reader should, however, be aware of the *caveat* that, even though most inventory problems turn out to be solved by some combination of probability distributions of demand and economic order quantity, each problem involves special features, and ready-made models are not often useful without modification.

PRICING AND INVENTORY
MODELS

In the economics of the firm as usually presented, the firm is confronted with demand and cost schedules. The quantity the firm will sell is determined by the point at which marginal revenues equal marginal costs, which maximizes profits. The price charged is found by referring to the demand schedule, which links a single quantity to each price.

The economic order quantity approach with certain demand is quite easy to reconcile with the economic model of price determination. The firm chooses the quantity it will sell over a period of time, setting price accordingly, so as to maximize profits, excluding inventory costs. It then determines the order quantity that minimizes inventory costs.

In most inventory models of variable demand, costs other than inventory are assumed to be linear, i.e., per unit purchase prices and selling costs do not vary as quantity changes. For each selling price, the firm faces not one quantity, as in the economic model of price determination, but a set of quantities. Each quantity in the set has a probability. For each quantity, we calculate the probability-adjusted marginal profit, i.e., the expected incremental difference between sale price and costs, and the probability-adjusted marginal loss, or expected incremental loss. The quantity chosen from the set of quantities for each price was that quantity which maximized total expected value. If this had been done for different prices, say 10 different prices, expected value-maximizing quantities would have emerged. The firm would charge the price associated with the set of quantities generating the *maximus maximorum*, the highest expected value of the 10 expected value-maximizing quantities.

The two major differences between the inventory model and the economic model of price determination are that the inventory model does not require the assumption of certain demand at each price and does assume that variable costs of production are linear. Otherwise, the firm is assumed to be achieving the same goal since, when profits and time periods are properly defined, maximizing profits over the long run is the same as maximizing the present value of net worth.

INVENTORY AND FIXED ASSETS

The optimal investment in inventory interacts with the optimal level of fixed assets. For example, the firm may acquire a computer in order to determine the optimal level of inventory. The net savings in this case would be the difference in the expected value of inventory if the computer is used and the expected value if some cruder approximation is attempted.

Fixed assets may affect the level of inventory. Consider a machine which, if used to produce large quantities of output, can produce at a lower per unit cost than existing equipment at the same level of output. However, the existing equipment can produce more cheaply than the new machine at low levels of output. The returns from adopting the new machine would be the result, primarily, of the difference between the expected value of inventory, net of carrying and ordering costs, with the new machine and the expected value of inventory, also net of inventory costs, for the existing equipment. The difference would occur because the new machine would produce large quantities at a lower per unit purchase cost than the old. This would reduce the cost of carrying inventory, increasing the economic order quantity and raising inventories. Also, the lower purchase cost would increase the conditional gain on each unit carried, increasing the quantity the firm would wish to stock for each demand period and tending to raise inventories. On the other hand, it may turn out that the setup costs (the equivalent of ordering costs) for a production run on the new equipment are higher than on the old. Though this would move in the direction of larger inventories, i.e., fewer orders, the net expected value of the inventory would be lower because of higher inventory costs.

An increase in the desired level of inventory, because of an increase in sales, for example, could change the level of fixed assets. Equipment proposals that would have been rejected earlier when demand was weak might be given favorable consideration in the face of strong demand. The calculation for the fixed assets is the same as in the example above. The difference between the expected value of optimal inventories with the new equipment and the expected value of optimal inventories with the existing fixed assets forms the basis for the returns of the new equipment. Then the S values are discounted by the cost of capital, and the new equipment is adopted if the net present value is positive.

CONCLUSION   Although the methods of calculating the expected value of inventory are varied and generally are different than the methods for calculating the present value of fixed assets, the decision variable is the same. Inventory is increased as long as the total expected value of inventory will rise. Fixed assets are increased as long as the net present value of each asset is positive. Both total expected value of inventory and net present value of fixed assets are increments to net worth, ignoring dividends. Thus, the general rule is that inventory and/or fixed asset investment will be expanded as long as the expected result is an increase in net worth.

SELECTED REFERENCES

Abramovitz, M.: *Inventories and Business Cycles*, National Bureau of Economic Research, New York, 1950.

Arrow, K., Harris T., and J. Marschak: "Optimal Inventory Policy," *Econometrica*, July, 1951.

Arrow, K., S. Karlin, and H. Scarf: *Studies in the Mathematical Theory of Inventory and Production*, Stanford, Cal., 1958.

Beckman, M., and J. Muth: "An Inventory Policy for the Case of Lagged Delivery," *Management Science*, Jan., 1956.

Dalleck, W., and R. Fetter: *Decision Models for Inventory Management*, Irwin, Homeward, Ill., 1961.

Dorfman, J.: "Operations Research," *American Economic Review*, Sept., 1960.

Eagle, A.: "Distribution of Seasonal Inventory of the Hawaiian Pineapple Company," *Operations Research*, June, 1957.

Metzler, L.: "The Nature and Stability of Inventory Cycles," *Review of Economic Statistics*, Aug., 1941.

Mills, E.: "The Theory of Inventory Decisions," *Econometrica*, Apr., 1957.

Nichol, W.: "Probability Analysis in the Theory of Demand, Net Revenue, and Price," *Journal of Political Economy*, Oct., 1941.

Savage, L.: "The Theory of Statistical Decision," *Journal of The American Statistical Association*, Mar., 1951.

Schlaiffer, R.: *Probability and Statistics for Business Decisions*, McGraw-Hill, New York, 1959.

Shaw, E.: "Elements of a Theory of Inventory," *Journal of Political Economy*, Aug., 1940.

Smithies, A.: "The Maximization of Profits over Time with Changing Cost and Demand Functions," *Econometrica*, Oct., 1939.

Whitin, T.: "Inventory Control and Price Theory," *Management Science*, Oct., 1955.

———: "Managerial Economics and the Firm," *American Economic Review, Papers and Proceedings, May*, 1960.

———: *The Theory of Inventory Management*, Princeton, N. J., 1953.

Trade
Credit Management

4

Trade credit arises because of sales between firms with cash payment postponed. Usually, the instrument recording the credit is simply an accounting entry: On the seller's books, the credit sale appears as an account receivable; on the buyer's books, as an account payable. In some industries, a promissory note records the credit. A note may also be used when a buyer fails to make payment within the agreed time. Typical credit periods are 30, 60, or 90 days, although longer terms may be offered.

Normally, interest is not directly charged on trade credit sales, although the selling firm is effectively making a loan to the buyer. It is not unusual for sellers to allow discounts if payment is made rapidly, say within 10, 20, or 30 days. From the buyer's point of view, failure to take cash discounts can be quite expensive. For example, when credit terms are 2/10, n/30—which means that a 2 per cent discount may be deducted from the bill if it is paid within 10 days, but that payment must be made within 30 days—, failure to take the discount means that the buyer is paying 2 per cent for an additional 20 days of credit. On an annual basis, this is equivalent to an interest rate of 36 per cent (2 per cent times 360/20).

Trade credit may also flow from buyer to seller in the form of advances. Advances have been quite common between defense manufacturers and the United States government. Private customers who buy all or most of the output of a firm may also supply advances.

Nonfinancial business corporations had some $94 billion of trade credit outstanding at the end of 1961. Over half of this, $58 billion, had been made to other nonfinancial business corporations, and the remainder had beenextended to other sectors of the economy, including unincorporated businesses. Typically, nonfinancial business corporations have been net trade creditors to the rest of the economy, i.e., the sector extends more trade credit than it receives. Table 4-1 shows that, within the nonfinancial corporate sector, there is considerable variation in the importance of trade credit, or accounts receivable, as an asset investment, and that, over time, it has become more important both as an asset investment and in relation to sales.

Table 4-1

ACCOUNTS RECEIVABLE AS A PER CENT OF TOTAL ASSETS
AND OF BUSINESS RECEIPTS FOR NONFINANCIAL BUSINESS
CORPORATIONS, BY SELECTED INDUSTRIES, 1948 AND 1960

Industry	ACCOUNTS RECEIVABLE ÷ TOTAL ASSETS, %		ACCOUNTS RECEIVABLE ÷ BUSINESS RECEIPTS, %	
	1948	1960	1948	1960
All manufacturing	14.41	16.90	8.98	12.16
Food	13.89	19.03	4.52	7.01
Apparel	25.05	30.89	8.56	11.46
Lumber	12.71	15.71	8.47	12.37
Chemicals	12.22	13.92	9.33	12.85
Petroleum and coal	12.76	13.68	11.96	15.11
Rubber	19.28	24.62	11.60	16.37
Primary metal	11.75	9.85	8.13	9.79
Electric machinery	17.80	24.55	11.92	16.08
Motor vehicles	10.12	9.44	5.60	6.33
Transportation and R.R.	4.19	6.25	8.47	10.37
Electric and gas utilities	2.65	3.07	10.00	10.07
Wholesale trade	31.58	35.54	8.67	11.66
Retail trade	19.63	23.79	6.95	8.60
Services	11.57	17.63	9.63	15.83

Source: *Corporation Income Tax Returns, Statistics of Income,* 1948–'49, 1960–'61, U.S. Government Printing Office.

THE TRADE CREDIT DECISION

In this section, we shall be concerned with identifying the determinants of the decision to invest in trade credit and the determinants of the credit terms. After an illustration of the basic factors, we shall turn to the following models:

1. the case of increasing demand;
2. optimal cash discount;
3. liquidation of excess inventories and utilization of excess plant by trade credit;

4. trade credit as an offset to seasonal demand.

In all these cases, credit risk will be assumed to be nonexistent. In other words, it is assumed certain that a buyer will pay on the due date of the trade credit. Though this is not realistic, it allows us to concentrate on the revenue and cost aspects of trade credit. In the next section, trade credit risk will be introduced, and we shall analyze its effect on the investment decision.

The decision variable will be as it has been with inventory and fixed assets: The firm will invest in trade credit if the net present value of the investment is positive. Investment will be undertaken as long as net worth will be larger with the investment than without it.

BASIC CASE

To illustrate the basic factors, except risk, which determine the trade credit investment, consider a firm approached by a customer who wishes to buy 100 units of a good for which the selling price is $2 per unit and costs are $1.50 per unit. The customer wishes to buy on credit, paying in three months.

Assume that the firm will not lose cash sales because of a stock shortage if it accepts this offer. The offer will be accepted if it generates a profit. To calculate the profit or loss, we must first reduce the $200 sale to its present value. If the cost of capital is 1 per cent a month, the present value of the sale is $194.20. Since the total cost is $150.00, the firm will make $44.20 by accepting the offer, increasing net worth by this amount.

The sale on trade credit is equivalent to cutting price. In this case, the effective price cut is from the normal price of $2 to $194.20/100 = $1.94. Generally, the size of the price cut is determined by the credit term, i.e., proposed collection period, and the cost of capital. For example, if the customer wanted credit terms of 40 months, the present value of the sale would be $134.40, and acceptance of these terms would involve the firm in a loss of $15.60. If the cost of capital for the three month sale were 25 per cent a month, the present value of the sale would be $102.40, and the firm would sustain a loss of $47.60 by accepting the offer.

Second, the accounting valuation of the credit sale is quite different from the economic valuation. The primary difference in the case with no credit risk is that the accounting valuation ignores the effect of the collection period and the cost of capital. Thus, accounts receivable will rise by $200 as a result of the sale. Assuming that the goods are carried at the full cost in inventory, inventory will fall by $150. The $50 remainder makes up gross income.

If accounting conventions allowed the use of present values, accounts receivable would be increased by $194.20 at the time of sale. Inventories would be decreased by $150, and the $44.20 difference would increase gross income and, ultimately, net worth. At the end of three months, the firm would receive cash of $200 in payment of the trade credit. Cash would rise by $200 and accounts receivable would fall by $194.20. The difference of $5.80 would be interest income for the use of funds invested in accounts receivable.

This approach, though novel, is helpful in understanding the nature of accounts receivable. The credit buyer is, in effect, selling a three-month bill to the firm. Because we assume that payment in three months is certain, the bill is similar to those issued by the United States Treasury. As with Treasury bills, the security is sold on a discount basis, i.e., the $200 is a maturity value, and the firm pays a lower price, which is determined by the interest rate, the cost of capital.

From the point of view of the buyer of goods, his liabilities, accounts payable specifically, have increased. If he could finance the purchase by issuing a different and cheaper liability, say a bank loan, he would. From the point of view of the seller of goods, an investment is made when he sells on credit. As with all investments, the account receivable must yield a positive expected net value if it is to be added to the firm's balance sheet.

Trade credit will be used when the cost of capital for the goods-buying, i.e., securities-issuing, firm is equal to, or higher than, the cost of capital for the goods-selling, i.e., securities-buying, firm. The differential between the two costs of capital should reflect the possibility that the acquisition costs, or the cost of floating securities, may be higher to the securities issuer in raising funds from sources other than trade credit. If the net cost of capital were only 0.5 per cent per month to the goods buyer, the goods buyer, i.e., securities seller, would ask for $196.05 for his three-month bill. The goods seller, or securities buyer, with a 1 per cent cost of capital would be unwilling to offer more than $194.20 for the bill. Therefore, no securities transaction would take place. The goods transaction would take place if the securities seller can sell his security, which now may take a different physical form than it would as trade credit, to another buyer at the minimum price of $196.05.

Is this really what happens? Or, is it simply a theoretical fable with no counterpart in reality? It is always dangerous to dismiss fables which make sense, even if there is no obvious real counterpart. Consider that, in the example, the goods seller would be just as well off accepting a cash sale at a discounted price as low as $1.942 per unit. If the goods buyer has a cost of capital of only 0.5 per cent a month, he can raise $194.20 by issuing a three-month security with a maturity value of about $198.12 instead of the $200 maturity of the trade credit security. So, when the goods buyer has a lower cost of capital than the goods seller, the goods buyer can save by financing through the issue of some other kind of liability, rather than trade credit.

It should be noted that the goods-selling firm can effectively cut price for a cash sale by means other than a direct price cut. All or part of the costs of shipping the goods can be absorbed by the seller, or *bonus* units can be added to the order if payment is for cash. The devices which an ingenious seller can use to disguise a price cut, and so avoid the reactions of competitors or the demands of other customers, are legion.

INCREASING DEMAND

Perhaps the most general reason for investing in trade credit is that the offer of trade credit terms increases demand. As has been indicated already, trade credit is not costless to the seller. And trade credit is not the only way a firm can increase demand. Even when competitors offer trade credit terms, the firm may choose to use advertising, pricing, increased services, or any combination of these and trade credit as means of retaining or increasing demand.

In the case of advertising, the firm will increase advertising expenditures as long as the expected profits from the increased demand, measured before deducting the added advertising costs, exceed the advertising expenditures required to generate the expected profits. So, too, in the case of trade credit. The firm will invest in trade credit as long as the expected net value of inventory is greater with trade credit than without it.

It is convenient to visualize the problem as that of deciding which of several trade credit policies will be adopted. For each trade credit policy, there is a separate probability schedule of demand. As the trade credit terms become more generous, the probability of selling larger quantities increases, but not necessarily in proportion to the improvement in trade credit terms. Also, as trade credit terms are expanded, the proportion of cash customers diminishes, and the proportion of customers buying on extended credit terms increases. With more customers buying on credit and the credit term extended, the present value of the selling price falls, reducing the expected value of demand. As long as the expected quantity of sales rises relatively more rapidly than the decline in the present value of the selling price, the net effect of extending more generous trade credit terms will increase the expected value of sales. At some point, further expansion of trade credit reduces the present value of the selling price by more than it increases demand, and the expected value of sales will fall. Thus, the firm will offer expanded credit terms as long as the net effect is to increase the expected value of sales.

Example of Increasing Demand. Assume a firm is selling a good at a price of $2, with a cost of production of $1. Each sale involves a variable selling expense of $0.50 per unit. Each unit not sold in the current selling period incurs an expected loss of $1. The cost of capital is 1 per cent a month.

On the basis of market surveys and past experience, the firm estimates that extending trade credit will favorably affect the probability distribution of demand. The demand distributions associated with three possible trade credit policies will be compared. The first policy is cash sales only. The second will allow credit extensions for a term of no longer than three months. Finally, we shall consider the probability distribution of demand associated with the policy of extending trade credit for periods as long as six months.

PROBABILITY DISTRIBUTIONS WITH

Quantity	All Cash Sales	Up to 3-month Credit	Up to 6-month Credit
0	0.01	0.0001	0.001
1	0.04	0.0009	0.009
2	0.10	0.006	0.01
3	0.15	0.04	0.01
4	0.18	0.10	0.02
5	0.22	0.15	0.09
6	0.16	0.18	0.15
7	0.11	0.22	0.17
8	0.02	0.16	0.22
9	0.006	0.11	0.20
10	0.003	0.03	0.10
11 or more	0.001	0.003	0.02

The conditional gain from a cash sale is $2 − $1 − $0.50 = $0.50. The loss if not sold is $1, regardless of credit. If the firm does not receive payment immediately, however, the conditional gain is the present value of the price, from which the current value of costs will be deducted. The present value of $2 received in one month is $1.98 when the cost of capital is 1 per cent per month. The conditional gain from a credit sale paid in one month is $1.98 − $1.50 = $0.48. The present value of the conditional gains for a cash sale with one-month, two-month, three-month, four-month, five-month, and six-month credit are presented below.

Collected	Present Value of Conditional Gain
Cash immediately	$0.50
At end of 1 month	0.48
At end of 2 months	0.46
At end of 3 months	0.44
At end of 4 months	0.42
At end of 5 months	0.40
At end of 6 months	0.38

The conditional gain under each of the probability distributions of demand shown above will depend upon the proportion of sales made to each of the types of customers represented. Suppose the firm estimates that the distribution will be as follows:

Customer Types	Up to 3-month Credit, %	Up to 6-month Credit, %
Cash	25	14.3
Pay at end of 1 month	25	14.3
Pay at end of 2 months	25	14.3
Pay at end of 3 months	25	14.3
Pay at end of 4 months		14.3
Pay at end of 5 months		14.3
Pay at end of 6 months		14.3

with, of course, all customers paying cash under the "all cash sales" policy. The average conditional gain with all cash sales would be $0.50. With the policy of selling on credit up to three months, the average conditional gain is the average of the conditional gain for cash sales and of the present values of the conditional gain from collections in one, two, and three months, each weighted by the proportion of customers in its class, i.e., 0.25($0.50) + 0.25($0.48) + 0.25($0.46) + 0.25($0.44) = $0.47. The same method is used to calculate the average conditional gain if sales are made on credit terms to six months, which is $0.44.

With the average conditional gain for each of the three trade credit policies as given above, and the conditional loss being $1 in all cases, it is possible to calculate the total expected value for each of the policies.

Given the probability distribution associated with each of the policies, we use the same method developed in calculating the optimal level of inventory with variable demand in the previous chapter. Under the cash sales policy, the firm would stock four units for each demand period, and the total expected value for the demand period would be $1.24. If credit sales are allowed for as long as three months, the firm would stock six units with a total expected value of $2.08. The total expected value with the policy of selling on credit for periods up to six months is $2.30, and the firm would stock seven units for each demand period.

Under the criterion of maximizing net worth, the firm would adopt the policy of making credit sales for as long as six months. It is important to remember that this is based on a set of asumptions concerning the probability distribution of demand and the distribution of customer types. While different assumptions would lead to different answers, the method would be the same.

THE VALUE OF ACCOUNTS RECEIVABLE   The value of accounts receivable on the balance sheet may be stated either in accounting values or as the expected increment to net worth. In the latter instance, it is the difference between the cash sales only policy and the policy of making sales on credit for periods up to six months. It is $2.30 − $1.24, or $1.06. This measures the expected increase in the firm's net worth for a single demand period as a result of making credit sales. If a demand period equals 1 day and there are 250 business days in a year, the annual value of the increment to net worth from accounts receivable would be $265.

What would be the average accounting value of accounts receivable? Sales will be $14 per business day (seven units @ $2), or $3,500 a year. Monthly sales will be approximately $292, 14.3 per cent of which are for cash and the remainder collected within a six-month period following sales. At the end of the first month, $250.29 of accounts receivable will be on the books. During the second month, the firm will invest in an additional $250.29 of accounts receivable and will collect $41.71 from sales of the first month, leaving accounts receivable at $458.87. During the third month, the firm will add $250.29 to accounts receivable from current sales, but will collect $41.71 from sales of the first and second months'. Accounts receivable will total $625.74 at the end of the third month. During the fourth month, credit sales will increase accounts receivable by another $250.29, but collections of approximately $41.71 from each of the preceding three months' sales will leave an accounts receivable balance of $750.90 at the end of the month. This will continue until, at the end of the seventh month, the balance will be approximately $875. This is the end-of-the-month balance which will prevail under the policy of selling on credit terms up to six months as long as the probability distribution of demand does not change and the distribution of credit customers remains as specified earlier.

The average level of accounts receivable would rise if:

1. the total volume of sales rose, with the proportion of credit sales held constant;
2. the proportion of customers paying in two or more months rose, and the proportion of those paying cash or in one month fell, with sales held constant.

And the converse is also true. If there are seasonal variations in demand, the level of accounts receivable will tend to rise following the peak in demand and fall following slack demand. This is in contrast to inventory where the accumulation of inventory precedes the peak demand and drops thereafter.

Annual credit sales in our example is 85.7 per cent of total sales, or $2,499,50. The average of accounts receivable is $875. In analyzing accounting statements, the liquidity, i.e., the speed with which a noncash asset is converted into cash, of accounts receivable is measured by taking the ratio of total credit sales to average accounts receivable. The resultant ratio is called the *turnover of accounts receivable*. In the example, the ratio would be $2,499.50/$875 = 2.88, i.e., accounts receivable turn over 2.88 times a year. The average age of accounts receivable in months is the reciprocal of the turnover multiplied by the number of months in a year. Thus, the average age of accounts receivable in the example is about 4.2 months. Interpreted, the average age indicates the average length of time the firm must wait between making a credit sale and collecting cash for the sale. When credit sales are not available for the computation, total sales are used instead. As a result, the turnover ratio is greater, and the average age less, than when cash sales are excluded. In the example using total sales, the turnover becomes four, and the average age becomes three months.

DISCOUNT POLICY

In order to encourage early payment of credit sales, the firm may offer a discount from the purchase price if payment is made before a specified date. We are interested only in those discounts which have, as the sole purpose, speeding payments. Under competitive circumstances, a very generous system of discounts for early payment may really be a way of disguising a price cut and so reducing the chance of retaliatory price cuts by competitors. Even when the discount policy had, as its original purpose, the aim of speeding up collections, it may become a means of cutting price when demand becomes slack. For example, the firm may allow a 2 per cent discount if payment is made within 30 days. Under conditions of slack demand, the firm may use the discount as a price cut by not enforcing the 30-day limit.

The size of a *collections speedup discount* is determined by the gain to the firm resulting from more rapid collections and the size of the discount required to achieve the speedup. The gain is simply the difference between the present value of the price with a normal collection period and the present value of the same price with an earlier collection caused by the discount. If the discount needed to speed collections exceeds the difference in present values of price, the firm is better off with no discounts. Ideally, the firm would like the discount to be very small and the difference in present values very large. However, it will offer larger discounts as long as the discount is less than the gain in present value of price.

As an example, let us use the data from the example of increasing demand. A customer who would normally pay for a good in three months offers the firm a conditional gain of $0.50 with a present value of $0.44, assuming the cost of capital to be 1 per cent a month. What would be the maximum discount the firm would be willing to offer the customer in order to make him pay at the end of two months? The present value of $0.50 in two months is $0.46, so the firm gains 0.02 if the customer pays one month earlier. Since the price of the good is $2, the discount should not exceed 1 per cent. To get the customer to pay two months earlier than he would in the absence of the discount, the discount should not exceed 2 per cent. A 3 per cent discount would be the maximum the firm would be willing to offer to convert a three-month payer to a cash customer. In trade credit jargon, this discount structure would be expressed, 3/cash, 2/30, 1/60, net/90.

More formally, the determination of the maximum discount is as follows:

$$\text{Price} \times \frac{1}{(1 + i)^n} - \text{costs} = PV^n,$$

where PV^n is the net present value of a credit sale which the firm expects to collect in period n. The maximum discount the firm will be willing to offer is the increase in present value resulting from an early collection. If the firm collects one period earlier than n, the increase in present value is

$$\text{Price} \times \frac{1}{(1 + i)^{n-1}} - \text{costs} - \text{price} \times \frac{1}{(1 + i)^n} - \text{costs} = PV^{n-1} - PV^n.$$

The maximum amount of discount, then, is $PV^{n-1} - PV^n$. In percentage terms, the maximum discount rate is $[PV^{n-1} - PV^n]/\text{price} = \text{maximum price}$ discount for one period earlier collection. The numerical example in the preceding paragraph is only approximately correct, since the precise credit structure to be offered a customer normally paying in three months is 2.9/cash, 1.9/one month, 0.9/two months, net/three months. For practical purposes, the rounded percentages given earlier are probably adequate. It should be noted, however, that the main determinant of the discount structure is the firm's cost of capital. It should also be noted that the customer will only take advantage of the discount if the customer's cost of capital is equal to or less than the firm's cost of capital.

All would be well if the firm could offer various discount structures to different customers. However, it may be impractical to discriminate between customers. The problem arises because a cash customer may insist that he be allowed the 3 per cent discount. Customers who normally pay in one month may insist upon the 2 per cent discount, and normal two-month payers may now insist upon the 1 per cent discount. From the firm's point of view, it would like to offer a normal two-month payer credit terms of 2/cash, 1/30, net/60, and to the normal one-month payer, terms of 1/cash, net/30; with the normal cash customer receiving no discount. However, attempts to discriminate may result in customers becoming angry and taking their business elsewhere.

If it cannot discriminate, the firm will offer a single set of discount terms, which will treat the cash customer better than if the firm could discriminate, but treat the normal two-month payer less favorably. Although it might appear that the single discount structure should be an average of the structures that would prevail if the firm could discriminate, this is not a necessary result. For example, cash customers may be less likely to switch to another firm than the credit customers. If so, the single discount structure will be more favorable to credit customers, and less favorable to cash customers, than would an average structure.

A complication to the problem may be caused by competition. Can the firm afford to offer discount terms less generous than those of its competitors? Perhaps, for there are many means of competing, and it may be more effective for the firm to compete with competitors' generous discounts by advertising, pricing, service, absorption of delivery costs, or any of a host of competitive tools rather than by imitating discount structures. However, when competition is strong and customers very conscious of discounts, the firm may find that not imitating the discounts of the competition leads to a lower expected value of accounts receivable than if the firm does imitate. In that case, it is in the best interests of the firm to meet the competition.

INVENTORY, FIXED ASSETS, AND CREDIT SALES

To this point, we have shown that, with appropriate demand conditions and cost of capital, the firm can increase the expected value of net worth by increasing sales through the extension of trade credit. One result of this is an increase in inventory, though not necessarily in direct proportion to the increase in sales. Another possible result could be an increase in fixed asset investment, justified by the increased production needed to meet higher sales. In this section, we shall be concerned with the opposite flow of causation, i.e., how a large inventory or investment in fixed assets can cause an increase in trade credit.

EXCESS INVENTORY

Consider a firm which has made a mistake in its forecasts of demand. As a result, it has an inventory of 10 units. The price of each unit is $2, the cost is $1, and there is a variable selling expense of $0.50 per unit. The loss, if the unit is not sold in this period, is $1. On the basis of revised forecasts, the firm estimates that the probability that demand will equal or exceed 10 units, with existing price and trade credit policy, is 0.01, so that the probability that the firm will incur a $1 loss is 0.99. Thus, the expected incremental value of the tenth unit is $0.01(0.50) - 0.99($1) =$ a loss of $0.985.

Should a customer appear who is interested in buying a unit at a price of $1.80, the firm is faced with this situation: If it makes the sale, it avoids an expected loss of $0.985; at the $1.80 price, the firm will net $0.30. Thus, by making the sale at the reduced price, the firm nets $0.30 and avoids an expected loss of $0.985. So, the sale is worth $1.285 in terms of increasing expected net worth above what it would be if the firm refuses the sale. The firm may still be unhappy about making the sale at the lower price because of fear of the reactions of competitors and other customers. If the reduced price sets off a wave of price reductions by competitors, or other customers insist on receiving the lower price, the firm may have to reduce price on the other nine units in stock, as well as on future stocks. It may seem better to refuse the sale and take the probable loss, because the losses that will result from cutting price could exceed $0.985.

Though not an inevitable conclusion, the firm may prefer to avoid the $0.985 loss in other ways than cutting price. One way is to sell on extended credit terms. Market reactions tend to be less sensitive to variations in credit terms than to variations in price. Yet, as shown earlier, selling on credit is the equivalent of cutting price. Thus, the firm might prefer to sell the unit at $2, but wait for, say, 12 months to receive payment. If the cost of capital is 1 per cent a month, the present value of $2 received in 12 months is $1.77, approximately. This is equivalent to reducing price by 11.5 per cent. The firm profits because it receives $1.77 less $1.50, or $0.27, and avoids the $0.985 expected loss. Thus, the sale for extended credit terms is worth $1.255. Though this is less than the gain from selling at a $1.80 price, the probability of reactions from the market is much lower, and the firm may prefer the trade credit route for dumping excess stocks to the price-cutting way.

EXCESS CAPACITY

In much the same way as the firm adds to accounts receivable by selling excess inventory on credit, it may increase accounts receivable in order to utilize fixed assets. If the firm is operating plant and equipment below capacity, the additional cost of producing more units can be well below normal per unit cost of production because the fixed costs of production will not change. In the long run, the firm must cover fixed costs. When operating below capacity, however, it can be profitable to produce units that will be sold below normal price.

For example, suppose that the variable costs of production are $0.50 per unit and total per unit costs are $1. As long as the firm can cover the $0.50 variable production cost and the $0.50 variable selling cost, it will be interested in producing more units.

The firm may be reluctant to encourage added sales by reducing price. Yet, it may try to encourage sales by offering credit terms that would be unprofitable if the firm were able to sell capacity production at normal prices and credit terms.

SEASONAL DEMAND

A more normal situation exists when the firm faces seasonal variations in demand. If the firm produces at an even rate over the year, it will accumulate stocks on which it incurs carrying costs during the off-peak period. On the other hand, if it produces at a greater rate before peak demand and then decreases production, production costs may rise. The higher production costs are caused by such factors as higher labor turnover due to seasonal demand, overtime and night-shift wage premiums, increased maintenance as equipment is used more intensively, etc.

Suppose that carrying costs, which include the cost of capital as well as warehousing and insurance charges, are 2 per cent per month on the cost of each unit. At an even rate of production, per unit costs are $1 and would be $1.10 at a seasonal rate of production. If the storage period with even production is four months, production cost plus carrying charges will be $1.082 per unit at the time of sale. It will be cheaper to produce at an even rate of production. Thus the firm will produce for storage as long as the added carrying costs are less than the difference in production costs.

Once the production decision has been made, the firm can reduce the effect of the carrying costs by selling either at a discounted price or on extended credit terms, or by a combination of the two. The firm would be willing to reduce the price by an amount up to the carrying costs for cash sale in the off-season. With a normal selling price of $2 and carrying costs of $0.082, the firm could sell immediately at an off-season price as low as $1.918 and be no worse off than it would be in carrying the unit for four months and then selling at $2.

An alternative, which the firm may prefer because of market reactions to price cutting, would be an immediate credit sale on extended terms. The credit sale would reduce the present value of the price. On the other hand, the firm would avoid the carrying costs. If the firm were to consider credit sales on extended terms, collections would have to occur soon enough so that the firm would be no worse off than if it waited for four months and sold for cash. The gain from a cash sale that might occur in four months is $2 − $1.082 − $0.50 (variable selling expense), or $0.418.

Now consider a credit sale to be collected five months hence, i.e., one month after a normal cash sale would occur. For the last one month of the credit term, the firm would be foregoing the $2 it would have received by selling for cash. Thus, it has $2 invested, C, for one month, which investment would have been avoided by selling for cash in four months.

At the time the normal cash sale would occur, the present value of $2 for one month at 1 per cent is $1.98. There is $1 production cost and the $0.50 selling cost to be deducted. The firm has avoided that part of the carrying charges consisting of such things as warehousing and insurance. But it has not avoided the portion of carrying charges made up of the cost of invested funds. The invested funds, including the variable selling costs $0.50 incurred at sale, are $1.50, and thus the cost of the invested funds is the cost of capital, 1 per cent per month. The costs then are 1 per cent of $1.50 for four months, or $0.062. The value earned by selling for one month's credit at the time of production is $1.98 − $1 − $0.50 − $0.062 = $0.418. This is exactly the same as if the firm were to wait for four months after production, and sell for cash. If the firm could make an immediate credit sale on terms of less than five months credit, it would be better off with the credit sale than waiting four months for a cash sale. Further, if the cash sale in four months is less than certain, as is usually the case, the firm would be better off with a certain credit sale right now, even if the credit term is five months. In the case of uncertain future sales, the $0.418 would be reduced by the probability of not making the sale. We are still assuming that a customer who promises to pay in five months is certain to make payment.

RISK

The value of trade credit is based on the fact that the pattern of product demand is different with trade credit than without. Whether and how much trade credit will be extended depends upon the degree to which demand is shifted through the extension of credit terms, the credit terms which have to be offered to generate a shift in demand, and the cost of capital. What happens to the trade credit decision when we drop the assumption that all credit buyers will pay bills on the promised date? Now the firm makes a decision from which there may be several consequences since the customer may pay after the promised date. In other words, dropping the assumption of a repayment date which is certain introduces risk into the problem.

The structure of the decision is changed very little by the introduction of risk. The present value of the price to be received some time after the sale is the variable affected. Without risk, the present value is certain and, therefore, has a single value. With risk, the present value will depend upon when the payment is made, and several possible collection periods may occur. There is some probability that the customer will pay on time. But there is also the probability that he will pay one month, two months, or more after the credit terms have expired. There is also the possibility of no payment at all. Each of these possibilities generates a different present value, and each present value has a probability of occurrence.

In addition to the effect of different collection periods, each of the present values will have different associated collection costs. As an account becomes overdue, the firm will exert increasingly strenuous, and costly, efforts to collect. These efforts run the gamut from a succession of letters with tones of growing urgency and irritation through personal calls, lawyers' letters, turning the account over to a collection agency to bringing the debtor into court. The extent of the collection effort will depend upon the costs of the efforts and the amount at stake. A lawsuit may make sense when a large amount of money is involved, but would not be used for a small account. Since the costs of collection increase with the length of the collection period, the net present value of a long overdue account declines not only because of the time period, but because of the high collection costs associated with it.

CREDIT INFORMATION

How may a firm judge whether a potential credit customer is or is not a good credit risk? There is available to the firm a surprisingly large amount of credit information ranging from the firm's experience with the customer through fairly elaborate and expensive credit checks.

If the firm has had previous experience with the customer, bad experiences in the past generally predict similar experiences in the future. Even without such experience, the firm's salesmen can provide general impressions of the condition of the customer. Even experiences with other customers provide some information of the credit risk. If similarly situated customers have recently become "slow payers," the odds are that the same conditions will make an unknown customer a slow payer.

The firm can receive information from the credit customer directly. Such information can include an audited set of recent operating statements, the name of the customer's bank of deposit, and the names of suppliers who have sold to the customer on credit. The latter are often willing to supply information, particularly on customers with whom they have had bad experience.

Operating statements can be used to indicate the amount of cash and liquid assets, such as marketable securities, accounts receivable, and merchandise inventory that the customer has. This provides some notion of the customer's ability to pay a debt when due. Also, the customer's short-term liabilities must be compared with the liquidity. Though profits are not as important as liquidity in evaluating the ability to pay currently maturing debt, profits give some idea of the liquidity of noncash assets. The liquidity of inventory for a customer taking losses is considerably less than for a customer with a profitable business.

The customer's bank can provide credit information also. Even if the bank is not the investigating firm's bank, the customer's bank will provide information about the size of deposits and any loan experience it has to the investigating firm's bank. This information consists of such things as reporting that the firm in question has, for example, an average balance in high four figures, meaning less than $10,000, but more than $4,000 or $5,000. If the customer's bank has made a loan to the customer, it will say so, indicating repayment experience and any other information the bank may have accumulated pursuant to investigating the loan application.

In addition to these sources, there are many local, regional, and national organizations whose business it is to provide credit information. Dun and Bradstreet is perhaps the best known of these, but most cities and many towns have local credit reporting agencies. The latter are usually affiliated with regional associations, which pool information, so that the firm may request information about customers who live in a different area. Some industries have specialized credit reporting agencies, such as those that specialize in credit information on retail furniture dealers, lumber yards, or hardware stores.

The amount of information the seller will require depends on the size of the credit requested, the state of competition, the seller's desire for new business, and the customer's delivery time requirements. However, information is not costless. The more information collected by the seller, the better he can evaluate risk, but the greater the cost of the evaluation. This is analogous to a quality control problem, in which the firm could be certain of having no bad pieces in a production lot by examining each piece. The costs associated with a 100 per cent sampling inspection are so high compared with the benefits of removing defects that most firms sample considerably less than all of the pieces in the lot. So, too, with credit information. At some point before complete exhaustion of all credit information sources, the value of new information becomes less than the cost of acquiring it, and the firm finds it profitable to evaluate on the basis of incomplete information. The amount of information collected will depend on the size of the credit being requested, since that determines the value of the information. In addition, more information will be required when initial information is adverse than when the initial information is favorable.

APPLYING
THE INFORMATION

The evaluation of credit risk must be essentially qualitative. The famous four C's of credit— capital, character, capacity, and conditions— still provide the best guidelines for credit evaluation. Despite this, we shall attempt to quantify the decision by assuming that the seller can combine the results of credit information, experience, and intuition into a subjective probability distribution for the possible collection periods associated with a particular credit sale. In effect, we shall assume, not unreasonably, that the credit manager can associate probabilities with the following classes of collection periods: the possibility that the customer will pay within the discount period; the possibility that the customer will miss the discount period, but will pay within the net credit term; the possibility that the customer will pay, but only after the expiration of the credit terms; the possibility that the customer will not pay or, what amounts to the same thing, that the proceeds of the collection will be equal to, or less than, the collection costs.

Assume the probability distribution takes the following form for a $200 sale with terms of 1/30, n/60:

Collection period	Probability
1 month or less	0.40
More than 1 month to 2 months	0.40
More than 2 months to 6 months	0.15
More than 6 months	0.05

Assume the firm makes no collection efforts during the credit term. So, the only expense during the credit term is the discount, if the buyer pays within the discount period. After the two-month credit term has expired, the credit manager estimates that $10 per month is expended for collections through the sixth month, i.e., the fourth month after the expiration of the credit term. An account which is more than four months overdue is turned over to a lawyer. Although some of these accounts do eventually pay, the costs of legal fees are sufficiently large that the firm receives nothing, on the average. Still, the credit manager believes that, even if it costs the firm more to collect funds than the proceeds from the collection, it is good policy to harass accounts which are more than six months overdue. The collection cost schedule then is:

Collection Period	Costs
1 month or less	$ 2
During 2nd month	0
3–6 months	10 per month
More than 6 months	200 flat loss

The credit manager assumes that the chances are even that a customer paying within the first month will pay at any time during the month. So, too, for a customer paying during the second month. Overdue customers who pay sometime during the third through sixth months are equally likely to pay at any time during that period. With this information, we can substitute the midpoint of each collection period class interval for the class interval. In other words, there is a 0.5 chance that the customer who pays in the discount period will pay in the first half of the month and a 0.5 chance that he will pay in the last half of the month. On the average, the customer will pay in 0.5 months if he takes a discount. The probability distribution can then be restated:

Midpoint of Collection Period	Probability
0.5 months	0.40
1.5 months	0.40
4.0 months	0.15
More than 6 months	0.05

If a customer pays during the discount period, the firm will collect $200 − $2 = $198, and will have to wait one-half month on the average. At a cost of capital of 1 per cent a month, the present value of the net proceeds is about $197. If collection occurs after the discount period, but before the expiration of the credit period, the firm will collect $200, but will wait 1.5 months, on the average, after the point of sale. The present value of the $200 is approximately $197. If the customer is a late payer—more than two months, but not over six months—, the firm will wait an average of four months. During the third month, the firm will incur collection costs of $10, which have a present value of

$$\frac{1}{(1.01)^3}\ \$10 = \$9.71.$$

During the fourth month, the firm will incur an additional $10 of collection expenses, but will collect the $200. The present value of the net $190 for the fourth month is $182.59. Thus a late payer will generate an average net present value of $182.59 − $9.71 = $172.88. An account which is written off costs the firm $10 collection expense during each of the third, fourth, fifth, and sixth months, as well as the $200 write-off which occurs at the end of the sixth month. The present value of these losses is $226.65.

Using the probabilities and the conditional present value for each of the four classes of collection periods, the expected present value of the credit sale is:

Collection Period	Conditional Present Value	Probability	Expected Present Value
1 month or less	$197.00	0.40	$78.80
During 2nd month	197.00	0.40	78.80
3–6 months	172.88	0.15	25.93
More than 6 months	−226.65	0.05	−11.33
		Expected net present value	$172.20

The expected present value is substituted for the certain present value used in the earlier examples. If the expected present value exceeds the costs, the sale will be made.

MEASURING RISK

The risk measurement for accounts receivable is the same as for the other assets—the standard deviation. If the costs of the sale in the example above were $150, the firm expects net worth to rise by $22.20 as a result of this credit sale. The actual profit may be as high as $47, if collected in either the first or second months, or as low as −$376.65 if uncollectible. The standard deviation is taken with respect to these conditional profits.

Conditional Profit	Expected Profit	Difference	(Difference)²	Probability	Probability Times (Difference)²
$ 47.00	$22.20	$ 24.80	$ 619.04	0.40	$ 247.62
47.00	22.20	24.80	619.04	0.40	247.62
22.88	22.20	0.68	0.46	0.15	0.05
−376.65	22.20	−398.85	159,081.32	0.05	7,954.07
				Variance	$8,449.36
				Standard deviation	91.92

The standard deviation is measured in the units of the conditional distribution. To convert it to a *pure* measure, we find the ratio of the standard deviation to the expected value, i.e., $91.92/$22.20 = $4.14.

The measurement of risk indicates the possible effect of risk on the firm. Although the firm expects to make a profit in the example, the average of the difference between what may occur and what is expected to occur exceeds the expected profit. Another way of putting this is to indicate that it will take almost 17 identical sales, each yielding the expected value of $22.20, to offset one customer who fails to pay and involves the firm in a total loss of $376.65. On this basis, the firm may well decide against making a sale such as described in the example, even though the expected value of the sale is positive. As will be shown later, the firm's decision will depend on its attitude toward risk and the kinds of risk embodied in its other assets, as well as the expected value of the transaction.

SUMMARY

Credit sales are similar in effect to price reductions in increasing or shifting demand. However, a credit sale may be less likely to induce retaliatory measures by competitors. Unlike a price cut, trade credit may result in high collection costs and a long collection period, both of which act to reduce the profitability of the credit sale. Investment in trade credit will occur when the expected present value of the sales price exceeds the cost of the goods sold.

SELECTED REFERENCES

Andrews, V., S. Friedland, and E. Shapiro; "Who Finances Small Business?" *Financing Small Business*, Federal Reserve System, 1958.

——: "Working Capital Financing of Small Business," *Law and Contemporary Problems*, Winter, 1959.

Butters, S., and J. Lintner: *The Effects of Taxes on Growing Enterprises*, Harvard, Cambridge, Mass., 1945.

Einzig, R.: "Credit From Large to Small Business," *Financing Small Business*, Federal Reserve System, 1958.

Jacoby, N., and R. Saulnier: *Business Finance and Banking*, National Bureau of Economic Research, New York, 1947.

Jacoby, N., and F. Weston: "Financial Policies for Regularizing Business Investment," *Regularization of Business Investment*, Princeton, N.J., 1954.

Merwin, C.: *Financing Small Corporations in Five Manufacturing Industries*, National Bureau of Economic Research, New York, 1942.

Saulnier, R., and N. Jacoby: *Accounts Receivable Financing*, National Bureau of Economic Research, New York, 1943.

"Trade Credit: A Factor in the Rationing of Capital," *Monthly Review of the Federal Reserve Bank of Kansas City*, June, 1957.

APPENDIX

Statement Analysis

In a competitive free enterprise economy, most of the information about the internal operations of the firm are privy to it. To attract external funds, however, information must be supplied to investors so that they may be able to evaluate the investment. Operating statements provide much, though not all, information of interest to investors. These statements are considered sufficiently important sources of information for the public that firms with securities traded on major securities exchanges are legally required to supply operating statements at regular intervals. Most institutional lenders, such as banks and insurance companies, require the submission of operating statements as part of a loan application. Non-financial corporations, in their role as extenders of trade credit, are in fact performing the function of a financial institution. Therefore, it should not be surprising that, when a trade credit request involves a substantial amount of funds, the trade credit issuer may ask for a set of recent operating statements.

Operating statement analysis can yield information on the safety, liquidity, profitability, and growth of the firm. Not all investors will place the same emphasis on each of these aspects. Long-term investors are primarily interested in the safety, profitability, and growth of the firm. Short-term investors are less interested in profitability and growth since their claims will have to be paid in the near future. But they are quite interested in the amount of cash and near-cash assets owned by the firm. The differences in interest are more a matter of degree than of kind. The profits, which the long-term investor hopes for, may never be forthcoming if the firm does not have enough liquidity to pay currently maturing obligations. On the other hand, the short-term assets of a firm may not be very liquid if the firm is unprofitable. In the illustrative analysis that follows, emphasis will be placed on liquidity. The profitability, safety, and growth of the firm, except as measured by liquidity, will be ignored for the time being.

To illustrate the analysis, two semiannual balance sheets and the interim income statement are presented in Exhibit 4-1. Though purposely simplified, they are similar to the operating statements which are commonly issued by actual firms.

WORKING CAPITAL ANALYSIS

The liquidity of a firm measures its ability to pay obligations as they mature. Inability to make such payments is technical insolvency, and this can be just as fatal to the firm as heavy losses over an extended period. Paradoxically, the firm with very profitable investment opportunities is more apt to have low liquidity and thus be prone to technical insolvency, than is a firm with few profitable opportunities. The profitable firm is continually tempted to invest all its funds in high-earning investments, whereas a stagnant firms sacrifices less in profits by holding liquid assets. Liquidity can be measured in a variety of ways. Clearly, cash on hand and on deposit in a bank is the most liquid asset. However, accounts

Exhibit 4-1

ABC MANUFACTURING CORPORATION

ASSETS	BALANCE SHEET AS OF	
	December 31, 1962	*June 30, 1963*
Cash	$100	$180
Accounts receivable, net	200	250
Merchandise inventory	300	330
Total current assets	$ 600	$ 760
Fixed assets, gross	$500	$550
Less accumulated depreciation	100	120
Net fixed assets	400	430
Total assets	$1,000	$1,190

LIABILITIES AND NET WORTH		
Accounts payable	$ 40	$ 60
Bank loan payable	60	50
Current portion of term loan	60	60
Other accruals payable	100	140
Total current liabilities	$ 260	$ 310
Term loan payable*	240	180
Total liabilities	$ 500	$ 490
Paid-in capital	$300	$300
Retained earnings	200	400
Total net worth	500	700
Total liabilities and net worth	$1,000	$1,190

INCOME STATEMENT FOR 6 MONTHS ENDING
JUNE 30, 1963

Sales	$2,000
Less cost of goods sold**	1,200
Gross income	$ 800
Other expenses	200
Net income before taxes	$ 600
Income taxes	310
Net income after taxes	$ 290
Dividends	90
To retained earnings	$ 200

*Term loan is repaid in semiannual installments of $60.
**Includes depreciation of $50

receivable are but one step away from becoming cash, and inventory need only be sold and the sales collected before it becomes cash. Thus, all current assets are, to varying degrees, indicators of liquidity.

Offsetting these are the current liabilities, those claims which the firm must pay within a year or less. As shown in the exhibit, these include such things as trade credit owed, short-term bank loans, and any portion of a long-term liability which must be paid in the near future. The accruals include wages and taxes payable.

The difference between current assets and current liabilities is called *working capital*—$340 in the earlier balance sheet and $450 in the more recent balance sheet. Working capital is an estimate of the liquidity, net of current obligations, available to the firm. However, it can be deceptive. If trade credit of $1,000 were extended to this firm, inventory and accounts payable would both rise by equal amounts. Working capital would be unchanged, even though the firm had substantially added to its current obligations.

As a result, working capital ratios are used to estimate the liquidity of the firm. The two best known of these are the *current ratio* and the *quick*, or *acid-test*, *ratio*. The former is simply the ratio of current assets to current liabilities and is 2.3 for the December balance sheet and 2.5 for the June balance sheet. The quick ratio is the same as the current ratio, except that inventory is omitted on the grounds that it is less liquid than the other current assets. In the example, the quick ratio for December is 1.2 and for June, 1.4. The difference in the changes between the current ratio and the quick ratio suggest that, over-all, the firm has increased its liquidity during the period. The improvement was not only due to an increase in current assets over current liabilities, but because accounts receivable and cash grew relatively more rapidly than inventory.

The length of time needed to convert inventory into sales may be roughly estimated by the average age of inventory. In the example, the average inventory is $315 [($300 + $330)/2]. The cost of goods sold represents the cost value of inventory sold during the last six months. Thus, average inventory is about 26 per cent of semiannual cost of sales, or, on the average, inventory is converted into sales in about 1.6 months (0.26 × 6 months).

The length of the collection period for accounts receivable may be found by estimating the average age of the receivables. Treating the sales figure as credit sales, this is

$$\frac{(\$200 + \$250)/2}{\$2,000} \times 6 \text{ months} = 0.7 \text{ months}.$$

Combining the two estimates, we can measure the length of time needed to convert inventory into cash, which is 1.6 months +0.7 months = 2.3 months. Although these are rough estimates subject, among other things, to seasonal variations in sales and collections, the results may be interpreted to indicate that the firm will be able to pay off a trade credit within three months using only funds generated by liquidating the inventory bought on credit.

A cash flow estimate may be made by comparing the funds generated from operations with current liabilities. Cash generated from operations may be estimated by summing profits, after taxes, and depreciation, which total $340. On an annual basis, assuming that the second half of the year will be the same as the first, the firm is expected to generate $680. Thus, the firm could pay all existing current liabilities with cash generated from operations. This, of course, is a biased estimate since some of the current liabilities, such as accounts payable and wages payable, are included among cost of goods sold and the other expenses. It is difficult to correct for the bias with statement analysis. We do not know how much of the wages payable and accounts payable are in cost of goods sold and how much in inventory. If all the wages represented by accruals and inventory represented by accounts payable are included in cost of goods sold, we have already deducted them in calculating the operating cash inflow, and the firm is in a more liquid condition that indicated by the cash flow analysis.

Another useful tool is the analysis of sources and uses of working capital. In effect, this tool is a re-creation of the transactions which took place over the accounting period, as indicated by the operating statements. However, instead of treating the individual current assets and current liabilities, these are lumped, and we are interested in the factors which have affected working capital. Exhibit 4-2 shows a form of work sheet used in sources and uses, or flow of funds, analysis. The analysis indicates that the only sources of working capital have been internal, depreciation and income, with no long-term loans or stock sales as sources. It also shows dividends to be the largest use of funds, with new plant and equipment a close second. A lender may be heartened to note that the term loan installment could have been met by reducing dividends to $30, without reducing asset acquisitions at all. Surprisingly, such an observation might be reassuring to a stockholder also.

How may the results of the various forms of analysis be interpreted to indicate the degree of risk a lender undertakes in making a loan to this firm? If the lender sets certain standards, interpretation is easy. For example, if the lender believes that the minimum acceptable current ratio is 2.5, the firm is barely acceptable.

Standards themselves are never absolute. In the period following World War II, most firms had a high degree of liquidity, and current ratios of 3.1 or better were quite common. As the postwar period progressed, the liquidity was used to acquire earning assets, and ratios of 2.1 are common today. The ratios are not only affected by trendlike movements as just described. During periods of rising business activity, liquidity ratios tend to fall as firms find it profitable to borrow in order to acquire earning assets. When the pace of economic activity slackens, liquidity positions improve. Finally, liquidity ratios vary at any time among firms in different industries and

Exhibit 4-2

FLOW OF FUNDS ANALYSIS FOR ABC MANUFACTURING CORPORATION FOR 6 MONTHS ENDING JUNE 30, 1963

ACCOUNT	TRIAL BALANCE, DECEMBER 31, 1962 Dr.	Cr.	ADJUSTMENTS TO NONWORKING CAPITAL ACCOUNTS Dr.	Cr.	TRIAL BALANCE, JUNE 30, 1963 Dr.	Cr.
Fixed assets	500	—	(e) 80	(d) 30	550	—
Accumulated depreciation	—	100	(d) 30	(c) 50	—	120
Term loan	—	240	(f) 60	—	—	180
Paid-in capital	—	300	—	—	—	300
Retained earnings	—	200	(b) 90	(a) 290	—	400
Working capital	340	—	(g) 110	—	450	—
Totals	840	840	370	370	1060	1060

ADJUSTMENTS TO WORKING CAPITAL

	Sources	Uses
After-tax profits	(a) 290	
Dividends		(b) 90
Depreciation	(c) 50	
Fixed asset acquisitions		(e) 80
Term loan payment		(f) 60
Totals:		
Sources of working capital	340	
Uses of working capital		230
Net increase in working capital		(g) 110
Totals	340	340

Explanations:
Entry (a)   To record net income after taxes.
Entry (b)   To record dividends.
Entry (c)   To record depreciation charged.
Entry (d)   This is the difference between the sum of the December accumulated depreciation total plus depreciation for the 6-month period and the June accumulated depreciation. It is an estimate of the fixed assets which have been disposed of and written off the books. Therefore, it reduces both accumulated depreciation and fixed assets.
Entry (e)   To record the gross additions to fixed assets, i.e., gross of write-offs.
Entry (f)   To record amortization of term loan, not interest.
Entry (g)   To transfer excess of sources of working capital over uses for 6-month period to working capital account.

Table 4-2

LIQUIDITY RATIOS FOR CORPORATIONS IN SELECTED MANUFACTURING INDUSTRIES AND SIZE GROUPS
FOURTH QUARTER 1948, 1955, 1963

INDUSTRY	CURRENT RATIO			QUICK RATIO			AGE OF RECEIVABLES, (MONTHS)			AGE OF INVENTORIES, (MONTHS)		
	1948	1955	1963	1948	1955	1963	1948	1955	1963	1948	1955	1963
All manufacturing	2.70	2.41	2.46	1.35	1.31	1.24	0.90	1.13	1.43	2.33	2.12	2.14
Food	2.54	2.47	2.36	1.10	1.14	1.06	0.57	0.69	0.88	1.68	1.52	1.57
Apparel	2.65	2.22	2.00	1.19	1.14	0.95	0.92	1.24	1.33	2.03	1.63	1.82
Lumber	2.38	2.76	2.37	1.32	1.45	1.19	0.96	1.17	1.30	2.18	2.01	1.81
Paper	2.55	2.65	2.69	1.35	1.68	1.41	0.80	0.97	1.53	2.04	1.52	2.46
Chemicals	2.84	2.71	2.82	1.45	1.57	1.49	0.95	1.20	1.60	2.68	2.26	2.20
Petroleum	2.33	2.66	2.41	1.34	1.72	1.56	0.99	1.21	1.76	0.96	1.52	1.44
Rubber	3.60	2.86	2.75	1.76	1.49	1.49	1.27	1.59	1.84	2.87	2.50	2.14
Primary metals	2.67	2.53	2.91	1.57	1.59	1.44	0.84	0.94	1.26	2.01	1.91	2.63
Electrical	2.52	2.29	2.41	1.22	1.19	0.95	1.22	1.52	1.81	2.60	2.19	2.50
Motor vehicles	2.35	1.72	2.11	1.27	1.04	1.09	0.54	0.67	0.94	1.98	1.85	1.82
SIZE GROUPS												
Under 1,000,000	2.38	2.06	1.88	1.24	1.18	1.11	0.87	1.11	1.28	1.49	1.26	1.21
1,000,000–5,000,000	2.70	2.49	2.25	1.36	1.28	1.16	0.93	1.12	1.36	1.98	1.80	1.81
5,000,000–100,000,000	2.81	2.66	2.73	1.36	1.37	1.35	0.95	1.21	1.55	2.52	2.33	2.38
100,000,000–over	2.67	2.34	2.52	1.35	1.30	1.25	0.86	1.10	1.44	2.57	2.36	2.36

Source: *Quarterly Financial Report of Manufacturing Corporations*, Federal Trade Commission–Securities and Exchange Commission, U.S. Government Printing Office, 4th Quarters 1948, 1955, and 1963.

different size classes. Small firms tend to have less liquidity than do larger firms. Some of these industry-size class/time differences are shown in Table 4-2.

The ratios and other forms of working capital analysis have little intrinsic meaning in terms of credit risk. As a result, comparative analysis must be used to evaluate credit risk. By analyzing a series of operating statements for a given firm, the lender can determine whether the borrower's liquidity has increased, declined, or remained constant over time. More important, a trade creditor can compare the ratios of one customer with those of several other customers to determine whether a particular customer offers substantially more credit risk than others. Some credit reporting agencies, such as Dun and Bradstreet, compile ratios for various industries which are made available to clients. These ratios are quite useful for the industry group is narrowly defined, assuring a high degree of homogeneity among the firms comprising the industry, and the ratios are reported in terms of quartile groupings. This allows the trade creditor to compare a particular customer's ratios with the ratios of 25 per cent of firms having the highest value of that particular ratio, the 25 per cent having the lowest value, etc.

Clearly, it is easier to calculate ratios than it is to evaluate them. This is even more obvious when we consider that the ratios offer only part of the information needed to evaluate risk. It should not be forgotten that risk is only one factor involved in making the trade credit decision.

Management of Cash
and Near-Cash Assets

5

In the last chapter, we discussed investment in trade credit, a financial asset, since it is a claim on some other economic unit. The discussion in this chapter also concerns a financial asset, cash. Cash includes currency held by the firm and checking deposits in commercial banks. Currency is either a debt of the United States government or of the Federal Reserve System, usually the latter since there are almost $30 billion of Federal Reserve Notes in circulation as compared with slightly more than $5 billion of Treasury currency. Demand deposits are debts of the commercial bank in which the deposits are made and are far more important quantitatively than is currency. In early 1963, demand deposits totaled approximately $118 billion.

In 1963, nonfinancial business corporations held about $31 billion in demand deposits and currency, slightly more than 20 per cent of the total money supply. As shown in Table 5-1, this is the third lowest percentage of the entire postwar period. The decline in the share of the total money supply held by nonfinancial corporate businesses was apparently caused by an increase in the interest rate paid on savings or time deposits. In 1960, non-financial business corporations held 2 per cent of time deposits in commercial banks. By 1961, the percentage had risen to 3.3 per cent, and, by 1962, corporate business firms held almost 8 per cent of commercial bank time deposits.

This shift illustrates an important point, which will be discussed at greater length in a later section of this chapter. There are a variety of near-cash assets, such as time deposits, which can fulfill some of the functions of cash.

Table 5-1

CASH BALANCES OF NONFINANCIAL
BUSINESS CORPORATIONS, 1947–1963,
IN BILLIONS OF DOLLARS
AND AS A RATIO TO THE MONEY SUPPLY

Year	Corporate Cash	Total Money Supply*	Cash/ Money Supply
1947.................	23.4	113.1	20.6
1948.................	23.6	111.5	21.1
1949.................	24.7	111.2	22.2
1950.................	26.2	116.4	22.5
1951.................	27.9	122.8	22.7
1952.................	28.7	127.5	22.5
1953.................	28.9	128.8	22.4
1954.................	30.9	132.3	23.3
1955.................	32.0	135.2	23.6
1956.................	32.1	136.9	23.4
1957.................	32.1	135.9	23.6
1958.................	33.8	141.2	23.9
1959.................	33.8	142.0	23.8
1960.................	33.1	141.2	23.4
1961.................	36.7	145.7	25.1
1962.................	30.7	147.9	20.7
1963.................	30.8	153.5	20.0

*Seasonally adjusted as of December.
Source: *Federal Reserve Bulletin*, Board of Governors of the Federal Reserve System.

Though a checking account balance reduces the costs of drawing checks, cash generally has no rate of earnings. Time deposits and other cash substitutes do earn interest. All other things being equal, an increase in the interest rates paid on near-cash assets will cause the firm to reduce cash holdings and shift to near-cash assets.

If the firm earns no interest on cash holdings, why is cash held? There are two kinds of penalties for inadequate cash balances. First, the firm will not be able to pay all obligations as they come due and may be forced to curtail operations. Without cash, the firm may not be able to pay workers and suppliers for services and materials needed to generate profits. Capital equipment may have to be foregone if the firm does not have enough cash to buy the equipment, and the profits to be generated by the foregone capital equipment will also be foregone. Even worse than the unrealized profits resulting from lack of liquidity, the firm may be forced out of existence if unable to pay creditors. Thus, the costs of illiquidity can be quite high. If the firm has cash, it will not have to forego profits nor will its existence be threatened by unsatisfied creditors. The increments to net worth which would have to be foregone in the absence of cash are properly viewed as the expected value of the cash balance. Economists frequently refer to this reason for holding cash as the *transactions* and *precautionary motives*.

The second reason for holding cash has to do with a peculiar property of financial assets with a fixed nominal value. The purchasing power of money varies inversely with the price level. If the price level falls by 50 per cent, a dollar can buy twice as much after the price level decline than it could before. The value of real assets, such as plant, equipment, and inventory, varies directly with the price level. A decline in the price level will bring about a decline in the expected value of real assets.

Accounts receivable share this characteristic with money. A customer who owes $100 before a decline in the price level will still owe $100 after the price level falls. However, the probability of collecting such an account may decrease when prices fall. In other words, the safety of most fixed-dollar-value financial assets depends upon how certain the holder of the asset is that the debtor will be able and willing to pay when the claim is due. Few firms are as good credit risks as is the United States government and its monetary agents. Thus, money and safe fixed-dollar-value financial assets, such as Treasury securities, may be held by the firm as a hedge against price level declines.

Later, we shall see that money is an even safer hedge against capital shrinkages caused by price declines than the safest of government securities. Economists refer to this reason for holding money as the *speculative motive* for holding cash. Of course, if prices are expected to rise, firms will not hold cash as a hedge. Instead they will prefer assets, the value of which will rise with the price level, such as real assets and variable-dollar-claim financial assets, i.e., common stocks.

The problem of cash management would be simpler if it were costless to hold cash. But each dollar of cash held is a dollar not used for another purpose. The firm could invest in other assets, reduce liabilities, or even make payments to owners with the cash balances. Cash balances will be held only if stockholders of the firm are better off with the cash balance than without it. In other words, the cost of holding cash is the cost of capital times the amount of investment in cash. And cash will be held as long as the expected value of the cash balance exceeds the cost. Thus, cash will be held if the holdings increase net worth.

TRANSACTIONS BALANCES

CASH BUDGETING

To understand the transactions and precautionary motives for holding cash, it is necessary first to understand the effect of the operations of the firm on cash. Exhibit 5-1 presents a projected income statement for a hypothetical firm. Exhibit 5-2 shows the same information by months. Underlying these projections are the sales forecasts, inventory and production-scheduling decisions, and trade credit decisions.

Exhibit 5-1

XYZ MANUFACTURING CORPORATION
PROJECTED INCOME STATEMENT FOR YEAR ENDING
DECEMBER 31, 1964
(Thousands of Dollars)

Sales		14,000
Less		
Wage and salary expense	6,520	
Materials costs	5,090	
Depreciation	1,970	
Operating expenses		13,580
Gross income		420
Less interest expense		114
Net income before taxes		306
Income taxes		159
Net income after taxes		147
Dividends		100
To retained earnings		47

It is assumed that all these decisions were made on the basis of maximizing the expected value of net worth.

COLLECTIONS

Income statements alone, however, give only limited information about cash flows. We know, for example, that depreciation expense does not represent a cash outflow. Exhibit 5-3 provides another example of the difference between profit flows and cash flows. Here, sales are translated into actual cash collections. It has been assumed that the firm expects to collect 20 per cent of sales in the month in which the sale is made. Forty per cent is expected to be collected in the month following the sale. Thirty per cent of any month's sales will be collected two months after the sale is made. And the remaining 10 per cent will be collected three months after the sale.

Thus, during the first three months of the year, the firm expects to collect not only from sales made during 1964, but also from sales made in 1963. At the end of the projection, part of the sales for the last three months are not expected to be collected until 1965. Since total expected collections are less than total expected sales, the investment in accounts receivable at the end of 1964 will be larger than at the end of 1963.

DISBURSEMENTS

Exhibit 5-4 takes the collection information and combines it with monthly details on cash disbursements. Here, too, the timing of cash flows does not coincide with the profit flows. It is assumed that wage and salary payments lag one-half month behind the period in which they are earned. Thus, the January wage and salary pay-

Exhibit 5-2

XYZ MANUFACTURING CORPORATION
PROJECTED MONTHLY INCOME STATEMENTS FOR 1964
(In Thousands of Dollars)

Account	Jan.	Feb.	Mar.	Apr.	May	June	July	Aug.	Sept.	Oct.	Nov.	Dec.	Total
Sales	1,000	900	900	1,100	1,200	1,400	900	600	1,200	1,400	1,600	1,800	14,000
Less wages and salaries	550	500	500	550	560	570	500	500	560	570	580	580	6,520
Materials	360	350	350	380	400	500	350	200	400	500	600	700	5,090
Depreciation	125	135	140	140	150	160	170	180	180	180	205	205	1,970
Interest	10	10	10	10	10	10	9	9	9	9	9	9	114
Net income before tax	−45	−95	−100	20	80	160	−129	−289	51	141	206	306	306
Quarterly taxable income	..	..	−240	..	..	260	..	..	−367	..	..	653	306
Previous losses	..	..	..	..	..	−240	..	..	−367	..	..	−367	306
Net Tax	..	..	0	..	..	11	..	..	0	..	..	148	159

Exhibit 5-3

COLLECTIONS FROM SALES FOR 1964
(In Thousands of Dollars)

	Jan.	Feb.	Mar.	Apr.	May	June	July	Aug.	Sept.	Oct.	Nov.	Dec.	Total
Cash sales	200	180	180	220	240	280	280	120	240	280	320	360	
Previous month	640	400	360	360	440	480	560	360	240	480	560	640	
2 months ago	360	480	300	270	270	330	360	420	270	180	360	420	
3 months ago	100	120	160	100	90	90	110	120	140	90	60	120	
Totals	1,300	1,180	1,000	950	1,040	1,180	1,210	1,020	890	1,030	1,300	1,540	13,640

Exhibit 5-4

XYZ MANUFACTURING CORPORATION
MONTHLY CASH FLOWS FOR 1964
(In Thousands of Dollars)

Account	Jan.	Feb.	Mar.	Apr.	May	June	July	Aug.	Sept.	Oct.	Nov.	Dec.	Totals
Collections	1,300	1,180	1,000	950	1,040	1,180	1,210	1,020	890	1,030	1,300	1,540	13,640
Wage and salary payments	500	525	500	525	555	565	535	500	530	565	575	580	6,455
Materials payments	600	360	350	350	380	400	500	350	200	400	500	600	4,990
Interest payments	...	...	...	...	...	60	...	...	...	...	...	54	114
Tax payments	...	...	10	...	...	125	...	...	...	...	...	11	146
Term loan amortization.	...	...	...	...	...	200	...	...	...	...	...	200	400
Bank loan repayment ..	...	...	...	...	50	...	...	...	...	...	...	...	50
Dividend payment	25	...	...	25	...	...	25	...	...	25	...	...	100
Fixed asset acquisitions.	310	470	200	...	400	...	510	...	220	...	420	...	2,530
Net cash flow..........	−135	−175	−60	50	−345	−170	−360	170	−60	40	−195	95	−1,145

ments figure of $500 represents one-half the wage and salary expenses incurred in January, and the remainder is one-half the expenses incurred in the preceding month.

It is assumed that bills for materials are paid one month after the materials are delivered. Thus, January's bills are shown in February. Just as the unpaid portion of the wage and salary expenses is reflected in a current liability, accrued wages and salaries, unpaid bills are reflected in accounts payable.

As of the writing of this chapter, corporations pay taxes quarterly, one-half year after having incurred the tax liability. Thus, the tax liability incurred over the first two quarters of 1964 is not reflected in the cash flow schedule until it is paid in December 1964. No tax payment is shown in September, since the firm expects to show a loss for the first quarter of 1964. Losses may be carried forward to offset profits for as long as five years, or carried back by recalculating past tax liabilities for as long as three years. The firm could have planned equal quarterly payments of 25 per cent of the 1964 estimated tax liability, with the first payment starting in September 1964. The payments planned for March and June of 1964 are for tax liabilities incurred in the last half of 1963.

Although interest is incurred over the year, actual payments are made semiannually. We have assumed that the interest is paid on the term loan.

Before turning to the nonincome statement items which affect cash flow, one other point should be made contrasting the effect of income statement items on cash. In the example, we have assumed that the firm does not plan either to accumulate or to diminish the investment in inventory. Had the firm planned to increase inventory investment, the labor, materials, and depreciation used for the inventory accumulation would not have been shown in the income statement, but would have been reflected in the cash flow schedule. On the other hand, if the firm planned to reduce inventory investment, the cost of the goods produced in the past, but sold in 1964, would be shown in the planned income statement. The cost would not affect cash in 1964, however, since the cash expenditures would have been made in the past when the goods were produced.

The installment payment on the term loan, the bank loan repayment, and the cash expenditures for the acquisition of fixed assets are not directly shown in the income statement. The loan payments do reduce interest, and the acquisition of fixed assets will increase depreciation expense. However, the information needed to reflect the cash impact of these transactions is not in the income statement.

The dividend payments shown in the cash budget reflect the payment to owners of part of profits. The January, 1964, planned disbursement reflects profits earned in 1963. Dividend payments for the last quarter of 1964 will not be made until 1965. As we shall see later, it is not unusual for firms to keep dividends at a stable level even though profits fluctuate.

In Exhibit 5-4, the cash flow is shown by months. If the firm preferred to ignore the monthly schedules and take only the annual cash flow into account, difficulties might ensue. Over the year, the firm expects to disburse $1,145,000 more than it receives from operations. If the firm plans to have $100,000 cash available each month to take care of the average monthly net outflow, it would run short of cash in each of the six months when the net cash outflow exceeds $100,000.

Even if the firm plans for cash on a monthly basis, it may have cash shortages. Suppose that the disbursements of $1,435,000 planned for January take place in the first half of the month, but the collections do not occur until the end of the month. If the firm plans on starting January with a cash balance equal to the expected net outflow for the month, $135,000, a substantial shortage will occur well before January 15.

To avoid the problem of intra-planning-period shortages, the firm must choose a time period short enough to avoid such fluctuations. The shorter the budget period, the less likely it is that the net cash outflow for any intra-period will exceed the net cash outflow for the period as a whole. On the other hand, the shorter the period, the more expenses are incurred in preparing budgets for the year. Preparing daily budgets would make little sense. The costs would be enormous. For most disbursement items, the firm will not incur severe penalties if it makes payments one day late. Weekly budgets would be less expensive, and the penalties for late payment are apt to be more severe if the payment is one week late than one day late. However, even weekly budgets may be unnecessary if disbursements come at the end of the week and receipts come at the beginning, or if receipts and disbursements are fairly well matched.

In the example, we have assumed that the firm has decided to use a monthly planning period. This decision implies that the probability of a cash deficit greater than the net cash flow's occurring within the month is small.

Exhibit 5-4 shows the effects of a set of production, financing, marketing, and capital expenditure plans on cash. Since these are plans, they are subject to revision if the cash effects of the plans are considered to be undesirable. Modification of the plans, however, would have the effect of reducing profits, i.e., the expected value of net worth. Thus, the firm will reduce or eliminate particular plans only if, as a result, the costs of financing the cash deficits will be reduced by an amount greater than the reduction in profits resulting from curtailment of the planned activities. The first step in making this determination is to estimate the costs of financing the cash deficits as initially projected.

Treat the cash flows shown in Exhibit 5-4 as certain. The flows can then be considered analogous to a demand for inventory, cash inventory instead of merchandise inventory. Given a certain demand, the firm wishes to stock cash inventories so that the total inventory costs of cash are minimized. The proposed solution will be similar to the economic order quantity method of determining the least cost order quantity in the instance of certain demand.

To carry out the analogy, we must consider the elements that enter the calculation. With merchandise inventory, total inventory costs were minimized when total carrying costs equaled total ordering costs. Are there analogous carrying costs and ordering costs associated with a cash inventory?

The carrying costs of cash are the product of the cost of capital and the average monthly cash balance. The higher the cost of capital, the higher the carrying costs of cash. Costs will vary directly, also, with the size of the cash balance.

The ordering costs associated with raising cash require some explanation. To raise funds, the firm must supply various kinds of information, such as past operating statements, budgets, etc., to potential investors. For certain types of funds, such as publicly traded securities, the information has to be quite extensive and detailed, requiring the use of lawyers, accountants, and other specialists. For small issues of common stock, the ordering costs, called *flotation costs*, can be as much as 25 per cent of the funds raised. Although the ordering costs vary depending upon the source of the funds, the amount of funds, and the length of time for which the funds are required, all fund raising requires some flotation, or ordering, costs. In later chapters, we shall be concerned with the flotation costs associated with specific sources of funds, but we shall simply assume a constant cost per order at this point.

Given a constant cost per order, total ordering costs are the product of the cost per order and the number of orders. With a large number of orders, ordering costs will rise, and the reverse is true, also. However, as the number of orders increase, the average cash balance, or inventory, will fall, reducing carrying costs. So carrying costs and ordering costs vary inversely in the case of cash, just as they do in the case of merchandise inventory.

It follows that total costs of financing cash deficits will be minimized when total ordering costs equal total carrying costs, just as was shown in Chapter 3 with merchandise inventory. The square root expression used for merchandise will not be developed for cash. It should be recalled that the use of the economic order quantity formula rested on the assumption that demand was approximately constant within the planning period. Though we assume demand for cash to be constant within a month, the planning period in this case is a year, and the cash budget clearly shows that demand varies from month to month.

Nonetheless, it is true that the total costs of cash will be at a minimum when total ordering costs equal total carrying costs. This is a useful guide in determining whether a given schedule of cash orders and disbursements is the best, i.e., the cheapest, possible within the limit that all cash deficits are to be financed in the month in which they occur.

As a first approximation, the firm might determine the costs of financing the deficits by ordering a sufficient amount of cash to cover any monthly outflow that exceeds the cash balance carried forward from the previous month. If the cost of capital is 2 per cent a month, the cost of orders is $3,000 per order, and we assume that no cash is carried forward from December of the preceding year, the costs of this schedule for the data shown in Exhibit 5-4 are $43,950. The method of calculation and the monthly schedule are shown in Exhibit 5-5.

As an alternative, the firm might try to minimize ordering costs by scheduling a single order for the year, large enough to meet the largest cumulative deficit. The cumulative deficit for the year is largest at the end of November, when it is $1,240,000. Ordering costs would be $3,000 for the year, but carrying costs would rise to $121,650 for a total of $124,650.

Inspection of Exhibit 5-5 reveals that a reduction in the total inventory costs of cash is possible. By ordering $60,000 in March, the firm incurs an ordering cost of $3,000. Should the $60,000 order be included with the February order, the ordering cost could be avoided for March, although carrying costs in February would rise by $0.02 \times \$60,000 = \$1,200$. Since the increase in carrying costs is less than the decrease in ordering costs, the firm would reschedule cash, increasing the February order to $235,000 and eliminating any order in March.

An additional saving is possible by reducing the cash balance brought forward from August to $60,000, perhaps by repaying debt. Since the average balance during September would become $30,000, carrying costs in September would fall by $2,200. This would mean that no balance would be carried over into October, which would reduce the ending October balance to $40,000, leaving the average balance in October at $20,000. Carrying costs for October would be reduced by $2,200. Thus, the firm can reduce carrying costs by a total of $4,400 if it reduces the ending cash balance in August to $60,000. The revised schedule is shown in Exhibit 5-6, with total costs reduced to $37,750.

The two adjustments are worthy of special note. The cash balance for February, in the first approximation, was too small, and costs could be reduced by increasing the balance. In the second case, the cash balance for September and October, as initially planned, was too large. The best cash balance is not necessarily the largest, the smallest, or even a constant one. It is the balance associated with minimum cash inventory costs.

If the various asset investments included in the plan have been properly evaluated, a reduction in the scale of asset investment, even if there is a

Exhibit 5-5
FIRST APPROXIMATION OF CASH SCHEDULE
(In Thousands of Dollars)

	Jan.	Feb.	Mar.	Apr.	May	June	July	Aug.	Sept.	Oct.	Nov.	Dec.
Cash from previous month	0.0	0.0	0.0	0.0	50.0	0.0	0.0	0.0	170.0	110.0	150.0	0.0
Orders for cash	135.0	175.0	60.0	0.0	295.0	170.0	360.0	0.0	0.0	0.0	45.0	0.0
Beginning balance	135.0	175.0	60.0	0.0	345.0	170.0	360.0	0.0	170.0	110.0	195.0	0.0
Cash flow	−135.0	−175.0	−60.0	+50.0	−345.0	−170.0	−360.0	+170.0	−60.0	+40.0	−195.0	+95.0
Ending balance	0.0	0.0	0.0	50.0	0.0	0.0	0.0	170.0	110.0	150.0	0.0	95.0
Average balance	67.5	87.5	30.0	25.0	172.5	85.0	180.0	85.0	140.0	130.0	97.5	47.5
Carrying costs	1.35	1.75	0.60	0.50	3.45	1.70	3.60	1.70	2.80	2.60	1.95	0.95
Ordering Costs	3.00	3.00	3.00	0.0	3.00	3.00	3.00	0.0	0.0	0.0	3.00	0.0
Total costs	4.35	4.75	3.60	0.50	6.45	4.70	6.60	1.70	2.80	2.60	4.95	0.95

Exhibit 5-6
OPTIMAL CASH SCHEDULE
(In Thousands of Dollars)

	Jan.	Feb.	Mar.	Apr.	May	June	July	Aug.	Sept.	Oct.	Nov.	Dec.
Cash from previous month	0.0	0.0	60.0	0.0	50.0	0.0	0.0	0.0	60.0	0.0	40.0	0.0
Orders for cash	135.0	235.0	0.0	0.0	295.0	170.0	360.0	0.0	0.0	0.0	155.0	0.0
Beginning balance	135.0	235.0	60.0	0.0	345.0	170.0	360.0	0.0	60.0	0.0	195.0	0.0
Cash flow	−135.0	−175.0	−60.0	+50.0	−345.0	−170.0	−360.0	+170.0	−60.0	+40.0	−195.0	+95.0
Ending balance	0.0	60.0	0.0	50.0	0.0	0.0	0.0	170.0	0.0	40.0	0.0	95.0
Average balance	67.5	147.5	30.0	25.0	172.5	85.0	180.0	85.0	30.0	20.0	97.5	47.5
Reductions in balance	—	—	—	—	—	—	—	110				
Carrying costs	1.35	2.95	0.60	0.50	3.45	1.40	3.60	1.70	0.60	0.40	1.95	0.95
Ordering costs	3.00	3.00	0.0	0.0	3.00	3.00	3.00	0.0	0.0	0.0	3.00	0.0
Total costs	4.35	5.95	0.60	0.50	6.45	4.70	6.60	1.70	0.60	0.40	4.95	0.95

reduction in the cost of financing cash deficits, will not be profitable. In order for an asset to be acceptable, its gross expected present value must exceed the cost of the asset. The cost includes the cash involved in the acquisition of the asset. By definition, therefore, an asset which is profitable when properly evaluated will be worth financing.

In evaluating the various earning asset investments, the firm included the cash involved in acquiring each asset in the cost of the asset, C, and reduced the expected returns by any cash disbursements, such as the payment of labor, etc., necessary to achieve the returns. Thus, the carrying costs of cash have already been included in the evaluation of the assets which contribute to the cash flows. Assuming that the expected net present value of each asset is positive, the carrying costs of the cash required to finance the various asset investments is, by definition, less than the increments to net worth generated by the assets.

Nonetheless, it is necessary to include the assets in the cash flow schedules. First, merely justifying the costs of cash does not guarantee that the cash will be available when needed. Second, if the firm generates net outflows of cash for a given period, the carrying costs are only a part of the costs of financing the cash deficits. Ordering costs must be included also. The ordering costs can not be included in the evaluation of individual assets because the optimal ordering schedule is determined not only by the cost of capital and the cost of each order, but by the total cash flows generated by asset investments and payments of liabilities. Thus, it may still be profitable for the firm to eliminate specific asset proposals on the grounds that the reduction in the *total* costs of cash will exceed the reduction in net worth if the asset is not acquired. In short, whenever the firm has to seek external sources of cash so that ordering costs may be incurred, i.e., whenever cash outflows exceed cash inflows, it may be profitable to reduce asset expenditures so as to reduce the cost of financing cash deficits.

REVISING
DISBURSEMENTS

Assuming a tax rate of 48 per cent, the after-tax costs of financing the cash deficits in the example are $16,770. This is the amount by which net worth will fall if the existing plans are retained. Given these data, should the firm alter plans, reducing disbursements and decreasing cash deficits and cost of financing?

The costs of financing cash flows may be reduced if the firm curtails disbursements by not paying financial obligations promptly. There are costs associated with this decision. As long as the costs of cash fall by more than the penalties and costs resulting from failure to meet obligations, the firm will postpone such disbursements as paying taxes, paying suppliers' bills, etc.

The costs of late payment may be simply the loss of a trade discount. If payments to suppliers are very late, the costs may be much larger, including such items as legal fees. In addition to the costs that may arise because the supplier takes legal action in order to collect, future trade credit may be unavailable. This may not affect the activities of the immediate year as much as it will the following year. With curtailed trade credit the firm is likely to have larger cash deficits to finance in the future. The present value of the higher costs of financing future cash deficits must be compared with the reduction in costs of financing the immediate year's deficits. If the latter exceed the former, the firm will become a slow payer. If not, it may still find it relatively profitable to lose discounts, but pay within the net credit period. The decision will depend on the size of the cash deficits, the cost of capital, and the cost of raising funds.

Other examples of ways of reducing cash deficits include late payment of taxes, the penalties for which can be quite high; late payment of interest and repayment of the term loan; and late payment of the bank loan. The penalties for failure to make financial payments when due may be low if the firm can persuade lenders to modify the original loan agreements. The bank might be willing to extend its loan from May to August, when a cash surplus is expected. This would reduce the cash order in May (see Exhibit 5-6) by $50,000 and reduce the carrying charges by $500. The penalty for such a postponement would be added interest costs from May to August.

If lenders are unwilling to modify loan agreements, the firm could still violate its agreements and make late payments. The penalties can be quite high since creditors can resort to courts of law to satisfy their claims. If, as is common, the term loan agreement states that when any payment is late, all payments become due, the firm may find itself forced into liquidating assets or losing control of the firm. Though it is unlikely that the firm will find it profitable to incur such penalties simply to reduce the costs of financing cash deficits, the decision rule would be the same as given earlier. The firm will delay financial payments as long as the costs of doing so are less than the reduction in costs resulting from reduced cash deficits.

THE CASH BALANCE
AFTER REVISION

As the firm revises its plans in order *not* just to minimize the costs of cash, but to maximize the expected value of net worth, the cash balance will vary. When cash deficits are reduced, cash balances vary, but not always downward.

If the February cash outflow in Exhibit 5-6 were reduced to $100,000, the firm would order $235,000 in January and carry the excess $100,000 over to finance the February outflow. This would be cheaper than making an order in February, since the ordering costs are $3,000 and the monthly carrying costs on $100,000 are $2,000. The January cash balance would rise to an average of $167,500, and the average cash balance for February would fall from the $147,500 shown in Exhibit 5-6 to $50,000.

If the ordering costs were lower, say $1,000 an order, the results would have been that the January order and balance would be unchanged, but

February's order would fall to $100,000, and the February average balance would be $50,000. The cash balance will reflect not only the size of the outflows, but the cost of capital and ordering costs.

SAFETY STOCKS

Given certainty with respect to flows, there is no need for a safety stock or precautionary balance of cash to meet unexpected needs. Yet, just as in the case of certain demand for inventories, a safety stock will be held if delivery time is uncertain. Variations in the time needed to raise money result from the possibility that a source of funds, such as a bank, may take longer than expected to process a loan application, or simply refuse all or part of the loan request. Time then is required either to present additional arguments to the lender or to find a new source of funds. During this time, cash demands may be presented which, in the absence of a safety stock, the firm will be unable to meet promptly. The temporary delay, even if for only a few days, can carry high penalties. For example, failure to meet a payroll on the normal payday may mean that vital workers will lose faith in the strength of the firm and seek employment elsewhere. The penalties in this case would be the costs of finding replacements and the associated costs of production slowdowns.

The size of the cash safety stock will be determined just as the merchandise safety stock was determined. The firm will have to estimate the probability distribution for delivery time. The penalty for each day of delay will be multiplied by the probability that the delay will occur. The cost of carrying a safety stock of cash for each day will have to be multiplied by the probability that the delay will not occur, i.e., the probability that the delivery time will be less. As long as the expected gain from holding an additional day's supply of cash exceeds the expected loss, the firm will add cash to the safety stock.

THE VALUE
OF THE CASH BALANCE

For fixed assets, inventories, and accounts receivable, an economic value was determined. This value equaled the cost of the asset plus its expected net present value. To fit these values into a balance sheet which recognizes expected gains, it is useful to consider the bookkeeping entries. Consider an asset with a cost of $100 and a net present value of $50. When the asset is acquired, the following entries would be made:

Debit		*Credit*	
Asset	$150	Cash	$100
		Net worth...............	50

From what has been said in the earlier parts of this chapter, it should be clear that the value of cash is not simply the nominal dollars in the cash balance. The firm will only stock, i.e., invest in, cash when the gains from being able to finance disbursements exceed the costs of holding the necessary cash balances. In other words, the asset cash has an economic value, which can differ from its purchase price just as can the other assets.

With this in mind, let us revise the accounting entry above. Assuming that the cash costs $10, the firm will make the following entry when it acquires the cash:

Debit	*Credit*
Cash $140	Source of funds $100
	Net worth 40

When the asset is acquired, the entry becomes:

Debit	*Credit*
Asset $140	Cash $140

The value of cash that is held for transactions purposes reflects the value of the asset that makes the cash worth holding. Further, the cost of the cash is charged against the asset, so that the net increment to net worth from acquiring the asset is the expected net present value of the asset, less the costs of the cash needed to finance the asset. The account *source of funds* is simply a general term which could refer specifically to a bank loan, a bond sale, or whatever means the firm has used to raise the cash. Specific sources of funds and the determinants of these sources will be considered in the latter half of this book.

The relationship between liabilities and the value of the transactions cash balance is similar to the relationship between cash and other assets. Take the relatively simple case of an account payable of $100 with a 2 per cent discount allowed if the firm pays within 30 days. If the firm fails to pay within the discount period, net worth is $2 less than if the discount were taken. If the cost of holding a sufficiently large cash balance to pay within the discount period is $1, the net value of the cash account is $1.

More generally, the net value of the cash balance needed to pay liabilities punctually is the difference between the penalties avoided by paying the obligations when due and the costs of the required cash balance. For all cases, the net value of the cash asset is the difference between the increments to net worth gained, or decrements to net worth avoided by carrying enough cash, and the costs of ordering and carrying the required amount of cash.

PRECAUTIONARY BALANCES

Since the cash flows generated by assets, such as inventory, accounts receivable, and equipment, are variable, the firm is unlikely to be certain of the magnitude of the cash flow. If the cash balance is insufficient, the firm will incur the penalties and other reductions in net worth which are associated with failure to make planned disbursements. On the other hand, if excess cash is held, the firm incurs a loss or decline in net worth because of high inventory costs of cash.

This is analogous to the problem confronting the firm in the case of merchandise inventory for which there is a variable demand. In the merchandise case, the firm picked the optimal level of inventory to have on hand by combining the probability distribution of demand, the conditional gain per unit, and the loss for each unsold unit. Where the good was storable, the optimal level of inventory was then adjusted to minimize the sum of ordering and carrying costs.

In the case of cash, the same approach is used. With variable inflows and outflows, the demand for cash balances are also variable and, on the basis of judgment and experience, can be associated with a probability distribution. The conditional gain associated with an increment to the cash balance reflects the penalties avoided by being able to make disbursements. The cost of capital times the unused cash is the conditional loss of stocking an unnecessary increment to the cash balance. The optimal level of cash for each month can then be determined by finding the balance at which the expected gain (conditional gain times probability that cash needs will equal or exceed the balance) equals the expected loss (conditional loss times the probability that the cash increment will not be needed).

As an illustration, assume that the probability distribution for cash needs in January from Exhibit 5-5 is:

Outflow	Probability
$132,000 or less	0.01
133,000	0.10
134,000	0.20
135,000	0.26
136,000	0.26
137,000	0.15
138,000 or more	0.02

The penalties for insufficient cash balances will vary depending upon the nature of the disbursement which has been delayed. For the sake of simplicity, assume that the penalty is a constant $100 per $1,000 shortage. The loss resulting from holding excess cash is the amount of excess cash times the monthly cost of capital. Assume the cost of capital to be 2 per cent per month, so that the penalty for each $1,000 of excess cash is $20. With these data, the optimal outflow for January is calculated in Exhibit 5-7.

The optimal cash balance for January is slightly more than $137,000. The same calculation would be made for each month, and the optimal cash need would replace the certain cash flow in a schedule similar to Exhibit 5-6 in order to schedule the least cost method of financing the cash needs.

Exhibit 5-7

DETERMINING THE OPTIMAL CASH OUTFLOW

Possible Cash Flows = Beginning Cash Balances (1)	Probability that Flows Will Equal or Exceed (2)	Conditional Incremental Gain (3)	Expected Incremental Gain (4) = (2) × (3)	Probability that Flows Will Be Less (5)	Conditional Incremental Loss (6)	Expected Incremental Loss (7) = (5) × (6)	Expected Incremental Value (8) = (4) − (7)
$132,000 or less	1.00	$13,200	$13,200	0.00	$264	0.0	$13,200.00
133,000	0.99	100	99	0.01	20	0.20	98.80
134,000	0.89	100	89	0.11	20	2.20	86.80
135,000	0.69	100	69	0.31	20	6.20	62.80
136,000	0.43	100	43	0.57	20	11.40	31.60
137,000	0.17	100	17	0.83	20	16.60	0.40
138,000 or more	0.02	100	2	0.98	20	19.60	−17.60

When it is expected that inflows will exceed outflows, as in March, the same approach is used. If the net inflow is certain, no cash need be supplied from external sources. Given a variable cash flow, the expected inflow may really be an outflow, in which case it may be wise to hold a beginning cash balance. Suppose that the probability that the March flows will be an outflow of $1,000 or more is 0.25. The expected gain from a beginning cash balance of $1,000 rather than a zero balance is $0.25 \times \$100$, assuming the penalties are the same as in Exhibit 5-7, or $25. The expected incremental loss is $0.75 \times \$20 = \$15$. In this case, because conditional gains are substantially larger than conditional losses, it is profitable to hold a $1,000 beginning balance in March, even though the odds are 3/1 that the actual outflow will be less than $1,000.

TRANSACTIONS VS. PRECAUTIONARY BALANCES

Using this approach to precautionary balances, it is virtually impossible to separate transactions from precautionary balances. They are both held for the same reasons and, except for the probability distribution, are determined by the same variables. If $135,000 would be the cash stocked for January under certainty, the additional $2,000, which would be held when the cash flow is uncertain, could be counted as the precautionary balance. However, there is little point in separating the two balances.

THE VALUE OF THE CASH BALANCE

The expected net value of the cash balance is the sum of the expected incremental gains less the expected incremental losses for each cash balance through the optimal balance. From Exhibit 5-7, it is the sum of column (8) for all positive expected incremental values, $13,480.40. It should be noted that the calculation is identical to that used for merchandise inventory in Chapter 3.

RISK AND THE CASH BALANCE

How can there be any risk attached to the cash balance? After all, if one holds a dollar for a month, he must still have a dollar at the end of the month. The risk is not with the balance, but is a result of the possibility that the actual net value of the cash balance may not be equal to the forecast value.

Suppose the firm stocks $137,000 in January and the actual outflow for January turns out to be $133,000. Although the expected net value of the cash balance is $13,480.40, the actual value will be less. The firm would have actually avoided penalties of $133 \times \$100 = \$13,300$. Four thousand dollars would be excess, involving a loss of $4 \times \$20 = \$80$. So, the actual value of the $137,000 cash balance, when needs are for only $133,000, is $13,300 - \$80 = \$13,220$. There is a distribution of possible actual values around the expected value. The expected value is the probability-weighted arithmetical mean of the actual values.

WITH BEGINNING CASH BALANCE = $137,000

Actual Outflow	Net Value of Cash Balance	Probability	Weighted Value
$132,000............	$13,100	0.01	$ 131.00
133,000............	13,220	0.10	1,322.00
134,000............	13,340	0.20	2,668.00
135,000............	13,460	0.26	3,499.60
136,000............	13,580	0.26	3,530.80
137,000............	13,700	0.15	2,055.00
138,000............	13,700	0.02	274.00
	Weighted mean = net expected value		$13,480.40

The standard deviation measures the variation of actual values around the expected value and, as before, will serve as a measure of risk. The standard deviation for the value of the January balance of $137,000 is $151.84 (variance = $23,055.84). To offset the effect of the units of measurement, the risk measure can be standardized by dividing it by the expected value, which is 0.011.

SPECULATIVE BALANCES

CASH AS AN
EARNING ASSET

The value attributed to cash as a transactions and precautionary balance is a mirror value, reflecting the fact that everyone is willing to accept cash in exchange for real assets and as payment for liabilities. The value of cash in this sense is the value of the asset acquired and the penalties avoided by paying financial obligations when due.

If the firm holds a dollar bill for one year, it will have only a dollar bill at the end of the year. In terms of other assets, however, the value of cash may have increased or fallen, depending upon what has happened to the price level. If prices have fallen, the value of cash will have risen, because everyone will be willing to accept less cash than before the price decline in exchange for other assets. In short, the purchasing power of cash will rise when prices fall.

Thus, the value of cash will vary inversely with the price level and, in this sense, cash can be viewed as an earning asset. To evaluate cash as an earning asset, the same technique is used as with a fixed asset. The cost of the investment, C, is M/P_1, where M is the nominal amount of dollars held for speculative purposes, and P_1 is the price level prevailing when the cash is invested. In order for the investment to be profitable, it must have a gross present value in excess of the cost, i.e., it must have a positive net present value. The gross present value of the cash asset is $(M/P_2) \times [1/(1+i)^n]$, where P_2 is the price level expected to prevail in the future and $1/(1+i)^n$ is the multiplier from Table 2-2.

If the cost of capital is 0.20, M is \$100, P_1 is 1 (a price index), and P_2 is expected to be 0.75 in one year, the gross present value of the \$100 cash investment is

$$\frac{\$100}{0.75}(0.833) = \$111.06,$$

and the investment will be accepted since it is larger than the cost

$$\frac{\$100}{1} = \$100.$$

The net present value of this investment is \$11.06. As long as this is true, the firm will accumulate cash as an earning asset, adding to the speculative cash balance.

Obviously, any decline in price does not suffice to justify holding cash. If the expected annual decline in the price level is from 1 to 0.85, a 15 per cent decline, a firm with a cost of capital of 20 per cent would lose \$2.01 by holding a speculative balance of \$100. In fact, the future price level must be less than $P_1/(1+i)^n$ if the speculative balance is to be profitable. This ratio indicates that firms with a high cost of capital are less likely to hold speculative balances than are firms with a low cost of capital, since the required future price level varies inversely with the cost of capital. Further, the longer the time span before prices fall, the less is the profit in holding speculative balances.

RISK

Certainty about future price changes is rather unlikely. The firm, however, can describe its beliefs about the future by using a probability distribution. A net present value would be calculated for each possible future price, or for the various lengths of time before a given price decline is reached. For each net present value, a probability is assigned. The sum of the products of each net present value multiplied by its probability yields the expected net present value. The standard deviation of the distribution of net present values is the measure of risk for the speculative balance.

SPECULATIVE,
TRANSACTIONS,
PRECAUTIONARY BALANCES

When prices are expected to fall by less than $P_1/(1+i)^n$, or are expected to rise, the desired level of speculative balances becomes a negative quantity. How can we hold a negative speculative balance? Since dollars held by the firm for speculative purposes are indistinguishable from the dollars held for precautionary and transactions purposes, speculative balances can become negative by reducing transactions and precautionary balances.

For example, a firm might calculate, in the absence of price level change considerations, that it should have a precautionary cash balance of at least $100. In its calculations, the firm has already considered the inventory costs of carrying such a balance. If prices are expected to remain constant, the precautionary balance will not be reduced. However, if prices are expected to rise, the firm will suffer a speculative loss by holding the precautionary balance.

A price rise of 5 per cent over the year will reduce the purchasing power of the $100 balance to $95.23 in terms of the initial prices. With a cost of capital of 24 per cent annually, the present value of the $4.77 loss is $3.85. Suppose that the firm had calculated the expected net value of the $100 balance at $0.50 a month. Using the monthly cost of capital as 2 per cent, the net present value of the precautionary balance over the year is about $5.29. Since this exceeds the present value of the loss due to price rises, the cash balance will remain unchanged.

Had the monthly expected value of holding a precautionary balance of $100 been only $0.35 per month, the present value of the precautionary balance for a year would be $3.70. Under these conditions, the firm would reduce the cash balance, because the combined effects of the value of the precautionary balance and the price rise would result in a loss, reducing the expected value of net worth by $0.15.

It is unlikely that the precautionary balance would be reduced to zero under these circumstances. As the balance is reduced, three things change. The expected loss due to the price rise falls as the balance falls. The costs of carrying and ordering cash fall as the balance falls. The penalties which the firm is likely to incur rise because of the smaller balance. At some point before the balance reaches zero, the present value of the expected monthly values of the lower precautionary balance will exceed the present value of the loss due to price rises.

Just as the precautionary and transactions balances may be reduced to reflect a desired negative speculative balance, the desire for a positive speculative balance may be satisfied by the transactions and precautionary balance. The point is, as has been said earlier, dollars in the cash balance cannot be separated in terms of their purposes. Dollars held for speculative purposes are available for transactions purposes. A balance held for transactions and precautionary purposes will increase in purchasing power when prices fall, just as if the balance had been held for speculative purposes. There is only one cash balance, although there are several reasons for holding it.

CASH AS A HEDGE

Even though the general price level is stable, the firm may suffer from adverse business conditions affecting the firm or the firm's industry only, with the remainder of the economy untouched. There are many examples of a particular industry confronted with a decline in demand while the rest of the economy prospers. In the early 1950's, the television industry suffered an industrial slump caused by a combination of overexpansion and a switch in consumers' tastes from large consoles to less expensive table models. Some industries, particularly in the consumer durable-goods area, appear to have periodic variations in demand. Events in one sector of the economy can adversely affect firms in other parts of the economy, such as the effects on the steel industry of a strike in the automobile industry.

Whatever the reasons, the effect of such a slump is a decline in the value of the earning assets of the firm and a resultant decline in the expected value of net worth. To the extent that the firm holds cash balances, the effect of declining asset values on net worth can be moderated. The effect of the asset-value decline on net worth depends upon the relative importance of earning assets among the assets of the balance sheet and upon the relative importance of net worth compared with liabilities. Since we are postponing a discussion of the capital structure, i.e., structure of liabilities and net worth, to a later part of the book, we shall assume net worth constitutes the entire capital structure of the firm.

With this assumption, the effect of a decline in the value of earning assets on net worth equals the percentage decline in asset value times the ratio of earning assets to total assets. If all assets are earning assets, a 10 per cent decline in the value of earning assets causes a 10 per cent decline in the value of net worth. If the firm holds 20 per cent of its assets in cash, with the remaining 80 per cent in earning assets, a 10 per cent decline in the value of earning assets will reduce the value of net worth by only 8 per cent.

Thus, even if the firm needs little or no cash for transactions or precautionary purposes and does not expect a general price deflation, it may carry speculative balances to moderate the effects of business reverses, in much the same way that one buys life insurance. The cost of this insurance is the carrying cost of the cash balance, i.e., the cost of capital times the balance.

Just as businessmen are apt to increase fire insurance coverage after another businessman suffers a fire loss against which he was underinsured, businessmen will tend to increase asset-value insurance when they anticipate reverses. Anticipation of reverses occurs frequently after reverses actually have been suffered. So, the composition of the asset structure of the firm tends to shift away from earning assets toward cash when business conditions worsen.

This is consistent with what has been said earlier about the decision process affecting investment in earning assets. When adverse business conditions are anticipated, the profitability of earning assets diminishes. If, under these conditions, the firm chooses not to distribute excess funds to owners or, dropping the assumption of zero liabilities for a moment, not to reduce debt, cash balances will automatically rise. The increased cash serves as a buffer, or insurance, against the expected adverse turn of events.

Even if a firm does not expect to suffer reverses, it may wish to insure against reverses anyhow. The amount of insurance, or speculative cash balance, carried will depend upon how remote the firm believes reverses to be and upon the premium i.e., carrying costs, of the insurance. A firm with a high cost of capital will tend to be relatively less liquid than a firm with a low cost of capital. Later on, we shall show that firms which have many profitable investment opportunities and are trying to grow rapidly are apt to have a higher marginal cost of capital than they would if they did not wish to acquire large amounts of funds. Because the premium for holding cash is high for such rapid-growth firms, they will tend to hold less cash insurance than they would if they were trying to grow less rapidly.

MARKETABLE SECURITIES

If borrowers could be found who were willing to sell the firm securities on which the firm would earn interest, but which could be converted into cash very quickly and with no chance of loss, the firm would convert a substantial portion of cash holdings into such securities.

Suppose the firm could buy at a price of $1,000 a security paying $50 in interest, maturing in one year, and with a redemption value of $1,000 at the maturity date. If the security were marketable at a guaranteed price of $1,000 any time before maturity, it would be an excellent substitute for cash. The cost of holding a $1,000 cash balance for a year is $240, assuming the cost of capital is 24 per cent on an annual basis. By investing the cash in this near-perfect cash substitute, the firm can reduce carrying costs to $190 ($240 − $50). The higher the interest rate paid on the security, or the lower the cost of capital, the more desirable the security will be. It is conceivable that a security could earn at a rate greater than the cost of capital, in which event the firm will use the security not just as a cash substitute, but as an earning-asset investment.

Since the security is marketable at a fixed price, it is an ideal substitute for either precautionary or speculative balances. If prices fall, the maturity value of the security is fixed, making it behave as if it were cash. If the value of the earning assets fall, the fixed value of the security moderates the effect on net worth just as cash would. If the firm needs cash because outflows unexpectedly exceed inflows, the security can be sold at the price paid for it, making it useful for precautionary purposes.

Assuming that the firm need pay no broker's fees when either selling or buying this admirable security, the cash balance will approach zero. The firm will simply buy securities as soon as it has ordered cash, and sell the securities day by day or as the need for cash arises. Ordering costs will be unchanged, but carrying costs will be reduced by the interest earned on the securities.

BROKER'S FEES AND TRANSACTIONS BALANCES

Let us approach reality by stages. First, the purchase and sale of a security normally involves a fee. Thus, if the firm tries to reduce carrying costs of transactions balances by investing all cash in the ideal security and selling off securities as cash needs arise, it normally will incur substantial costs in the form of broker's fees.

Keep all the assumptions except that each sale and each purchase of a security involves a broker's fee of $1 per $1,000 security. Consider a firm which has calculated that it should order $30,000 of cash every 30 days, to be spent at a rate of $1,000 a day. Assume the carrying costs are 2 per cent of the average balance, or $300. Ordering costs are also $300. If the firm tried to reduce the carrying costs by investing the entire $30,000 in securities and selling off $1,000 daily to meet cash needs, it would incur a cost of $30 in the purchase of the securities and $30 in the sale, or $60.00.

With an annual yield of $40 per security, 4 per cent, the firm would earn interest of $3.33 for each security held for 30 days, or 0.11 per day. The average security, however, will be held for only 15 days. Thus interest earned will be $49.95, or $1.65 × 30. The zero cash balance costs can be portrayed as follows:

Ordering costs of cash, prior to securities purchase	$300.00
Carrying costs	300.00
Costs without securities	$600.00
Less interest on securities	− 49.95
	$550.05
Plus costs of buying and selling securities	+ 60.00
Costs of meeting transactions needs with zero cash balance	$610.05

The firm is $10.05 worse off with zero cash balances than it would have been with zero securities.

In this case, cash balance with some securities would be better than either no securities or no cash. Should the firm invest half the cash balance in securities, buying and selling costs would fall to $30. The securities would not be sold until the cash balance of $15,000 had been exhausted, i.e., the average security would earn interest for 22.5 days instead of 15, making the interest earned 22.5 days × $0.11 × 15 securities = $37.13. Since the return from the securities exceeds the buying and selling costs, the surplus $7.13 reduces the carrying costs of financing the transactions needs.

The 50-50 mixture of securities and cash is not optimal. The cost of the last security is the cost of buying it and selling it 15 days later, a total of $2. The last security added would be sold 15 days after purchase, earning only $15 \times \$0.11$, or about $1.65. It is not profitable to substitute it for cash since it costs $0.35 more than it yields.

The optimal mixture can be found by considering the number of days a security must be held until its interest equals the costs of buying and selling it. In this example, the security must be held for about 19 days, i.e., $2 ÷ $0.11. Therefore, the firm should begin the 30-day period with eleven $1,000 securities and $19,000 in cash. The costs of buying and selling the securities will be $22. The interest earned will average $2.71 for each of the 11 securities (the first security sold will earn $2.09, and the last security will earn $3.33, which averages $2.71), for a total of $29.81. This reduces the costs of financing the transactions needs by $7.81 and is $0.35 better than if the firm held half the transactions needs in securities.

The general rule is that a security will be substituted for cash as long as the interest earned from the security exceeds any costs associated with acquiring and disposing of the security. As has been shown, precautionary balances are inseparable from transactions balances. So the rule will apply to precautionary balances. It also applies to speculative balances, but is not ordinarily important in this case because a security substituted for a speculative balance will be held long enough so that the interest earned will exceed the cost of purchase and sale.

CAPITAL LOSSES

A security with a maturity, or redemption, value of $1,000 which pays $40 a year is said to have a *coupon* rate of 4 per cent. If the market rate is 3 per cent, a security with a 4 per cent coupon rate will sell for more than its maturity value. The simplest illustration is that of a permanent security that will never be redeemed. This kind of security, of which there are no American examples, is called a *consol*. Its market value is simply the ratio of its annual dollar yield to the market rate of interest. If the yield is $40 per annum and the market rate is 4 per cent, the value of the consol is $1,000. With a market rate of 3 per cent, the value of the consol rises to $40/0.03, or $1,333.33. At a market rate of 5 per cent, the value of the consol will fall to $800.

Changing market interest rates have a similar effect on securities with a definite maturity date. The effect is damped, however, to a greater or lesser extent depending on when the security is to be redeemed. If the market rate should rise to 5 per cent, it is unlikely that the price of a bond yielding $40 a year would fall to $800 if the bond is to mature in, say, one year. Such a decline would make the bond a terrific bargain. By investing $800 today, the investor would receive interest of $40 plus $1,000 in one year. Assume that the interest is paid at the end of the year (usually interest is paid semi-annually or quarterly). The rate of return on the investment is over 30 per cent. An excellent return when the market rate is only 5 per cent. The proximity of the maturity date in this example would indicate that price should fall to $1,040 × 1/1.05 = $990.48. If the redemption date were two years away, the price should be $40 × 1/1.05 + $1,040 × 1/(1.05)² = = $981.40.

Of course, the actual values of a security are determined by supply and demand, not a present-value formula. But, if securities similar to the one in question are selling at 5 per cent, the market value of the security will not be far off the value indicated by the formula.

When a firm buys a security, it takes the risk that the interest rate will rise. Even if the firm holds the security until maturity, thus avoiding the sale at below maturity value, it has suffered a loss since the funds could have been invested at the higher interest rate. To some degree, the risk is offset by the chance that interest rates will fall, allowing the firm a capital gain. Though the chance of interest rate rises may be equal to the chance of a fall, this is not necessarily the case.

The behavior of investors with asymmetrical interest rate expectations tends to justify their expectations. When everyone expects interest rates to rise, holders of securities try to avoid capital losses by selling their holdings, and few buyers appear. As a result, the supply of securities exceeds the demand, the prices of securities fall, and market interest rates rise. The converse occurs when everyone anticipates a rate decline.

Hedging Via the Maturity Structure. The risk of interest rate rises can be reduced by shifting securities from those maturing in the far future to those of shorter term. As an example of this process, consider a security with a $1,000 maturity value and a coupon rate of 4 per cent. At a 4 per cent market rate, the security sells for $1,000 regardless of when it matures. Should the interest rate rise to 5 per cent, the price of the security would fall to $922.10 if it matures in 10 years, but would fall to only $990.40 if it matures in 1 year. Conversely, long-term securities show larger capital gains than do short-term securities when interest rates fall.

A speculator on the securities markets may shift his holdings to long-term maturities when he expects a fall in interest rates. He is apt to shift to cash when he expects a rise in interest rates. The firm, in using securities as a substitute for cash, is not speculating on interest rate movements. Nonetheless, the firm is apt to avoid securities when interest rates are expected to rise, stay primarily in short-term securities normally, and shift somewhat to longer term securities when interest rates are expected to fall. Table 5-2 indicates the propensity of nonfinancial business corporations to stay in the short end of the market.

Table 5-2

RELATIVE DISTRIBUTION OF MARKETABLE GOVERNMENT
SECURITIES BY MATURITY CLASSES FOR ALL HOLDERS
AND NONFINANCIAL BUSINESS CORPORATIONS
DECEMBER 31, 1962

Maturity Class	All Holders, %	Nonfinancial Business Corporations, %
less than 1 year	43	84.0
1– 5 years	30	14.0
5–10 years	17	1.0
10–20 years	2	0.3
20 + years	8	0.7
Totals	100	100.0

Source: *Federal Reserve Bulletin*, December, 1964.

Sensitivity of Security Prices to Interest Rates. The arithmetic of interest rate–price relationships operates so that the absolute size of a capital loss resulting from a small interest rate rise, say of 0.1 per cent, results in a larger capital loss when interest rates are low rather than when they are high. The price of a 4 per cent coupon rate bond maturing in 30 years will fall from $1,449.60 to $1,421.30 when the interest rate moves from 2 per cent to 2.1 per cent, a capital loss of $28.30. When the interest rate rises from 5.8 per cent to 5.9 per cent, the same bond will fall from a price of $745.50 to $734.20, a loss of only $11.30. Thus, although capital losses depend on the maturity of the security, the size of the loss is affected by the absolute level of the interest rate, also. The converse holds for gains. Gains are larger when the rate falls from a low rate than from a high level.

THE SECURITIES
PORTFOLIO

From the previous discussion, the following would seem to hold: (1) Holdings of liquid assets will rarely be completely in the form of cash, nor completely in the form of marketable securities. It is not only a matter of buying and selling costs, but also of holding cash as a hedge against interest rate rises. (2) The securities held by business corporations as cash substitutes will be primarily short-term. However, when rates are expected to fall, the prospect of the gain may tempt the firm to speculate by extending the average maturity of the securities held.

The firm will tend to prefer securities issued by safe borrowers, borrowers who can be depended upon to pay interest and principal when due. The safest borrower is the United States government. Reflecting this, the rates on government securities tend to be lower than on the securities of other issuers for comparable maturities (see Table 5-3).

Table 5-3
YIELDS ON CASH-SUBSTITUTE SECURITIES, 1960-1963
(Per Cent Per Annum)

Period	Prime Coml Paper, 4-6 Months[1]	Finance Co. Paper Placed Directly, 3-6 Months[2]	Prime Bankers' Acceptances, 90 Days[1]	U.S. Government Securities (Taxable)[3] 3-Month Bills Rate on New Issue	3-Month Bills Market Yield	6-Month Bills Rate on New Issue	6-Month Bills Market Yield	9- to 12-Month Issues Bills (Market Yield)	9- to 12-Month Issues Other[4]	3- to 5-Year Issues[5]	United States (Long-term)	Government Bonds Total[6]	State and Local Aaa	State and Local Baa
1960	3.85	3.54	3.51	2.928	2.87	3.247	3.20	3.41	3.55	3.99	4.01	3.69	3.26	4.22
1961	2.97	2.68	2.81	2.378	2.36	2.605	2.59	2.81	2.91	3.60	3.90	3.60	3.27	4.01
1962	3.26	3.07	3.01	2.778	2.77	2.908	2.90	3.01	3.02	3.57	3.95	3.30	3.03	3.67
1962, Mar.	3.25	3.02	3.00	2.719	2.72	2.883	2.87	2.98	2.99	3.55	4.01	3.30	3.03	3.66
Apr.	3.20	3.09	3.00	2.735	2.73	2.838	2.83	2.90	2.94	3.48	3.89	3.21	2.98	3.55
May.	3.16	2.95	2.91	2.694	2.68	2.789	2.78	2.91	2.98	3.53	3.88	3.21	2.98	3.55
June	3.25	3.02	2.90	2.719	2.73	2.804	2.80	2.89	3.02	3.51	3.90	3.31	3.06	3.65
July	3.36	3.20	3.07	2.945	2.92	3.085	3.08	3.17	3.23	3.71	4.02	3.37	3.10	3.72
Aug.	3.30	3.12	3.11	2.837	2.82	3.005	2.99	3.10	3.13	3.57	3.97	3.38	3.10	3.74
Sept.	3.34	3.13	3.09	2.792	2.78	2.947	2.93	2.99	3.00	3.56	3.94	3.28	3.01	3.66
Oct.	3.27	3.04	3.03	2.751	2.74	2.859	2.84	2.90	2.90	3.46	3.89	3.21	2.94	3.62
Nov.	3.23	3.08	3.00	2.803	2.83	2.875	2.89	2.94	2.92	3.46	3.87	3.15	2.89	3.53
Dec.	3.29	3.16	3.00	2.856	2.87	2.908	2.91	2.94	2.95	3.44	3.87	3.22	2.93	3.57
1963, Jan.	3.34	3.18	3.07	2.914	2.91	2.962	2.96	3.00	2.97	3.47	3.88	3.22	2.95	3.56
Feb.	3.25	3.13	3.13	2.916	2.92	2.970	2.98	3.00	2.89	3.48	3.92	3.24	2.99	3.57
Mar.	3.34	3.15	3.13	2.897	2.89	2.950	2.95	2.97	2.99	3.50	3.93	3.21	2.97	3.56
Week ending: 1963, Mar. 2	3.25	3.13	3.13	2.870	2.90	2.922	2.94	2.98	2.93	3.50	3.94	3.25	3.02	3.57
9	3.25	3.13	3.13	2.897	2.89	2.938	2.93	2.97	2.99	3.49	3.92	3.25	3.02	3.57
16	3.38	3.13	3.13	2.870	2.88	2.931	2.94	2.95	2.97	3.49	3.93	3.23	2.98	3.57
23	3.38	3.13	3.13	2.902	2.90	2.955	2.96	2.97	2.99	3.51	3.94	3.18	2.93	3.55
30	3.38	3.23	3.13	2.919	2.91	2.977	2.98	2.99	3.01	3.53	3.95	3.19	2.93	3.55
											4-11	20	5	5

[1] Averages of daily offering rates of dealers.
[2] Averages of daily rates, published by finance cos., for varying maturities in the 90-179 day range.
[3] Except for new bill issues, yields are averages computed from daily closing bid prices.
[4] Certificates of indebtedness and selected note and bond issues.
[5] Selected note and bond issues.
[6] Includes bonds rated Aaa and Aa, data for which are not shown separately. Because of a limited number of suitable issues, the number of corporate bonds in some groups has varied somewhat.

NOTE.—Annual yields are averages of monthly or quarterly data. Monthly and weekly yields are computed as follows: U.S. Govt. bonds: averages of daily figures for bonds maturing or callable in 10 years or more.

Source: Federal Reserve Bulletin, Board of Governors of the Federal Reserve System April, 1963.

Prime commercial paper represents short-term negotiable promissory notes issued by prime risk corporations, usually engaged in financing the sales and purchases of consumer goods, such as automobiles, washing machines, etc. The issuers may be independent sales finance companies or finance companies, such as the General Motors Acceptance Corporation, associated with, and controlled by, a nonfinancial business corporation. Though it is not common, a nonfinancial business corporation with a strong financial position may raise funds in the commercial paper market. The paper is distributed through commercial paper dealers and is sold on a discount basis. Instead of receiving an explicit payment, the buyer pays a price below the maturity value of the commercial paper. The difference between the price paid and the maturity value is the gain. For example, paper maturing in four months with a maturity value of $1,000 would sell at a price of $1,000 \times 1/[(1 + 0.04)/3] = $986.85 to yield an annual rate of 4 per cent.

Directly placed finance company paper is similar to commercial paper, except that the dealer is eliminated. Financial officers of nonfinancial firms who wish to substitute securities for cash holdings approach, or are approached by, sales finance companies. Often, the maturity of the promissory note can be adjusted to coincide with the time when the lender will need cash. The advantage in this is that the lending corporation need take no interest rate risk, since the paper will be held until it matures. Also, dealers' commissions are avoided both in purchase and resale. These advantages are reflected in the lower rates generally prevailing for directly placed paper as compared with commercial paper.

Government securities come in a variety of maturity classes. New issue rates on bills vary somewhat from the yields on outstanding issues. Three factors cause this. First, the new bills are sold to dealers in government securities on a bid basis and are not put on the general market directly by the government. The actual market yield on securities fluctuates, usually slightly, from transaction to transaction. Thus, the bid rate may not coincide precisely with the average yield for outstanding bills.

Second, the value of a bill tends to rise, ignoring interest rate changes, as it approaches maturity. The bills are sold on a discount basis, so the increase in value as the bill approaches maturity is purely a matter of the arithmetic of discounting. When a large number of the outstanding bills are approaching maturity, a new issue will sell at a higher yield than the outstanding bills. The yield difference reflects the fact that the holder of a new bill has longer to wait for maturity than he would with an older bill.

Third, and always important in explaining interest rate movements, is the supply of, and demand for, bills. If the Treasury issues a large number of new bills, there is a tendency for the new bill yield to be higher than existing bills because supply temporarily exceeds demand. The differential in this case cannot become too large, or holders of old bills will find it profitable to sell their old bills and buy the new, higher-yielding bills. This kind of activity is called *arbitrage* and works to eliminate differentials among the yields of similar securities.

Table 5-3 indicates that long-term securities tend to have higher yields than short-term. All other things being equal, long-term yields will tend to exceed short-term yields because the latter are less susceptible to capital losses resulting from interest rate fluctuations. The differential is increased when it is expected that rates are going to rise, and can be reduced, or even reversed, if it is expected that rates are going to fall.

State and local government bonds are usually long-term. However, the interest earned on these bonds is tax-exempt. As a result, a taxpayer in a 48 per cent tax bracket, which is the bracket for all business corporations with an income in excess of $25,000, would view a 3 per cent, tax-exempt yield as being the equivalent of a 5.77 per cent yield on a similar risk, similar maturity bond, the interest on which is subject to taxes.

Table 5-4 shows the securities used as cash substitutes by nonfinancial business corporations. Although not a security, time deposits have been included. The interest rate on time deposits reduces the carrying costs of cash just as the interest on securities. There are no fees associated with purchase and redemption of time deposits. In addition, there is no direct risk of capital loss since the time deposit can be redeemed at its fixed value. The issuer of time deposits is a commercial bank and the deposits are insured by the Federal Deposit Insurance Corporation. As of Nov. 1964, time deposit interest rates applicable to business corporations were:

$4\frac{1}{2}$ per cent for deposits payable in 90 days or more,
4 per cent for deposits payable in less than 90 days.

This represents an increase for the longer-term holders of time deposits over rates prevailing prior to late 1964.

Although Treasury securities constitute the largest part of the cash-substitute or near-cash balances, the relative importance of United States securities fell erratically from almost 95 per cent in 1945 to about 59 per cent in 1962. By 1962, nonfinancial business corporations held $3 billion fewer government securities than in 1945. The decline in United States holdings accompanied a general increase in the over-all level of near-cash assets.

The most dramatic increase is the increase in time deposits, which was noted at the beginning of the chapter. Time deposits in 1962 rose 72 per cent over the 1961 balances, and by almost 700 per cent of the 1945 balances. Most of this can be attributed to the increase in time deposit rates.

Most of the other shifts can be explained similarly. For example, there was a sharp decline of $3 billion in the holdings of Treasury securities between 1959 and 1960. About $1.3 billion reflected a shift out of securities. The remainder of the shift resulted in an increase in time deposits and

Table 5-4

NONFINANCIAL BUSINESS CORPORATION HOLDINGS
OF TIME DEPOSITS, TREASURY SECURITIES, STATE
AND LOCAL GOVERNMENT OBLIGATIONS, AND COMMERCIAL
AND SALES FINANCE COMPANY PAPER, 1945–1962
(In Billions of Dollars)

Year End Date,	Treasury	State and and Local	Commercial and Sales Finance Paper	Time Deposits	Total
1945	22.2	0.3	...	0.9	23.4
1946	15.3	0.3	... *	0.9	16.5
1947	14.1	0.4	0.1	0.9	15.4
1948	14.7	0.4	0.3	0.9	16.3
1949	16.7	0.5	0.6	0.9	18.7
1950	19.6	0.5	0.6	0.9	21.6
1951	20.7	0.6	0.9	0.9	23.1
1952	19.9	0.7	1.2	0.9	22.7
1953	21.5	0.8	1.4	0.9	24.6
1954	19.1	1.0	1.2	1.1	22.4
1955	23.5	1.2	1.2	1.0	26.9
1956	19.2	1.3	1.4	1.0	22.9
1957	19.2	1.5	1.6	1.0	23.3
1958	19.0	2.0	1.7	1.6	24.3
1959	23.4	2.6	2.1	1.5	29.6
1960	20.4	2.9	2.7	2.3	28.3
1961	19.5	3.3	2.8	3.6	29.2
1962	19.2	3.8	3.5	6.2	32.7
1963	19.9	2.4	4.4	10.3	37.0

*Less than $50,000.
Source: Federal Reserve Bulletin (October, 1964), Board of Governors of the Federal Reserve System.

other securities. About $600 million were added to the holdings of commercial and sales finance paper. As of December, 1959, the rate on directly placed sales finance paper was 0.32 more than the yield on three-month Treasury bills. By December, 1960, the differential had grown to 0.72. From such small changes in yield differences, major portfolio shifts are made.

EXPECTED VALUE AND RISK
OF CASH SUBSTITUTES

Since the securities discussed are substitutes for cash, the expected value of the securities is derived from the expected value of the cash. If the net expected value of a $1,000 cash balance is $500, the value of securities bought as a substitute will be the $1,000 cost plus the $500 net value plus the advantage in reduced carrying charges resulting from earning interest on the securities. Thus, with a 4 per cent interest rate, the value of the securities will be $1,540, ignoring brokers' fees, if the firm plans to hold the securities for a year.

The risk, or standard deviation, associated with the original cash balance is transferred to the securities used as the cash substitute: In addition to this, there is the risk associated with the security itself. Assuming that the issuer will be able to meet the financial obligations of the security, the firm still has an interest rate risk. If rates rise, the firm suffers a capital loss. The loss may easily be larger than the interest the firm expects to earn. As has been indicated, the firm can moderate this risk by holding short-term securities, which usually involves accepting a lower interest rate. However, short-term securities do not completely remove the risk of capital losses.

To assess the interest rate risk, the firm must prepare a probability distribution of interest rates that are expected to prevail when the security is sold. For interest rates higher than that prevailing at the time of purchase, a capital loss is incurred. For interest rates lower, a capital gain is made. The present value of each capital gain or loss must be added to the present value of the interest earned. This is a list of the conditional gains or possibilities resulting from substituting a security for cash. Each of the conditional gains is associated with a probability, the probability that the interest rate will be at a certain level when the security is sold. The summation of the products of the conditional gains and the associated probabilities yields the expected value of the security. The expected value is equivalent to the $40 added to the value of the cash balance in the example at the beginning of this section.

The risk of the security is the standard deviation of the conditional values around the expected value. For reasons that will be given in the next chapter, the over-all risk of the security is not necessarily the sum of the risk associated with the cash balance plus the interest rate risk. That sum is the maximum risk. As will be shown later, the total risk of a cash-substitute security may be lower than the sum of the risk of the cash balance plus the risk of interest rate variations.

SELECTED REFERENCES

Baumol, W. J.: "The Transactions Demand for Cash: An Inventory-Theoretic Approach," *Quarterly Journal of Economics*, Nov., 1952.
Frazer, W. J.: "Large Manufacturing Corporations as Suppliers of Funds to the United States Government Security Market," *Journal of Finance*, Dec., 1958.
Hansen, A.: *Monetary Theory and Fiscal Policy*, Harvard, Cambridge, Mass., 1949.
Hicks, J. R.: *Value and Capital*, Oxford, London, 1946.
Jacobs, D. P.: "The Marketable Security Portfolios of Non-financial Corporations, Investment Practices and Trends," *Journal of Finance*, Sept., 1960.
Keynes, J. M.: *The General Theory of Employment, Money, and Interest*, Harcourt, New York, 1936.
———: *A Treatise on Money*, Harcourt, New York, 1953.

Lutz, F. A.: *Corporate Cash Balances 1914–43, Manufacturing and Trade*, National Bureau of Economic Research, New York, 1945.

————: *The Theory of Investment of the Firm*, Princeton, N.J., 1951.

Madden, J. T., M. Nadler, and S. Heller,: *Money Market Primer*, Ronald, New York, 1948.

Tobin, J.: "The Interest-Elasticity of Transactions Demand for Cash," *Review of Economics and Statistics*, Aug., 1956.

The Asset Portfolio:
Risk and Return

6

In the last four chapters, we have considered the major kinds of assets in which nonfinancial business corporations invest. The important conclusions drawn from this detailed discussion are:

1. The individual assets may be evaluated in terms of profitability, in which profit becomes expected profit under conditions of risk and expected profit becomes expected net present value when the income stream generated by the asset occurs over time rather than at a single point in time;

2. The expected net present value of an asset usually cannot be considered apart from the other asset investments made by the firm. The value of a fixed asset investment affects the value of the inventory investment. The value of inventories will depend upon the value of credit sales, or accounts receivable, in which the firm plans to invest; and the value of the cash balance is affected by all the other assets. Thus, it is essential to consider all the assets combined, the portfolio of asset investments, as well as the individual assets.

In this chapter, we shall be concerned with the effects of the cost of capital and risk on the choice of the asset portfolio.

THE COST OF CAPITAL

In general, the cost of capital and the total funds invested vary inversely. For an individual asset, however, the relationship is not variable. Although the expected net present value of any asset varies inversely with the cost of capital, the asset investment will be made as long as expected net present value is positive. The decision is of a "go–no go" nature. If the present value of an asset is zero at a cost of capital of 20 per cent, the asset will be adopted as long as the cost of capital is less than 20 per cent. And it will be rejected when the cost of capital is equal to, or more than, 20 per cent. The nature of the investment decision for a particular asset tends to make the demand schedule for investment funds shift in a discontinuous fashion. For example, at all costs of capital below 10 per cent, the firm may find assets requiring investments totaling $1,000,000 profitable. At 10 per cent, an asset costing $100,000 may become unprofitable. There may be no further decline in the demand for assets until the cost of capital reaches 14 per cent, at which point other assets become unprofitable, etc., resulting in a discontinuous demand for funds.

Further, it does not follow that the total investment funds demanded will become smaller as the cost of capital rises. As was shown in Chapter 2, a rising cost of capital reduces the expected net present value of long-lived assets more than it reduces the value of short-lived assets. To some extent, then, the firm will substitute short-lived for long-lived assets as the cost of capital rises. However, the funds needed for short-term investments are not necessarily less than the funds needed for long-term investments. Thus, the investment funds demanded may actually increase at times when the cost of capital rises.

Figure 6–1 shows hypothetical supply and demand schedules. SS' represents the supply curve of funds to the firm. As additional funds are needed, the cost of capital rises. The numbered dots represent asset portfolios. The location point for each portfolio is determined by the amount of investment funds needed to acquire the portfolio and the highest cost of capital at which the portfolio is profitable. For example, portfolio 6 requires OU of funds and is profitable when the cost of capital is OC or less.

The firm will not invest in portfolio 6 because the cost of capital for OU funds exceeds OC. At OC, the firm can acquire only OT in funds. For the same reason, the firm will not adopt portfolios 7 or 8 either. The only portfolios involving funds which can be acquired at a cost of capital equal to, or less than, the minimum cost of capital at which the portfolios remain profitable are portfolios 1, 2, 3, 4, and 5. Portfolio 5 requires OS in funds. OS funds can be acquired at a cost of capital of OB. This is less than the minimum cost of capital at which 5 remains profitable, OD.

The firm will consider only those asset portfolios which lie to the left of the supply curve. But, of the five in the illustration, the firm can choose only one. Which one will be chosen?

In the absence of risk, the firm would calculate the total net present value of each portfolio. For a given portfolio, the total net present value is simply the sum of the net present values of each asset in the portfolio. The cost of capital used to discount the income streams for each asset is

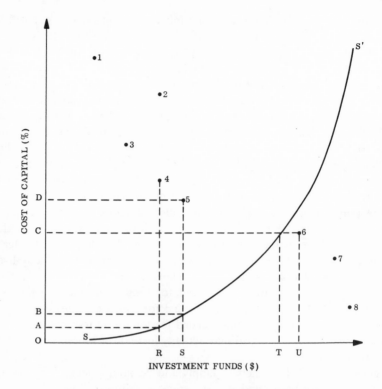

Figure 6-1. Hypothetical Supply and Demand Schedules

the lowest cost of capital for the funds needed to buy the portfolio. Thus, the cost of capital used for portfolio 5 is *OB*. For portfolio 4, the cost of capital would be *OA*, which is the cost of capital required to raise *OR* funds. The portfolio adopted would be that with the largest total net present value. Incidentally, we have not used the word "expected" in this case since, with certainty, actual and expected values are identical by definition.

If risk exists, the portfolio decision is more complex. For example, the most profitable portfolio may be the riskiest. It would be quite rational for the firm to prefer a less risky asset portfolio even though it is less profitable. This is the same kind of rationality that makes firms and individuals spend money on fire and casualty insurance. With asset portfolios, the insurance premium takes the form of a reduction in the total expected net present value of the portfolio.

RISK

The risk of an individual asset is measured by the standard deviation of probability distribution of the conditional values of that asset. It follows that the risk of a group of assets, an asset portfolio, may be measured by the standard deviation of the probability distribution of conditional values for the portfolio.

Unlike the expected value of a portfolio, the portfolio risk is not usually the sum of the asset risks. A simple example will demonstrate this point. Consider an asset with the following probability distribution:

Probability	Conditional Value
0.2	$1
0.6	2
0.2	3

The expected value of the asset is $2, and the standard deviation is approximately $0.633.

Next, consider another asset with an identical probability distribution of conditional values, and, hence, an identical expected value and standard deviation. To determine the standard deviation of an asset portfolio consisting of these two assets, we must first know the degree to which they are related. Suppose that they are identical inventory items. In that case, when the actual value of the first asset is $1, the actual value of the second asset will be $1, and the actual values will coincide at all points. Thus, a portfolio consisting of the two identical assets would have a probability distribution as follows:

Probability	Conditional Value
0.2	$2
0.6	4
0.2	6

The expected value of the portfolio would be $4, twice the expected value of each asset, and the standard deviation would also be twice the standard deviation of each asset, 1.266. This illustrates the point that, when assets are perfectly correlated, the standard deviation of the portfolio is the weighted sum of the standard deviations of the assets. The weight for each asset is the ratio of the funds invested in the asset to the funds invested in the total asset portfolio.

But suppose the assets are not identical. Suppose they vary inversely, so that when the actual value of the first asset is $1, the actual value of the second asset will be $3; when the first asset's actual value is $2, the same value will hold for the second asset; and when the actual value of the first asset is $3, the value of the second will be $1. This relationship is referred to as *perfect negative correlation*, as contrasted to the first situation, which would be called *perfect positive correlation*. If the assets were perfectly negatively correlated, the probability distribution of the portfolio would be:

Probability	Conditional Value
0.2	$4
0.6	4
0.2	4

The expected value of the portfolio would still be \$4, but the standard deviation would be zero, i.e., the portfolio would be riskless despite the fact that each of its component assets is risky.

Thus, to determine the standard deviation of an asset portfolio, we must know the standard deviations of the assets included and the degree of correlation between them. The covariance is a measure which includes both the effects of the standard deviations and correlation. It is defined as

$$(6\text{-}1) \qquad\qquad Cov_{xy} = r_{xy}SD_xSD_y,$$

where the left-hand term is the covariance between assets x and y, r_{xy} is the degree of correlation between x and y varying from $+1$ for perfect positive correlation and -1 for perfect negative correlation, and the SD terms refer to the standard deviation for x and y.

Few portfolios consist of only two assets. The approach used in the simple arithmetic illustrations above is too tedious for an asset portfolio consisting of many assets. The standard deviation of an asset portfolio of n assets may be defined generally as the square root of the following:

$$a(aCov_{AA} + bCov_{AB} + cCov_{AC} + \cdots + nCov_{AN})$$
$$+ b(aCov_{BA} + bCov_{BB} + cCov_{BC} + \cdots + nCov_{BN})$$
$$+ c(aCov_{CA} + bCov_{CB} + cCov_{CC} + \cdots + nCov_{CN})$$

(6-2)
$$\cdot$$
$$\cdot$$
$$\cdot$$

$$+ n(aCov_{NA} + bCov_{NB} + cCov_{NC} + \cdots + nCov_{NN})$$
$$= \text{variance of the portfolio.}$$

The lower case letters refer to the proportion of total investment in each asset, e.g., a is the ratio of the investment in assset A to the total investment in assets A through N. The Cov_{AA} is the variance SD^2 of asset A, as is clear from Eq. (6-1) above.

An arithmetic example may prove useful. Consider four assets A, B, C, and D. The basic data needed to determine the risk of a portfolio containing these four assets are the proportion of total investment in each asset, the standard deviation of each asset, and the correlations among the assets. These are:

Asset	Proportion of Invested Funds	Standard Deviation
A......................	0.2	1
B......................	0.3	2
C......................	0.4	3
D	0.1	4

CORRELATIONS

	A	B	C	D
A........ +1	+1	−0.4	+0.7
B........ —	+1	−0.4	+0.7
C........ —	—	+1.0	−0.6
D ...... —	—	—	+1.0

From these data, we can compute the covariances, remembering that the correlation coefficient between A and B is the same as the correlation coefficient between B and A. The covariances are:

COVARIANCES

	A	B	C	D
A........ +1.0	+2.0	−1.2	+2.8
B........ +2.0	+4.0	−2.4	+5.6
C........ −1.2	−2.4	+9.0	−7.2
D ...... +2.8	+5.6	−7.2	+16.0

Substituting the covariances and the weights into Eq. (6–2), we have

$$0.2[0.2(1) + 0.3(2) + 0.4(-1.2) + 0.1(2.8)]$$
$$+ 0.3[0.2(2) + 0.3(4) + 0.4(-2.4) + 0.1(5.6)]$$
$$+ 0.4[0.2(-1.2) + 0.3(-2.4) + 0.4(9) + 0.1(-7.2)]$$
$$+ 0.1[0.2(2.8) + 0.3(5.6) + 0.4(-7.2) + 0.1(16)] = 0.524,$$

which is the variance of the portfolio. The standard deviation is about 0.7, substantially below the standard deviation of any of the individual assets.

The contribution of each asset to the total risk of the portfolio is determined not only by the risk of the asset and the proportion of total funds invested in the asset, but by the correlation between the probability distribution of returns of that asset with each of the other assets.

Asset C in the example makes the point. It is the second most risky asset, i.e., it has the second largest standard deviation. A greater share of funds are invested in this risky asset than in any of the others. Nonetheless, if the firm did not invest in asset C, and the amounts invested in the other assets were unchanged, the standard deviation of the portfolio would rise to 1.87. The reason for this is that asset C is negatively correlated with all of the other assets.

Lest it be thought that negatively correlated assets are essential to what may be called the *diversification* effect, the 1.87 standard deviation of the "C-less" portfolio is less than the weighted average of the standard deviations of A, B, and D, which is 2.01. The diversification effect is very slight without asset C, as would be expected since A and B are perfectly positively correlated. Yet, it still exists. As long as some of the assets in the portfolio are not perfectly positively correlated, the diversification effect occurs.

ASSET CORRELATIONS

Rather than measuring the various correlations that exist among the assets comprising the asset portfolio, it is useful and simpler to consider the correlation between each asset and a meaningful indicator of the firm's activity. The volume of sales could be used as such an indicator.

Inventory. The actual value of inventory and sales volume tend to be very positively correlated. As sales fall, inventory turnover falls. The longer the time needed to sell inventory, the larger are the carrying costs, and the smaller the gain from the sale. With declining sales, prices may have to be reduced, also serving to reduce the gain from selling the inventory. Rising sales tend to increase the actual gain, as actual carrying costs fall and higher prices may be charged.

Accounts Receivable. The actual value of accounts receivable also tends to be positively correlated with sales, but not as well as inventories. Rising sales reflect good times not only for the seller, but also for the buyer. As a result, collection periods tend to be shorter, increasing the actual value of accounts receivable because of the shortening of collection period and the reduction of collection expenses. On the other hand, the collection period tends to lengthen when sales decline.

Fixed Assets. Sales and the actual value of fixed assets are positively correlated, but the degree of correlation depends on the life of the assets. The actual value of long-lived assets will be little affected by a short-term increase in sales. For relatively short-lived fixed assets, the actual asset values will be more closely related to the value of sales.

Cash. The relationships between the actual value of cash and the volume of sales is not as clear as with inventories, accounts receivable, and fixed assets. The value of transactions and precautionary balances depends on the relationships between cash inflows and outflows as sales vary.

If the firm believes that the sales increase is apt to be of short duration, it is not likely to increase investment in fixed assets and, because of strong demand, it may be able to hold accounts receivable constant. In this case, cash inflows may rise more rapidly than outflows, and a given transactions and precautionary cash balance will be less needed, hence less valuable.

Because of an increase in sales, however, the firm may increase asset investments in both inventory and fixed assets beyond what had been originally planned. Should the added investments be large enough, the actual cash deficits may exceed the planned deficits, increasing the value of the transactions and precautionary balances.

When sales decline, the value of the transactions and precautionary balances may either rise or fall, again depending on the relationship of actual inflows and outflows. Inflows diminish because of declining cash sales and a lengthening collection period. The firm may also be forced to invest in riskier accounts receivable in order to maintain sales.

On the outflow side, investment in inventories may be cut back, reducing materials and wage disbursements. Fixed asset expenditures may be postponed or canceled. If profits decline, income tax payments will fall, but, because of the tax payment schedule, not until six months after the decline in profits.

If the net effect of the changes in cash flows tends to increase the cash deficits, the actual value of the transactions and precautionary balances will be negatively correlated with sales. On the other hand, if reduced activity reduces the cash deficits, the correlation will be positive, though far from perfect.

The actual value of the speculative cash balance will either be uncorrelated with sales, or negatively correlated. If, as the sales of the firm rise, a general price inflation also occurs, the actual value of the speculative balance will fall. The actual value of the speculative balance will rise when sales fall if the general price level varies with the firm's sales.

Though it is not unlikely that the sales of the firm will reflect the general state of the economy, rising in prosperity and falling in recession, the correlation between sales and, as a measure of prosperity and recession, gross national product is apt to be less than perfect. Further, the relationship between GNP and the price level is positive, but far from perfect. GNP can and has risen with no appreciable increase in prices, and has fallen with little change in the price level. Thus, the actual value of speculative balance tends to be uncorrelated or negatively correlated with changes in the firm's sales.

At the end of the previous chapter, we discussed the role of cash as a hedge against variations in the value of earning assets. The hedge function of cash may be considered more meaningfully in the context of the analysis of risk.

Cash held as a hedge has an expected value of zero. Barring changes in the price level, the actual value of the cash hedge is equal to the expected value, i.e., the standard deviation is also zero. Thus, by definition, the correlation between the actual values of the cash hedge and the actual values of other assets is zero. Whether such cash balances will be carried or not depends on the firm's attitude toward risk and the cost of carrying the cash balance. The latter may be viewed as an insurance premium, and cash will be held as a hedge if the disutility caused by paying the premium, i.e., reducing the expected value of net worth, is less than the utility of reducing the risk of the asset portfolio.

Marketable Securities. Marketable securities may provide a hedge distinct from their role as cash substitutes. Although most firms tend to share in prosperity and recession, they do not share equally. Some firms produce goods for which there is a very good market in prosperous times and a very poor market in recessions. An example might be custom-made luxury automobiles. Such goods are said to be highly *income-elastic*, i.e., sales respond sharply to changes in national income. The products of other firms may be less income-elastic. Sales do not fluctuate sharply with changes in the over-all level of economic activity. Food may be an example of an industry with low income-elasticity.

A firm whose sales are, for example, highly income elastic may invest in the securities of firms with a low income elasticity. In a recession, the value of the securities are likely to fall less sharply than the value of the firm's earning assets. In prosperity, the value of the securities will rise by less than the value of the earning assets. Thus, the value of such securities tend to be weakly correlated with the value of earning assets, and such securities would serve to reduce the risk of the asset portfolio. Marketable securities are not as good for hedging as cash because the value of the securities will vary inversely with the market interest rate, whereas the value of the cash hedge will only vary if the price level changes. But, unlike cash, the securities provide income, through interest and dividend payments, to offset the carrying costs.

Rather than diversifying by holding the securities of other firms, the firm may decide to acquire the earning assets needed to enter other industries. This may be more attractive than holding securities if the net expected value of the assets exceed the value of the securities. We shall return to this later when we discuss mergers.

SELECTING THE ASSET PORTFOLIO

In Figure 6–1, the firm has to choose among five portfolios, all of which are acceptable, given the cost of capital schedule, SS'. With the risk relationship developed in the previous section, the expected value and the risk associated with each asset portfolio can be paired. This has been done in Figure 6–2.

Each of the numbered dots represents one of the acceptable portfolios which were shown in Figure 6–1. Ignoring the other lines in Figure 6–2 for the moment, we can compare the portfolios in terms of both risk and expected value. Portfolios 1 and 4 have the same expected value, but 4 has a greater risk. Unless the firm is willing to accept risk gratuitously, portfolio 4 would be immediately rejected. Portfolios 2 and 5 have the same risk, but 5 has a larger net expected value. For a given level of risk, it seems reasonable to assume that the firm would seek the highest expected value and, therefore, would reject portfolio 2.

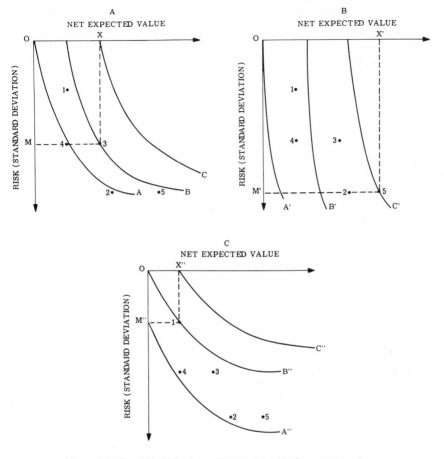

Figure 6-2. Portfolio Selection with Changing Preference Functions

CRITICISMS

The portfolio choice, given preference functions, is determined by the first two moments of the distribution of possible portfolio values, i.e., by the mean and the standard deviation. With normal distributions, the distribution is specified precisely by the first two moments. However, there is no reason to assume that the probability distributions with which we are dealing are normal. With distributions that are not normal, the mean and standard deviation are insufficient to describe the distribution completely. Distributions with identical mean and standard deviations can be quite different. The differences exist with respect to the third moment, or skewness, roughly the relationship between the arithmetic mean and the median of the distribution which are equal in a normal distribution, and the fourth moment, or *kurtosis*, the degree of peakedness of the distribution. Skewness is probably the more important difference.

Given two portfolio distributions *A* and *B*, both with means, expected values, of $1,000,000 and standard deviations of $200,000, *A* may have an extreme value of $-$ $1,000,000 while *B* has $-$ $5,000 as its lowest conditional value. The probability associated with the $-$ $1,000,000 can be low enough so that both distributions have the same means and standard deviations. Nonetheless, the firm could rationally reject *A* and prefer *B*. By the method of calculation shown earlier, however, the firm would have no preference between the two portfolios.

On the other hand, the problem almost vanishes if we assume that the firm rejects individual assets which have extremely dangerous conditional values. As argued earlier, the firm may be unwilling to invest in an asset which has a probability of loss sufficiently large, say, to bankrupt the firm. It is true that many assets, each of which is acceptable to the firm, can be combined into a portfolio which has unacceptable extreme values. But for this to happen, the assets must have fairly high positive intercorrelations; otherwise there will not be a linear combination of asset risks, and the effect of combination will be, as shown earlier, to reduce over-all risk. If there are strong intercorrelations, there is a good chance that the over-all standard deviation of the portfolio will be sufficiently high for the portfolio to be rejected on the basis of the first two moments of the distribution.

Finally, the inclusion of the third and other moments of the distribution would make the already tedious portfolio calculation almost unworkable. Even on a very large scale computer, a portfolio selection program using only the first two moments can take up intolerably large amounts of time.

To sum up, the method described for selection of the portfolio is weak in that it does not consider skewness and kurtosis. However, it is improbable that considering the third and fourth moments of the distribution will make any difference. And, with the current state of knowledge in computation techniques, it is impracticable to go beyond the mean and the standard deviation. Nonetheless, we have not disposed of the theoretical validity of the criticisms. They are theoretically valid, but practically unimportant.

THE PREFERENCE
FUNCTION

The three lines, *A*, *B*, and *C*, shown in Figure 6–2(a), represent the firm's attitude toward risk and profits. Each line is an indifference curve. As long as the firm is on a given line, say line *A*, it does not care at what specific point it is. The slope of the indifference curve is the ratio of the change in risk to the change in expected value. The higher the ratio, i.e., the steeper the indifference curve, the more willing is the firm to accept risk in order to gain expected value. A very steep curve would reflect the attitude of a gambler. A very flat curve reflects an unwillingness to accept risk unless the increment to expected value is very large.

Line *B* is preferred to line *A*, and line *C* is preferred to line *B*. Note that at a given level of risk, a portfolio falling on *B* provides a higher expected value than a point on A. So too, in comparing B and C, points on C are preferred to points on B. Holding expected value constant, a portfolio on C has less risk than a portfolio on B. Similarly, a portfolio on C is preferred to a portfolio on B.

In Figure 6–2(a), portfolio 3 places the firm on the highest indifference curve attainable, given the portfolio alternatives. Portfolio 3 is neither the most profitable portfolio, which is 5, nor is it the safest, which is 1. Thus, the portfolio selected by the firm is not necessarily the one which maximizes profits nor the one minimizing risk.

Figures 6–2(b) and 6–2(c) indicate other possible attitudes of firm. In Figure 6–2(b), the preference curves are steeper, indicating a greater willingness to assume risk. The asset portfolio chosen is 5, the profit-maximizing choice. Figure 6–2(c) represents a timid firm, unwilling to assume risk. Here the preferred portfolio is 1, the risk-minimizing choice.

Different firms facing the same opportunities may have quite different attitudes toward risk because of a combination of objective situations as well as subjective attitudes. A firm with total resources of $10,000 is apt to view a loss of $10,000 as being more damaging to the firm than a gain of $10,000 will be beneficial. In this situation, the firm might avoid any asset with a possible loss of $10,000 no matter how small the probability of loss. On the other hand, a firm with resources of $1,000,000 might be willing to invest in an asset with an equiprobable loss or gain of $10,000. In short, the impact of a loss may not be measurable in money, but in the ability of the firm to absorb the loss.

Two assumptions. It may be argued that a still better choice for the timid firm lies at the origin O. A portfolio at the origin is possible, but such a portfolio, consisting mainly of cash and short-term government securities, would convert the firm from being, for example, a manufacturer to being some sort of supersafe investment company. We assume the firm will only consider portfolios within a range of types of economic activity, and that the portfolios shown are the only potentially acceptable ones.

It is also mathematically possible to develop intermediate portfolios, consisting of combinations of those shown in the figures. Such combinations could be superior to the basic portfolios from which the combinations would be selected. With some asset portfolios, consisting mainly of securities, such combinations are possible in reality. With real assets, the combinations are limited. For example, a portfolio consisting of half of portfolio 1 and half of portfolio 3 may imply the firm invests in half a steel mill. The problem is that real assets are technologically or economically lumpy. We have assumed that the 5 portfolios shown are the only ones that are feasible.

To sum up, the choice of the asset portfolio depends on the cost of capital schedule, the funds required by the various portfolios, the projected returns of the individual assets, the dispersion of these returns around the expected value, the correlations among the probability distributions of the individual assets, and the attitude of the firm toward risk. The last point is in turn affected by the "personality" of management and the resources of the firm.

CONTROL OF ASSET INVESTMENT

The methods that have been discussed over the last five chapters are fairly new, most of them having been developed after World War II. As a result, the methods are not yet in general use. However, instances of the adoption of these methods, as reported in journals such as *Management Science* and *Operations Research*, indicate that firms can often make substantially better decisions with the new methods than with more traditional decision techniques.

In this section, we shall examine two of the traditional techniques that have been used to evaluate asset investment policies. The first of these is *break-even* analysis; second is *asset turnover*.

BREAK-EVEN ANALYSIS

Break-even analysis is aimed at determining the production level at which costs equal revenues. At lower levels of production, the firm incurs losses. At higher levels, profits are made. An asset investment which raises the break-even point is, in the absence of other considerations, undesirable.

Revenues are defined as a constant price times the level of production. If Q is production in number of units, and p is price, revenues are pQ.

Costs are divided into two groups, variable and fixed. Fixed costs are those which are insensitive to variations in output. They include the wages of supervisory and managerial personnel, depreciation, interest payments, etc. Variable costs are assumed to change linearly with output, i.e., the variable costs *per unit* are assumed to be fixed. If v is variable costs per unit, vQ is total variable costs. F will signify fixed costs.

Sometimes, a third category of costs, semivariable costs, are added. Semivariable costs will remain fixed over a range of output, and then will jump to a higher level, forming a series of steps as output increases. Simplicity is a major virtue of break-even analysis, and this virtue is lost with a complex cost function. Therefore, we shall treat only variable costs and fixed costs. Total costs TC are equal to $F + vQ$.

The break-even point exists where revenues equal total costs and thus is the level Q where

$$F + vQ = pQ,$$

or where

$$Q = \frac{F}{p - v}.$$

From this equation, it can be seen that the break-even point will vary directly with the level of fixed costs, inversely with price, and directly with per unit variable costs.

Given a firm with $F = \$100$, $p = \$1$, and $v = \$0.50$, the break-even level of output is 200 units. A change in asset investments, raising F to 150, and reducing v to 0.30, will raise the break-even point to about 214 units. If the firm is so naive as to consider no other factors, the change will be rejected because it raises the break-even point.

However, suppose the firm typically sells 500 units. The profit, using the same notation, is

$$\text{Profit} = Q(p - v) - F.$$

With the original cost relationships, the profit for 500 units would be $150. Under the proposed change, the profit becomes $200. In fact, the profit will be greater under the proposed change for quantities in excess of 250 units.

Then, one weakness of break-even analysis is that it does not focus directly on profits. Of course, if the firm is likely to produce in the range of the break-even quantity, an increased break-even point is a relevant consideration. However, if output typically is above break-even points, concern with the break-even point is irrelevant.

On a mechanical level, another weakness is that the analysis assumes a constant difference between price and per unit variable costs, i.e., a standard markup over variable costs. If the markup has to be reduced in order to sell more units of a single product, or if the firm produces several products with different markups, the analysis will not yield a unique break-even point.

Break-even analysis can be useful as a means of raising questions about investment proposals, rather than as a decision device. To be used in this fashion, however, concern must be with profits, not with break-even points. Otherwise, investments which do not affect, or reduce, the break-even point may not be properly evaluated. Moving from profit analysis to the present value of a stream of returns and the effect of risk leads us back to the tools which were developed earlier in this book.

ASSET TURNOVER

The asset-turnover ratio is the ratio of sales to assets. Its significance can be seen more clearly by combining the asset-turnover ratio with the operating margin. The operating margin is the ratio of earnings before interest and taxes to sales. Interest is not deducted since interest expense depends on how the firm decides to finance assets, not on the assets themselves. Combining the two ratios, we have

$$\frac{\text{Sales}}{\text{assets}} \frac{\text{earnings before interest and taxes}}{\text{sales}}$$

$$= \frac{\text{earnings before interest and taxes}}{\text{assets}}$$

$$= \text{the before-tax rate of return on assets.}$$

With a constant operating margin, a decrease in turnover results in a reduction in the rate of return on assets. To avoid reducing the rate of return on assets, new assets must increase sales so as to maintain the turnover ratio and/or increase the operating margin to offset the decline in turnover.

Although earnings before interest and taxes are important, the present value of the cash flow is more important. The latter embraces the former and considers future returns as well. Nonetheless, the turnover ratio itself can be quite useful in setting the direction of asset evaluation. It can be misleading since managerial attention will not be drawn to assets which have no effect on turnover or actually reduce turnover, even though such investments are not necessarily profitable.

SELECTED REFERENCES

Davis, T. C.: *How the du Pont Organization Appraises its Performance*, Financial Management Series, No. 94, American Management Association, New York, 1950.

Dean, J.: "Cost Structure of Enterprises and Break-even Analysis," *American Economic Review*, May, 1948.

Farrar, D. E.: *The Investment Decision under Uncertainty*, Prentice-Hall, Englewood Cliffs, N.Y., 1962.

Kalecki, M.: "The Principle of Increasing Risk," *Economica*, Nov., 1937.

Lutz, F.: *The Theory of Investment of the Firm*, Princeton, N.Y., 1951.

Markowitz, H.: *Portfolio Selection: Efficient Diversification of Investments*, Wiley, New York, 1951.

Robbins, S., and F. Foster: "Profit Planning and the Finance Function," *Journal of Finance*, Dec., 1957.

THE CAPITAL STRUCTURE

PART

The Capital Structure:
Introduction

7
The asset portfolio is bought through the use of funds. These funds are acquired either internally, as with retained earnings and depreciation, or externally, by the firm's selling financial claims to the income and cash flows which the firm hopes will be generated by the assets. The liquidation of assets to provide funds for the acquisition of other assets, as by reducing cash balances or selling near-cash assets, will be considered a negative use of funds, rather than a source. We have already considered the determinants of asset investment decisions. The decision to disinvest is the mirror image of the decision to invest, i.e., the firm will shift the composition of the asset portfolio when the results are a more desirable mixture of expected value and risk.

In this and the next three chapters, attention will be focussed on the determinants of the structure of internal funds and financial claims chosen by the firm. This structure will be called the *capital structure* of the firm.

The capital structure chosen by the firm depends on the cash flow generated by the asset portfolio. However, the future cash flow generated by an asset portfolio is, at best, a matter of judgment. There are three possible groups who are party to the choice of capital structure. First, of course, is the management of the firm. Second are the stockholders. Third are the firm's creditors. The capital structure will depend on the judgment that each of these groups has about the future cash flow.

Even if the firm chooses to finance all assets from internal sources, it can only escape the influence of one group, the creditors. As will be shown later, the stockholders can impose their influence on the firm, even if the firm does not issue additional shares of stock.

If the creditor and ownership groups disagree with the firm's judgment about the future cash flow, and if the beliefs of these two groups are less optimistic than that of the firm, they can virtually veto a unilateral capital structure decision made by the firm. The management of a firm is selling financial claims when it chooses a capital structure. As with any merchant, the firm has to be reasonably certain that there are willing customers for the financial wares which it hopes to market.

In some cases, the firm may design a particular financial instrument jointly with the customer. This is the case in what is called a *direct placement loan* made to one or a few lenders. Such direct placements include most short-term loans and an increasing number of longer-term loans. When the firm has to sell a financial claim to a large number of investors, as is usually the case with a stock issue, management may call in a marketing expert with special knowledge about the wants of buyers for that instrument. This financial marketing expert is called an *investment banker* and performs other services, to be discussed later, in addition to providing marketing advice.

Since the discussion of the determinants of the capital structure will continue through Chapter 10, an outline may be useful. Topics will be studied in the following order:

1. The remainder of this chapter will be devoted to the characteristics and relative importance of the various types of financial claims.
2. Chapter 8 will focus on the choice between debt and equity claims.
3. Chapter 9 will concentrate on the maturity structure of debt.
4. Chapter 10 will contain an analysis of the cost of capital and its role in the determination of the capital structure.

It is difficult to discuss these matters without considering the nature and needs of the buyers of financial claims and of the markets and institutional framework of the financial economy. However, a detailed analysis of the financial markets and institutions will not be undertaken at this point.

FINANCIAL INSTRUMENTS

The instruments used in corporate finance reflect not only the needs of the firm, but the needs of the buyers of the claims. The firm will find it advantageous to design instruments for which there is a large demand, since this may make funds available cheaply. As a result, there is considerable diversity in the spectrum of such instruments. I shall use a set of classifications in this discussion to maintain a semblance of order. But, it will become obvious that firms and the buyers of financial claims are compelled by no law of nature or man to stay within the classifications. Further, all instruments will not be considered, only the most important. However, the factors that make a particular instrument important today can and do change. Thus, 10 years from now, the important financial instruments may include some that are insignificant or nonexistent today.

A COMPARISON
OF DEBT AND EQUITY

Purchasers of equity instruments are stockholders. Those who hold debt claims are creditors.

Preference to Income. Creditors have a prior claim to the income stream over owners. This means that interest must be paid before dividends can be declared.

Preference to Assets. Rarely is it profitable to buy any kind of financial claim on a corporation that is likely to be forced out of business. Nonetheless, business firms do fail, and investors do lose money as a result of such failures. The claims of creditors must be met before any of the assets of a dissolved firm are distributed among the owners.

If a firm is forced to reorganize its capital structure, usually because its income stream is inadequate to meet the existing structure of financial obligations, investors may be required to accept claims with less rigid requirements and, perhaps, yielding less income. Some investors may be completely eliminated in such a reorganization. Creditors usually are favored by the courts, which superintend such reorganizations, whereas stockholders are apt to bear the greater loss.

Fixedness of Claims. Most debtors have a specified and fixed claim to the income stream and cash flows. Interest payments are usually set in the loan agreement, as are repayment rates. Normally, the creditor cannot receive any more regardless of how large the income stream becomes.

In contrast, the most important class of owners, the common stockholders, have an unrestricted right to the income stream after all creditor expenses have been deducted. True, the firm usually does not distribute all earnings, but the retained earnings tend to increase the market value of the common stock and definitely increase the book value of common stock (the ratio of paid-in capital plus retained earnings to the number of common shares outstanding).

Two borderline cases illustrate how difficult it is to generalize about classes of financial claims. *Income bonds* carry an interest rate, as do most bonds. However, the interest is paid only if earnings are adequate to cover the payment. The income bond claim to the income stream is subordinate to the claims of other bondholders. Interest not earned in one year carries over as a liability, i.e., interest is cumulative. Cumulated interest on income bonds can be a real problem to a firm which has had a run of profitless years, since dividends cannot be paid to stockholders as long as there are cumulated arrearages of interest. Still, this is less of a problem than is caused by normal bonds on which the regular payment of interest is obligatory whether or not earnings are sufficient. Debt repayment requirements are just as rigid for income bonds as for ordinary bonds.

Preferred stock is the other borderline case. The preferred stock dividend is partly or completely fixed, limiting the preferred stockholder's claim to the income stream. As with income bonds, payment of the preferred dividend is not obligatory. Unlike the income bond case, the firm does not have to pay a preferred dividend even if earnings are sufficient, but common stock dividends cannot be paid until the preferred stockholders have been paid. Most modern preferred stock issues have a cumulative feature; i.e., dividends not paid in one year are cumulated, and all cumulated and current preferred dividends must be paid before the common stockholder can receive any dividends. Preferred stock can also be participating, i.e., share in profits on a basis roughly equivalent to common stock.

The role of preferred stock in corporate finance is today relatively unimportant. Despite minor recessions, the economic environment since World War II has been stable in the United States. Thus, the safety provided by preferred stock probably seems less important to firms than was the case when memories of the depression of the '30's were fresher. If a firm has trouble and cumulates preferred dividends, ridding itself of the dividend arrearage so as to be able to attract new equity funds can be almost as difficult as if the arrearages were on bond interest. Also, preferred dividends are not tax-deductible, so that the firm must earn a larger before-tax income in order to pay a given level of preferred dividends than it would have to earn in order to pay the same amount of interest, which is tax-deductible.

Preferred stock is usually considered to be an alternative to long-term debt. Most long-term debt is held by financial institutions. As of the end of 1962, there were outstanding $182.3 billion of corporate and foreign bonds, mainly corporate, and mortgages other than for 1–4 family residences. Over 72 per cent of this long-term debt was held by financial institutions, $95 billion held by insurance companies alone. Most of these institutions are regulated to varying degrees in the amount and kind of equity investments they can hold and generally prefer debt instruments. Thus, a significant factor in the diminution of the importance of preferred stock has been the nature of the supply of funds, which has favored debt issues. Table 7–1 shows the new corporate issues of preferred and common stock since 1950.

CONTROL OF THE FIRM

Stockholders are owners of the firm and, as such, have the right to affect the firm's policies. The most obvious means of control is through the exercise of the right to vote for members of the board of directors. Each share of stock is entitled to one vote. The laws of some states require, and many corporations allow, cumulative voting.

Table 7-1

COMMON AND PREFERRED STOCK ISSUES SUBJECT
TO THE SECURITIES ACT OF 1933, 1949–JUNE 1962
(In Millions of Dollars)

Year	Common Stock	Preferred Stock
1949	736.4	424.7
1950	810.7	630.8
1951	1212.5	837.7
1952	1368.6	564.5
1953	1326.0	488.6
1954	1212.7	815.9
1955	2185.2	635.1
1956	2301.1	635.5
1957	2516.2	410.5
1958	1334.1	571.5
1959	2027.1	531.2
1960	1664.1	408.5
1961	3272.5	449.3
1962 to June	950.1	196.2

Source: Annual Report of the Securities and Exchange
Commission, 1962.

In this case, the stockholder may cast one vote per share per director to be
elected. If four directors are to be elected, one share of stock is entitled to
four votes. The four votes can be spread among the directors, or cumulated
and voted for one director. In this fashion, minority stockholders can concentrate their votes on one or two directors and gain some representation
on the board of directors.

The power of the voting privilege for the individual stockholder depends
on the number of shares he holds. Most stockholders have very small
holdings, as is shown by Table 7–2 and consequently have little individual
effect on corporate elections.

Table 7-2

RELATIVE HOLDINGS OF MARKETABLE STOCK BY INDIVIDUALS,
BY SIZE CLASS OF HOLDINGS, AS OF 1949

Size Class of Stockholdings	Per Cent of Individual Holders	Per Cent of Total Individual Holdings
Under $ 1,000	54.8	1.0
$ 1,000– 4,999	22.9	4.0
5,000– 24,999	16.0	13.0
25,000– 99,999	5.1	17.0
100,000 and over	1.1	65.0

Source: Adapted from Table XVI-3,   J. Butters, L. Thompson, and
L. Bollinger, *Effects of Taxation: Investments by Individuals*,
Harvard, Cambridge, Mass., 1953.

The Securities and Exchange Commission (SEC) regulates various financial aspects of corporate life for those corporations issuing financial claims to the public. Some 2,388 corporations must submit proxy information to the Commission prior to mailing proxies to stockholders. Proxies are requests to stockholders asking them to sign their voting rights over to the group sending the proxy for purposes of a particular corporate election. Not all proxy requests involve the election of directors but, during fiscal 1962, the SEC reports, in its *Annual Report*, that 1,807 corporations solicited proxies from their stockholders for the election of directors. Only 17 of the companies had proxy contests, i.e., had opposing groups soliciting proxies. Management won nine of the cases, nonmanagement groups won five, one case was settled by negotiation between the contending groups, and two cases had not been settled as of June 30, 1962. In short, it is rare that a proxy fight occurs. When it does, existing management apparently has a definite edge.

All of this suggests that the voting power of the stockholder is not very important generally. We shall see later that stockholders do affect managerial policy, but by "voting with their feet," i.e., selling stock when they are dissatisfied.

All classes of stock have voting rights unless the corporate charter specifically denies them these rights. Preferred stockholders usually are denied voting rights. Sometimes, there is a provision allowing the preferred stockholders voting rights when preferred dividends have not been paid over a period of time. Though somewhat unusual today, common stock may be classified, with the voting right denied to certain classes of common. The original purpose of such classification was to allow a small group to retain control, at the same time allowing the firm to issue securities with the characteristics of common stock.

Ford Motor Company provides an interesting example of a modern-day usage of classified common stock. It has three classifications: class A, which comprised about 32 per cent of total common shares issued as of December 31, 1962; class B, which represented about 7 per cent of common issued; and Common Stock making up almost 61 per cent of the issued common shares. Class A stock is nonvoting and is held by the Ford Foundation. When the Foundation sells shares of Ford stock, the sold shares are converted into Common Stock. Class B and Common Stock are voting shares, entitled to one vote per share. However, Common Stock has an aggregate voting power proportional to the importance of Common Stock to all issued common stock, amounting to about 60 per cent at the end of 1962. Class B stock has an aggregate voting power equal to the remainder, about 40 per cent in 1962. In effect, the class B stock votes both its own shares and the nonvoting class A shares.

Creditors affect managerial policy, in a sense controlling the firm, in several ways. The firm must behave so as to make potential creditors willing to become actual creditors. The creditors frequently set conditions, other than interest payments and debt redemption dates, which affect the firm's policies. For example, lenders may restrict the total amount of debt which the firm can incur, will specify the minimum ratio of current assets to current liabilities, restrict the amount of dividends which can be paid, specify that the nature of the business be not altered and that major assets be not sold, etc. These conditions are set with the aim of protecting the creditors and, quite often, do not impose a policy which the firm would not follow anyhow. Nonetheless, these side restrictions can hamper a firm's activities, perhaps, more than can a minority stockholder.

Taxation   Interest payments on debt are considered a cost of business, and are deductible for income tax purposes. Dividend payments are considered a distribution of profits and are not deductible for tax purposes.

With a marginal tax rate of 48 per cent, the firm must earn $1.92 before taxes in order to pay $1 in dividends. To make the same interest payment, the firm need earn only $1 before taxes. Of course, the repayment of debt is not considered an expense and is not tax-deductible. However, the repayment of debt does not rely on the income stream only, but on the cash flow as well as on the proceeds of any borrowing or stock sales the firm undertakes.

PREFERENCE
AMONG CREDITORS

All creditors are preferred for income and assets over all owners. Some creditors may have preference over other creditors, either with a claim to specific assets or for both assets and income. The former occurs when the firm pledges, or mortgages, certain assets as security for a loan. The preferred lender has the right to seize the pledged assets if the conditions of the loan agreement are not met. Such seizure is subject to court supervision to prevent secured creditors from damaging the firm or the interests of other creditors by seizing assets other than those which were pledged.

The kinds of assets pledged are generally, but not necessarily, related to the maturity of the loan sought. Assets pledged to secure long-term loans are usually long-lived, such as plant and equipment. Inventory and accounts receivable may serve as security for short-term loans.

Few creditors want the assets which are pledged, the hope is that the possibility of seizure will put pressure on the firm to meet the conditions of the loan agreement. Therefore, assets which are essential to the firm's operations are better security than assets which are dispensable. Thus, rolling stock for railroads and modern plant for other businesses are often used as security.

The value of the asset to the firm is one safeguard, but an asset which has little or no resale value, e.g., highly specialized machine tools, is not as useful as is an asset for which there is a ready market.

In order to claim an asset, the creditor must be able to identify the asset. The precise requirements for identification vary according to state law. For large fixed assets or for equipment which can be identified by character and manufacturer's number, there is little problem. Short-term loans, however, are often secured by accounts receivable and/or inventory. In the case of accounts receivable, ledger notations can serve as identification. For inventory, particularly when the security consists of a large number of items, the inventory may be segregated from the rest of the firm's assets by keeping the inventory in a public warehouse or by creating a *field warehouse* on the borrowing firm's premises. When inventory is warehoused so that it can be easily identified and controlled by the lender, the firm must receive a release from the lender each time inventory is to be withdrawn from the warehouse.

SUBORDINATED DEBT

Preference among creditors may exist without pledging specific assets as security for some creditors. The firm may issue subordinated debentures, which is unsecured debt with a prior right to assets over owners, but subordinate to other creditors. Subordinated debentures are used mostly, but not exclusively, by sales and commercial finance companies. These financial institutions rely on commercial banks and the sale of commercial paper for a good deal of their financing. In order to provide the security required by these short-term lenders and still issue long-term debt, finance companies issue the subordinated debentures. The subordinated income debenture, or bond, is attractive to industrial companies since it is, in effect, a preferred stock the "dividend" on which is deductible for income tax purposes.

Unowned Assets. When security is important to a creditor, he is apt to insist on protection provided by asset segregation (as in inventory warehousing), frequent inspections of pledged assets, recording of mortgage claims, etc. Both protection and ease of seizure are stronger if the creditor simply takes or retains title to the assets used as security. In this case, of course, the creditor is not a creditor at all. He owns the asset and leases its use to the firm.

From the firm's point of view, leasing is a means of finance. The firm's alternative to leasing assets is to purchase the assets and use them as security for a loan. Leasing is a source of funds to the firm, and the lessor is a kind of creditor.

The financial instrument in this case is a lease. The terms of the lease are as binding as the terms of a loan agreement. Indeed, seizure of the leased asset is much easier for a lessor than for a creditor. So, the penalties for failing to meet lease obligations are at least more certain and can occur more rapidly than when a secured loan agreement is used for financing.

The lessor is a creditor of the firm just as a bank or other lender. Should the leased asset be seized and liquidated and the proceeds from the asset be insufficient to cover the firm's liabilities under the lease, the lessor stands as a general creditor to claims on assets. Lease terms can, though this is not common, restrict the firm as to payment of dividends, the creation of debt, and the ratio of current assets to current liabilities, just as is done in loan agreements. Such restrictions are appropriate, since they affect the firm's ability to meet the lease payments. We shall consider the variables affecting the firm's decision to buy or lease assets in Chapter 10.

DEBT MATURITY

Debt which matures, i.e., must be paid, within one year is short-term. Debt maturing in more than one year is long-term. Sometimes, debt with a maturity date more than 1 year, but less than 15 years, from the date of issue is called *term debt*.

Short-term debt includes accruals, such as wages payable, trade debt, and that portion of long-term debt which is payable within one year. The institutional sources of short-term debt are commercial banks, sales and commercial finance companies, and the commercial paper market.

Too much reliance can be placed on the formal distinction of maturity dates. Short-term bank loans can be renewed, sometimes, quite easily. Inventory loans made by banks or commercial finance companies can revolve, i.e., be renewed as inventory, which is sold, is replaced by new inventory. Indeed, arrangements can exist in which a loan, originated as an inventory loan, becomes secured by accounts receivable after the inventory is sold and then comes full cycle when the receivable is collected and new inventory is purchased. Even the accruals can become permanent since the firm will be incurring trade debt as it purchases, wages payable as it employs labor, and taxes payable as it earns income. To the extent that short-term debt can be refinanced, keeping in mind that a short-term lender does not have to renew a loan, such debt can be a permanent part of the firm's capital structure.

Unlike short-term indebtedness for which accruals and trade debt arising from normal operations are quite important, long-term debt typically arises from financial arrangements separate from the normal operations of the firm. Long-term lenders include banks, insurance companies, pension funds, mutual funds, nonprofit institutions, and households. As was true of the maturity structure of government interest rates (see Table 5-3), long-term interest rates have been higher than short-term rates in the United States during most of this century.

Just as short-term debt may be permanent despite the maturity date, long-term debt can, at least partially, be short-term. Most long-term corporate debt provides for a partial or complete repayment of principal prior to the maturity date. Some bond issues mature serially, i.e., the maturity dates of a serial bond issue vary, with some of the bonds maturing after 1 or 2 years, and others not maturing for perhaps 20 or 25 years.

Even more common is a *sinking fund* provision attached to the loan agreement. At one time, the sinking fund provision required the firm to set aside a certain amount of funds each year to insure the repayment of the bond issue when it matured. However, this was both costly, since the firm had to segregate the sinking fund assets, which were usually held in the form of securities, and risky, since the value of the sinking fund assets were as susceptible to variations as are any securities. In addition, there was the possibility of deliberate fraud by a firm which wished to avoid setting funds aside for debt redemption purposes.

Modern sinking funds require the firm to redeem some portion of the indebtedness each year directly by making payments to the creditors. Some loan agreements call for complete redemption by sinking fund payments by the maturity date. Others provide for partial repayment with a *balloon payment* due at maturity. The timing of sinking fund payments is jointly determined by the requirements of the firm and the requirements of buyers of the financial claims, as well as by the supply and demand conditions in the market for financial claims.

When sinking fund provisions are included in a loan agreement between the firm and one or a few buyers, as occurs when the firm borrows from financial institutions, the cancellation of debt is quite simple. The firm makes a payment, for example, to a life insurance company, which includes both interest and debt redemption. In this case, the term *sinking fund* may not even be used. When debt is publicly marketed and there is a large number of holders, partial debt repayment can be a problem. The proportion of the debt redeemed by a given dollar sinking fund payment will depend on the market price of the debt, and the very fact that the firm is buying up its own debt claims will tend to elevate the market price.

To avoid this, debt agreements which include sinking fund provisions usually also include a *call* feature. The call feature allows the firm to require that debt holders surrender their debt claims to the firm at the call price. Failure to do so does not extinguish the debt, but the firm does not have to pay interest on a claim after it has been called. The call price is determined in the loan agreement. Usually the firm pays a price in excess of the maturity value of the debt, with the size of the premium varying with the number of years to maturity. Should the call price exceed the market price, the firm will fulfill the sinking fund provision by buying up the bonds or notes in the market, rather than by calling the debt. The call privilege allows the firm some flexibility in adjusting its capital structure if changing conditions require modifications.

PLACEMENT

Financial claims can be sold to one or a few buyers, or they can be issued to the public at large. The former method of sale is called *direct*, or *private*, *placement*, while the latter is called *public placement*.

Except for commerical paper, the short-term debt claims of nonfinancial business corporations are directly placed. The buyers of short-term direct placements are commercial banks, sales finance companies, and commercial finance companies.

Commercial paper is issued through commercial paper dealers. The paper is sold at a discount, rather than at an interest rate. This source is more important for sales and commercial finance companies than for nonfinancial corporations. The seller of these claims must be an excellent credit risk.

Public Placements. Between 60 and 70 per cent of long-term financial claims other than internal funds, those maturing in one year or more from the date of issue, are placed publicly. Public placements are usually marketed through investment bankers, who provide advice, a marketing organization, and may underwrite the issue, i.e., insure the firm against receiving less than a specified price for the issue.

New issues are normally sold in what is called an *over-the-counter market*, which consists of thousands of security dealers and brokers throughout the country. They attempt to distribute new issues as rapidly as possible through their customer networks. In addition, brokers and dealers take positions, i.e., sell inventories, and make markets for securities. After a security has been traded for a period, it may be listed on an organized securities exchange, the largest of which is the New York Stock Exchange. Listing will depend on the size of the company, its age, and profits. Most bond and preferred stock transactions, however, and about one-third of the market activity in common stocks are completed over the counter.

Regulation of Securities Issues. The Securities Act of 1933 sets forth requirements made of all interstate public issuers of securities, except governments and other special cases. Requirements are not aimed at approval of securities, but at full disclosure of all material facts. It is sometimes called the "truth law."

Under the law, a firm making a public issue of securities must register the securities with the Securities and Exchange Commission prior to sale. The registration statement is a lengthy and detailed account, including financial, legal, and technical information about the issuer, the underwriting, and the proposed uses of the funds to be generated. Since all who participate in the preparation of the statement may be sued by a purchaser who suffers a loss because of inaccurate or incomplete information, the registration statement is prepared very carefully. The registration statement must be filed with the SEC at least 20 days prior to the proposed date of issuance. At any time during the 20-day period or thereafter, the SEC can issue a *stop order*, stopping the distribution, and request additional information if it believes that the registration statment does not fully comply with the law. For issues of less than $300,000, a shorter version of the registration statement is permitted.

After the 20-day period or after amendments have been filed with the

SEC, the securities may be sold. The sale must be accompanied by a prospectus, which is an abridged version of the registration statement. Distribution of a prospectus prior to the effective date of the registration is permitted providing it states that the prospectus is not an offer to sell or the solicitation of a request to buy. Because the warning is printed in red ink, it is often called a *red-herring prospectus*.

The Securities Exchange Act of 1934 is a logical extension of the 1933 Act. Whereas the 1933 Act requires full disclosure for new securities, the 1934 Act requires full disclosure for existing securities listed on organized exchanges. This involves filing a statement similar to the registration statement and, also, periodic reports on changes that take place. Similar regulation is envisioned for securities on the over-the-counter market.

In addition to requiring disclosure of listed securities, the Securities Exchange Act gives the SEC control over proxy machinery, provides for the regulation of national securities exchanges, requires that corporate "insiders," such as officers, directors, and major stockholders, file monthly reports of changes in their holdings of the company's stock. Stockholders can force insiders to pay to the corporation any short-term gains made by trading in the firm's securities.

The Act also gives the SEC the power to prohibit securities prices manipulation. The various practices that have been prohibited include all those that lead to false price movements, except when an investment banker pegs the price as part of the process of issuing securities. It should be noted that securities exchanges themselves forbid such actions by their members.

In addition to the federal laws regulating the issuance and trading of securities, most states also have regulations. These are generally not as demanding as the federal laws. There are three broad classifications of laws: fraud laws, providing penalties for securities issuance and trading the result of which defrauds the buyer or seller; distributor-registration laws, which require that brokers and dealers be registered with the state authority; and laws which require *approval* of the issuer. The last may be an abbreviated version of the federal registration requirements or the securities may be registered by notification alone. The latter course is available only to strong companies with well-established reputations and to public utilities. Federal laws do not preempt the regulation area so that, for interstate issues, both state and federal regulations must be met.

Private Placements.   Private placements of long-term claims have become more important since World War II than before. This is shown in Table 7-3. Usually the customers are financial institutions, such as insurance companies, pension funds, and even commercial banks. Although an investment banker may be used as a *middleman* between the issuing firm and the purchasing institutions, the functions of the investment banker are much more limited for private placements than for public placements. Underwriting is not necessary for private placements, nor is the marketing organization

SUMMARY OF CORPORATE SECURITIES* PUBLICLY OFFERED AND PRIVATELY PLACED IN EACH YEAR 1934–JUNE, 1962
(In Millions of Dollars)

Calendar Year	TOTAL			PUBLIC OFFERINGS			PRIVATE PLACEMENTS			PRIVATE PLACEMENTS AS % OF TOTAL	
	All Issues	Debt Issues	Equity Issues	All Issues	Debt Issues	Equity Issues	All Issues	Debt Issues	Equity Issues	All Issues	Debt Issues
1934	397	372	25	305	280	25	92	92	0	23.2	24.7
1935	2,332	2,225	108	1,945	1,840	106	387	385	2	16.6	17.3
1936	4,752	4,029	543	4,199	3,660	539	373	369	4	8.2	9.2
1937	2,309	1,618	691	1,979	1,291	688	330	327	3	14.3	20.2
1938	2,155	2,044	111	1,463	1,353	110	692	691	1	32.1	33.8
1939	2,164	1,979	185	1,458	1,276	181	706	703	4	32.6	35.5
1940	2,677	2,386	291	1,912	1,628	284	765	758	7	28.6	31.8
1941	2,667	2,389	277	1,854	1,578	276	813	811	2	30.5	33.9
1942	1,062	917	146	642	506	136	420	411	9	39.5	44.8
1943	1,170	990	180	798	621	178	372	369	3	31.8	37.3
1944	3,202	2,670	532	2,415	1,892	524	787	778	9	24.6	29.1
1945	6,011	4,855	1,155	4,989	3,851	1,138	1,022	1,004	18	17.0	20.7
1946	6,900	4,882	2,018	4,983	3,019	1,963	1,917	1,863	54	27.8	38.2
1947	6,577	5,036	1,541	4,342	2,889	1,452	2,235	2,147	88	34.0	42.6
1948	7,078	5,973	1,106	3,991	2,965	1,028	3,087	3,008	79	43.6	50.4
1949	6,052	4,890	1,161	3,550	2,437	1,112	2,502	2,453	49	41.3	50.2
1950	6,362	4,920	1,442	3,681	2,360	1,321	2,680	2,560	120	42.1	52.0
1951	7,741	5,691	2,050	4,326	2,364	1,962	3,415	3,326	88	44.1	58.4
1952	9,534	7,601	1,933	5,533	3,645	1,888	4,002	3,957	45	42.0	52.1
1953	8,898	7,083	1,815	5,580	3,856	1,725	3,318	3,228	90	37.3	45.6
1954	9,516	7,488	2,029	5,848	4,003	1,844	3,668	3,484	184	38.5	46.5
1955	10,240	7,420	2,820	6,763	4,119	2,644	3,477	3,301	176	34.0	44.5
1956	10,939	8,002	2,937	7,053	4,225	2,827	3,886	3,777	109	35.5	47.2
1957	12,884	9,957	2,927	8,959	6,118	2,841	3,925	3,839	86	30.5	38.6
1958	11,558	9,653	1,906	8,068	6,332	1,736	3,490	3,320	170	30.2	34.4
1959	9,748	7,190	2,558	5,993	3,557	2,436	3,755	3,632	122	38.5	50.5
1960	10,154	8,081	2,073	6,657	4,806	1,851	3,497	3,275	221	34.4	40.5
1961	13,147	9,425	3,722	8,149	4,706	3,443	4,999	4,720	279	38.0	50.1
1962 (Jan.–June)	5,628	4,482	1,146	3,646	2,544	1,102	1,982	1,938	45	35.2	43.2

Source: Securities and Exchange Commission, *Annual Report for 1962.*
*Covers issues in excess of $100,000 for all corporations, not just nonfinancial business corporations.

important. This tends to reduce the costs of issuing private placements. Further, the firm is required by law to supply fairly detailed information when selling claims to the public, particularly for issues in excess of $300,000. The costs of providing this information are avoided by private placement. It is not clear that this is a real saving since the purchasers of private placements may require the same information as would have to be provided for a public issue.

It will be noted in Table 7-3 that privately placed equity issues are relatively insignificant compared with privately placed debt. Most of the equity issues are for small businesses. Even publicly issued equities appear to be less important than debt. Part of this is more apparent than real. Common stock issues have no maturity date, i.e., they represent permanent claims on the firm which can be canceled only if the firm buys its own stock, dies, i.e., loses its identity, or goes through a reorganization. The debt claims are for all debt issues with a maturity date no less than one year from the issue date. As debt matures, the corporation will issue new debt to raise the funds needed to repay the old debt. In a sense, then, the same debt is represented in several years as the firm turns debt over. As a result, the data on new issues gives the false impression that firms use much more debt than equity.

CONVERTIBILITY

Among the various features the firm can use to attract buyers for its financial claims is the conversion privilege. This applies to bonds and preferred stocks and allows the holder to convert the debt or preferred stock claim to a common stock claim.

The conversion price is set at the time the debt or preferred stock is issued. There may be a schedule of conversion prices, rising as time passes. Initially, the conversion prices is above market. If the common stock price rises over time, it can become profitable to convert the bond or preferred stock into common. There are at least two related aspects of convertibility which attract buyers: first, the profits that can be made by converting when the market price is above the conversion price; second the opportunity allowed the holder to sell the convertible security at a capital gain, since the price of the bond or preferred stock will reflect the value of the common stock when the market price of common exceeds the conversion price. If a preferred stock has an investment value of $100 as a preferred stock, but has a conversion clause allowing an exchange of three shares of common for one share of preferred, the price of the preferred will remain at $100 as long as the price of the common is $33.33 or less. If the price of the common rises to, say, $40, the price of the preferred will rise to approximately $120, the $20 increase being the value of the conversion privilege.

Sometimes, firms will issue convertible securities as an indirect means of issuing common stock. This is apt to be true under two circumstances:

when the market for senior claims is relatively stronger than the market for common stock; and when the firm wishes to avoid the temporary decline in common stock prices usually associated with a new issue of common stock. The price decline is undesirable since the firm has to issue more shares of common in order to net a given amount of money. By using a convertible security, the firm is assured that new shares of common stock will be issued when the price of common is high, with the maximum number of new common shares to be issued determined by the conversion ratio.

When a firm uses convertible issues as a means of issuing common stock indirectly, the bond or preferred stock will usually be callable. If holders of the convertible issue are reluctant to convert when the market price is favorable, because they prefer the greater security of the convertible issue or because they hope that the price of the common will rise still higher, the firm can force conversion by threatening to call the convertible issue. This is only effective if the call price is below the conversion value of the security being called.

CAPITAL STRUCTURE FLOWS

There are many ways of viewing the capital structure of the firm. In this section, we shall study the net inflows of funds to nonfinancial business corporations. They appear in Table 7-4.

Net inflows are estimates of net changes in liability or net worth accounts. For example, the category "corporate bonds" shows a net inflow of $4.2 billion for 1962. The gross flows, from which the net flow is derived, could have involved the redemption or repayment of $5 billion of bonds and new issues worth $9.2 billion. The difference between the gross inflow and the gross outflow is the net inflow, or if preceded by —, the net outflow. The difference between gross flows and net flows is the primary reason for differences between the data in Table 7-3, which shows new issues gross of any reductions in debt or equity outstanding, and Table 7-4.

Unlike Table 7-3, the data on net flows do provide insight in the relative importance of various kinds of funds in the capital structure. Table 7-3 cannot be used this way since it deals with the gross issues of long-term securities and takes no account of the retirement and cancellation of outstanding securities.

The data in Table 7-4 include all liabilities and net worth items except accruals and taxes payable. Long-term sources are corporate bonds, corporate stock, mortgages, a small part of other bank loans, and retained earnings and depreciation. Trade debt, profit tax accruals, commercial paper and finance company loans, and most other bank loans are short-term.

The most obvious fact in the table is that the greatest source has been

Table 7-4

ANNUAL FLOWS OF SOURCES OF FUNDS
FOR NONFINANCIAL BUSINESS CORPORATIONS, 1950-62
(In Billions of Dollars)

Sources	1950	1951	1952	1953	1954	1955	1956	1957	1958	1959	1960	1961	1962
Corporate bonds	1.6	3.3	4.7	3.4	3.5	2.8	3.7	6.3	5.7	3.0	3.5	4.6	4.2
Corporate stock	1.4	2.2	2.3	1.8	1.6	2.0	2.3	2.4	2.3	2.3	1.8	2.7	0.5
Mortgages	1.4	0.1	1.9	0.9	1.8	1.6	1.4	1.4	2.5	2.5	2.2	3.0	4.4
Other bank loans	3.1	3.2	0.9	*	−0.7	3.0	5.3	2.0	0.4	3.7	2.6	1.6	2.6
Commercial paper and finance company loans	0.3	0.3	0.2	0.1	*	0.3	0.1	0.6	0.2	0.7	1.5	0.7	1.1
Trade debt	6.3	3.4	3.0	−0.3	2.0	8.9	4.3	−0.1	2.7	2.9	−2.7	2.1	*
Federal, State and local profits tax accruals	7.4	4.4	−3.3	0.6	−3.1	4.7	0.6	−0.7	−2.7	4.5	−1.5	—	0.3
Retained earnings and depreciation	24.5	24.5	16.8	21.0	17.9	29.5	24.9	26.3	25.2	35.2	29.7	32.1	36.6
Total sources	46.0	41.4	27.5	27.5	22.6	52.8	41.4	38.2	36.3	54.8	37.1	46.8	49.7

*Less than $50,000,000.
Source: *Flow of Funds, Accounts, 1955–62, 1963 Supplement*, Board of Governors of the Federal Reserve System.

internal—retained earnings and depreciation. Internal funds have provided well over 50 per cent of all sources for each of the years included in the table.

Less important quantitatively have been the so-called "automatic sources" —trade debt and tax accruals. These are automatic in the sense that they reflect the activity and profitability of business firms automatically. As the firm earns profits, profit tax accruals rise. As the firm purchases goods, trade debt rises. Both of these sources reflect business conditions and, as a result, fluctuate more widely than do any of the other sources. In 1950, 1951, 1955, and 1959, the two sources summed were more important than any of the other sources, except internal sources.

In the first chapter it was shown that internal financing was adequate to finance most capital expenditures. The sources in Table 7-4 finance not only capital expenditures, but increases in financial asset holdings. Sources other than internal and automatic, all of which require some formal financial arrangement apart from the firm's normal operations, are relatively unimportant. During the period 1950 through 1962, over 75 per cent of increases in assets were financed by internal and automatic sources.

At this point, a detailed discussion of annual variations among the different sources would be tedious and not very informative. The factors that determine the variations are demand and supply. The over-all demand for funds is the demand for assets and has been discussed in detail in Chapters 2 through 7. The determinants of the particular proportion of funds, i.e., capital structure, desired by the firm will be discussed in the next three chapters. The factors that determine the supply of funds to the firm will be the subject matter of most of the book from Chapter 11 on.

SELECTED REFERENCES

Butters, J., Thompson, and L. Bollinger; *Effects of Taxation: Investments by Individuals*, Harvard, Cambridge, Mass., 1953.

Corey, E.: *Direct Placement of Securities*, Harvard Cambridge, Mass., 1951.

Dewing, A.: *Financial Policy of Corporations*, 4th ed., Ronald, New York, 1941.

Gerstenberg, C.: *Financial Organization and Management*, 4th rev. ed., Prentice-Hall, Englewood Cliffs, N.J., 1959.

Hickman, C.: *The Volume of Corporate Bond Financing*, Princeton, N. J., 1953.

Perlo, V.: " 'People's Capitalism' and Stock-Ownership," *American Economic Review*, June, 1958.

Shapiro, E.: "The Postwar Market for Corporate Securities," *Journal of Finance*, May, 1959.

Smith, D.: *Effects of Taxation: Corporate Financial Policy*, Harvard, Cambridge, Mass., 1952.

Soldofsky, R.: "The Size and Maturity of Direct-Placement Loans," *Journal of Finance*, Mar., 1960.

Winn, W., and A. Hess, "The Value of the Call Privilege," *Journal of Finance*, May, 1959.

The Capital Structure :
Debt and Equity

8 In this chapter, we shall compare the effects of debt, common stock, and internal financing on the income stream and on cash flows.

It is convenient to illustrate the analysis with numerical examples. To avoid confusion, we shall use the same basic situation for the various examples in the chapter. The problem will be how to finance asset acquisitions costing $500,000, which are expected to add $60,000 annually to income before interest and taxes and $50,000 each year to depreciation. Without the acquisitions, the balance sheet and income statement will be

BALANCE SHEET NET OF NEW ASSETS

Assets	$5,000,000
Liabilities	$2,000,000
Preferred stock, 6%	500,000
Common stock, $10 par value	1,000,000
Capital surplus..................................	800,000
Retained earnings	700,000
Liabilities and net worth	$5,000,000

INCOME STATEMENT NET OF NEW ASSETS

Sales	$10,000,000
Operating costs*	8,380,000
Earnings before interest and taxes	$ 1,620,000
Interest	100,000
Earnings before taxes	$ 1,520,000
Taxes (22% on first $25,000 and 48% on all over)	723,100
Earnings after taxes	796,900
Preferred dividends	30,000
Available to stockholders........................	$ 766,900

*Including depreciation, $860,000.

Assume that $500,000 of the liabilities must be paid within the year. Since par value is the value assigned to each share of common stock in the corporate charter, there are 100,000 shares of common stock outstanding. Note that par value has no necessary relationship to market value or book value. For example, the book value of the common stock is total assets less all prior claims, i.e., $5,000,000 − ($2,000,000 + $500,000) = $2,500,000, divided by the number of shares. In this case, book value is $25 per share. A market value of $60 would not be unreasonably high for the common stock in this example, since the earnings per share (eps) after taxes and preferred dividends are $766,900/100,000 shares = approximately $7.67 per share, and it is not unusual for the ratio of market price to eps to be 10/1 or higher.

DEBT AND EQUITY

LEVERAGE AND PROFITS

The existing assets earn $1,620,000 prior to taxes and financing charges (interest and preferred dividends). The rate of return on the asset investment is $1,620,000/$5,000,000 = 32.4 per cent. If the entire asset portfolio had been financed by common stock and retained earnings, the rate of return on net worth before taxes would have been 32.4 per cent also, and the after-tax rate of return would have been approximately 17 per cent (about 52 per cent of the before-tax rate of return). The actual after-tax rate of return on total net worth, including preferred stock is $796,900/$3,000,000 = 26.6 per cent, substantially above the 17 per cent rate that would have been earned with no debt.

If the firm had used no preferred stock, but had $2,000,000 of debt, the rate of return on the increased level of common stock and retained earnings would have been 26.6 per cent. The actual rate of return on common stock and retained earnings is $766,900/$2,500,000 = 30.7 per cent, again above the rate which would have prevailed with no preferred stock.

The reason for the effect of debt and preferred stock in *levering* the rate of return on the common stockholders' investment, which includes the retained earnings, lies in the fixedness of the firm's obligations to the preferred stockholders and to the creditors. Once the fixed interest payments, taxes, and preferred dividends have been deducted, the remainder of the income stream belongs to the common stockholder. If the rate of return on assets exceeds the interest rate and the preferred dividend rate, the rate of return to the common stockholder is levered above what it would be in the absence of debt and preferred stock financing.

To see this simply, ignore the preferred stock for the moment. The relationship among the rate of return on assets, the debt financing, and the rate of return to common stockholders is

(8–1)
$$e = \frac{t(aA - dD)}{A - D},$$

where e is the rate of return on common stock and retained earnings invest-ment, t is 1 minus the marginal income tax rate, a is the rate of return on the asset portfolio, A is the dollars invested in the asset portfolio, d is the interest rate on debt financing, D is the dollars of debt financing. It follows that, ignoring preferred stock, $A - D$ is the investment of the common stockholders.

When a is greater than d, e will be levered. The extent of the leverage will depend upon the size of D compared with A. The larger is D, the greater the leverage. If the new asset acquisitions are financed one-half by debt-bearing interest of 6 per cent annually, and one-half by equity, the value of e for the new assets would be

$$\frac{0.52[0.12(\$500,000) - 0.06(\$250,000)]}{\$500,000 - \$250,000} = 9.36 \text{ per cent.}$$

If none of the assets were financed by debt, the rate of return to stock-holders of the new investments would be

$$\frac{0.48[0.12(\$500,000)]}{\$500,000} = 6.24 \text{ per cent.}$$

LEVERAGE AND RISK

Figure 8–1 shows the relationship between the rate of return on owners' investment and the amount of 6 per cent debt used to finance a $500,000 investment. The vertical axis measures the rate of return on owner's investment. The horizontal axis measures $A - D$, the amount of ownership investment. The maximum value for $A - D$ is, of course, $500,000. The uppermost curve illustrates the relation-ship when the rate of return on assets is 12 per cent. As shown in the arithmetic examples, the rate of return to owners becomes increasingly levered when the amount of debt rises (moving to the left in the graph) relative to equity and when a is greater than d.

The leverage effect, however, depends not only on the proportion of debt used, but on the difference between a and d. When a is 8 per cent, the leverage effect still exists, but it is weaker than when a was 12 per cent. The second curve from the top shows the relationship between e and $A - D$ when $a = 8$ per cent. The straight line labeled "$a = 6$ per cent" indicates that, regardless of the proportion of debt used, there is no leverage effect when $a = d$.

When the rate of return on the asset portfolio is less than the interest rate, leverage occurs, but in the wrong direction. The two lower curves illustrate negative leverage. The lowest curve shows the degree of negative

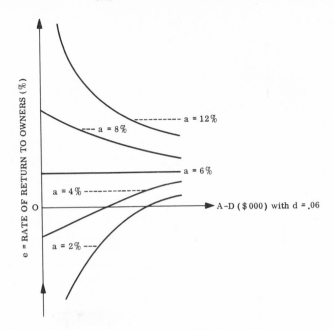

Figure 8-1. The effect on the rate of return to owners of varying debt levels with varying asset returns. (Interest rate on debt is 6 per cent and total investment is $500,000)

leverage when $a = 2$ per cent. Despite the fact that the investments are earning a positive return, owners suffer losses as long as debt exceeds approximately two hundred thousand dollars. At any positive level of debt, the rate of return to owners is less than it would be in the absence of debt when a is less than d.

Figure 8–1 also shows the instability of earnings created by debt. Suppose the firm decides to finance the asset investments using $50,000 of equity $A - D$ and $450,000 of 6 per cent debt. The rate of return to the owners would vary between about 32 per cent and -16 per cent, whereas the return on assets varies only between 12 per cent and 2 per cent. The diagram shows that the extent of the instability added to the owners' income stream depends on the amount of debt used, as well as on the variability of the return on assets.

All three parties to the capital structure—the managers, the owners, and the creditors—,then, have reason to be concerned about the degree of debt financing used by the firm. With a high degree of debt financing and a low rate of return on assets, not only will the rate of return to owners fall, but the firm may not earn enough to meet the interest payments due on debt. However, evaluation of the financial risk introduced by the use of debt is not usually applied to a single group of asset acquisitions, but to the entire capital structure of the firm.

Equation 8–2 expresses the leverage relationship for the entire capital structure for any firm:

(8-2)
$$e = \frac{t(aA - d_1 D_1 - d_2 D_2 - \cdots - d_n D_n) - pP}{A - (D_1 + D_2 + \cdots + D_n + P)},$$

where the subscripts refer to different classes of debt and interest rates, P is the dollar amount of preferred stock, and p is the preferred dividend rate. It should be noted that for some kinds of debt, particularly accruals and trade debt paid within the discount period, d can be zero. Preferred dividends, unlike debt, are not deductible for tax purposes and so are shown in the numerator outside the parenthesis.

If the firm should decide to divide the financing for the new assets evenly between 6 per cent debt and equity, treating the interest rate on existing debt as 5 per cent (the ratio of existing interest payments to liabilities), the leverage expression would be as follows:

[8-2(a)]
$$e = \frac{0.52[a(\$5,500,000) - 0.05(\$2,000,000) - 0.06(\$250,000) - \$25,000] - 0.06(\$500,000) + \$19,500}{\$5,500,000 - (\$2,000,000 + \$250,000 + \$500,000)}.$$

Since the 48 per cent tax rate applies only to income over \$25,000, the \$25,000 is deducted within the taxable income parenthesis. This initial income is taxed at a 22 per cent rate, i.e., the tax on the first \$25,000 is \$5,500, which is deducted from the \$25,000 outside the parenthesis in the numerator.

If the firm's earnings before taxes and interest are \$1,620,000 on the existing assets and \$60,000 on the new assets, the value for a will be 30.6 per cent, and the after-tax rate of return to the owners' investment will be 28.7 per cent. Without any debt or preferred stock, e would be only 16 per cent. Both debt and preferred stock provide leverage, but the effect of preferred stock is weaker because preferred dividends are not deductible for tax purposes.

Given the capital structure, what is the effect of changing a values on the rate of return to owners? Specifically, it would be useful to know how low a may fall before negative leverage effects are encountered. Figure 8–2 answers this question. The steeper solid line shows the relationship between a and e, given the capital structure described above. The dashed flatter line shows the relationship if neither debt nor preferred stock were used. Negative leverage begins below the intersection of the two lines. The more debt in the capital structure, the steeper the line relating a and e, and the reverse. Also, as more debt is used, the levered line shifts to the right, raising the level of a at which negative leverage begins.

Although the decision on capital structure is not made solely on the probability of negative leverage, this does play a role in the decision.

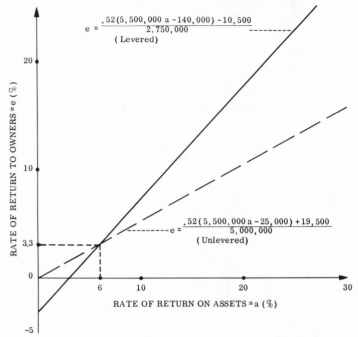

Figure 8-2. Break-even analysis for financial leverage.

Obviously, the point is unimportant if the firm has never experienced a rate of return on assets below, say, 20 per cent and if the firm believes it extremely unlikely that a will ever fall below 20 per cent. But, if the firm has experienced values of a around 6 per cent, a high proportion of debt will not be attractive to managers, owners, or creditors.

SAFETY TESTS

The capacity of a firm to hold debt in its capital structure is sometimes tested by two operating statement ratios: the ratio of earnings before interest and taxes to interest, called the *times interest earned*; and the ratio of debt to equity. A large times-interest-earned ratio and a low debt/equity ratio would indicate a safe firm, and the reverse. Though the firm does not operate with the goal of achieving safe ratios, it will have difficulty acquiring funds on good terms if times interest earned and the debt/equity ratio are at what creditors feel are unsafe levels. Stockholders also may be unhappy in this event.

The definition of safe levels varies among industries over time and, to some extent, among creditors. During periods of prosperity and stability, creditors may be willing to tolerate more debt in the capital structure than during recessions. Further, in stable industries, such as public utilities, more debt is tolerated than in less stable industries. Table 8-1 shows debt/equity and times-interest-earned ratios for selected industries.

Table 8-1

DEBT/EQUITY AND TIMES-INTEREST-EARNED RATIOS
FOR SELECTED INDUSTRIES, 1948 AND 1960

Industry	LONG-TERM DEBT/EQUITY		TOTAL DEBT AND PREFERRED STOCK/COMMON EQUITY		EARNINGS BEFORE INTEREST AND TAXES/INTEREST	
	1948	1960	1948	1960	1948	1960
All manufacturing	0.2622	0.2460	0.5492	0.6888	38.43	15.80
Food and kindred products	0.2513	0.2202	0.6079	0.7039	20.51	13.67
Apparel and fabric products	0.2343	0.1943	0.7222	1.1444	21.14	9.31
Lumber and wood products (except furniture)	0.2426	0.2782	0.4419	0.6530	40.78	6.22
Paper and allied products	0.2650	0.2888	0.5189	0.5534	49.96	15.01
Chemicals and allied products	0.2452	0.2396	0.5508	0.5518	44.80	22.60
Petroleum and coat products	0.2569	0.1944	0.4547	0.4111	36.97	14.10
Rubber products	0.4683	0.3498	0.9463	0.7702	27.46	15.47
Primary metal industries	0.2702	0.3497	0.6325	0.6615	27.21	10.39
Electrical machinery and equipment	0.3868	0.3560	0.6768	0.7675	38.56	15.64
Motor vehicles and equipment (except electrical)	0.1515	0.1244	0.4516	0.4621	112.63	54.48
Transportation, including railroads	0.6014	0.6807	0.9442	0.9822	70.05	4.57
Electric and gas utilities	0.9211	1.1794	1.4797	1.8902	6.938	4.78
Wholesale trade	0.2706	0.2707	0.8946	1.1939	24.41	7.75
Retail trade	0.2661	0.2878	0.8729	0.9579	36.52	8.08
Services	0.5214	0.8460	0.7761	1.6858	12.78	5.38

Sources: Statistics of Income: Corporation Income Tax Returns, 1948, 1960–'61.

In the usual version, the debt/equity ratio is the ratio of long-term debt to total equity, i.e., including preferred stock. Although short-term debt and accruals provide leverage just as long-term debt, current liabilities are usually omitted from the ratio. The firm is assumed to be able to adjust the short-term part of the capital structure rapidly when the rate of return on assets declines. Short-term debt may be permanent if the firm finds it cheaper than long-term debt. In this case, the firm may have little more flexibility in adjusting the short-term portion of its capital structure than it has with the long-term portion.

Preferred stock is treated as if it were common stock since, in the eyes of creditors, all stock has a junior claim to income. This treatment is questionable despite its general acceptance. Failure to pay preferred dividends will lead to large arrearages if the preferred are cumulative. The arrearages can make it virtually impossible for the firm to sell new common stock following a period of losses just when the firm may be in great need of new funds. Without new asset investments, the income stream may be so small as to threaten the position of creditors as well as of owners. Although preferred stockholders have a claim subordinate to that of creditors, the position of creditors may be adversely affected indirectly by the existence of preferred dividend arrearages.

CASH FLOW

In addition to the difference between debt and equity as they affect the rate of return on equity investment, the types of financing will have different effects on the cash flow of the firm. The payment of interest on debt is obligatory. Though firms are reluctant to stir up stockholder unrest by cutting dividends, the payment of dividends is not as rigid a requirement as are interest payments. Both interest payments and dividend payments usually come out of the income stream of the firm. However, they are both cash payments and, in a very real sense, come out of the firm's cash balance.

This can perhaps be appreciated more by considering that, even if the income stream is insufficient to cover interest payments, the firm will pay interest providing it has sufficient cash. Indeed, even dividend payments may be larger than earnings after taxes when the firm has had temporary business reverses, but is reluctant to cut dividends below past levels. On the other hand, the income stream may be quite large and, if the firm wishes to increase asset holdings substantially, the firm may prefer to cut dividends rather than to raise the cash needed to maintain a past level of dividend payments. The ability of the firm to make any payment depends fundamentally on the availability of cash.

Another, and perhaps more important, aspect of the differential effects debt and equity on the firm's cash flow is that debt has to be repaid while equity does not. Creditors, owners, and management may properly be concerned about the ability of the firm to meet the repayment obligation. One test of the firm's ability to meet repayment obligations is to compare the cash flow with the debt obligation. This is somewhat like the use of the times-interest-earned ratio. Instead of testing the adequacy of the income stream to meet interest obligations, we test the adequacy of the cash flow to meet repayment obligations.

Turning to the illustrative example used earlier, the new assets are expected to generate $60,000 earnings before interest and taxes, EBIT, and depreciation is to be $50,000 per annum. If half the financing is to come from 6 per cent debt, the after-tax cash flow generated by the new assets is expected to be

EBIT	$60,000
Interest	15,000
Taxable income	$45,000
Taxes, 48%	21,600
After-tax earnings	$23,400
Depreciation	50,000
After-tax cash flow	$73,400

Suppose that the debt financing is to be repaid in five equal annual installments of $50,000 each. The debt repayment is covered 1.5 times in the first year. Coverage will improve over time as the interest payments decline because the outstanding debt is being reduced annually. How low may EBIT fall before the adequacy of the cash flow coverage is endangered. Equation 8–3 shows the basic relationship between EBIT and cash flow.

(8–3) $$\text{Cash flow} = t(\text{EBIT} - dD) + \text{depreciation}.$$

If the minimally acceptable cash flow is equal to the repayment or sinking fund requirements, we substitute sinking fund for cash flow, and solve Eq. (8–3) for EBIT.

(8–4) $$\text{EBIT} = \frac{\text{sinking fund} + t(dD) - \text{depreciation}}{t}.$$

Substituting the numbers from the example into Eq. 8–4, we have

$$\$15,000 = \frac{\$50,000 + 0.52(\$15,000) - \$50,000}{0.52}.$$

Since the depreciation on the new assets is adequate to cover sinking fund requirements, the firm need only have EBIT sufficient to cover interest payments. When depreciation is less than sinking fund requirements, EBIT must rise by the difference divided by 0.52. For example, if depreciation in the example were only $40,000, the level of EBIT required to cover debt payments would rise from $15,000 to $34,231, an increase of more than $19,000 in EBIT needed to cover an after-tax difference of only $10,000.

Evaluation of the results indicate that the expected EBIT level is four times larger than the EBIT minimum needed to cover debt requirements. Since this takes into account the effect of income taxes, it is much more accurate than the 1.5 ratio of after-tax cash flow to sinking fund requirements used earlier. Whether or not the proposed financing pattern is too risky depends upon how likely the managers, creditors, and owners view a 75 per cent decline in EBIT, as well as upon their willingness to take risks.

Though it is useful to evaluate the effect of a particular asset investment and its financing on the cash flow, it is more meaningful to consider the over-all capital structure and cash flow of the firm. Even if the cash flow generated by a particular asset is inadequate to cover financing requirements, the cash flow generated by the other assets may be more than adequate. With the proposed asset investment and financing of 50 per cent of the cost of the new assets by 6 per cent debt, the firm's cash flow will be

EBIT	$1,680,000
Interest	115,000
Taxable income	$1,565,000
Taxes	744,700
After-tax earnings	$ 820,300
Less preferred dividends	30,000
Available to common holders	$ 790,300
Depreciation	910,000
Cash flow	$1,700,300

As indicated earlier, $500,000 of existing liabilities must be paid annually, which brings total debt repayment requirements to $550,000. Rather than solving for the minimum EBIT in the cash flow Eq. 8–4, we can calculate the required level of EBIT as follows:

After-tax charges	
Debt repayment	$550,000
Preferred dividends	30,000
Total	$580,000
Less depreciation	910,000
Required after-tax income (loss)	−$330,000
Taxes (ignore loss carry-forward or -back)	0
Required before tax income	−$330,000
Plus interest	115,000
Required EBIT	−$215,000

In this example, because depreciation is large relative to the after-tax charges, the firm can have a negative EBIT of −$215,000 and still meet its financial obligations. EBIT would have to fall by 112 per cent of the expected level, or $1,680,000, before the cash flow would be inadequate.

DIVIDENDS

Common stockholders may not view the negative value of EBIT with equanimity. Although the payment of common stock dividends is not a legal obligation of the firm, most firms are reluctant to reduce dividends. Figure 8–3 compares earnings after taxes with cash dividend payments for nonfinancial business corporations annually for the period 1946–'62. The most casual of glances indicates that dividend payments have been far more stable than have earnings after taxes. During the recession periods 1948–'49, 1953–'54, 1957–'58, and 1959–'60, the decline in earnings far exceeded the decline in dividends. In fact, the dividend decline is virtually imperceptible in most cases. Also, firms seem reluctant to raise dividends rapidly in response to increases in earnings. The evidence strongly suggests that firms view common stock dividend payments as, at least, semifixed financial obligations.

If the firm in the example has been paying dividends of $3 a share, i.e., $300,000 total, this charge should be included in the calculation of the

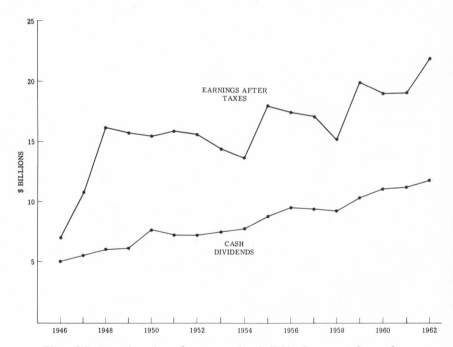

Figure 8-3. Annual earnings after taxes and cash dividend payments for nonfinancial business coporations, 1946–1962. Source: Board of Governors of the Federal Reserve System.

required cash flow. Further, if the firm proposes to finance half the new asset investments by common stock issue, each new share will receive $3 in dividends since it is impossible for the firm to discriminate among new and old holders of a given class of stock. Assume that the firm will net, after paying the costs of distribution, $50 for each new share sold. To raise half the $500,000 needed for the new investments by common stock issue would require issuing 5,000 shares of new stock. This would add $15,000 to dividend requirements, assuming that the firm wishes to retain the $3 dividend. With total common dividend requirements of $315,000, what is the lowest level of EBIT needed to cover all the firm's financial obligations?

After-tax charges
Debt repayment	$550,000
Common stock dividends	315,000
Preferred dividends	30,000
Total	$895,000
Less depreciation	910,000
Required after-tax income (loss)	−$ 15,000
Tax	0
Required before-tax income (loss)	−$ 15,000
Plus interest	115,000
Required minimum EBIT	$100,000

Although the minimum EBIT including dividend payments is still substantially below the expected EBIT, it is clear that dividend payments do make a real difference in determining the adequacy of a given cash flow. In our example, dividend payments require less after-tax cash flow than does 6 per cent, 5-year debt. However, suppose dividends had been $6 per share, and the debt was to be repaid over 25 years in equal installments. Then, each $50 share of stock would require $6 in after-tax cash flow in order to maintain the dividend, or $6/0.52 = $11.54 in EBIT. Each $50 of debt would require $2 in after-tax cash flow for a sinking fund and $3 in before-tax income for interest payments, or $2/0.52 + $3 = $6.85 in earnings before taxes, interest, and depreciation. Thus, it is well within the realm of possibility that common stock financing can require a larger cash flow than does debt.

INTERNAL FUNDS

Internal funds provide advantages similar to the leverage effect of debt, but without increasing the variability of the owners' share of the income stream. Further, the use of internal funds does not increase the level of required EBIT as do both stock and debt financing.

The leverage effect of internal funds can be seen by revising Eq. 8–1 so that, instead of showing the effects of various financing methods on the rate of return to owners, it shows the effect on the eps (earnings per share) of common stock. This is done in Eq. 8–6.

$$(8\text{–}6) \qquad \text{eps} = \frac{t(aA - dD)}{Sh},$$

where Sh is the number of shares. The equation can be modified to include several kinds of debt and preferred stock, as in Eq. 8–2, by substituting Sh for $A - (D_1 + D_2 + \cdots + D_n + P)$ in the denominator and solving for eps instead of e.

When either debt or internal funds are used to finance an asset, the denominator of Eq. 8–6 is unchanged. In the case of debt, positive leverage occurs when the assets generate an EBIT greater than the interest payments on the debt, i.e., eps rises. With internal funds, any increase in EBIT generated by the new assets will increase eps. With debt, when the EBIT generated by the new assets is less than the interest payments, eps will fall and will be as unstable as was the rate of return to owners, e. But with internal funds, eps will be upwardly unstable only.

To see this more clearly, let us return to the example of the $500,000 of investments, which were expected to generate a rate of return on assets of 12 per cent. Assume that half the assets will be financed by common stock at $50 per share. If the remainder is financed by 6 per cent debt, eps on the new assets for all common stockholders will be

$$\frac{0.52[0.12(\$500,000) - 0.06(\$250,000)]}{105,000 \text{ shares}} = \$0.223.$$

If, instead of using common stock financing, internal funds were used, the results would be

$$\frac{0.52[0.12(\$500,000) - 0.06(\$250,000)]}{100,000 \text{ shares}} = \$0.234.$$

Thus, internal funds are superior to common stock financing in affecting eps.

If the entire new investment were financed by internal funds, eps would be

$$\frac{0.52[0.12(\$500,000)]}{100,000 \text{ shares}} = \$0.312.$$

So, internal funds can be superior to debt in affecting eps.

Next, suppose that the rate of return on assets fell to 5 per cent. If the firm had financed the investment half with 6 per cent debt and half with internal funds, eps would be

$$\frac{0.52[0.05(\$500,000) - 0.06(\$250,000)]}{100,000 \text{ shares}} = \$0.052.$$

If the firm had financed the investment entirely with internal funds, eps would be

$$\frac{0.52[0.05(\$500,000)]}{100,000 \text{ shares}} = \$0.13.$$

Not only are retained earnings superior to debt when assets are generating high earnings, retained earnings are even more desirable when earnings are unfavorable. If the entire investment had been financed with stock, the eps, at a 5 per cent rate of return on assets, would be

$$\frac{0.52[0.05(\$500,000)]}{110,000 \text{ shares}} = \$0.118.$$

The additional 10,000 shares result from raising $500,000 through stock issue. Even in adversity, internal funds are superior to common stock in their effect on eps.

DETERMINANTS AND CHARACTERISTICS

Throughout this chapter, we have been concerned not with the determinants of the capital structure, but with describing the characteristics of debt, common stock, and internal financing. The firm does not operate to maximize the rate of return to owners. After all, this is simply the ratio of after-tax earnings to the book value of common stock. The book value of common stock has no necessary relationship to the actual value of common stock.

Earnings per share are somewhat less artificial, but are still subject to accounting decisions such as those that affect the level of depreciation charges. The market value of the firm's net worth, or equity, accounts is the market value of the firm's common stock. Common stock values reflect current and past earnings, but they also reflect expected future earnings, the number and quality of alternative securities which the stockholder can purchase, and general expectations such as those concerned with the general price level.

We have assumed throughout this book that the firm is trying to achieve some optimal mixture of the expected value of net worth, which is more nearly market value than book value or any other observable valuation, and risk. The characteristics of the different methods of financing will affect the decisions of the firm as it tries to achieve the desired level of net worth. Under some circumstances, achieving the desired net worth goal may mean maximizing the rate of return to the owners, avoiding the possibility of negative leverage and of maximizing the after-tax cash flow, or maximizing eps. In general, however, achieving the optimal level of the expected value of net worth does not necessarily involve achieving any of the aims mentioned above. Knowledge of the various characteristics described in this chapter, and the next, is useful, indeed indispensable, in making rational capital structure decisions. But minimizing bad characteristics or maximizing good characteristics will not necessarily be consistent with optimizing the expected value of net worth. Means should not be confused with ends.

SELECTED REFERENCES

Dobrovolsky, S.: "Economics of Corporate Internal and External Financing," *Journal of Finance*, Mar., 1958.

Hunt, P.: "A Proposal for Precise Definitions of 'Trading on the Equity' and 'Leverage,' " *Journal of Finance*, Sept., 1961.

Sussman, M.: "A Note on the Implications of Periodic 'Cash Flow,' " *Journal of Finance*, Dec., 1962.

The Capital Structure :
Term Aspects

9

When the firm wishes to borrow, it has a wide variety of debt alternatives. These alternatives differ: in interest rates; whether or not they are secured by assets; if they are secured, in the ratio of the principal amount of the loan to the value of the assets used as security; in the nature of restrictions placed on the firm with respect to the required level of working capital and payment of dividends; and in the terms of the loan. In this chapter, we shall concentrate on the factors underlying the choice with respect to the term of the loan.

It may be well to repeat a point made in Chapter 7. Since short-term loans can be renewed or replaced with other short-term loans, they can be as permanent as long-term financing. It is therefore appropriate to treat short- and long-term debt financing as substitutes, or alternatives.

Table 9-1 illustrates the relative permanence of short-term financing. The first two items, corporate bonds and mortgages, are long-term sources of funds. The third item, bank loans not elsewhere classified, is primarily short-term, as are trade debt and loans from commercial and sales finance companies.

INTEREST RATES
AND THE TERM STRUCTURE

Is there an interest rate differential between short- and long-term debt? The evidence, such as it is, indicates that long-

Table 9-1

OUTSTANDING BALANCES FOR SELECTED LIABILITIES
OF NONFINANCIAL BUSINESS CORPORATIONS, ANNUALLY, 1956–1962
(In Billions of Dollars)

Year	Corporate Bonds	Mortgages	Bank Loans n.e.c.*	Loans from Sales and Commercial Finance Companies	Trade Debt
1956	56.4	19.2	24.0	3.2	47.9
1957	62.7	20.6	26.0	3.8	46.8
1958	68.4	23.1	26.4	4.0	49.5
1959	71.4	25.6	31.2	4.5	50.6
1960	74.9	27.8	33.8	6.1	51.0
1961	79.1	30.8	35.4	6.7	53.2
1962	83.2	35.2	38.0	7.8	53.4

*Not elsewhere classified.
Source: *Flow of Fund Accounts*, 1945–'62, 1963 Supplement, Board of Governors of the Federal Reserve System.

term debt has been somewhat more expensive than short-term debt during most of this century. Before presenting the evidence, let us look at the problems involved in deciding whether or not there is a differential.

If we are to compare the interest rates on short- and long-term debt, it is essential that the only difference between the two debts is the term. For example, the interest rate on a five-year term loan which is secured by a first mortgage on highly salable assets can be compared with the interest rate on an unsecured six-month bank loan, but the difference between the two rates will reflect not only term, but also the security.

To arrive at an accurate notion of term interest rate differentials, we must make comparisons for nearly identical firms. Yet, one of the points made in Chapter 6 was that even firms engaged in essentially the same kind of business activities may have different asset portfolios, depending on how they view the future and their willingness to gamble.

The selection of the asset portfolio involves rather subtle points of difference. Simply discovering firms which have identical product lines is enormously difficult. Compare Ford and General Motors. Both produce similar motor cars, appliances, and even computers. But GM in addition is the largest producer of diesel locomotives in the United States. Should investors view the securities of these two firms as near-identical?

Even electric power companies, which produce homogeneous products, are quite different. Some utility companies operate in states where the regulatory commissions, which set the price of power, are very sympathetic to the company's problems. In other states, rate increases are hard to come by. Some areas are characterized by rapid industrial and population growth, while others are stagnant. One utility may be located near inexpensive fuel or water resources. Another utility may have to pay high transport costs in order to acquire coal or oil as fuel for the electric generators.

The best way to view the term pattern of interest rates is to find a firm which issues a large number of securities with different maturities. Unfortunately, there is no such firm. However, the United States government does fit this description. It will be recalled that Table 5-3 showed the yields on taxable U.S. securities maturing at different points. In 1962, the average yield on three-month U.S. securities averaged 2.77 per cent, and the yield on long-term government bonds was 3.95 per cent.

Table 9-2 shows quarterly estimates of basic yields for corporate debt maturing from 1 to 40 years for 1952–1957. A basic yield differs from a market yield, and both may differ from the coupon rate. The coupon rate is the ratio of annual interest to maturity value of a bond. A bond which pays $40 annually with a maturity value of $1,000 has a 4 per cent coupon rate. If the bond is selling at $900, it has a 4.44 per cent market rate ($40/$900). Yet neither the coupon nor the market rates distinguish between securities which mature at different times. The basic yield is the discount rate which equates the present value of future interest payments and maturity value to the market price. A bond with a maturity value of $1,000, payable in one year, paying $40 interest per annum semiannually, and selling at $900, has a basic yield of about 15 per cent. If the same security were to mature in six months, the basic yield would be approximately 26 per cent.

The table shows the same kind of term interest rate difference shown for government securities—a tendency for rates to rise as the term of the security increases. It will be noted the the estimates most liable to error, those marked with a dagger, occur in the shorter term securities. Short-term basic yield estimates are weak because there are relatively few price quotations, inactive trading, and, as a result, considerable sensitivity to minor changes in demand and supply. The differences in the term-yield pattern shown in table 9-2 are smaller than the differences shown in Table 5-3, the government structure, primarily because the data in Table 5-3 are market yields.

The evidence indicates that, for comparable securities, there is a tendency for interest rates to rise with the term of the loan. However, the interest rate differential is far from impressive. From Table 9-2, the difference between 1-year securities and 40-year securities ranged from 0.28 per cent in the first quarter of 1957 to only 0.60 per cent in the first quarter of 1953. On this basis, it seems quite unlikely that term interest rate differentials play an important part in determining the term structure of debt.

FLEXIBILITY AND COSTS

FLEXIBILITY

When the firm finances assets through long-term debt, it enters into a relatively rigid loan agreement. Long-term lenders, particularly institutional lenders such as life insurance companies, usually require the payment of penalties if the firm wishes to make early

Table 9-2
BASIC YIELDS BY QUARTERS*
YEARS TO MATURITY

	1	2	3	4	5	6	8	10	12	14	15	20	25	30	40
1952															
1st....	2.73†	2.73†	2.73†	2.73†	2.73†	2.73†	2.73†	2.73	2.77	2.80	2.81	2.88	2.94	3.00	3.09
2d....	‡	‡	‡	‡	2.70	2.71	2.74	2.76	2.78	2.80	2.81	2.87	2.94	3.00	3.08
3d....	‡	‡	‡	‡	2.80	2.80	2.80	2.80	2.82	2.84	2.85	2.90	3.00	3.05	3.10
4th....	‡	‡	‡	‡	2.77	2.78	2.80	2.82	2.84	2.85	2.86	2.91	2.96	3.00	3.09
1953															
1st....	2.62†	2.65†	2.69†	2.72†	2.75†	2.78†	2.83	2.88	2.92	2.95	2.97	3.05	3.11	3.15	3.22
2d....	‡	‡	‡	‡	3.02	3.05	3.07	3.10	3.13	3.16	3.17	3.25	3.33	3.40	3.53
3d....	‡	‡	‡	‡	2.95	2.96	2.98	3.00	3.04	3.07	3.09	3.13	3.26	3.35	3.45
4th....	‡	‡	‡	‡	2.75	2.77	2.81	2.85	2.89	2.93	2.94	3.03	3.08	3.12	3.20
1954															
1st....	2.40	2.43	2.46	2.49	2.52	2.55	2.60	2.66	2.71	2.76	2.78	2.88	2.95	3.00	3.05
2d....	‡	‡	‡	‡	2.55	2.57	2.60	2.65	2.67	2.72	2.73	2.81	2.89	2.95	3.02
3d....	‡	‡	‡	‡	2.50	2.52	2.54	2.60	2.63	2.67	2.69	2.77	2.86	2.94	3.02
4th....	‡	‡	‡	‡	2.54	2.57	2.60	2.64	2.67	2.70	2.72	2.81	2.88	2.95	3.04
1955															
1st....	‡	‡	‡	‡	2.70	2.72	2.76	2.80	2.83	2.87	2.88	2.95	3.00	3.04	3.10
2d....	‡	‡	‡	‡	2.80	2.81	2.83	2.85	2.87	2.89	2.90	2.95	3.00	3.11	3.18
3d....	‡	‡	‡	‡	2.84	2.85	2.88	2.90	2.92	2.95	2.96	3.02	3.08	3.14	3.25
4th....	‡	‡	‡	‡	2.85	2.87	2.90	2.93	2.95	2.98	2.99	3.04	3.08	3.11	3.15
1956															
1st....	2.70	2.72	2.74	2.76	2.78	2.80	2.83	2.86	2.89	2.92	2.93	2.99	3.04	3.09	3.17
2d....	‡	‡	‡	‡	3.10	3.11	3.12	3.14	3.15	3.16	3.17	3.21	3.25	3.29	3.35
3d....	‡	4.05†	3.92†	3.80†	3.69†	3.60†	3.43†	3.31†	3.24	3.24	3.25	3.32	3.39	3.46	3.60
4th....	‡	‡	‡	‡	3.65	3.65	3.65	3.65	3.65	3.65	3.65	3.65	3.65	3.65	3.65†
1957															
1st....	3.50†	3.50†	3.50†	3.50†	3.50†	3.50	3.50	3.50	3.50	3.50	3.50	3.50†	3.60	3.68	3.78
2d....	‡	‡	‡	‡	3.65	3.65	3.65	3.65	3.65	3.65	3.65	3.65	3.65	3.65	3.65†
3d....	‡	‡	‡	‡	4.00	4.00	4.00	4.00	4.00	4.00	4.00	4.00	4.00	4.00	4.00
4th....	‡	4.75†	4.50†	4.30†	4.18†	4.10†	4.04†	4.00	4.00	4.00	4.00	4.00	4.00	4.00	4.00
1958															
1st....	3.21†	3.22†	3.23	3.24†	3.25†	3.27	3.30	3.33	3.36	3.39	3.40	3.47	3.54	3.61	3.75

*These yields have been derived from averages of high and low sale prices of the best-grade corporate bonds for the central month of each quarter—i.e., Feb., May, Aug., and Nov. Originally, the annual series was constructed from averages of monthly high and low prices for Jan., Feb., and Mar.; but for 1951 and subsequent years, only high and low prices for Feb. have been used.

†More than usually liable to error.

‡Reliable estimates impossible in this area.

Source: Durand, D.: "A Quarterly Series of Corporate Basic Yields, 1952–'57, and Some Attendant Reservations," *Journal of Finance,* Sept., 1958.

repayment. With bonds, the penalty may take the form of a high call price, so that the firm may have to pay more than the maturity value if the bond is called. When the bonds are publicly held, the firm can extinguish debt by purchasing the bonds on the open market. However, should the firm make large bond purchases over a short period of time, the firm's actions will tend to force up the price of the bonds.

With term loans or mortgages, rapid repayment is either not allowed or allowed at a penalty, which tends to be high in the early years of the loan agreement, but diminishes over time. This is similar to the penalties an individual usually must pay if he wishes to repay a home mortgage loan sooner than is required by the loan agreement.

The penalties exist partly because the lender incurs costs each time his investment portfolio must be adjusted. Institutional lenders continually have cash inflows from the payment of life insurance premiums, pension payments, etc. In order to fulfill the terms of their "borrowing" agreements, such as the payment of life insurance claims, the lenders must be able to invest the cash inflows profitably. When an investment, which was supposed to be outstanding for 10 years, is paid in 2 years, the financial institution must go to the trouble of reinvesting the funds. Two kinds of costs are involved. First, there are the acquisition costs of a new investment. Financial institutions often make payments to loan brokers, or agents, who discover and prepare lending opportunities. This is roughly equivalent to the broker's fee paid by individuals when they buy or sell stock. Second, there is often a time lag between when a loan is repaid and when the funds can be reinvested. During this time, the lender either receives no earnings on the funds or, if the funds are temporarily invested in short-term government securities or commercial paper, receives very low returns.

Another factor which makes long-term lenders demand penalties for rapid repayment is the likelihood that rapid repayment will occur during periods when interest rates are low. Borrowers will tend to refinance using low interest rate debt to replace higher interest rate debt. There are two aspects to this problem. First, the lender who has received rapid payment of high interest rate debt in a period of low interest rates will be able to reinvest the funds only at a lower interest rate. Second, as interest rates fall, the lender who holds high interest rate securities enjoys a capital gain. This is the same kind of capital gain that was discussed with respect to the firm's holdings of marketable securities in Chapter 5. When the borrower is allowed to repay rapidly with no penalty, the lender loses the capital gain. In effect, the penalty offsets the loss of capital gain.

The rigidity of long-term debt may be viewed in terms of its effects on leverage. When the rate of return on assets falls below the interest rate, the firm with short-term debt can revise its balance sheet to avoid the negative leverage effects more easily than can the firm with long-term debt. The short-term debt can be rapidly repaid, and the composition and quantity of assets altered so as to, at least, moderate the effects of negative leverage. The firm with long-term debt can do the same thing, but it will usually have to pay a penalty for early repayment. The penalty may be large enough to reduce the present value of net worth by more than will the effects of the negative leverage. In this case, the firm will suffer with the negative leverage as the lesser of two evils. Even if the penalties are not this large, the price of getting rid of negative leverage will be larger for the firm with long-term debt than for the firm with short-term debt.

COSTS OF FLOTATION

Table 9-3 shows the cost of flotation of long-term debt issued to the public as a percentage of the gross selling price of the debt, classified by the size of the issue. It is readily apparent that large issues are relatively cheaper to sell than are small issues. Yet, the cheapest issue costs over 1 per cent of the gross proceeds of the securities sale.

Table 9-3

COST OF FLOTATION AS PERCENTAGE OF GROSS PROCEEDS
FOR BONDS, NOTES, AND DEBENTURES REGISTERED WITH
THE SECURITIES AND EXCHANGE COMMISSION,
1951, 1953, AND 1955, BY SIZE OF ISSUE

Size of Issue (In Millions of Dollars)	Flotation Cost as Per cent of Proceeds	Number of Issues
Under 0.5	—	0
0.5– 0.99	11.5	5
1.0– 1.99	8.2	15
2.0– 4.99	3.8	29
5.0– 9.99	1.8	44
10.0–19.99	1.5	72
20.0–49.99	1.3	79
50.0 and over	1.2	21

Source: Table 5, *Cost of Flotation of Corporate Securities, 1951–1955*, Securities and Exchange Commission, US. Gov. Printing Office, 1957.

To my knowledge, there are no comparable flotation cost data available for short-term debt issues. Since most short-term debt is directly placed, however, we can get a rough idea of the magnitudes probably involved by considering the flotation costs of long-term direct placements of debt. Table 9-4 compares flotation costs for private and public placements of long-term debt by size of issue for the five years immediately following World War II. The data on the public issues may be compared with the similar data for 1951, 1953, and 1955 shown in Table 9-3. Considering that the size classes are not the same in both tables and that the data on the very small issues, say below $2 million, are not reliable because of the few observations, costs as a percentage of gross proceeds of flotation appear to be surprisingly stable.

Table 9-4

COMPARISON OF COST OF FLOTATION
FOR PRIVATELY PLACED AND PUBLICLY OFFERED SECURITIES
BONDS, NOTES, AND DEBENTURES OFFERED BY INVESTMENT BANKERS
(PER CENT OF PROCEEDS)

Size of Issue ($000)	PRIVATELY PLACED ISSUES 1947, 1949–'50				PUBLICLY OFFERED ISSUES[1] 1945–'49			
	No. of Issues	Total Costs	Compen- sation	Other Expenses[2]	No. of Issues	Total Costs	Compen- sation	Other Expenses
0–499	145	3.05	1.69	1.37	4	10.21	7.34	2.88
500–999	162	2.24	1.29	0.96	8	8.72	5.51	3.21
1,000–2,999[3]	207	1.45	0.37	0.58	12	5.61	3.52	2.09
3,000–4,999[4]	51	1.13	0.61	0.52	61	2.69	1.41	1.28
5,000–9,999	68	0.89	0.55	0.34	72	1.91	0.88	1.03
10,000–24,999[5] ..	49	0.54	0.31	0.23	77	1.72	0.99	0.73
25,000 and over[6]	30	0.42	0.22	0.19	126	1.15	0.72	0.43

[1]Data taken from, "Cost of Flotation 1945–1949." Slightly different size intervals, as noted in footnotes 3—6, were used in that compilation but are close enough for purposes of comparison.
[2]Covers only issues sold by agents or finders.
[3]The data on public offerings cover issues between $1 million and $2 million in size.
[4]The data on public offerings cover issues between $2 million and $5 million in size.
[5]The data on public offerings cover issues between $10 million and $20 million in size.
[6]The data on public offerings cover issues between $20 million and over in size.
Source: *Privately Placed Securities—Cost of Flotation*, Securities and Exchange Commission, Washington, D.C., 1952.

The major difference between the costs of flotation for private placements and public placements is compensation paid to the investment banker. In a public issue, the investment banker often underwrites the issue, i.e., insures the issuer of receiving a given price. This important and risky function is not performed for private placements. In the private placement, the investment banker is a finder of customers for the securities, i.e., simply a salesman. Normally, an investment banker is not used in a short-term private placement, and so there would be no compensation. However, most of the other expenses would be similar for private placements of either short- or long-term variety. If anything, we would expect the costs of floating a short-term private placement to be somewhat less than the other expenses of the long-term issue because the risk to the lender is somewhat less for short-run loans.

The cost-of-flotation advantage of short-term debt can turn into a disadvantage fairly rapidly, if the financing is more or less continuous. A firm which finances $1 million for a year using 30-day notes enters into 12 separate financing arrangements within the year. If the flotation cost per arrangement is as low as 0.2 per cent of the financing, the firm will incur $24,000 total flotation costs over the year, equivalent to about a 2.4 per cent cost of flotation. If this continues over a five-year period, the firm will have spent $120,000 in flotation costs. Even if we reduce the funds by discounting to find the present value of the flotation costs spread over five years, it is likely that the present value will exceed the flotation costs of even a publicly offered debt long-term issue.

CASH BALANCE EFFECTS

Recall in Exhibit 5-4 that the repayment of debt, both for the bank loan and the term loan, was counted as part of the monthly cash outflows. For the month of June, the firm would have generated a net cash surplus had it not been for the $200,000 term-loan amortization payment. As a result, the firm had to borrow $170,000 in June and incurred ordering and carrying costs totaling $4,700 for that one month. Without the term loan, the average balance for the month of June would have been $15,000 instead of $85,000.

The point is that, since debt repayment is a cash outflow, the firm that finances its cash deficits by short-term means increases the average cash balance, raising costs and reducing the expected value of net worth. The following example may help. Imagine a firm which budgets a January cash deficit of $100,000, but has cash in-flows equal to cash outflows for the rest of the year. It should be noted that many factors contribute to a cash deficit, including payment for materials, labor, acquisition of plant and equipment, payment of dividends, etc. The firm may decide to borrow short-term and, when asked the purpose of the loan, is likely to point only to the short-term factors contributing to the deficit, such as payments for materials. The inventory may even be used as collateral or security for the loan. However, the operations of the firm will not generate repayment of the short-term loan within the year.

To make the case extreme, assume the short-term loan is for 30-days. This means that the firm will have to order funds from some source, perhaps different sources, not once but 12 times. The ordering costs (= flotation costs) have already been discussed. Ignoring speculative and precautionary motives for holding cash, the firm would have had a $50,000 transactions cash balance for January and a zero average cash balance for the remaining 11 months if the loan were long-term. With the 30-day loan, the firm will have to hold an average cash balance of almost $50,000 each month. If the loan were for three months, the firm would have an average balance of $50,000 in January, nothing in February or March, $50,000 in April, nothing in May and June, etc. With a six-month loan, the firm would have a zero cash balance in all months but January and July. The shorter the term of the loan, the larger the cash balance, the larger the costs of carrying cash for the year, and the smaller the expected value of net worth.

This problem is analogous to that faced by the United States Treasury in managing the public debt. With a good part of the permanent debt in short-term securities, the Treasury is almost continually refinancing the debt, which of course is just what happens to the firm when it has to replace short-term debt. The turnover costs for the Treasury are sufficiently high that the

Treasury has been trying to extend the average maturity of the public debt since the end of World War II. Since the Treasury must have funds to repay the old debt prior to the maturity of the debt, new debt is sold prior to the maturity of existing debt, raising the average cash balance held by the Treasury above what it would be with a longer term public debt.

In recent years, the Treasury has on occasion attempted to persuade holders of maturing debt to accept new debt in return. This sharply reduces the costs of the new debt and economizes on the average cash balance. The firm may be able to persuade lenders to renew short-term obligations, or the firm may persuade a commercial bank to extend a *line of credit*. In either case, flotation costs are sharply reduced, and the necessary cash balance for short-term financing is also reduced.

The line of credit is an arrangement whereby the firm makes a single formal application for a maximum amount of short-term funds to be extended at various times over a year. The bank is not obligated to extend these funds, but most banks view the agreement as binding unless the condition of the borrower changes radically. The firm is usually required to submit a planned borrowing and repayment schedule reflecting the kind of information found in Exhibit 5–6. If the agreement is made, funds are granted with a minimum of notification, providing the firm stays somewhere close to the schedule. The firm pays interest on the funds actually borrowed, but usually is charged a fee by the bank for the line of credit arrangement. The line of credit agreement is not a very good substitute for long-term financing since the lender anticipates that the arrangement will end within a year with all loans paid up.

Similar arrangements can be made with sales and commercial finance companies, by which the firm can use inventory or accounts receivable collateral as security for short-term loans, replacing inventory and accounts as they are sold and collected. Both the line of credit arrangements with commercial banks and the revolving security arrangements are sometimes called *revolving credits*. They serve to reduce the costs of flotation and large cash balances usually associated with continuous short-term financing. In addition, the firm may feel that there is less risk of an abrupt stoppage to the availability of short-term funds with revolving credit arrangements than with one-shot short-term financing agreements.

WORKING CAPITAL EFFECTS Given an asset portfolio, the choice between long- and short-term financing will affect the firm's working capital position. Creditors are concerned about working capital because it is a gauge of the firm's ability to pay currently maturing obligations. The short-term creditors are concerned because they want to be paid. The long-term creditors and owners are concerned because failure to pay currently maturing obligations can place all financial claims in jeopardy. And the managers are concerned because they presumably are interested in maintaining the firm as a going concern. To see the effects of the term-structure decision on working capital, let us return to the example which was used in discussing the transactions cash balance in Chapter 5. Exhibit 9-1 shows the beginning and ending balance sheets for the firm in 1964. The ending balance sheet reflects all the plans shown in Exhibits 5-1, 5-2, 5-3, 5-4, and 5-6, as well as those discussed in the text in Chapter 5.

Exhibit 9-1

**XYZ MANUFACTURING CORPORATION,
ACTUAL BALANCE SHEET FOR DECEMBER 31, 1963,
AND PROJECTED BALANCE SHEET FOR DECEMBER 31, 1964**
(In Thousands of Dollars)

ASSETS	DEC. 31, 1963		DEC. 31, 1964	
Cash		0		95
Accounts receivable		1,860		2,220
Merchandise inventory		2,140		2,140
Total current assets		4,000		4,455
Gross fixed assets	10,000		12,530	
Reserve for depreciation	2,000		3,970	
Net fixed assets		8,000		8,560
Total assets		12,000		13,015

LIABILITIES AND NET WORTH				
Accounts payable		600		700
Wages payable		250		315
Taxes payable		135		148
Interest payable		114		114
Dividends payable		25		25
Short-term bank loan		50		0
Current portion of term loan		400		400
Total current liabilities		1,574		1,702
Term loan payable		2,000		1,600
Total liabilities		3,574		3,302
Paid-in capital	4,000		4,000	
Retained earnings	4,426		4,473	
Net worth		8,426		8,473
Required new financing	—	—	—	1,240
Total liabilities, net worth and new financing		12,000		13,015

The new financing required is the sum of the annual cash flow ($1,145 thousand from Exhibit 5-4) plus the increase in cash for December. Another way of looking at the new financing required is

Increase in current assets	$	+455,000
Increase in net fixed assets		+560,000
Increase in total assets	$	1,015,000
Less increase in current liabilities	.. −	128,000
Increase in net worth	−	47,000
Plus decrease in long-term debt	.... +	400,000
Required new financing	$	1,240,000

It should be noted that over half of the increase in current assets was financed by the automatic increase of trade debt and accruals. The financial problem is caused by the increase in assets and the decrease in long-term debt. By showing the increase in *net* fixed assets, we are saying that depreciation funds financed $1,970,000 of the gross fixed asset expansion, which totaled $2,530,000.

The working capital measures for the firm at the beginning of the year were

Working capital	$2,426,000
Current ratio	2.54
Quick ratio	1.18

The working capital measures for the end of the year will depend on how the firm decides to finance the changes in the balance sheet. It makes little difference for working capital purposes whether the firm finances through equity or long-term debt. It makes a good deal of difference whether the firm uses long-term financing or short-term financing. Look at the effects of three different methods of acquiring the new financing:

	All Short-term	*Half Short-term*	*All Long-term*
Working capital	$1,513,000	$2,133,000	$2,753,000
Current ratio	1.51	1.92	2.62
Quick ratio	0.79	1.00	1.36

If the ratios and level of working capital for the beginning of the year are considered minimally acceptable to creditors, the firm may have little alternative but to use long-term sources, not necessarily debt, for the new financing. However, creditors, owners, and managers may be willing to accept lower ratios. In this event, the firm will be able to use a good deal of short-term financing if it wishes.

The phrase "if it wishes" is very important. The effect of the financing method on working capital operates as a restriction, not a goal. The firm does not usually wish to achieve some level of working capital. Rather, there is some level of working capital, or current ratio, which it must exceed. Thus, the firm may not use short-term debt for reasons having to do with flotation costs, additional cash costs, or the risk associated with short-term debt renewals, even though it could use short-term debt according to the working capital criterion.

RISK AND THE TERM-STRUCTURE CHOICE   Ignoring the cost factors, the firm which decides between long-term and short-term debt is deciding between inflexibility, on the one hand, and the risk of being cut off from desirable credit sources, on the other.

Long-term Debt and Inflexibility. Suppose the firm finds it advisable to reduce the level of asset holdings. Some of the current liabilities such as accounts payable and wages payable will automatically be reduced as the firm curtails inventory investment. The proceeds from the reduction of inventory investment will be used partly to pay these liabilities. The funds generated by the liquidation of assets can also be used to repay other short-term liabilities such as bank loans, loans from commercial finance companies, etc., as these liabilities come due.

With long-term debt, the firm has three alternatives. It can use the proceeds from liquidating assets to repay the debt before it is due, and incur the penalties for so doing. It can invest the proceeds from liquidating the assets in cash or securities and pay the long-term debt as it comes due. Or, it can retain the asset investment, liquidating the assets only as the long-term debt comes due.

Each of these alternatives may be costly, i.e., reduce the present value of net worth. The first alternative clearly reduces net worth by forcing the firm to make larger debt payments than it would with short-term debt. The second alternative will be costly if the expected gross present value of investment in cash or securities is less than the investment cost of these financial assets. And the final alternative may be costly if the expected net present value of the earning assets is negative, i.e., the gross present value is less than the cash sacrificed. Ignoring risk, the firm will choose the alternative which involves the least loss, or maximum gain. However, the choice is apt to be different with long-term debt in the capital structure than without it.

This problem is one that may occur periodically with the firm that operates seasonally either because of the nature of demand or because of supply conditions. A firm faced with seasonal variations in the level of asset holdings can use long-term debt to finance seasonal asset levels if it is willing to shift from real assets to financial assets, such as cash at the seasonal low. Since the rate of return on liquid financial assets may well be lower than the interest rate on long-term debt, this particular means of financing seasonal assets can become quite expensive. The tendency will be for short-term assets to be financed by short-term sources of funds.

Problems of Short-term Debt. The firm which relies on short-term debt financing may escape the problems listed above, only to encounter other problems. Consider a firm which finances inventory through trade credit, accruals, and short-term bank loans. The trade credit and accruals will revolve automatically as the firm employs workers and orders materials. The short-term loan will require some formal request for funds made to the commercial bank, which request may be rejected or the size of the new loan reduced. The refusal or reduction could reflect changes that have taken place in the creditworthiness of the firm, the condition of the lending bank, or the general economic environment.

Whatever the reason, the firm would be forced to adjust its capital structure and/or its asset portfolio. The simplest adjustment would be to find another bank or other short-term lender. But it may be necessary to incur higher interest costs and/or service charges, particularly if the new source of funds requires that the inventory be used as security, in order to attract the new funds. On the asset side, the firm may be able to divert cash outflows from the purchase of other assets or the payment of dividends to the financing of inventory. Or, the firm may have sufficient cash or other liquid assets in precautionary and speculative balances to finance the inventory.

If the firm had been at an optimal balance sheet position with the bank loan, the removal of the bank loan should result in a less desirable balance sheet however the firm decides to replace the bank loan. The reason for this is that the replacement balance sheet was available to the firm before it originally decided on using the short-term bank loan—it was available, but rejected.

If the firm uses short-term funds to finance long-term assets, it runs the risk of interest rates rising. As the short-term funds come due, they must be replaced with higher cost funds, reducing the expected value of net worth. To be sure, if interest rates fall, the firm can enjoy a windfall gain by financing long-lived assets with short-term funds. However, it would be quite rational for the firm to eschew interest rate speculation and prefer to concentrate on profitable management of its assets. The result would be that long-term assets will tend to be financed by long-term sources of funds.

EQUITY ISSUES
AND INTERNAL FUNDS

As a permanent means of financing, equity issues and internal funds may be compared with long-term debt. Stock, depreciation, and retained earnings are not as risky as long-term debt in terms of negative leverage. As shown in Table 9-5, stock issues have substantially higher flotation costs than debt. There are no flotation costs for internal funds.

STOCK FLEXIBILITY

In terms of flexibility, common stock may be more of a problem than long-term debt. If the firm issues common stock, the proceeds of which are invested in assets that turn out to be insufficiently profitable to maintain earnings per share, the firm has diluted the ownership interest. This is a particularly serious problem if earnings per share would have been higher had the financing been done through internal funds or debt. Correction of the capital structure will require that the asset investment be liquidated and the proceeds used to buy up the "excess" shares, that the stock financing be replaced by internal funds, or that the asset investment be liquidated and reinvested in more profitable assets. If the last alternative is not available, the firm must somehow reduce the number of outstanding common shares or suffer with an unhappy group of stockholders.

Reduction of common shares outstanding is done by purchasing shares

Table 9-5

COST OF FLOTATION
REGISTERED ISSUES OFFERED TO THE GENERAL PUBLIC
CLASSIFIED BY SIZE OF ISSUE AND TYPE OF SECURITY,
1951, 1953, AND 1955
(Per cent of Proceeds)

Size of Issue (In Millions of Dollars)	Preferred Stock	Common Stock
COST OF FLOTATION		
Under 0.6	—	27.15
0.5– 0.9	12.63	21.76
1.0– 1.9	8.07	13.58
2.0– 4.9	4.88	9.97
5.0– 9.9	3.72	6.17
10.0–19.9	2.92	4.66
20.0–49.9	3.20	5.37
50.0 and over	2.51	—
Total	4.34	10.28
COMPENSATION		
Under 0.5	—	20.99
0.5– 0.9	8.67	17.12
1.0– 1.9	5.98	11.27
2.0– 4.9	3.83	8.47
5.0– 9.9	2.93	5.31
10.0–19.9	2.40	4.20
20.0–49.9	2.84	4.98
50.0 and over	2.12	—
Total[1]	3.34	8.75
EXPENSES		
Under 0.5	—	6.16
0.5–0.9	3.96	4.64
1.0–1.9	2.09	2.31
2.0– 4.9	1.05	1.50
5.0– 9.9	0.79	0.86
10.0–19.9	0.52	0.46
20.0–49.9	0.35	0.38
50.0 and over	0.38	—
Total[1]	1.22	1.85

[1]Median percentages. Means of all issues are not used because they are distorted by the weight of large issues for which costs in relation to proceeds are small.

NOTE: Per cents have been rounded and will not necessarily add to totals.

Source: *Cost of Flotation of Corporate Securities*, 1951–1955, Securities and Exchange Commission, U.S. Gov. Printing Office, 1957.

on the market or by soliciting offers of stock from stockholders. The latter approach may be favored since it can result in a lower price per purchased share than if the firm bids up the price on the market.

Firms are reluctant to become involved in the purchase of their own stock, which is called *treasury stock* when repurchased, because of insufficient profitability. A firm that redeems debt before maturity may do so because of insufficient profitability, but the ability to repay debt can be interpreted as a sign of financial strength. The repurchase of common stock, however, is not viewed favorably. Indeed, firms that purchase their own shares are often viewed with suspicion because this has been a device by which unscrupulous promoters have, in years past, bilked the company and its stockholders of funds. For example, stock can be purchased by the corporation at a price of $100 and then issued to a majority stockholder or favored member of the management group at a price of, say, $50 with the firm absorbing the $50 loss. Some states forbid corporations to deal in their own securities. Most states do not allow a corporation to buy its own stock if the accounting value of net worth is negative.

FLEXIBILITY
OF INTERNAL FUNDS

Internal financing in one sense is considerably less flexible than either debt or stock. The amount of internal financing that the firm can use is limited ultimately by the amount of internal funds generated. The firm which generates earnings of $100,000 after taxes and $200,000 in depreciation has a maximum of $300,000 of internal funds available. Internal funds cannot be raised in the way stock funds and debt funds can.

On the other hand, when the firm wants to reduce asset investments, internal financing is more flexible than other sources, with the possible exception of short-term debt. The firm can reduce the amount of internal financing in its capital structure simply by using the funds, made available through the liquidation of assets, to increase dividend payments. As long as the retained earnings account in the balance sheet is positive, the dividends can be charged against it. If the firm wishes to reduce asset investments and internal financing beyond the point at which cumulated retained earnings are exhausted, the dividends are charged against paid-in capital (capital stock and capital surplus accounts) and are labeled *liquidation dividends.*

CONCLUSION

In the absence of risk, the capital structure choice would be relatively simple. Given the expected value of the asset portfolio, the firm would choose that combination of short-term debt, long-term debt, stock issue, and internal funds which would maximize the expected value of net worth. Leverage, flotation costs, the effects of the debt structure on the cash balance, interest rates, and the term structure of the asset portfolio—all these play a role in the decision.

In a dynamic world, the capital structure choice leads not to a single result, but to a range of possible results. The firm chooses a balance sheet today, but tomorrow's balance sheet may be quite different. This is not to say that the immediate choice is unimportant. In the last two chapters, I have stressed the point that the alternatives available to the firm in the future are limited by the choices it makes today. Debt financing today may mean that the firm foregoes debt financing next year because the debt/equity ratio has been pushed to its limit. Long-term financing today may force the firm to retain a given aggregate level of asset investment tomorrow.

When the firm makes its capital structure choice, it is really making two choices. The first is for an immediate balance sheet. The second is for a range of choices of future balance sheets. A good decision is one which considers both the immediate effects and possible future effects. The capital structure choice thus is analogous to the asset choice under risk, in which the firm will not necessarily attempt to achieve the highest level of expected value of net worth, but will choose a capital structure providing the most desirable mixture of return and risk available to it.

SELECTED REFERENCES

Durand, D.: "*Basic Yields of Corporate Bonds*, 1900–1942, National Bureau of Economic Research, New York, 1942.

———: "A Quarterly Series of Corporate Basic Yields, 1952–'57, and Some Attendant Reservations," *Journal of Finance*, Sept., 1958.

———, and W. Winn: *Basic Yields of Bonds*, 1926–1947: *Their Measurement and Pattern*, National Bureau of Economic Research, New York, 1947.

Securities Exchange Commission, *Cost of Flotation of Corporate Securities*, 1951–1955, U.S. Gov. Printing Office, 1957.

———, *Privately Placed Securities—Cost of Flotation*, U.S. Gov. Printing Office, 1952.

The Cost of Capital
and the Balance Sheet Decision

10

The cost of capital plays a very important role in determining the asset portfolio. No asset will be acquired unless the future returns of that asset have a gross present value in excess of the cost of the asset. The gross present value is determined by discounting the future returns, with the cost of capital as the discount rate. In this way, the cost of capital serves as a cutoff rate in evaluating asset investments.

Until now, we have not been ready to enter a detailed discussion of the determinants of the cost of capital and have made do with a simple, though accurate, definition. The cost of capital has been defined as the rate of return which the firm must earn on its investments so as to leave undamaged the interests of the stockholder. In this chapter, that definition will not be altered, simply amplified.

The three main questions that will be investigated in this chapter are: What is meant by "the interests of the stockholders?" What are the forces that will impel management to operate in the stockholders' interests when the corporation is not controlled by a dominant stockholder or group of stockholders? What are the problems encountered in measuring the cost of capital? In addition to answering these questions, an attempt will be made to bring together the materials on the debt/equity problem and the term characteristics of the capital structure to see whether the capital structure has an effect on the cost of capital and the choice of asset portfolio.

THE COST OF CAPITAL
AND THE OWNER-MANAGER

Before turning to the complex case of the firm with many stockholders, none of whom have significant control over management, consider the corporation in which ownership and management are blended in one man. To make the case more directly applicable to the case of many stockholders, assume that the owner-manager functions purely at the policy level and draws no salary. His decisions will be guided by what he believes is best for himself.

The household-owner has a balance sheet, and he is assumed to make decisions which will optimize the value of the balance sheet to him. We shall ignore the capital structure of his balance sheet, except to note that he can legitimately view corporate indebtedness as different than personal indebtedness, even though he is the sole owner. The reason for this is that his personal liability is limited for corporate indebtedness, whereas it is complete for personal debt.

For that part of the household asset portfolio made up of nonfinancial assets, such as a house and durable consumer goods, the choice of acquisitions is based on tastes, cost, and the income of the household. Financial assets, aside from transactions and precautionary cash balances, are held because of yield. The yield is attractive because it permits the household to acquire consumer goods in the future. In effect, the purchase of financial assets is really the purchase of future consumer goods and services. The purchase cost of financial assets is the sacrifice of current consumer goods and services. Viewed this way, the yield on financial assets is

$$\frac{\text{increase in future consumption}}{\text{decrease in current consumption}} - 1.$$

Although this yield would generally be expected to be greater than zero for the exchange of consumption over time, there are cases in which it may be negative. Professional athletes, who earn high salaries currently but anticipate a decline in future income, may prefer to curtail already high levels of current consumption and transfer this to the future, even if the quantity of future goods gained is less than the quantity of current goods sacrificed, i.e., even if the yield is negative.

When financial assets are viewed this way, they fit into the theory of demand very easily. The demand for additional future goods (= financial assets) will depend upon the quantity of current goods, the price of current goods, the quantity of future goods which the household already has, and the price of additional future goods. The larger the quantity of current consumer goods, the more likely it is that there will be a demand for more future goods, which means that the rich are more likely to invest than the poor. On the other hand, if there is a large supply of future goods already on the household's balance sheet, the demand for added quantities will be less than if only a small quantity of future goods are owned, and the reverse. Finally, all other things equal, if the price of future goods relative to current goods prices is high, the demand for future goods will be less than if the relative prices favored future goods. Since the price of future goods is roughly the inverse of the yield on financial assets, this means that the higher the yields on financial assets, the greater the demand.

Risk adds another dimension to the demand for financial assets. Financial assets for which the variance of the distribution of conditional returns is small will sell at higher prices, i.e., lower yields, than will financial assets with very large variances. Since the household deals with the risk of the entire asset portfolio, the problem is not just of variances, but of covariances. Financial assets with moderate variances will sell at higher or lower yields depending upon the covariances of the financial asset with all other assets. If the distribution of returns for the financial asset is highly correlated with the returns of other assets in the portfolio, its contribution to risk will be high, and the household would require a higher yield in order to buy it than if its returns were weakly or negatively correlated with the returns of other assets.

With respect to a specific financial asset, the household will consider all these factors. If risk and the substitution between current consumption goods and future consumption goods are equal, as between two financial assets, the household will choose the one with the higher yield. More generally, ignoring risk and substitution, the household will invest in a financial asset only if it will yield at a rate at least equal to the rate available on alternative investments. The yield will have to be higher if the asset adds to the total risk of the asset portfolio, if the household already has a large quantity of financial assets, or if the prices of current consumption goods are low relative to the prices of financial assets.

MEASURING
THE COST OF CAPITAL

The main variables mentioned will above all affect the cost of capital. To repeat, these variables are the prices of all other goods, future or current, the quantities of all other goods, the tastes of the household, and the risk added to the portfolio by the financial asset. The latter is a function not only of variance of the financial asset in question, but of the covariances between it and all other assets. An analysis including all of these variables, even for a single household, is enormously complex. Therefore, some very strong simplifying assumptions will be made initially. They are:

1. There is an absence of all risk on all possible expenditures of the household.

2. Yields on alternative expenditures or investments are constant.
3. The composition of the household's balance sheet will not affect its demand for financial assets.

The first assumption removes the need for considering the effect of the financial asset on the risk of the portfolio. The second assumption allows us to ignore changes which take place in the market places of the economy. And the third assumption allows us to ignore the household's tastes as these are affected by increasing or decreasing investment in the firm. Later, these assumptions can be removed.

If the household is to buy the firm at all, if it is to make the initial investment necessary for it to become a household-owner, the present value of the returns of the firm must at least equal the cost C of buying the firm. The rate at which the returns will be discounted is determined by the owner on the basis of his tastes and alternate opportunities. The rate will be defined as i_K, and the returns as E. The cost of capital will be i. Thus, using the same formulation as was used for fixed assets in Chapter 2,

$$C \leq E_1 \frac{1}{1 + i_K} + E_2 \frac{1}{(1 + i_K)^2} + \cdots + E_n \frac{1}{(1 + i_K)^n}.$$

This is rather a cumbersome formulation for what will be done in this section and can be simplified if we assume that all E's are equal, that they are received continuously over the years and not just at the end of each, and, finally, that n, the life of the investment, is very large. With these assumptions, made just to simplify calculations, we can approximate the minimum present value above as

$$C = \frac{E}{i_K}$$

The cost of capital is the ratio of required earnings to investment and, in this case, equals the capitalization rate, i.e.,

$$i = \frac{E}{C} = i_K$$

External Equity Investment. If the household is to be the sole owner of the firm, external equity investment can come only if the household invests more money in the firm. Using b as the rate of change in earnings, so that bE is the increase in earnings, the household will make the added investment only if it promises to yield additional earnings such that the present value of the added earnings equals the added funds invested. Thus,

$$C = \frac{bE}{i_K}.$$

And the cost of capital, which, in this and all succeeding cases, is the ratio of the required change in earnings to the change in investment, is

$$i = \frac{bE}{C} = i_K.$$

It will also be of interest to define the required rate of increase in earnings. Solving the equation for b, we have

$$b = \frac{i_K C}{E}.$$

Retained Earnings. Although, until now, it has not been made explicit, all earnings are assumed to be paid out as dividends. If the household-owner considers retaining in the firm a portion of earnings, mE, the reduction of value in the household's holdings will equal the present value of the retained earnings. In other words, the cost of retaining earnings is

$$C = \frac{mE}{i_K}.$$

Earnings must increase by enough that the value of the holdings do not decline, or

$$\frac{bE}{i_K} = \frac{mE}{i_K}.$$

Solving for the cost of capital, we have

$$i = \frac{mE}{C} = i_K,$$

and for the required rate of increase in earnings

$$b = m .$$

As an aside, it is worth noting that the gross present value of the firm to the household, before dividend reduction, is

$$V = \frac{E}{i_K}.$$

After dividend reduction, the value is

$$V = \frac{E}{i_K} + \frac{mE}{i_K},$$

since

$$\frac{mE}{i_K} = \frac{bE}{i_K}.$$

The first term in the value expression represents dividends. The second term represents retained earnings. Both terms are used to determine value. The significance of this, which really seems obvious, is that you will often encounter debates in the literature of finance between proponents of an "earnings approach" and of a "dividends approach" for determining stock values. Both are important.

The effect of a differential between the way in which dividends and capital gains are taxed as personal income can affect the required growth in earnings. If capital gains are taxed at a rate g that is lower than the rate at which dividends are taxed, t, the growth rate of earnings is modified as follows: The capital gain is bE/i_k, and after taxes, it is

$$\left[1 - g\right]\frac{bE}{i_K}.$$

The after-tax reduction in dividends is

$$\left[1 - t\right]\frac{mE}{i_K}.$$

For the after-tax capital gain to equal the after-tax reduction in dividends,

$$\left[1 - g\right]\frac{bE}{i_K} = \left[1 - t\right]\frac{mE}{i_K}.$$

Solving for b, we have

$$b = \frac{1 - t}{1 - g}\left[\frac{mE}{E}\right].$$

If the tax on dividends is greater than the tax on capital gains, the ratio of $1 - t/1 - g$ will be less than unity, and this will reduce b below its level on a before-tax basis. This situation encourages the retention of earnings. In the case of large numbers of owners, who have many different tax rates for their personal incomes, it is unlikely that the tax differential effect can be used with any degree of precision.

Debt. If the firm should borrow an amount D at an interest rate d, assuming the firm would refinance the debt so that, in effect, it is a permanent loan, earnings available to owners will fall by the amount of the interest payments. The value of the owner's holdings will decline by

$$\frac{dD}{i_K} = C,$$

the present value of the interest payments. This then is the cost of debt. Earnings must rise so that the present value of the increase in earnings at least equals the cost. Thus,

$$\frac{bE}{i_K} = \frac{dD}{i_K}.$$

The cost of capital is

$$i = \frac{bE}{dD/i_K} = i_K,$$

keeping in mind that

$$\frac{dD}{i_K} = C.$$

The required growth in earnings is

$$b = \frac{dD}{E}.$$

REMOVING THE ASSUMPTIONS The main effect of removing the three assumptions made at the beginning of this section is to allow i_K to vary so that $i_K \neq i$.

If E is not certain, the household-owner will treat it as a random variable subject to a probability distribution. The expected value of the distribution, $\bar{E}$, will be used for determining present value. Now, however, the present value will have a variance or risk measure. When an investment is made by the firm, regardless of how it is financed, the variance of the expected returns will usually be affected. If the variance increases, the risk of the household's investment increases, and the owner will require a higher rate of return than before the investment was made. It is, of course, possible that the new investment will actually reduce the risk of the over-all investment if the new investment's returns are weakly correlated with the existing returns. If you recall the discussion in Chapter 6, most assets for a firm in a given area of activity are more or less highly correlated, so that the reduction in risk will usually not occur through the covariance effect, but only if the new investment itself is less risky than the existing investments. Other effects of risk on the cost of capital are associated with specific methods of financing and will be handled under separate headings.

By removing the second assumption, yields on all alternate assets for the household are constant, the possibility that i_k will vary and not equal i arises again. If alternate yields rise, the household will require that the yield from the investment in the firm also rise. Should alternate yields fall, the cost of capital for the firm falls. There are no effects on i_k associated with specific methods of financing that arise from relaxing the second assumption.

Relaxation of the third assumption, that the composition of the household's balance sheet will not affect its demand for financial assets, again leads to the possibility of variations in i_k and between i_k and i. If the firm grows, regardless of how the growth is financed, the value of the household-owner's equity in the firm will also grow. Assume that it grows more rapidly than the rest of the household's asset portfolio. In this case, the owner may find that, at the given yield, he has enough invested in the firm, or perhaps too much for his tastes, and would prefer holding less investment in the firm and more in other things. The required yield from the firm must rise if the owner is to accept more growth. On the other hand, the holdings of other assets may grow more rapidly than the equity interest in the firm, and this may lead to a reduction in the cost of capital.

There exists the possibility of a combined *risk-growth in portfolio* effect. Even if it is assumed that the added assets for the firm are no more risky than the existing assets, the larger holdings of the owner may increase the risk of his personal asset portfolio. As the owner's equity share grows, the added value of the equity asset is perfectly correlated with the old value of the equity asset. As the equity asset grows then, the owner's personal asset portfolio loses diversification, i.e., becomes more risky. This is not a necessary result since the equity asset may be much less risky than the other assets in the household portfolio, or it may be negatively correlated with the other assets. Nonetheless, the added risk is a possibility, and the effect would be that the owner would require a higher yield for additions to the firm.

EXTERNAL EQUITY FINANCING WITH CHANGING
As before, the owner is considering investing more of his money in the firm. If he does this, his investment in the firm grows as part of his personal asset portfolio, and, because of his tastes and or because of the loss of diversification, he will invest more in the firm only at a higher yield, i_k', on the total investment.

If the rate had not been increased, the minimally acceptable value of the owner's investment, including the added investment would have been

$$\frac{\bar{E} + i_K C}{i_K} = V.$$

Now, the added earnings $i_k C$ will be insufficient to maintain value. Instead, we have

$$\frac{\bar{E} + b\bar{E}}{i_K'} = V.$$

By what rate must earnings increase at the new capitalization rate if the value of holdings, including the added investment, is not to decline? To determine this, set the old value equation equal to the new value, and solve for b.

$$\frac{\bar{E} + i_K C}{i_K} = \frac{\bar{E} + b\bar{E}}{i'_K}.$$

$$b = \frac{i'_k(\bar{E} + i_k C)}{i_k \bar{E}} - 1$$

The required rate of increase before the increase in the capitalization rate was

$$b = \frac{i_K C}{\bar{E}}.$$

The numerator of the new formulation will be larger than the numerator of the old formulation when $i'_k > i_k$. The denominator of the new fraction is smaller than the old if $i_k < 1$, which would be normal. With a larger numerator and a smaller denominator, the required rate of increase in earnings will be larger with i'_k than it was with i_k.

But what is the cost of capital? Is it i_k? Or, i'_k? Actually, it depends on both. The cost of capital is the ratio of the required increase in earnings to the cost of the additional funds invested, i.e.

$$i = \frac{b\bar{E}}{C}.$$

With an increased capitalization rate, we substitute the term for b given above so that

$$i = \frac{\left[\frac{i'_k(\bar{E} + i_k C)}{i_k \bar{E}} - 1 \right] \bar{E}}{C}.$$

If there had been no change in the capitalization rate, the equation for the cost of capital could be simplified to show that $i = i_k$. With the change, the greater the increase in the capitalization rate, the larger will be the increase in the cost of capital.

Consider the following small arithmetic example where $\bar{E} = \$1$, $i_k = 0.1$, $i'_k = 0.2$, and C, the added investment \$10. The value of the total investment before the rise in the capitalization rate would have been

$$\frac{\$1 + 0.1(\$10)}{0.1} = \$20,$$

and the required increase in earnings, $b\bar{E}$, would have been \$1.

With the new capitalization rate, the increase in earnings will have to be \$3 to yield the same value since

$$\frac{\$1 + 3(\$1)}{0.2} = \$20.$$

The cost of capital under the old capitalization rate was

$$0.1 = \frac{1(\$1)}{\$10}.$$

Under the new rate, the required increase in earnings is $3, though the cost of the investment is still $10, so the cost of capital is

$$0.3 = \frac{3(\$1)}{\$10}.$$

which is higher than i_k or i_k'. (It is just coincidence that the cost of capital happens to be the sum of the old and the new capitalization rates. Try it by changing i_k' to 0.3.)

EARNINGS RETENTION AND A CHANGING CAPITALIZATION RATE

The retention of earnings is the equivalent of added investment in the firm, if personal tax differences are ignored. Therefore, the household-owner could require a higher capitalization as a result of earnings retention for the same reasons that would apply in the case of increased external investment. Assume i_k rises to i_k'. Using the same approach as above, we first set the value of the firm with i_k equal to the value with a change in i_k.

$$\frac{\bar{E} + b\bar{E}}{i_k'} = \frac{\bar{E} + m\bar{E}}{i_k}.$$

Solving for b,

$$b = \frac{i_k'(\bar{E} + m\bar{E})}{i_k\bar{E}} - 1.$$

With no change in i_k,

$$b = m$$

Since $i_k'/i_k > 1$ by definition, the required rate of increase of earnings with an increase in the capitalization rate will exceed the rate of increase when the capitalization rate remains unchanged.

The cost of capital is $i = b\bar{E}/C$. Substituting the expression for b given above and the present value of the retained earnings $(m\bar{E}/i_k')$ for C, the cost of capital expression, with changing capitalization rates, is

$$i = \frac{\left[\dfrac{i'_k(\bar{E} + m\bar{E})}{i_k\bar{E}} - 1\right]\bar{E}}{m\bar{E}/i'_k},$$

where

$$\frac{m\bar{E}}{i'_k} = C.$$

The cost of capital will equal the *new* capitalization rate only if the new capitalization rate equals the old rate. When, as in this section, it is assumed that $i'_k > i_k$, $i > i'_k$.

Once more a numerical example will help in determining the cost of capital. Using the same figures for $\bar{E}$, i_k, and i'_k as in the previous example, let $mE = 0.5$. Without the increase in the capitalization rate, the value of the owner's interest would have had to e

$$V = \frac{\$1 + \$0.5}{0.1} = \$15.$$

Since the cost of the investment is $0.5/0.1 = \$5$, and the required increase in earnings is $\$0.5$, the cost of capital is $\$0.5/\$5 = 0.1$.

With the new capitalization rate, the increase in earnings must be twice the old earnings from the equation for b, so

$$V = \frac{\$1 + 2(\$1)}{0.2} = \$15.$$

The cost of the investment is now $mE/i'_k = 0.5/0.2 = \$2.50$. The increase in earnings required is $\$2$, so the cost of capital is $\$2/\$2.50 = 0.8$.

DEBT FINANCING WITH CHANGING CAPITALIZATION RATES Given variable and uncertain earnings, debt financing can result in negative leverage. Therefore, it would not be surprising if the household-owner requires a higher capitalization with debt than without it. In effect, debt reduces the stability of his income from the firm. It, of course, is not inevitable that he will require a higher capitalization rate, but it is reasonable.

With the old capitalization rate, the condition necessary to maintain the value of the firm to the household-owner was that

$$\frac{\bar{E} + dD}{i_k} = V.$$

The value of the firm with the new capitalization rate is

$$\frac{\bar{E} + b\bar{E}}{i'_k} = V.$$

Setting the two expressions equal and solving for b, we find

$$b = \frac{i'_k/i_k(\bar{E} + Dd) - \bar{E}}{\bar{E}},$$

which will be larger than the value for b under the old capitalization rate as long as $i'_k > i_k$.

The cost of capital with debt is

$$i = \frac{b\bar{E}}{dD/i'_k}.$$

Substituting the expression for b,

$$i = \frac{\left[\dfrac{i'_k/i_k(\bar{E} + dD) - \bar{E}}{\bar{E}}\right]\bar{E}}{dD/i'_k} = \frac{i'_k/i_k(\bar{E} + dD) - \bar{E}}{dD/i'_k}.$$

When i'_k is larger than i_K, the numerator of the expression increases and the denominator becomes smaller, both working to increase the cost of capital. It is possible to show that $i > i'_k$ when $i'_k > i_k$.

As an arithmetic example, keep the same values for $\bar{E}$, i_k, and i'_k as before, and set D at \$5 and d at 0.05. The value of the equity under the old capitalization rate would have been

$$\$12.50 = \frac{\$1 + 0.05(\$5)}{0.1}.$$

And the cost of capital is the ratio of the increase in earnings required, \$0.25, to the present value of the interest payments, \$2.50, or 0.10.

Under the new capitalization rate,

$$b = \frac{0.2/0.1(\$1 + \$0.25) - \$1}{\$1} = 1.5.$$

Therefore bE will equal \$1.50. The cost of the debt is the present value of the interest payments under the new capitalization rate,

$$\frac{\$0.25}{0.2} = \$1.25,$$

so the cost of capital is

$$\frac{\$1.50}{\$1.25} = 1.20, \text{ or } 120 \text{ per cent.}$$

The differences in the costs of capital under the numerical examples, 0.3 for external equity, 0.8 for retained earnings, and 1.2 for debt, reflect the amounts invested as contrasted to the rise in capitalization rate. All three methods in the example resulted in the same capitalization rate increase. However, the cost of the external equity investment was $10, the cost of the retained earnings was $5 under the old capitalization rate, and the cost of the debt was $2.50 under the old capitalization rate. Thus, the differences merely reflect the particular numbers chosen for the examples.

One final point concerning *corporate* taxation: Corporate income taxes have been ignored in this analysis to keep the algebraic manipulations as simple as possible, although the effect of differential *personal* income tax rates on capital gains vs. dividends were considered. The corporate income tax favors debt over any kind of equity financing. Since interest payments are deductible for tax purposes, the owner pays only $(1 - c) \, dD$, where c is the corporate tax rate. All dividends are paid from after-tax dollars.

THE COST OF CAPITAL
WITH MANY OWNERS

In this case, it shall be assumed that there are many owners, but one of them controls the actions of the corporation and will be referred to as the *owner-manager*. Legally, control is certain when the owner-manager holds more than 50 per cent of the voting stock. When, however, the remaining ownership is highly fragmented, ownership of considerably less than 50 per cent can give control.

Where there was only one owner, the cost of capital posed no great problems, even when capitalization rates changed. It may be difficult to show the cost of capital in a simple formula when the i_k value changes, but as long as the owner knows what his personal capitalization rate is, he has no problem in using the cost of capital as a means of making investment decisions.

Why should it be different when there are many owners? Why doesn't the controlling owner operate the firm as if he were the sole owner? The major reason is that the value of the owner-manager's holdings are no longer the present value of the returns expected by him, discounted by his personal capitalization rate. Instead, the equity shares are traded in a market, and the value of the owner-manager's holdings is determined by the price set in the market.

The market price is determined by the interactions of all the holders of the stock and the potential holders. Each of these has a balance sheet of his own, personal preferences and attitudes toward current consumption vs. future consumption, and, to some extent, different alternative opportunities. To make matters worse, each may have his own set of expectations about the future earnings of the firm.

As the price of the stock increases, existing holders may be tempted to sell some or all of their holdings. As the price of the stock declines, new holders appear, attracted by the lower price (= higher yield). To know what the market price will be, using the same methods as were used in the case of the single owner, requires that the owner-manager shall have information on each actual and potential stockholder's tastes, balance sheets, alternative opportunities, and expectations with respect to the firm. Obviously, this is impossible.

On the other hand, if the owner-manager ignores the other owners and uses his personal data to make investment decisions, the result may be catastrophic. If he assumes $i = 0.1$ but it turns out that the market action makes $i = 0.2$ as the result of an investment-financing decision, the value of the owner-manager's holdings will plummet. If, after a few disastrous attempts at picking an i which is too low, he becomes overly conservative and picks i values which are higher than reality, investment opportunities are rejected. Persisting in this conservative policy, the result may be that the expected earnings of the firm are reduced in the eyes of the owner-manager and for the market as a whole. Price will fall and the owner-manager may find that his inaction has, in fact, resulted in as high a capitalization as he had initially assumed.

Since it is impossible to determine the appropriate capitalization rate by reviewing the information on innumerable individuals and it is dangerous to ignore their reactions, the owner-manager has little recourse but to attempt, by analysis of the market as an aggregate, to estimate the i value that will result from a given financial decision. One way to do this is to seek a valuation formula which will predict reactions of the market. For example, in calculating the effects of debt financing, the owner-manager may use the *net income* method.

Under the net income method, the value of the firm to owners, V, is

$$V = \frac{\bar{E} - dD}{i_k}.$$

The total value of the firm, V_f, is the value to owners plus the indebtedness of the firm, D, or

$$V_f = D + V.$$

The capitalization rate for the total firm is

$$i_f = \frac{\bar{E}}{V_f}.$$

It is specifically assumed that i_k remains constant, which is the underlying behavioral assumption necessary to convert an equation into a formula. With this assumption

$$i_f = \frac{\bar{E}}{[(\bar{E} - dD)/i] + D}.$$

As long as the interest rate d is less than i_k, dD/i_k will grow less rapidly than D. As D increases, i_f will therefore fall, since the denominator of the

i_f equation will rise more rapidly than the numerator. Thus, the value of the firm will rise with its indebtedness as long as added earnings equal added interest payments.

A moment's consideration indicates that the net income method is nothing more than what was done in calculating the cost of capital with debt financing under the assumption that i_k is constant. If, in fact, i_k remains constant, the method yields accurate results. But there is nothing in the formula which indicates whether i_k will rise or fall. It is simply assumed that i_k is constant and therefore $i_k = i$.

An alternative method, which does not assume a constant i_k, is the *net operating income* approach. The value of the firm once again is

$$\frac{\bar{E}}{i_f} = V_f.$$

The owners' share of this value is found by

$$V_f - D = V.$$

The value of i_k is defined as

$$i_k = \frac{\bar{E} - dD}{V}.$$

Now, assuming that i_f remains constant, the value of i_k may be redefined as

$$i_k = \frac{\bar{E} - dD}{\dfrac{\bar{E}}{i_f} - D}$$

Since i_f is assumed constant, i_k becomes larger as D becomes larger. In contrast to the net income method, which assumes that the stability and quality of the owners' earnings are not affected by debt as long as interest payments are covered, the net operating income approach assumes that any debt leads to a deterioration in the quality of owners' earnings and results in an increased i_k, and, therefore, an increased i.

Which method is correct? Either could be for different firms and at different times. Or, it is equally likely that some intermediate effect could occur with no change in i_k until some critical point is passed. One thing is clear. Formula approaches to valuation are no more accurate than the behavioral assumptions on which they are based. They do not answer the question the owner-manager poses, i.e., "Will debt increase i_k and by how much?"

Without formulas, the owner-manager has to turn to straightforward judgments about the reaction of the market to changes in the capital structure. He may turn to investment bankers and other capital market experts for opinions. He may analyze what happened to other similar firms which altered capital structure. But, fundamentally, he has to make an estimate or a decision on what he expects to happen. Once this is done, the rest is simple. If he judges that i_k *will* remain unchanged, the approach is that specified in the equations in which the cost of capital was analyzed with unchanging i_k values. If he judges that a new rate will prevail i_k, the remainder of the task is described by the equations in which we analyzed the cost of capital for the household-owner with changing i_k values. If he makes a bad estimate, the results are the same as when estimates are made for the returns expected on assets. If he underestimates i_k, the market value of his stock falls and he loses. If he overestimates i_k, he rejects what are really profitable investment opportunities, and his equity values do not appreciate in value as they would with a correct evaluation.

One helpful factor in this situation is that the market is not equally sensitive to all changes. Certain variables, such as earnings per share and dividends are key changes. Changes in these usually change the expectations of the market about the firm and so affect i_k. Large changes in other variables, such as major increases in debt or stock issues, can also result in variations of the capitalization rate. However, small changes in debt and in other variables which are not of main importance in the minds of investors may have little impact on i_k.

The expectations of the market are highly volatile. A cut in dividends may result in a worsening of expectations, which can lead to an increase in i_k. If, however, the firm shows strength subsequently, expectations may improve, and i_k decline. Therefore, it is not irrational for the owner-manager to undertake investment activities even if they should not be undertaken under a straightforward cost of capital analysis. In effect, the owner-manager is betting that the performance of the firm will shift expectations and, in the long-run, justify the investment. This of course involves something of a gamble and can be costly if the owner-manager is wrong. It is not unreasonable, however, if the argument that expectations are strongly keyed to current performance is accepted.

MANAGEMENT CONTROL

In many firms, no single stockholder has sufficient ownership to exert individually any effect on management policies. In large, publicly owned corporations, no single stockholder may own as much as 10 per cent of the outstanding shares. Management effectively controls the firm. With the stockholder-manager, his unwillingness to suffer personal value declines because of declining share prices was sufficient to assure us that the interests of minority stockholders would not be violated. What assurance is there that management will be at all concerned about stockholder interests when management has no significant stockholdings, and no stockholder has any appreciable share of the total ownership? There are at least four factors which work to assure stockholder protection. First is the law which protects stockholders against losses caused willfully or through unreasonably bad judgment. Generally, this is no assurance that management will operate so as to maintain the stock price. It protects against fraud, embezzlement, and other criminal acts of management. Given the uncertainties of business, it is difficult to prove bad judgment and render management liable for losses.

Second is the ethical responsibility of managers to stockholders. The cynics among us would be unwilling to accept this as a substantial assurance that managers will act in the stockholders' interests. The effectiveness of ethical responsibility may be a matter of question, but it exists to some extent. Unfortunately, we are talking of a specific kind of behavior, not a general feeling of responsibility. The cost-of-capital criterion requires that the firm make no investments or use no means of financing which will result in a stock price decline. Under the sway of ethical responsibility, management may do what it considers to be the best for the stockholders, but the stockholders may disagree. As a result, they sell off shares, and the price of the stock falls. Thus, one does not have to be a cynic to question managerial ethics as an assurance that the cost-of-capital criterion will be used.

For the firm which has profitable opportunities requiring more funds than are generated internally, maintaining the stock price is more than a matter of law or ethics. If stock prices are weak and falling because of investment or financing errors, the firm is virtually stopped from issuing new shares of stock. It can raise funds from debt sources, but ultimately the debt/equity ratio and the times-interest-earned coverage will deteriorate, and even debt will be unavailable. A growing company will have to issue new equity from time to time and must, therefore, sustain the price or the growth rate in price of the company's stock. Under these circumstances, the cost-of-capital criterion will be followed.

Finally, even if the firm is not growing rapidly, it will follow the cost-of-capital criterion to avoid a stockholder revolt. As was indicated earlier, proxy wars are extraordinarily expensive, and usually the management group has the odds on its side. However, if mismanagement drives the stock price down, existing stockholders are willing to sell their shares or to turn their votes over to others than existing management. These conditions attract people who will want to take over the existing management. A proxy fight with a large corporation costs a lot, and the chances of winning are slight. But the rewards of victory are also large. Shifts in management policy may be all that is required to raise the stock price. The gain in price is taxable as capital gains if stock is held for as little as six months.

Complete victory is not necessary. With cumulative voting, it is possible for an outside group to get some representation on the board of directors. Often the very threat of a proxy war, to say nothing of the partial victory of acquiring minority representation on the board, is all that is required to change the policies of management. The strategies and tactics involved in battling an e isting management are varied, complex, and often subtle. One of the most interesting inside stories of the methods open to minority stock-holders is recounted in *My Life in Court* * by Louis Nizer, who was involved in the proxy fight over Loew's Incorporated during 1956 and 1957. The story illustrates the ability of a minority to take over management, using a variety of threats, legal action, hazing, and even a management consultant's report. In this case, the threat of a proxy war was enough to secure half the board representation for the minority group.

THE COST OF CAPITAL AND STOCK MARKET MOVEMENTS

So far, we have dicussed the cost of capital as affected by asset portfolio and capital structure changes in the firm. Stock prices can and do change apart from anything that happens to the individual firm. There are all kinds of explanations offered for changes in the stock market ranging from astrological configurations through descriptions of the changes in the general level of stock prices as essentially random variations. Generally, it seems safe to say that no one has demonstrated a consistent ability to forecast the level of stock prices. Figure 10–1 presents a combination of monthly and weekly stock price indexes from 1960 through March, 1963.

Looking at the peaks and valleys in Figure 10–1, it would seem unreasonable to expect the firm to be able to forecast these changes. However, these general changes do affect the cost of capital for common stock issues. When stock prices are low, a new issue of common stock is apt to push prices down even further. Many more shares would have to be issued in order to raise a given amount of funds. The rate of return required to support even the low price level prevailing prior to the new issue will be quite high, if only because of the large number of new shares.

When stock prices are high, the reasoning about common stock issues is not always symmetrical with the reasoning when prices are low. If the firm believes its price to be abnormally high, it may not wish to issue new common stock for fear of having an irate group of disappointed new stockholders when the price drops to a more normal level. This sounds peculiar, but it is consistent with the relatively low significance of common stock issues as a means of financing, which has been noted previously.

If the changes in the stock price of a firm seem primarily related to temporary general market conditions, the cost of capital of all but common stock may be treated as unchanged. If the market changes seem more or less permanent, they reflect a basic change in the preferences of stockholders. A permanent decline in stock prices may be viewed as a sign that the public has little faith in the future earning power of business firms. The cost of capital has risen. On the asset side of the balance sheet, this means that

*Doubleday, 1961.

acceptable investments must generate larger dollar returns. As a result, the asset portfolio will grow less rapidly than it would, given a lower cost of capital. Changes in the capital structure caused by a rising cost of capital are harder to predict. If assets are liquidated because of insufficient profitability, the cash is apt to be used to reduce debt and to reduce retained earnings by maintaining dividends in the face of low earnings. However, if the firm still has profitable investments, there seems little reason to suppose that the relative desirability of different sources of funds will change.

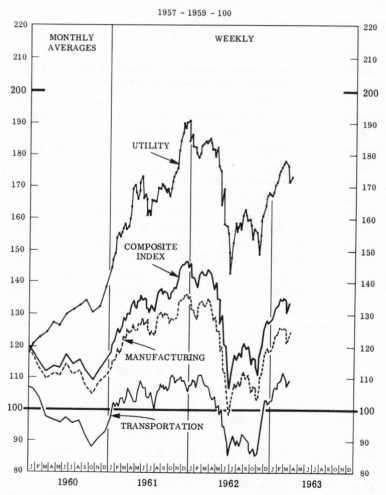

S. E. C. STOCK PRICE INDEXES

Indexes of 300 Stocks on N. Y. S. E.

1957 – 1959 – 100

Figure 10-1. Source: Statistical Bulletin, March 1963, U.S. Securities and Exchange Commission

In short, the effects of general stock price movements on the cost of capital will depend upon whether the changes are viewed as temporary or permanent. Temporary changes will affect the cost of capital of common stock, raising the cost when prices are low and, perhaps to a lesser degree, when they are high also. Permanent changes will increase the cost of capital when the change is downward, and lower the cost of capital when the change is upward. The growth rate of the asset portfolio will tend to vary inversely with the cost of capital changes. However, there is no obvious reason for supposing that the *relative* costs of different sources of funds will change.

Stock Price Maximization. In this chapter we developed the definition of the cost of capital as the discount rate used to evaluate asset investments which will maintain the price of the firm's stock or, in a growing economy, maintain the growth rate of the firm's stock price so that it does not fall behind the prices of competing securities. This does not imply that management will operate to maximize the price of the stock.

In a perfectly competitive economy with no risk, stock price maximization results from maximizing earnings and, under conditions of long-run equilibrium, to maximize earnings means to earn zero profits, net of economic rents. Firms which do not maximize earnings generate losses and eventually fail.

In a world such as ours, where oligopoly is dominant, firms which do not maximize earnings can continue to exist and just earn lower profits than are possible. Further, maximizing earnings will not maximize stock prices under conditions of risk. A safe stock earning $10 per share may be preferred rationally to a much riskier stock earning $12 per share. Even with low earnings, very risky stock may enjoy a high price if the probability distribution of its returns are negatively correlated to the returns of most other stocks, because it will reduce portfolio risk. However, these arguments do not explain why firms do not necessarily maximize stock prices; they simply indicate that stock price maximization under conditions of risk and imperfect competition is difficult.

In an imperfectly competitive economy, given a management with insignificant stockholdings in the firm, there is no necessary reason for a firm to maximize stock price any more than there is reason for a firm to maximize profits. Stockholders will not necessarily be unhappy about a stock price below its theoretical maximum, unless there are other similar stocks with higher prices. Just as consumers buy goods produced in imperfectly competitive industries at a price which is perhaps higher than it would be under perfect competition, stockholders will be willing to buy and hold stocks in an oligopolistic industry at a price below what it would be if the industry were perfectly competitive. The theoretical alternatives are irrelevant because they are not available. Thus, where management has goals, such as perhaps maximizing sales, which do not necessarily coincide with stock price maximization, but do not involve violation of the cost of capital criterion, stock prices will not and do not have to be maximized.

MEASURING THE COST OF CAPITAL

As indicated earlier, to know the cost of capital implies knowledge of a considerable quantity of detailed information about stockholders and potential stockholders. Such knowledge is impossible to come by in a firm with widely dispersed ownership. However, it does not seem unreasonable for a management, which understands the characteristics of the asset portfolio, the various elements of the capital structure, and the securities markets, to estimate the cost of capital. On the whole, I believe that this is the best way to measure the cost of capital.

The resulting measure has a subjective base and will be little better than the judgment of management. This hardly seems to be a major objection. Managerial compensation at the higher levels of management would appear to be largely based on the quality of judgment, i.e., the ability to make good decisions in difficult areas. The problem that does emerge is that the subjective cost of capital may not be used as intelligently as it might. Management may use judgment where formula techniques are at least as accurate. Management should use judgment in estimating the future returns of an asset investment and the probability distribution of the returns. Management should also judge the cost of capital. Given these two judgments, the decision as to whether it pays to invest in an asset is not a matter of judgment, but simply of calculating the net present value and standard deviation of the proposed asset.

Whether it is due to the unwillingness of firms to state a subjective estimate of the cost of capital in terms of a percentage, or to something else, there has been a good deal of effort spent in deriving formula approximations of the cost of capital. Such approaches result in estimates which are more or less wrong. But this is not an indictment. A poor estimate may be better than no estimate. Some of the methods to be reviewed in this section are very bad. Some seem to have a reasonable basis. It will turn out that those approaches which rely heavily on mechanical manipulation of objective data, such as given in normal balance sheets and income statements, are very bad. The better methods are really not formulas so much as means of manipulating what are, at heart, subjective judgments.

The Average Cost of Capital. The average cost of capital is almost pure formula. The firm considers its existing capital structure, measuring each source of funds as a percentage of the total capital structure. Next, it notes the interest cost of each source. For privately placed debt, the contract or coupon interest rate is used. For marketed debt, either the coupon rate or the market yield is used. For preferred stock, either the coupon yield, the ratio of the dollar dividend to the par value of preferred, is used or the market yield, the ratio of the dollar dividend to the market price. For common stock, the ratio of dividend to price, the dividend yield, is used, or the ratio of after-tax earnings per share to price is used. The interest costs are converted to an after-tax basis by multiplying the pretax charges, such as bond interest, by 1 minus the tax rate. After-tax charges, such as preferred dividends, common dividends, or common earnings per share, are, of course, left alone. Each tax-adjusted cost is multiplied or weighted by the importance of the source of funds in the capital structure. The products of the weights and costs are summed, and the resulting weighted average is used as the cost of capital. Exhibit 10-1 presents a simplified example.

Exhibit 10-1

CALCULATION OF THE WEIGHTED COST OF CAPITAL

Capital Structure (1)	Weights (2)	Before-tax Costs, % (3)	After-tax Costs,* % (4)	(2) × (4), % (5)
Debt	0.20	6	3.12	0.62
Common stock**	0.40	–	10.00	4.00
Retained earnings	0.40	–	10.00	4.00
Cost of capital	—	–	—	8.62

*Assumed tax rate is 48 per cent.
**Earnings/price ratio used as cost estimate for both stock and retained earnings.

The result is a single measure of the cost of capital. This is used to evaluate the prospective additions to the asset portfolio, even though the new assets may change the risk of the portfolio. It cannot be used to decide which of the sources of funds is cheapest. The firm, however, could use the unweighted individual costs as cost of capital estimates for particular sources.

There are many criticisms that can be made of the assumptions underlying this approach. More important are the results of using the weighted cost of capital. First, the method generates at best an erratic cost of capital estimate. For example, suppose the firm in Exhibit 10-1 decided to go ahead with an investment using 6 per cent debt, raising the debt proportion to 0.33 and reducing stock and retained earnings proportions each to 0.33. If the stockholders are satisfied that the investment is good and that the added risk of the debt is negligible, the true cost of capital will remain unchanged. With the new weights, however, the weighted cost of capital will fall from 8.62 to 7.96 per cent. Had the firm used either stock or retained earnings, the weighted cost of capital would have risen, even if the true cost of capital were unchanged. The problem is that these arbitrary fluctuations in the weighted cost of capital can result in rejection of asset investments which should be accepted, or vice versa.

Second, the method ties the firm to the past in making future decisions. The result will be that a mistake in one period can cause a chain of errors. Suppose the true cost of capital is really 10 per cent. The firm decides to use a weighted average approach and, as a result, finances a new investment with 6 per cent debt, again changing the weights to 0.33 for each source. This time, however, the stockholders are quite concerned about the debt/ equity ratio. As a result, the supply of stock offered exceeds the demand at the current price, and the price falls. Assume it falls until the earnings /price ratio is 15 per cent and that this is the new true cost of capital also. Using the new weights and the new earnings/price ratio, the weighted cost of capital is 10.9 per cent. The larger gap between the weighted cost of capital and the true cost makes it more likely that investments will be chosen which, when discounted by the *true* cost of capital, would be unprofitable. Further, if the firm persists in its folly, it will finance new investments by added debt because it is cheaper than either stock or retained earnings according to the weighted cost of capital criterion. Of course, this will simply drive the stock price down further and increase the true cost of capital. It is even possible for the weighted cost of capital to fall while the true cost rises.

The Income/Capital Structure Ratio. This method yields a single cost of capital measure also. However, it is based on more sophisticated arguments than the average cost of capital. The numerator of the ratio is earnings after taxes plus the after-tax interest costs of debt. The denominator is the market value of the capital structure. Where no market value exists, as with accruals and trade debt, the balance sheet value is used.

The basis for using this measure lies in the neoclassical theory of the firm. The value of a firm is the market value of its assets as a going concern. However, this value is generally unknown. In fact, it is the kind of value we discussed in the early chapters of this book, referring to it as the gross present value. Although the market value of the assets of the firm are unknown, the market value of the capital instruments, such as bonds and stock, which divide the income stream generated by the assets, are known, at least sometimes. And the market value of the capital instruments equals the market value of assets according to the principles of double-entry accounting. The ratio then reflects the price which debt and equity holders are willing to pay for a claim to the firm's income stream. If the firm is a poor risk, the price paid will be low, and the ratio will be high. If the firm is a good risk, the reverse will be true.

The ratio will not be affected by the capital structure. The reason for this is that security holders will adjust their personal portfolios to the financial situation of the firm so as to leave the ratio unchanged.

One example of this process should suffice. The firm which finances an asset through debt provides its stockholders with an opportunity to enjoy levered earnings. If the stockholders are impressed with the profit possibility more than with the risk of negative leverage, the price of the stock should rise. If it does rise, it will be higher than the stock price of another firm which is the *risk-equivalent* of the first firm, but has not used debt. The stock of the levered firm will be sold and the proceeds used to buy the cheaper stock of the unlevered company. Since the stockholders in the example like leverage, not only will the stockholders use the proceeds from the sale of the levered stocks to buy the unlevered stocks, but they will pledge their unlevered stocks as collateral for loans. The funds from these loans will be used to buy more shares of unlevered stock. This procedure will continue as long as the difference between the levered and unlevered stock prices is larger than would be accounted for by a risk premium, because of the debt, and the tax advantage of interest payments over dividend payments. In effect, the stockholders who love leverage are free to lever their own balance sheets if the firm will not. The result is that it makes no difference whether or not the firm uses leverage. Similar examples can be developed for any capital structure decision of the firm. In all cases, the optimal capital structure, as measured by risk and profit, is built in the investor's portfolio rather than in the firm's.

There are several objections that can be raised to this approach to the cost of capital. Some are relatively unimportant, such as the need to have established risk-equivalent classes of firms, with some unanimity among investors and firms as to the identity and composition of these groups. More important is the challenge that this approach brings to the distinction made between investors and firms. Firms exist to undertake activities that investors are unwilling or unable to undertake themselves. On the asset side, everyone agrees that the reason investors buy securities in steel companies is that, given the required knowledge for efficient operations and capital requirements, most investors do better buying securities than they would operating their own steel companies.

Much the same is true on the capital structure side—but this is where the proponents of the income/capital structure ratio measurement of the cost of capital disagree. In many of the capital structure adjustments required of investors for the ratio approach to work, the investor must add debt to his personal capital structure. This raises two questions: Is debt available to individuals on the same terms as it is available to corporations? Are investors indifferent as between personal indebtedness and corporate indebtedness?

The answer to the first question depends partly on who the investor is, and what corporation is involved. An investor with personal assets of $10 million may be able to borrow funds on much the same terms as a corporation with assets of the same amount. But few investors are this wealthy, and many corporations have assets in excess of $10 million. Most investors have to borrow funds at a higher interest rate and/or for a shorter term than do corporations. The firm which borrows funds to finance plant and equipment purchases can do so for periods of perhaps 30 years. The stockholder who wishes to lever his stockholdings can use the stock as collateral only for a short-term loan. If stock prices should fall during the term of the loan, the lender will request that either the loan be reduced, or the collateral be increased. It was precisely this kind of whipsaw that wiped out the savings of thousands of stockholders in 1929.

The second question can be answered by turning to the comparative terms on which equity funds are available to corporations and to individuals. An individual can sell equity shares only by entering into a partnership. Unlike the purchase of corporate stock, equity investment in a partnership places the personal assets of the investor in jeopardy if the business assets are insufficient to meet the claims of creditors. It is possible to have a limited partnership in which one or more of the partners can retain limited liability, i.e., be liable for business debts only to the extent of his investment in the partnership. The limited partner must forego any role in the management of the partnership. Some states recognize limited partnership associations. However, the legal ambiguities, lack of marketability of partnership shares, and organization problems surrounding these forms of organizations have made them largely useless for major industrial activities. One of the major virtues of the corporation is the limitation of liability.

This not only differentiates between the conditions under which individuals and corporations can acquire equity funds, it differentiates between the conditions under which corporations and individuals can acquire debt. The individual risks all of his personal assets on a personal loan. If the corporation borrows, the individual stockholder risks only his stockholdings in the corporation.

To summarize, the corporation serves as an intermediary between the investor and the real world. It affects the profitability and risk of investment on the assets side by enabling individuals to buy small pieces of capital equipment and know-how. It operates on the capital structure side by enabling the stockholder indirect access to funds under terms which most stockholders could not duplicate on their own. Further, it modifies capital structure risks because of the limitation of legal liability. Thus, debt is less risky for the individual if the corporation does the borrowing than if the individual does the borrowing directly. On the basis of these arguments, it appears reasonable to reject the ratio of income to capital structure as a reasonably accurate approximation of the cost of capital. More important, it seems clear that the capital structure will affect the cost of capital.

The Earnings/Price Ratio. The earnings/price ratio (e/p) is the ratio of earnings, after taxes and preferred dividends, to the market price of the stock. Its inverse, the price/earnings ratio is often used in financial analysis as a measure of the attitude of stockholders to the company. A high price /earnings ratio indicates that stockholders are willing to pay a high price for each dollar of earnings generated by the firm. The reverse is true for a low price/earnings ratio. Thus, a high e/p would be associated with a firm whose earnings are not valued highly, and a low e/p indicates that earnings are valued highly.

The cost of capital is not the e/p ratio, but the additional pretax earnings needed to maintain the stock price, divided by the dollars invested in the project. If either the asset investment or the means of financing increases the risk to the stockholder, e/p will rise. This will increase the cost of capital. To see this more clearly, consider a firm which has 100,000 shares of stock outstanding, e/p = 0.1, the tax rate is 0.48, after-tax eps = $10, and earnings before taxes is $1,923,077. Since eps = $10 and e/p = 0.1, the market price is $100. The firm wishes to raise $1,000,000 using 6 per cent bonds, common stock, or retained earnings. To net $1,000,000 (after flotation) from bond issue, the firm will have to issue $1,100,000 of bonds. Net proceeds of $1,000,000 from stock requires issuing 11,111 new shares. Exhibit 10-2 shows the cost of capital for each of these sources, first, assuming e/p = 0.10 and, second, assuming e/p = 0.11.

At any given e/p ratio, 6 per cent debt has a lower cost of capital than either the common stock financing or retained earnings. Partly, this is because interest charges are tax-deductible, while the required earnings for common stock and retained earnings are post-tax charges. Partly, the apparent superiority of debt is simply that the stock and retained earnings must generate 10 per cent after taxes when e/p is unchanged, while debt has to generate only 6 per cent before taxes. The superiority of debt is a result of the numbers chosen for the example and the fact that interest is tax-deductible. It does not follow that debt is always to be preferred. The real alternatives may be 6 per cent debt, which would result in a new e/p of 0.20, or equity financing with no change in e/p.

It should also be noted in the example that the use of retained earnings requires a price increase equal to the earnings retained, even when e/p is unchanged. If stockholders value a retained earning dollar as highly as a dividend dollar, the value of the stock must rise by as much as the stockholders' cash balance would have risen if the dividend had been paid.

The key variable in determining which source to use is the e/p which will prevail after the financing. Given that, the rest is simply a matter of arithmetic. It is the responsibility of the firm to estimate the effects of financing and investment patterns on e/p. Thus, the e/p. ratio approximation to the cost of capital requires a high degree of subjective evaluation, or judgment. This is not a criticism since estimating the cost of capital is an appropriate area for judgment.

As a measure of the comparative cost of capital, i.e., the cost of capital of different methods of financing, the e/p approach is good. The only inadequacy is that it places no cost on depreciation funds financing. This can be corrected simply by using the ratio of cash flow per share to price, rather than e/p. Instead of being concerned with the required amount of pretax earnings, we would measure the required amount of pretax cash

Exhibit 10-2

EXAMPLES OF COST OF CAPITAL CALCULATIONS USING THE EARNINGS/PRICE RATIO

Method of financing	COMMON				RETAINED			
	Stock	Stock	Bonds	Bonds	Earnings	Bonds	Earnings	Earnings
Expected e/p after financing	0.10	0.11	0.10	0.11	0.10	0.11	0.10	0.11
Required price	$100.00	$100.00	$100.00	$100.00	$110.00	$100.00	$110.00	$110.00
Required eps	$ 10.00	$ 11.00	$ 10.00	$ 11.00	$ 11.00	$ 11.00	$ 11.00	$ 12.00
Earnings after taxes	$1,111	$1,222	$1,000	$1,100	$1,100	$1,100	$1,100	$1,210
Earnings before taxes	2,137	2,350	1,923	2,115	2,115	2,115	2,115	2,327
Earnings before taxes and new interest	2,137	2,350	1,990	2,182	2,115	2,182	2,115	2,327
Old earnings before taxes	1,923	1,923	1,923	1,923	1,923	1,923	1,923	1,923
Required change in earnings before taxes	214	427	67	259	192	259	192	404
Required change/investment = cost of capital	21%	43%	7%	26%	19%	26%	19%	40%

flow. Thus, if there is no change in the cash flow/price ratio, the pretax cost of capital for the use of depreciation funds would be: $EBT/0.52 +$ depreciation, where EBT is earnings before taxes.

This approach to the cost of capital, however, is not useful as an absolute measure. The absolute value of the cost of capital is what is required if we are to use the cost of capital to discount future dollar returns and costs associated with asset investments. To see this, look at Table 10-1 which compares eps, dividends per share (dps), and market prices for four similar, though far from identical, companies.

Table 10-1

PER SHARE EARNINGS, DIVIDENDS, AND STOCK PRICE RANGES
FOR FOUR COMPANIES, 1962

Company	eps	ops	PRICE		E/P	
			High	Low	High	Low
Control Data Corporation	$0.39	none	52	22-1/2	0.0075	0.0173
General Electric Company	3.10*	$2	78-1/2	54-1/4	0.0395	0.0571
International Business Machines	8.72	3	578-1/2	300	0.0151	0.0291
Minneapolis-Honeywell Regulator	3.50*	2	133-1/4	70-1/8	0.0263	0.0499

*Estimated

Source: *Standard & Poor's Stock Guide, February 1963*, Standard & Poor's Corporation, New York.

All four companies manufacture electronic equipment, including computers. General Electric, IBM, and Minneaplis-Honeywell are well-known companies with established reputations. Control Data is a young company and, compared with the other three, undiversified. It has never paid dividends. Most investors would probably consider it the riskiest of the four companies. Yet, its e/p ratio is the lowest of the three companies. Using the e/p approach to the cost of capital, Control Data would have the lowest cost of capital for all investments and financing which do not change e/p. According to this estimate, Control Data is permitted to make investments which are far less profitable than are GE, IBM, or Minneapolis-Honeywell. This does not appear to be reasonable.

The e/p ratio reflects the expectations of investors with respect to particular firms. Control Data is a new company in a field which has enormous potential. It has demonstrated its ability to generate profits, and the e/p reflects the expectation that future profits will far exceed current levels. The other companies, because they are well established already, do not have a future which is likely to be remarkably better than what already exists. The very low e/p for Control Data does not indicate that stockholders will be satisfied with low rates of return. Rather, it is a sign that they expect very high rates of return.

If the future were to be simply a copy of the present, e/p would not be a bad index of the cost of capital. However, expectations for some firms may be far different than what have so far been experienced. This is reflected in e/p. It follows that the absolute value of the cost of capital as estimated with the e/p approach will tend to be too high for firms with unhappy prospects and too low for firms which have a future brighter than the present.

The Historic Rate of Return.   The firm may reason that, if it can do at least as well in the future as it has in the past, stockholders should be content to hold their shares. Any potential investment must then generate a positive expected net present value when discounted by some measure of past profitability, such as the rate of return on equity.

In its simplest version, the approach can be misleading for firms like Control Data, in which stockholders have invested expecting rising profitability. However, this weakness can be overcome by adjusting the historic rate for growth. If last year's rate of return on equity was 15 per cent and the rate of return on equity has shown an average growth rate of 10 per cent per annum, the cost of capital could be approximated at 16.5 per cent. If similar firms are earning 20 per cent, the firm may use the 20 per cent as its estimate.

The e/p method of estimating the cost of capital is unsatisfactory because it does not provide a good investment discount factor. It is useful as a measure of the relative costs of capital for different sources of funds. The historic rate of return may provide a useful discount factor for evaluating assets, but it is a very poor measure of the relative costs of capital because it ignores changes in risk. This can be corrected by estimating the required increase in rate of return in order to justify the risks of a changed capital structure. Thus, the firm could estimate that, with an unchanged capital structure, the cost of capital would be 16.5 per cent. With more debt, stock, or smaller dividends, the rate would be 25 per cent.

If these modifications are made to the historic rate of return, it becomes essentially a nonformula subjective measure of the cost of capital. Though it lacks the scientific appearance of the calculated cost of capital, it can be a far more accurate estimate of the true cost of capital.

CHOOSING THE BALANCE SHEET

This section is a modification of the part of Chapter 6 concerned with the choice of asset portfolio. In Chapter 6, the only capital structure factor considered was the cost of capital. We can now place the asset portfolio choice in a larger frame and consider the simultaneous selection of asset portfolio and capital structure—i.e., the choice of balance sheet.

The asset portfolio and the capital structure must be chosen simultaneously because they interact. The present value of the assets will depend upon the cost of capital. This will be partly determined by the risk of capital structure. The need for cash will also depend upon the term structure of capital with more cash needed if the firm finances with short-term debt than if with long-term. The risk of the capital structure is not independent of the asset portfolio. Relatively inflexible long-term debt is less risky if used to finance assets with a stable earning power. Also, safe assets reduce the risk of dilution of earnings if common stock is used for financing. And the expected value of net worth is reduced by the interest payments made for debt.

RESTRICTIONS
ON BALANCE
SHEET CHOICE

Cost of Capital. The cost of capital serves in choosing the balance sheet as it did in choosing the asset portfolio. It provides a restriction. The firm will not select any balance sheet in which the net expected value of the assets is not positive when discounted by the cost of capital.

Creditors. In addition to this restriction, there are various creditor restrictions. To qualify for desirable debt funds, the firm must meet the creditors' requirements as reflected in current ratios, debt/equity ratios, times-interest-earned coverage, etc. The firm cannot select a balance sheet using unsecured bank loans as a source of funds if that balance sheet does not also meet the safety requirements of the bank. These limits are usually not inflexible. The bank may be willing to accept a low current ratio if, say 80 per cent of the current assets are cash. Similarly, a high debt/equity ratio may be acceptable if the times-interest-earned coverage is very large. Whatever the requirements, the firm must be consistent. If it plans to use a particular source of credit, the balance sheet must meet the requirements set forth by that source.

Management. Some balance sheets will be rejected because they do not satisfy the cost of capital criterion, others, because they do not meet the restrictions set by creditors. Still others, which are satisfactory in terms of both cost of capital and creditors' requirements, may be rejected by management.

Risk and expected value are extremely useful variables for investment and financing decisions. However, they do not reflect necessarily the full range of management's aversions and aspirations.

For example, the management of a firm is unlikely to view business failure with equanimity. If a loss of $1 million means that the firm will go out of existence, the loss would not be treated on a par with the possibility of a $1 million gain, even if both events had identical probabilities. Though some firms may be able to choose a balance sheet with a zero probability of business failure, most firms have to accept some positive probability of business failure in order to get a balance sheet with adequate profits. The firm could reject, however, any balance sheet where the probability of failure exceeded some limit, say 10 per cent. Note that a balance sheet rejected for this reason might in all other respects be quite desirable, with a high expected value and a low standard deviation.

Business failure is an extreme case. There are many situations which management prefers to avoid that are less extreme. Although creditors may require certain safety ratios, the firm may be even more stringent in wanting high current ratios or low debt/equity ratios. Balance sheets with a high probability of ratios unsatisfactory to management may be rejected.

Aversions and aspirations are hard to separate. The firm may aspire to accomplish most of its financing through internal sources because it has an aversion to debt or external financing of any kind. Balance sheet choices which involve a high probability of external financing may thus be rejected. The firm may aim to maintain a given level of dps or eps, and would reject balance sheets in which reduced dps or eps have too high a probability, even though the particular balance sheet may meet the criteria of owners and creditors.

Within the limits set by the cost of capital and creditors, management is free to choose among available balance sheets to achieve a variety of goals, not all of which are necessarily profit maximizing. Management may wish to achieve some growth rate in sales, assets, or profits, and will prefer balance sheets which have a high probability of achieving such goals. The firm may wish to achieve or maintain a share of the market for their product. Balance sheets, otherwise acceptable, which do not show a high probability of accomplishing this aim, may be rejected regardless of their expected values and risks.

THE CAPITAL STRUCTURE, RISK, AND EXPECTED VALUE

After rejecting balance sheets which do not meet the criteria of the cost of capital, creditors' restrictions, and management's aims and aversions, the selection of the optimal balance sheet from those remaining will follow the procedure described in Chapter 6. The balance sheet chosen will be that which has a combination of expected value and risk that places the firm on the highest attainable preference or indifference curve. Although we have been discussing the effects of capital structure choices in this and the last three chapters, it may be desirable to summarize the impact of the choice of capital structure on risk and expected value.

Expected Value and Capital Structure. Interest payments and flotation costs reduce expected value in two ways. First, such payments are direct deductions, after taking taxes into account, from profits. Second, interest payments are cash disbursements and become reflected in the firm's cash flow projections. As a result, either the number of orders for cash or the average cash balance will rise, increasing the costs of the cash account and consequently reducing the expected value of net worth.

What is true of interest payments is also true of preferred dividends. The major difference is that preferred dividends are not tax-deductible. This not only means a larger direct after-tax deduction from the expected value of net worth than with interest, it increases cash disbursements more than interest. Since interest payments are tax-deductible, a rise in interest payments is reflected in a decline in tax payments, although the decline will not occur until two quarters later because of the tax payment schedule.

Unlike interest payments and preferred dividends, common dividends are not properly an expense, although the flotation costs of common stock are. Using the cost of capital criterion, earnings are retained only when the stockholders are no worse off than if the earnings had been paid out in cash dividends. Although common dividends are not deducted directly from the expected value of net worth, they do add to cash disbursements and increase the costs of cash. As a result, common dividends indirectly reduce the expected value of net worth

The repayment of debt is not an expense of the firm and is not deducted directly from the expected value of net worth. However, the repayment of debt is a cash disbursement, increasing the costs of cash and, in this fashion, reducing the expected value of net worth. Short-term debt involves larger cash costs than long-term debt because of the more rapid rate of repayment.

Risk and the Capital Structure. Debt amplifies the risk of the basic asset portfolio because of leverage, as was shown in Chapter 8. Both long-term debt and short-term debt add some special risks. Long-term debt presents the negative leverage problem, while offering the firm little flexibility in adjusting the capital structure as a response to adverse business conditions. Short-term debt offers flexibility, but perhaps too much flexibility. Changes in either the condition of the firm or the condition of the economy can make it difficult for the firm to refinance maturing short-term debt with new short-term debt.

Even common stock adds risk to the asset portfolio. The risk here is that earnings may be diluted. If retained earnings had been used, the decline in eps, which would occur when earnings fall in any event, would be far less than with stock issue.

Of the various sources, internal funds provide virtually no risk beyond what is embodied in the asset portfolio. If the actual value of the asset portfolio is low or negative, the firm will be better off, as far as the effect on stock prices and flexibility are concerned, with internal funds than with any other source.

Since many balance sheets are excluded because they fail to meet the demands of creditors, owners, and managers, there are far fewer balance sheet choices available for selection than there were asset portfolios. Further, the effects of capital structure on risk and expected value will eliminate still more balance sheets than might have been acceptable for consideration as pure asset portfolios. Those asset portfolios that, as balance sheets, are still efficient choices, i.e., they provide the least risk of any balance sheet which does not have a larger expected value, are apt to have very different risk and expected value characteristics in their balance sheet form than they did simply as asset portfolios. The assets in the optimal balance sheet thus may be quite different than the assets that would have been selected without capital structure influences.

To the extent that asset portfolios are safe, capital structures can be risky. One example of this is provided by the gas and electric utility companies. The safety of their assets lies in the fact that such utilities operate in protected markets and sell a product the demand for which is relatively stable. A large part of the capital structure of such companies is in the form of long-term debt, as was shown in Table 8-1. Thus, the choice of either asset portfolio or capital structure separately is apt to result, at the very least, in nonoptimal balance sheets. The reverse is also true.

THE SUPPLY OF FUNDS   Although we cannot generalize about the absolute costs of capital for various sources of funds, it is possible to generalize about the relative costs. From the point of view of the firm, certain sources will appear cheaper than others, if only because the cost of capital is not sensitive to these sources.

Depreciation will tend to be the cheapest source of funds. The reason for this is that depreciation does not involve the firm in fixed cash charges or in the possibility of negative leverage. Further, except when a firm is in process of liquidating its asset portfolio, depreciation is not distributed to stockholders.

Retained earnings share many of the characteristics of depreciation. Fixed charges are avoided, as is negative leverage. However, a reduction in dividends, or a failure to increase dividends in line with similar firms, may have an adverse effect on stock price. Thus, if the use of retained earnings involves a reduction in dividends, the cost of capital associated with such financing can be quite high. Low-cost retained earnings are restricted to that share of earnings not needed to meet normal dividend payments.

Accruals, trade debt, and short-term debt are probably the next least costly sources of funds. Creditors will take action to prevent excessive use of these sources, and stockholders may react adversely, raising the cost of capital, should the working capital position of the firm be substantially weakened as a result of excessive short-term debt financing.

Long-term debt would be next in order of ascending costs. If long-term debt does not raise the debt/equity ratio above that of similar firms, it is unlikely that the cost of capital will rise as a result of long-term debt financing. However, if business expectations are not favorable, the use of long-term debt can result in a stock price decline as stockholders become fearful of negative leverage.

Common stock is probably the most expensive source of finance, assuming internal funds are available without reduction of dividends, and also assuming that the debt/equity ratio and the working capital position of the firm are within tolerable limits. In addition to the high costs of flotation, the immediate effect of a stock issue is a decline in price, as the *floating* supply of stock will exceed demand until the stock finds its way into the portfolios of permanent investors. The new stockholders have a proportionate claim to both old and new earnings as well as to all future earnings. Thus, an increase of 10 per cent in outstanding common shares means that total earnings must rise by 10 per cent if eps are not to fall. Further, if existing stockholders have been anticipating a 10 per cent rate of growth in eps, the growth rate of total earnings will have to rise to 11 per cent in order to maintain the 10 per cent growth rate in eps. Finally, unlike any of the alternate sources of financing, there is no possibility of a favorable leverage effect with common stock.

If these arguments hold, the capital structure of the firm will reflect the growth rate as well as the risk of its asset portfolio. A firm increasing its asset holdings at a low rate will tend to rely primarily on internal funds. Debt will be used moderately, if needed, but the debt/equity ratio may actually improve if retained earnings exceed new debt. The working capital ratio may also improve if the new assets are current assets and/or if the debt used is long-term. A rapidly growing firm will be forced to finance with common stock since it will fully utilize all internal funds within dividend limits, as well as debt funds within the limitations of acceptable debt/equity and working capital ratios. A rising debt/equity ratio is an indication that the firm has been growing at a more rapid rate than can be financed by internal funds and moderate debt increases. We shall return to a discussion of the capital structure and the growth rate in Chapter 16, where the data for all nonfinancial corporations will be considered as a reflection of the corporate growth rate.

SELECTED REFERENCES

Benishay, H.: "Variability in Earnings-Price Ratios of Corporate Securities," *American Economic Review*, Mar., 1961.

——: "Variability in Earnings-Price Ratios: Reply," *American Economic Review*, Mar., 1962.

Bodenheimer, D.: "On the Problem of Capital Budgeting," *Journal of Finance*, Dec., 1959.

Darling, P.: "A Surrogative Measure of Business Confidence and its Relation to Stock Prices," *Journal of Finance*, Dec., 1955.

———: "The Influence of Expectation and Liquidity on Dividend Policy," *Review of Economics and Statistics*, June, 1957.

Dean, N.: *Capital Budgeting*, Columbia, New York, 1951.

Durand, D.: "The Cost of Debt and Equity Funds for Business," *Conference on Research in Business Finance*, National Bureau of Economic Research, Sns, New York, 1952.

Gordon, M.: "Dividends, Earnings and Stock Prices," *Review of Economics and Statistics*, May, 1959.

———: *The Investment, Financing and Valuation of the Corporation*, Irwin, Homewood, Ill., 1962.

———: "The Savings, Investment and Valuation of a Corporation," *Review of Economics and Statistics*, Feb., 1962.

———: "Security and a Financial Theory of Investment," *Quarterly Journal of Economics*, Aug., 1960.

———, and E. Shapiro: "Capital Equipment Analysis: The Required Rate of Profit," *Journal of Business*, Oct., 1955.

———: "Variability in Earnings-Price Ratios: Comment," *American Economic Review*, Mar., 1962.

Harkavy, O.: "The Relation between Retained Earnings and Common Stock Prices for Large Listed Corporations," *Journal of Finance*, Sept., 1953.

Modigliani, F., and M. Miller: "The Cost of Capital, Corporation Finance, and Theory of Investment," *American Economic Review*, June, 1958.

———: "The Cost of Capital, Corporation Finance, and Theory of Investment: Reply," *American Economic Review*, Sept., 1959.

———: "Dividend Policy, Growth and the Valuation of Shares," *Journal of Business*, Oct., 1961.

———, F., and M. Miller: "Taxes and the Cost of Capital: A Correction," *American Economic Review*, June, 1963.

Solomon, E.: "Measuring a Company's Cost of Capital," *Journal of Business*, Oct., 1955.

———: *The Theory of Financial Management*, Columbia, New York, 1963.

Lintner, R. "Distribution of Incomes of Corporations among Dividends, Retained Earnings, and Taxes," *American Economic Review*, May, 1956.

———: "Optimal Dividends and Corporate Growth under Uncertainty," *Journal of Finance*, Feb., 1964.

APPENDIX A

Leasing Assets and the Cost of Capital

Almost all fixed assets from typewriters through machinery to land and plant are available on lease terms. Manufacturers, distributors, builders, and real estate companies offer their goods and services on lease terms as well as through straight purchase. Though a great increase in kinds of equipment available on lease terms has occurred in the period since World War II, certain leasing activities have been in existence for many years. Leasing of land and buildings is of course quite old. Leasing of tranportation equipment is quite traditional in the railroad industry. Bus companies and airlines commonly lease the vehicles they use.

Those who sell products and services may offer leases directly and through subsidiary leasing companies. In the the direct lease, the lessor may be willing to take more risk or offer better terms than would an independent leasing company or other financial institution. The reason for this is the same that leads sellers to accept trade credit risks that banks and other financial institutions would not consider. Manufacturers, however, may offer lease terms in the expectation that the leases can be sold to a financial insititution or used as security for loans. When this is so, the manufacturer has to apply the same credit standards that would be applied by the financial institution.

The lessor acts as an intermediary between the user of the equipment, the lessee, and financial institutions. The lessor uses the lease agreement, the physical assets, and the lessor's general creditworthiness as a basis for borrowing from banks, insurance companies, pension funds, and other financial institutions. If the user bought the equipment, he could borrow directly, using the asset and his own general creditworthiness. Leasing companies can act as intermediaries because they may offer the financial institution a diversified group of leases and better creditworthiness than the lessee. In addition, the lease company has two assets to serve as security for loans: It can make short-term loans on the basis of lease payments which are currently payable; it can borrow on the physical assets which have been leased. If the user-firm purchased the equipment, it could use only the physical asset as security for loans. This point is not important for a user-firm with substantial ability to borrow on an unsecured basis.

The decision to buy or lease assets is relatively complex. There is no reason to believe that either decision will be correct in all cases. We shall use an example to illustrate the differences between leasing and buying and to demonstrate an analytic technique for arriving at the correct decision.

The asset costs $100 and has an expected life of three years. Cash flow before depreciation and taxes, but after all other operating expenses, is expected to be $70 per annum. If the asset is purchased, the firm will depreciate using the sum-of-the-years-digits technique, i.e., depreciation will be 0.5 of original cost the first year, 0.33 the second year, and 0.17 the last year. Initially, we shall assume that the asset is worthless at the end of three years. Tax rate is 48 per cent.

If purchased, the firm will finance the acquisition by a three-year 6 per cent unsecured loan, to be repaid in three annual installments with interest and principal summing to a constant $37.41 a year. The division between interest and principal annually is

End of Year	Interest	Principal	Total
1	$ 6.00	$ 31.41	$ 37.41
2	4.11	33.30	37.41
3	2.12	35.29	37.41
Totals $12.23		$100.00	$112.23

If we ignore the effects of the payments on the ordering costs of cash and ignore flotation costs, the after-tax cash flow for this asset, if purchased, will be

Year	Gross Flow	Depreciation	Interest	Income Before Taxes	Income After Taxes	Debt Repayment	Depreciation	After Tax Cash Flow
1	$70	$50	$6.00	$14.00	$ 7.28	$31.41	$50	$25.87
2	70	33	4.11	32.89	17.10	33.30	33	16.80
3	70	17	2.12	50.88	26.46	35.29	17	8.17

In this case, the repayment of the financing has been deducted from the cash flow and the cost of the asset, C, is zero. Had half the asset been financed by debt with the debt payments subtracted from the after-tax cash flow, C would be $50. The original cost of the asset is reduced by the amount of the debt repayment, not interest, which has been deducted from the cash flow. In this case, the present value of the after-tax cash flow is the net present value. At a cost of capital of 0.10, it is $43.53.

Lease payments are usually made in advance. Assume a lease involving three equal annual payments of $35.30. This provides the lessor with a 6 per cent return. The firm would pay $35.30 at the beginning of each year. The annual cash flow for the lessee under this arrangement is

Year	Gross Flow	Lease Payment	Before-Tax Flow	After-Tax Flow
1	$70	$35.30	$34.70	$18.04
2	70	35.30	34.70	18.04
3	70	35.30	70.00	36.40

Depreciation is not deducted by the lessee because the asset is owned by the lessor. Interest and debt repayment are not separated because both are tax-deductible when a legitimate lease exists. If the lease is not written carefully, the tax authorities may treat the arrangement as a conditional sales agreement. This would require a complete recalculation of the tax liability under the assumption that the lessee becomes the owner. Among the criteria of a legitimate lease is that it be for no longer than 30 years, that the lessor receive a reasonable rate of return on the lease, between 6 and 10 per cent, and that, if the lessee has the option of purchasing the asset at the end of the lease, the purchase price reflect a reasonable market value.

In the example, the lease payment is not deducted from the third year because payments are in advance. The third year payment occurs at the end of the second year and is deducted at that point. The cost C of the leased asset is the cost of the first year's lease payment adjusted for taxes, i.e., $0.52 \times \$35.30 = \$18.36$. At a cost of capital of 0.10, the gross present value of the after-tax cash flow is $58.64. The net present value is $58.64 − \$18.36 = \$40.28$. In this case, the firm would buy, because the net present value of acquiring the asset by purchase is $3.25 more than if the asset were leased. It is of some interest to note that, merely by shifting the lease payments from advance payments to payments made in arrears (at the end of each of the three years), the net present value would be $44.85 for leasing, slightly more valuable than the purchase net present value.

Other slight changes in the leasing agreement would suffice to make it more profitable than the purchase. One variable in which slight changes would make little difference is the interest rate used for both leasing and buying. The interest rate used by the lessor would have to be less than half the 6 per cent charged for the three-year loan before leasing would be advantageous.

The cost of capital is an important variable. It is reasonably clear that, under either lease or purchase, the firm becomes involved in a fixed obligation, the magnitude of which is similar under either alternative. Under the purchase, the firm would show the three-year loan in its liabilities. The liability is as great under the lease, but most firms do not show the lease obligation as a liability.

Two reasons for the different attitude of stockholders toward leases and loans are ignorance and unfamiliarity: ignorance because the lease is not recorded; unfamiliarity because it may not be as clear that a lease is just as fixed a claim to the income stream and the assets of the firm as is a loan. As a result, the cost of capital for purchases of assets financed by debt may be larger than for lease-financed asset acquisitions.

When a firm owns an asset, any gain in disposal value of that asset accrues to the firm. If it leases the asset, the capital gain goes to the lessor. For most equipment, salvage value usually does not result in a capital gain. Indeed, obsolescence may result in a capital loss. With land and building, however, capital gains are quite possible. To offset this advantage to owning, the lessee and lessor can negotiate lower lease payments for assets where capital gains seem likely. But not all capital gains can be foreseen, and the firm using an asset, the resale value of which may soar because of a large windfall gain, may prefer to own the asset rather than lease it.

The lease used in the example is called a *net lease*. Under a net lease, the lessee pays taxes, maintenance, and other expenses directly associated with the leased asset. The lessor's function is purely financial, and the lease is a financial instrument similar to a bond. It is not uncommon for the lessor to provide other services as well as the financial service, with the cost of these services included in the lease rental.

Often, the lessor cannot perform services such as paying property taxes on the leased asset any more efficiently than can the lessee. Sometimes the lessor can provide maintenance more cheaply. However, it is usually possible to buy maintenance separate from a lease by entering into a maintenance service contract when buying the asset. Even if the gross lease services cannot be performed more efficiently by the lessor than by the lessee, the lessor may be able to provide the services more cheaply if the lessor firm has access to cheaper sources of funds. The only solution is to compare the net present value of an asset purchase with the net present value of a gross lease.

If assets are leased and the lease allows the lessee to cancel the lease with no side payments, the firm may be enabled to use assets with little risk. If the assets turn out to be unprofitable, the firm can return them to the lessor. In effect, the lessee shifts the asset risk from himself to the lessor. Since free insurance is, to say the least, uncommon, the rentals in cancelable leases contain an insurance premium. The relevant question is not whether such risk insurance is free, but whether the insurance premium is less than if the firm purchased the asset and took the risk on a "self-insurance" basis. Can the lessor assume risks at a lower cost than would prevail if the lessee absorbed the risk? This is possible under at least two conditions.

First, if the asset is widely used by many firms, the lessor may be able to transfer the use of the asset from one firm to another at minimal cost. Computer equipment is an example. One firm may decide to abandon the equipment to some other firm. The transfer can be effected at less cost than if the original lessee had owned the equipment and tried to sell it on the secondhand market, because the lessor has better knowledge of the secondhand market and can offer lease terms to a new user.

Second, even if the leased asset is highly specialized so that there is no substantial secondhand market, the lessor may be able to absorb the loss of a canceled lease more easily than the user-firm could absorb the loss of an unprofitable asset. The argument here is based on pure insurance principles. If the lessor has cancelable lease agreements with many firms, it can foresee that some of these agreements will be canceled, resulting in a loss to the lessor. The individual cancellation will result in a loss to the lessor equal to the loss that the using firm would incur if it owned the asset. Since the lessor cannot predict which of the leases will be canceled, it will spread the cost of the anticipated losses due to cancellation among all the lease agreements. As long as the lessor does not expect all leases to be canceled, there is a good chance that the *cancellation-loss insurance premium* included in the rental payments will be less than the loss the firm would suffer if it owned the asset.

To sum up, there is no a priori reason for believing leases to be more or less costly than purchases of assets. Each case must be analyzed separately, with all relevant services and costs included in the cash flows. The firm will buy if the net present value of the after-tax cash flow for purchasing assets exceeds the net present value of the after-tax cash flow for leasing. Otherwise, it will lease.

SELECTED REFERENCES

Anthony, R. N., and S. Schwartz: *Office Equipment: Buy or Rent?* Management Analysis Center, Boston, 1957.

Leasing of Industrial Equipment, Bulletin No. 21, Council for Technological Advancement, Washington, D.C., 1954.

Taxation of Leasing, Bulletin No. 3660, Machinery and Allied Products Institute, Washington, D.C., 1960.

Treynor, J., and R. Vancil: *Machine Tool Leasing*, Management Analysis Center, Boston, 1956.

Vancil, R., and R. N. Anthony: "The Financial Community Looks at Leasing," *Harvard Business Review*, Nov.–Dec., 1959.

APPENDIX B

Mergers and Business Failures

MERGERS

The normal way to increase the asset portfolio is to buy assets from another firm whose business it is to sell such assets, as with buying a machine tool from a machine tool manufacturer; or to build assets, as in the case of a plant. An alternative exists to this approach—the acquisition of another firm which already has the assets the acquiring firm wishes. Such acquisitions can take a number of forms: If the acquiring firm simply absorbs the other firm, with the identity of the acquired firm lost in the acquisition, the form is called a *statutory merger;* if both acquiring and acquired firms lose their identities in a new firm, the form is called a *statutory consolidation;* if the acquired firm retains its identity but control passes to the acquiring firm, the acquired firm becomes a *subsidiary* and the acquiring firm is referred to as the *parent corporation*. A *holding company* is a parent firm whose asset portfolio consists almost completely of the stocks of its subsidiaries. In the following discussion, the acquisition of one firm by another, regardless if it be by merger, consolidation, or via the holding company device, will be referred to as a *merger*. Despite the inaccuracy, the usage is common and is justified for the sake of simplicity.

The model for the merger decision is the same as that used for fixed assets. In fact, the alternative to merger often is normal plant and equipment acquisition. If the risks of the alternatives are equal, the firm will choose the route providing the higher net present value. Where the risks differ, the choice will depend on which alternative provides the more desirable combination of risk and return.

From the point of view of the buying firm, certain advantages may be associated with merger rather than the ordinary means of increasing assets. If the acquired firm had been or, after the acquisition of the new assets, would have been a competitor, competition is reduced. As a result, the assets acquired by merger are likely to be more profitable than if acquired by other means and/or less risky.

Another advantage that may accrue from merger is that the assets absorbed with the absorbed firm constitute a going concern. The absorbing firm buys not only the assets, but the experience, administrative organization, etc., of the old firm. In some cases, this may be a liability, but it is apt to be an asset when the absorbing firm is adding to its product mixture, moving into a new market, or developing some other new function, as opposed to expansion of existing operations. Another advantage of the going concern is that the absorbing firm may have access to more accurate estimates of costs and demand with a firm that has been in operation for a time than it would if it started from scratch with new assets. This should work to reduce the variance of estimates, reducing risk.

Still another reason for preferring merger is that the cost may be lower than for buying new assets, or the income stream may be greater. There are several factors which make either of these possibilities highly probable.

The area of income taxation can have several effects on the price of a firm or the income stream to be derived from acquiring a firm, most of which work to make merger more desirable than the normal means of acquiring assets. The value of the firm absorbed is presumably the present value of its expected future returns. If the owners of the firm choose to remain as owners, they will realize these returns, but the returns will be subject to normal corporate taxation, and the dividends generated will be taxed as ordinary income. However, if the owners sell the firm, they receive the present value of the firm's expected future returns, but taxed as a capital gain, i.e., at half the tax rate which would be applied to normal income.

Taxation pushes in the direction of merger for firms which are sustaining losses, providing that the losses are not expected to continue indefinitely. The value of such a firm to another firm may be higher than to the existing owners. The losses currently being generated can be carried forward to reduce future taxable profits, providing the profits are generated within five years of when the loss is incurred. By merging the losing firm with a firm earning profits, the two firms can present consolidated operating statements for tax purposes, and the losses of one can reduce the tax liability of the other immediately. An example may clarify this argument. Assume a corporate tax rate structure of 22 per cent on the first $25,000 of taxable income and 48 per cent on all income in excess of $25,000. A firm that generates a $1 loss today can reduce its taxable income by the loss, providing it earns income within five years of the loss. If it earns profits next year, today's loss will reduce next year's income tax liability by either 22 per cent or 48 per cent of the loss, depending on whether earnings are above $25,000 or not. If earnings are $25,000 or below, today's $1 loss saves $0.22 next year. If earnings exceed $25,000, today's loss saves $0.48 next year. All else aside, it is obvious that a tax loss is more valuable to a large corporation whose earnings exceed $25,000 than to a small firm. Assume that the firm sustaining the loss, expects the 48 per cent rate to apply next year. Nonetheless, the present value of today's loss is less than $0.48 because the firm has to wait a year. At a discount rate of 10 per cent, the present value of $0.48 next year is less than $0.44. To the firm which has a current profit, the value of the loss would be the full $0.48 when consolidated with its profits. The scene for a merger is set with the absorbing firm's reservation price of less than $0.48 per dollar of loss and the absorbed firm's reservation price of $0.44 or more. The further off, or the less certain, are future profits, the greater the gap between what a profit-making firm would be willing to pay for the loss-taking firm and the minimum price the loss-taking firm would be willing to accept.

It isn't even necessary that the loss-taking firm even have a real prospect of profit to make a desirable candidate for merger. Given a sufficiently low price, the gross present value of the tax reductions resulting from the losses could be sufficiently large to make the merger profitable to the absorbing firm. If a portion of the losses result from depreciation, the losing firm is an even better buy, for then the actual cash flows resulting from the combination of depreciation with the tax saving will be even larger.

The particular magical quality of our tax structure which converts loss into gains is not the only, nor necessarily the major, reason for mergers. A relatively undiversified firm, even if highly profitable, may be willing to be absorbed by a larger, more diversified firm in order to reduce risk. In this instance, the income stream of the smaller firm is valued more highly by the larger firm, because the stream is less risky after the merger than before.

Other factors which lead to the merger of small firms into larger ones rely on economies of scale. The economies may relate to production, marketing, management, or finance. In any of these, the existence of economies of scale make the present value of a small firm larger if merged than as an independent firm.

The actual medium of exchange in a merger may be cash, stock, other securities, or some combination of these. In a statutory merger, the absorbing company may exchange its stock for the stock of the absorbed firm. In a statutory consolidation, both firms may exchange their stock for the stock of the new corporation. Even if there is a simple sale of assets, payment for the assets may be in securities. From the point of view of the buying firm, the use of securities as a medium of exchange is desirable in that it conserves cash. The selling firm may prefer securities, also, since this postpones capital gains tax payments as well as to provide a means by which the sellers can hold a share of the presumably superior income stream resulting from the merger. In addition to such payments, and particularly with the absorption of a small, new firm, the absorbing firm may offer managerial contracts to the officers of the absorbed corporation. These provide the absorbing firm with continuity of management for the absorbed firm and may be an important factor in convincing the officers of the absorbed corporation to agree to the merger.

Regardless of the medium of exchange used, the major problem in effecting merger is determining the value of the absorbed corporation. Where there is an exchange of securitites, the problem of valuation extends to the absorbing firm as well, since the question is: How many shares of A corporation stock equal one share of B corporation stock? Basically, the problem is solved by bargaining, and the results reflect not only the value of the merger to each party, but also the abilities of the bargainers.

Presumably, the market value of each company's stock would determine the values relative to each other. However, such is not always the case. If one company's stock is not actively traded, or is, perhaps, held by a closed group so that it is not traded at all, it is quite difficult to determine fair values. Even where the stocks are actively traded, it can always be argued that current market price is temporarily low or temporarily high, depending upon who is doing the arguing. Such arguments cannot be easily disproved, and they may well be true. The mere rumor of an impending merger could send the price of a firm's stock up, and this can hardly be viewed as reflecting the value of the firm. Other valuation methods, such as calling in professional appraisers, are not foolproof, since the valuations placed can and do vary from appraiser to appraiser.

Valuation is particularly important in statutory mergers or consolidations. Not only the officers of the corporations have to agree that the valuation is fair, most of the stockholders of both firms also have to agree. State laws vary, but it is common for the law to require that two-thirds of the stockholders of both corporations must agree to a proposed merger or consolidation. Even with this approval, individual stockholders may object. Procedure for treating the complaints of minority stockholders vary, but typically the dissenting stockholders have to be bought out. The value of their shares can be set by voluntary agreement or by a court of law. Where valuation is high or dissentors numerous, the cost of purchasing dissenting shares may make the merger infeasible.

The purchase of assets without statutory merger provides the buying firm the chance to buy only the assets it wants. Further, it does not have to absorb the liabilities of the selling firm. This may be quite important if the selling firm got into difficulties because of an inappropriate capital structure. Also, stockholder assent to a purchase of assets is limited to stockholders of the selling firm only.

Under some circumstances, the easiest way to effect a merger is through the holding company device. Effective control may be acquired with considerably less than even 51 per cent of stock ownership in the subsidiary. However, to achieve the advantages of filing a consolidated return for all of the controlled corporations, 80 per cent or more of the stock of the subsidiaries must be owned by the parent. Also, stockholder approval is usually not necessary if control is achieved via the holding company device.

Mergers are affected by public policy if competition is substantially lessened as a result. Under Section 7 of the Clayton Act, either the Federal Trade Commission can file a complaint or the Department of Justice can bring suit against mergers which are believed to violate the law. However, the definition of what is meant by substantially lessening competition is determined by judicial decision on a case-by-case basis. Except where mergers involve major competitors in a given market, antitrust policy is usually not relevant.

BUSINESS FAILURE

In 1963, the business failure rate was relatively low. On the average, 1,198 firms failed each month. Though most of these firms were small, their current liabilities averaged almost $113 million per month during 1963. On a monthly basis, almost six firms failed each month for every thousand firms in existence. Thus, some understanding of the legal procedures followed in business failure is important. Even if "your" firm does not fail, it is not unlikely that one of its debtor customers will, and then the problem of how to recover the debt arises. Practically speaking, this is a highly technical problem involving experts in law and credit management. The purpose here is simply to discuss the rationale underlying the processes of reorganization and liquidation and to outline the major legislation and legal procedures involved.

Traditionally, the primary cause for failure has been placed at the door of management, often properly so. Inept or dishonest managers can drive a firm to failure. Blaming management solely for business failure is, however, naive. There are almost no business decisions which enjoy a single-valued probability distribution of expectations. Even following the best procedures, actual values resulting from business decisions can turn out to be disastrous, even though such a turn of luck seemed highly improbable when the decision was made. General economic conditions also play an important role. In 1933, 31.822 firms failed out of a total of less than 2.1 millions in existence. In 1960, there were about 2.7 millions of firms, but only 15,445 failures. Incidentally, the 1933 definition of failure excludes certain classes of discontinuances which are included in 1960.

Business failure can be defined in many ways. Two distinctions seem to be particularly important. A business is technically insolvent if it is unable to pay its currently maturing obligations. A business is insolvent in the bankruptcy sense if a reasonable valuation of assets indicates that they are less than liabilities, i.e., if net worth is negative. Both problems are important, but the cure for technical insolvency is often considerably milder than the cure called for if the firm is insolvent in the bankruptcy sense.

Prior to the depression of the '30's, the sole aim of reorganization and bankruptcy proceedings was to protect creditors. This is still an important purpose. However, the depression indicated that public policy should be broadened. Large numbers of business owners suffered losses which might have been avoided or reduced with less harsh legal procedures. Further, the adverse impact of a high rate of business liquidation on employment was also a factor in modifying reorganization procedures. Current laws, as embodied in Chapter 10 of the Bankruptcy Act, provide for representation of stockholders in the preparation of the reorganization plan and careful judicial review of the plan. Under Chapter 11, the owners of the firm cannot be adversely affected by the reorganization. Under the equity receivership procedure that prevailed prior to 1934, liquidation was a more likely result than reorganization. Reorganization plans were prepared to satsify insiders in the creditor group with little control by the court and no evaluation of the plan was made by a disinterested party. Dissenters who disagreed with the reorganization had to be "bought off" and, if sufficient dissent existed, the plan could not be adopted. By the time a plan was accepted, the firm might well be beyond reorganization.

Modern reorganization procedures can be unofficial or made through the courts. The plan can be voluntary, i.e., begun by the debtor firm, or involuntary, i.e., begun by creditors. All reorganization plans involve elements of composition and extension. Composition refers to a scaling down of financial claims. For example, creditors may be asked to accept $0.50 for each dollar owed by the debtor, or bondholders may have to accept preferred stock. Extension refers to an extension of maturity dates.

The simplest, cheapest, and most rapid form of reorganization is one in which creditors voluntarily accept composition and extension without recourse to the courts. This type of reorganization is usually associated with technical insolvency. The agency through which the composition and extension agreement is reached is often an adjustment bureau set up by a credit men's association or a trade association. The debtor is left in control of the firm. However, creditors can insist upon safeguards and would not agree to the composition and extension unless the moral risk were slight. One of the problems of informal composition and extension agreements is that a dissenting creditor can block the agreement unless bought off. Further, once the debtor has admitted that he cannot meet his obligations, some of the creditors may band together and attempt to force the debtor into bankruptcy. Nonetheless, the informal and rapid procedures of composition and extension agreement, are often ideal from the point of view of both debtor and creditors. The agreement can be reached rapidly enough so that the firm's deterioration can be halted. The legal fees are low enough so that the creditor usually nets more from the debtor than if formal court procedures were followed.

Chapter 11 of the Bankruptcy Act is the closest legal equivalent to the informal composition and extension system. It applies both to corporations and unincorporated enterprises and can only be started by the debtor, i.e., it is voluntary. The reorganization plan can only affect unsecured creditors and usually involves a scaling down of unsecured creditors' claims. The court may or may not appoint a receiver or trustee to take over the properties in question during the court procedures. A receiver will be appointed if there is a possibility that a creditor may sue under another bankruptcy provision. The receivership protects the business properties from legal harassment during the period when a reorganization is being planned and also tries to rehabilitate properties where necessary. The receiver can be the owner of the business in a Chapter 11 proceeding. The court conducts meetings with owner and creditors. Following this, the owner submits a reorganization plan which, if approved by the court and by a majority of each debtor class affected, is adopted. The court then appoints a receiver, trustee, or disbursing agent, representing the court, to carry out the reorganization. Obviously, a firm which is insolvent in the bankruptcy sense is unlikely to benefit from a Chapter 11 reorganization.

A Chapter 10 reorganization is usually much more far-reaching. It may be commenced voluntarily by the debtor or by three or more creditors with claims totaling $5,000 or more. A disinterested trustee must be appointed by the court if debts exceed $250,000 and may be appointed even for smaller debts. A co-trustee from the management of the company is appointed to aid in operation of the firm. As with a Chapter 11 reorganization, the court effectively takes title, and creditors may not harass the firm with additional suits. Committees are formed representing each class of creditor and stockholder. The trustee confers with the committees and prepares a plan, which is presented to the court. A Chapter 10 reorganization plan usually involves an exchange of securities, with the various creditor groups accepting smaller claims or more junior claims in return for their old claims. Very often, the old stockholders are wiped out. Provisions are included for the selection of a new management. The SEC may prepare an advisory report on the proposed reorganization and must do so when debts exceed $3 million. Following this, the court approves the plan if it is fair and feasible.

There has been considerable discussion of the criteria of fairness. One criterion is absolute priority, which means that the old stockholder group can have no interest in the reorganized company unless the projected earnings and capitalization of the new company meet the claims of the old creditors completely. Since projected earnings for a firm that has gone through a Chapter 10 reorganization are, quite properly, very conservative, it often turns out, after the new corporation has been in operation, that the old stockholders could have received some consideration. The doctrine of relative priority would provide a contingent claim for the old stockholders, sometimes involving the investment of additional funds. Supreme Court cases have upheld the doctrine of absolute priority.

The primary criterion of feasibility is that the new corporation be able to meet fixed charges on its income. In addition, of course, the reorganization plan should provide for correction of other problems, such as obsolete plant, worthless inventories, or ineffective management.

Chapter 10 proceedings can lead to corporate liquidation, if liquidation will provide more adequately for creditors' claims than will reorganization. However, liquidation can take place in other ways. One method is assignment of the assets of the debtor company to an assignee or trustee, who is to dispose of the assets and distribute the proceeds on a pro rata basis among the creditors. An assignment does not necessarily relieve the debtor of any remaining obligation. However, if creditors accept payment as payment in full, the debtor is cleared of further claims. At any rate, the debtor can petition the courts to be declared bankrupt, in which event a procedure is commenced which terminates in the clearance of the debtor from further claims resulting from the bankrupt corporation. Railroads are subject to different laws of reorganization than other firms.

As indicated, the debtor may voluntarily petition for bankruptcy. An involuntary petition may be filed by creditors providing: The debts of the insolvent firm are equal to or greater than $1,000; the petitioning creditor be owed at least $500 if the total number of creditors is less than 12, or, if the number of creditors is 12 or greater, there must be at least 3 creditor petitioners with an aggregate claim of at least $500; the debtor must have committed one or more of the six acts of bankruptcy during the preceding four months. The six acts of bankruptcy are: concealment or fraudulent conveyance of property, which consists of either hiding assets with intent to defraud creditors or transferring property to someone with inadequate payment with intent to defraud creditors; preferential transfer, which is the transfer of assets by an insolvent debtor to a creditor, providing the creditor with more than he would receive under a liquidation; permitting a creditor to place a legal lien, or claim, on property and not discharging the claim within 30 days; making a general assignment of assets for the benefit of creditors; appointing a receiver or trustee to take charge of his property; admitting in writing that he is unable to pay his debts and is willing to be judged bankrupt.

Following the petition of bankruptcy, the court declares the debtor to be bankrupt. The case is then assigned to a referee in bankruptcy, a lawyer acting for the judge. To safeguard the creditors' interests, the judge or referee may appoint a receiver to act as custodian of the property until a trustee is appointed. The trustee is elected by the creditors and works with the creditors' committee to liquidate the assets. Any sale of property at less than 75 per cent of appraised value must be consented to by the court. After all bankruptcy expenses have been met, any remaining funds may be distributed as dividends to the creditors. Following the submission of the trustee's report, if no fraud is involved, the debtor is discharged of bankruptcy and is free to reenter business free of past obligations. Under the National Bankruptcy Act, no debtor may receive a bankruptcy discharge more than every six years.

Bankruptcy proceedings are lengthy and expensive. Creditors receive very little, unsecured creditors often receiving nothing. The net yield is probably as much a commentary on the severity of the condition of a firm reaching the stage of bankruptcy, as on the administration of the bankruptcy procedures.

SELECTED REFERENCES

Butters, J. K., J. Lintner, W. L. Cary, and P. Niland: *Effects of Taxation: Corporate Mergers*, Harvard, Cambridge, Mass., 1951.
Calkins, F. J.: "Corporate Reorganizations under Chapter X: A Post-Mortem," *Journal of Finance*, June, 1948.
———: "Feasibility of Plans of Corporate Reorganization under Chapter X," *Journal of Finance*, May, 1948.
Federal Trade Commission, *Report on Corporate Mergers and Acquisitions*, U.S. Government Printing Office, 1955.
Lintner, J., and J. K. Butters: "Effects of Mergers on Industrial Concentration, 1940–'47," *Review of Economics and Statistics*, Feb., 1950.
Markham, J.: "Summary of the Evidence and Findings on Mergers," *Business Concentration and Price Problems*, Princeton, N.J., 1955.
Walter, J. E.: "Determinants of Technical Solvency," *Journal of Business*, Jan., 1957.
Watson, ETP, "Distribution of New Securities in Section 77 Reorganizations," *Journal of Finance*, Dec., 1950.
Weston, J. F., *The Role of Mergers in the Growth of Large Firms*, U. of Cal., Berkley, 1953.

THE FINANCIAL
ECONOMY

The Financial Economy :
The Accounting Relationships

11

So far, we have viewed the problems of finance through the glasses of the firm: a "microfinancial" approach. The micro approach provides insights into the adaptive mechanism of the firm, i.e., how the firm reacts to external factors to achieve an optimal balance sheet, but provides little information on the processes by which the factors external to the firm change. In this and the next several chapters we shall focus on these processes.

To accomplish this, finance must be viewed in the large. Our prime concern will shift from the individual firm to all business corporations, and to the financial economy. The Board of Governors of the Federal Reserve System provides a very convenient analytic framework in its Flow of Funds Accounts. The concepts underlying the accounts will be explored in this and the next two chapters.

This is not the first time we have encountered the term flow of funds. In the Appendix to Chapter 4, flow of funds analysis was illustrated as applied to the individual firm. The Federal Reserve approach is very similar to this. Each entity in the economy is viewed as having a balance sheet and an income statement. Funds are used as a means of investing in assets. Thus, changes in assets are changes in the *uses* of funds. Since assets may decrease as well as increase, uses may be either positive or negative. Liabilities, net worth, and the reserve for depreciation account, all of which have a credit balance typically, are considered *sources* of funds. Since these accounts may decrease as well as increase, sources may be positive, as when borrowing occurs, or negative, as when debt is repaid.

Uses of funds are divided into two main groups—real and financial. Real uses are related to nonfinancial assets, such as inventories and plant and equipment. Financial assets include money and accounts receivable, as well as securities owned. Sources of funds are also divided into two groups—internal and financial. Internal sources include capital consumption, i.e., depreciation and accidental damage to fixed assets, and retained earnings. Financial, or external, sources include all other liability and net worth items, such as bank loans, accounts payable, common stock, term loans, and accruals.

One equality is readily apparent: Uses equal sources. Another way of putting it is

Real uses + financial uses = internal sources + financial sources.

The Federal Reserve Board manipulates this equation algebraically by subtracting financial sources from both sides of the equation so that

Real uses + (financial uses − financial sources) = internal sources.

Further, the Board makes the following definitions:

Financial uses − financial sources = net financial investment.
Real uses = private capital expenditures.
Private capital expenditures + net financial investment = gross investment.
Retained earnings = net savings.
Depreciation + accidental damage to fixed assets = capital consumption.
Net savings + capital consumption = gross savings.

Using these definitions, we have

Private capital expenditures + net financial investment = Gross savings,

or

Gross investment = gross savings.

It may be easier to understand the equations and their relationship to the operating statements by an example. In the Appendix to Chapter 4, Exhibit 4-1 presents operating statements for a hypothetical firm. Exhibit 4-2 illustrates how these data can be analyzed to show the sources and uses of working capital. In Exhibit 11-1, the operating statements are analyzed to show the sources and uses of funds.

The illustration might be interpreted as follows: During the period analyzed, the firm spent $110 on real assets; however, internal funds came to $250; the surplus of $140 was used to reduce indebtedness, to increase the cash balance, and was invested in accounts receivable. The reason that

Exhibit 11-1

SOURCES AND USES OF FUNDS FOR ABC MANUFACTURING
CORPORATION, SIX-MONTH PERIOD ENDING JUNE 30, 1963

	Uses	Sources
A. Gross savings = B + C................................$ ...		$250
B. Capital consumption		50
C. Net savings		200
D. Gross investment = E + H	250	
E. Private capital expenditures = F + G	110	
F. Plant & equipment expenditures	80	
G. Change in inventories	30	
H. Net financial investment = I − J	140	
I. Changes in financial assets	130	
J. Changes in liabilities		−10
K. Money..	80	
L. Trade credit	50	20
M. Bank loans		−10
N. Term loans		−60
O. Paid-in capital		
P. Accruals		40

both a source and use entry appear for trade credit is to reflect both accounts
receivable, a use, and accounts payable, a source.

SECTORS

A simple compilation of the balance sheets of
all entities in the economy would result in a
meaningless total balance sheet. Not only do we
want to know whether assets are increasing or
decreasing and whether the changes in assets are being financed by internal
or external sources, but we would like to know who is borrowing and who
is lending. Are assets growing because households are buying more houses
or because firms are constructing more plant facilities?

Even more confusing would be a listing of the individual operating
statements. There are millions of economic entities in our society, and the
detail would be meaningless.

Obviously, some compromise between totaling all data and totaling none
is required. The point of compromise involves partial aggregation of the
operating statements, with the separation, or sectoring, of operating statements based on a principle which makes sense to those who use the data.
The criterion for sectoring could be location, size, or type of activity of
the entities.

The Federal Reserve has chosen type of activity as the basis for sectoring.
The economy is divided into 11 sectors, and the flow of funds analysis is
presented on an aggregated basis for each sector. The sectors are

1. Consumer and nonprofit, which includes all households and nonprofit institutions such as colleges and churches;
2. Farm business, which includes all commercial farm operations, incorporated or unincorporated;
3. Noncorporate, nonfarm, nonfinancial business, which includes all unincorporated businesses, except farms and unincorporated financial firms such as securities brokerage firms;
4. Corporate nonfinancial business, which includes all business corporations, except incorporated farms and financial corporations such as banks and insurance companies;
5. Federal government, which includes the fiscal and financial operations of the government, but excludes the monetary functions of the Federal government;
6. State and local governments, which includes the fiscal and financial operations of state, county, city, school district, and other governmental units, except Federal government;
7. Commercial banking, which includes the operations of all commercial banks, the United States central bank, which is the Federal Reserve System, and the monetary functions of the United States Treasury;
8. Savings institutions, which include all thrift institutions, including mutual savings banks, savings and loan associations, and credit unions;
9. Insurance, which includes life and casualty insurance companies;
10. Finance not elsewhere classified, which includes investment banking, securities brokers, investment funds, and all other financial institutions not included as banks, savings institutions, and insurance companies;
11. Rest of the world, which sector is necessary to have a complete picture of the economy and includes all export and import activities, as well as the purchases and sales of foreign securities by domestic entities and the purchases and sales of United States securities by foreigners.

The Federal Reserve's choice of sectors is arbitrary. It could be far more detailed, showing, for example, the industrial breakdown of nonfinancial businesses and separating households from nonprofit institutions. We shall move in the other direction. For purposes of simplifying the analysis of the accounts, we shall aggregate the sectors into households, businesses, governments, the rest of the world, the monetary sector, and the nonbanking financial sectors. When the analysis has been completed, we shall return to the greater detail of the Federal Reserve sectoring.

CONSOLIDATION
AND NETTING

Consolidation. The flow of funds for each sector is largely consolidated by the Federal Reserve Board. The claims of one nonfinancial business corporation against another, for example, are subtracted from the financial assets of the company which owns the claim and from the liabilities of the company which sold the claim. What emerges from this is a consolidated measure of intersectoral transactions, with all intrasectoral transactions removed.

Income statements will also be consolidated within the sector. The purchases of equipment by one firm from another will be shown neither as a sale nor as an expenditure. Instead, the selling firm will record payments to another sector for the labor and raw materials needed to manufacture the equipment, or, if the equipment was manufactured in an earlier period and sold from inventory, it will be recorded as a decrease in the seller's inventory investment. The purchase will be recorded as an investment in real assets by the buyer.

Netting. Netting of accounts differs from consolidation, although both have the effect of destroying information. Consolidation destroys the information on how much investment is financed within the same sector. Netting destroys the gross changes that have occurred in an account. For example, if households sell $1 million of corporate stock, and other households purchase $2 million of corporate stock, the net effect on the common stock account for households is an increase of $1 million. Yet, the gross figure is a very useful indicator of what is happening in the economy.

The less homogeneous a transaction classification is, the more troublesome is netting. The Federal Reserve Board lumps the stock issues of nonfinancial business corporations with the stock issues of all other corporations, including banks, mutual funds, and stock of corporations of foreign countries. When the stock account is netted for sectors, it is impossible to tell which of the stock-issuing sectors is being financed by the sector buying the stock.

For better or worse, the Federal Reserve Board does net and does consolidate. We shall follow this practice also, since it would be foolish to develop a full-information analytic system with no quantitative counterpart when there is a quantitative counterpart to a system providing somewhat less information.

AN INDIRECT APPROACH
TO THE FLOW OF FUNDS

Despite the complaining tone of the paragraphs above, the quantity of data on our financial economy provided by the Flow-of-Funds Accounts is staggering. The data are presented in a matrix of interlocking accounts both within and between sectors. In short, the Flow-of-Funds present a substantial portion of a *tableau economique* for the United States on a quarterly basis.

Rather than race to the presentation of the matrix and then try to explain what it all means, the approach will be to start with a very simple general system and gradually add to it, finally arriving at the actual system used by the Federal Reserve. The first model, or system, will be for only two sectors, a household sector that provides labor, land, and some capital to the firm sector, which produces the goods and services that are purchased by the households.

Two versions of the two-sector model will be shown. In the first, the only external financing will be represented by the investment of household-owners in the firms, as partners or sole proprietors may invest funds in a firm. The second model will permit a wider range of external financing, including consumer finance, debt, and stock financing. Both versions will allow internal financing.

The second system will add a government sector to the firms and households. The government sector will tax households and firms, borrow from households and firms, and buy goods and services from households and firms. However, it will have no monetary functions.

The third system will add a fourth sector, the rest of the world. This foreign sector will buy and sell goods and services to all the domestic sectors. In addition, it will sell and buy debt and equity claims.

The three systems describe the operations of what may be termed the real sectors of the financial economy. These are the sectors which operate primarily to produce and consume real goods and services, as contrasted to sectors which operate mainly to produce financial services, such as banks and insurance companies. In this chapter, we shall concentrate on the accounting structure of the flow-of-funds for the real sectors. Chapter 12 will contain a theoretical model for the real sectors. The nature of U.S. financial institutions will be treated in Chapters 13, 14, and 15. The final chapter will be devoted to analyzing the post-war growth patterns of U.S. corporations as seen in the flow-of-funds' accounts and the behavior of capital markets.

Algebraic notation will be used to express the relationships between and within the sectors. This poses the problem of remembering the meaning of symbols, or abbreviations. However, the symbols will be mnemonic, and a glossary will precede each sections describing the new symbols to be introduced in that section. To reduce the number of symbols, subscripts will be used to indicate the sector involved. For example, I_h will indicate the capital expenditures of the household sector, while I_f will indicate capital expenditures made by firms. Financial assets will usually have two subscripts. The left subscript will refer to the sector holding the financial asset, and the subscript to the right of the symbol will indicate which sector issued the financial claim. Thus, $_hE_f$ will indicate stock or equity shares issued by firms and held by households. And $_fB_h$ will indicate debt owed by households and held by business firms. The two-subscript system will not be needed until the model has more than two sectors.

Arithmetic examples of the flow of funds will be shown for each model of the real sectors. We shall not, however, be able to turn to actual data until the monetary and financial sectors have been covered. The real sectors not only hold claims on each other, but hold claims on financial and monetary institutions, and vice versa. In Chapters 12 through 15, actual data will be used, and the actual data associated with all sectors will be treated in Chapter 16.

As a result of postponing the inclusion of the monetary and financial sectors until after the real sectors have been considered, the money supply used for the real sectors will be peculiar. It may be viewed as a gold system. Until the rest of the world is introduced, the domestic money supply will be fixed, so that one sector will be able to increase cash holdings only to the extent that other sectors decrease cash holdings. A more familiar money supply will be introduced in chapter 12.

THE TWO-SECTOR
INTERNALLY FINANCED MODEL

The two sectors are households and firms. Firms produce goods and services, which they sell to each other and to households. Interfirm transactions are consolidated outside the equations. Firms also buy labor services and property rights from households. There is no borrowing for either firms or households. Firms do not sell marketable ownership shares. However, firms are owned by households, and the owner-households may increase investment in firms just as a single proprietor or partner might invest funds in the single proprietorship or partnership. The owner-ship claims to the firms are not marketable except by selling the entire firm. Otherwise, all financing for firms is accomplished by retained earnings or depreciation, and for households, by saving or depreciation. The economy, thus, is almost completely financed internally.

GLOSSARY

Subscript h stands for households, and subscript f, for firms. The subscript will appear to the right only of nonfinancial assets and retained earnings, indicating the sector owing these items. For financial claims, the subscript at the right will indicate the issuing sector and the left subscript will indicate the sector owning the financial claim.

TA	Total assets
M	Cash or money
E	Nonmarketable paid-in investment by household-owners to firms
CD	Consumer durable goods net of depreciation
RH	Residential housing net of depreciation
RD	Reserve for depreciation
TL	Total liabilities and net worth

RE Cumulated total of retained earnings, or earned surplus
Q Inventory
PE Plant and equipment, net of depreciation
GI Gross investment
I Capital expenditures
NFI Net financial investment
FA Financial assets, i.e., total assets — real assets
FL Financial liabilities, i.e., total liabilities and net worth minus earned surplus
NS Net savings
GS Gross savings
CR Current receipts
C Expenditures on current account: for households, nondurable consumption payment; for firms, current payment for goods produced and sold during the period
D Capital consumption allowance

The letter d appearing before a balance sheet item indicates change, i.e., dPE is the change in plant and equipment holdings, or the amount invested in plant and equipment during the period being considered.

BALANCE SHEETS— HOUSEHOLDS

$$(11\text{-}1) \quad TA_h = {}_hM + {}_hE_f + CD + RH - RD_h$$

$$(11\text{-}2) \quad TL_h = RE_h$$

$$(11\text{-}3) \quad TA_h = TL_h$$

BALANCE SHEETS— FIRMS

$$(11\text{-}4) \quad TA_f = {}_fM + Q + PE - RD_f$$

$$(11\text{-}5) \quad TL_f = E_f + RE_f$$

$$(11\text{-}6) \quad TA_f = TL_f$$

USES OF FUNDS— HOUSEHOLDS

$$(11\text{-}7) \quad GI_h = I_h + NFI_h$$

$$(11\text{-}8) \quad I_h = dCD + dRH$$

$$(11\text{-}9) \quad NFI_h = d_h FA - dFL_h$$

$$(11\text{-}10) \quad dFA_h = d_h M + dE_f$$

$$(11\text{-}11) \quad dFL_h = 0, \text{ because there are no household financial liabilities in this model}$$

USES OF FUNDS— FIRMS

$$(11\text{-}12) \quad GI_f = I_f + NFI_f$$

$$(11\text{-}13) \quad I_f = dQ + dPE$$

$$(11\text{-}14) \quad NFI_f = d_f FA - dFL_f$$

$$(11\text{-}15) \quad dFA_f = d_f M$$

$$(11\text{-}16) \quad dFL_f = dE_f$$

SOURCES OF FUNDS— HOUSEHOLDS

$$(11\text{--}17) \quad CR_h = C_f + I_f = CR_f - NFI_f$$

$$(11\text{--}18) \quad NS_h = CR_h - C_h - D_h$$

$$(11\text{--}19) \quad GS_h = NS_h + D_h$$

SOURCES OF FUNDS— FIRMS

$$(11\text{--}20) \quad CR_f = C_h + I_h = CR_h - NFI_h$$

$$(11\text{--}21) \quad NS_f = CR_f - C_f - D_f$$

$$(11\text{--}22) \quad GS_f = NS_f + D_f$$

The Circular Flow. Note the circularity in Eq. (11–17) and (11–20). In a two-sector economy, the only way in which one sector can receive payments is to be paid them by the other sector. Thus, firms pay households for labor services, etc., and these payments are deducted from the firms' receipts. The firms' receipts, however, come from the households. The depreciation and net savings are potential leakages from the system and can only reenter via real investment.

INTRASECTORAL EQUALITIES— HOUSEHOLDS

$$(11\text{--}23) \quad dTL_h = NS_h$$

$$(11\text{--}24) \quad dTA_h = d_h M + d_h E_f + [(dCD + dRH) - D_h]$$

$$(11\text{--}25) \quad dTL_h = dTA_h, \text{ from Eq. (11–3),}$$

which becomes

$$(11\text{--}26) \quad NS_h + D_h = d_h M + d_h E_f + dCD + dRH$$

when we substitute Eqs. (11–23) and (11–24) into Eq. (11–25) and add D_h to both sides. From Eq. (11–19), the left-hand side of Eq. (11–26) is household gross savings. From Eqs. (11–7), (11–8), and (11–9), the right-hand side of Eq. (11–26) is household gross investment. Therefore,

$$(11\text{--}27) \quad GS_h = GI_h.$$

INTRASECTORAL EQUALITIES— FIRMS

$$(11\text{--}28) \quad dTL_f = dE_f + NS_f$$

$$(11\text{--}29) \quad dTA_f = d_f M + dQ + dPE - D_f$$

$$(11\text{--}30) \quad dTL_f = dTA_f, \text{ by multiplying both sides of Eq. (11–6) by } d.$$

It follows that

$$(11\text{--}31) \qquad d_f M + dQ + dPE - D_f = dE_f + NS_f.$$

By adding D_f to both sides and subtracting dE_f from both sides, we have

$$d_f M - dE_f + dQ + dPE = NS_f + D_f.$$

From Eq. (11–22), the right-hand side of the above is gross savings for the firm. From eq. (11–12) through (11–16), the left-hand side is gross investment for the firm. Therefore,

$$(11\text{–}32) \qquad GI_f = GS_f.$$

The General Equality of Gross Savings and Gross Investment. The equality of gross savings and gross investment proved above will hold for any sector which is added, and it will hold for households and firms regardless of the assets, liabilities, and net worth items that will be added as the models become more complex. Changes in assets are uses of funds, no matter how many assets are added to the balance sheet. Changes in real assets are capital expenditures, and changes in financial assets are financial investment. On the other side of the balance sheet, changes in financial liabilities are deducted from changes in financial assets to arrive at net financial investment. This is true no matter how varied the financial liabilities become. The remaining portion of the right-hand side of the balance sheet consists of internally generated funds, or gross savings.

INTERSECTORAL BALANCES

The equality of gross savings and gross investment for each sector of the economy indicates that, for the entire economy,

$$(11\text{–}33) \qquad GS = GI.$$

In the two-sector model, the money supply is fixed, so that

$$(11\text{–}34) \qquad d_h M = -d_f M.$$

Also, the purchase of nonmarketable ownership shares by households will equal the sale of such shares by firms, i.e.,

$$(11\text{–}35) \qquad d_h E_f = dE_f.$$

Combining Eqs. (11–32) and (11–33), we have

$$(11\text{–}36) \qquad d_h M + d_h E_f = -(d_f M - dE_f).$$

Equations (11–9), (11–10) and (11–11) show that the left-hand side of the equation is net financial investment for households. Equations (11–14), (11–15), and (11–16) tell us that the right-hand side of Eq. (11–36) is net financial investment for firms preceded by a minus sign, so that

$$(11\text{–}37) \qquad NFI_h + NFI_f = 0.$$

In a two-sector economy with a fixed money supply, the conclusion that net financial investment for the entire economy must be zero can be reached intuitively. The nonmonetary financial assets held by one sector must be the financial liabilities of the other sector. This will hold even when other financial assets, hence financial liabilities, are added. And it will hold even when the economy is expanded beyond two sectors. It will also hold when the money supply becomes variable for, then, cash holdings will constitute a financial claim on the monetary sector and will cancel out for the entire economy.

The Importance of Net Financial Investment. If net financial investment sums to zero for the entire economy, why bother with it? To answer this question, recall the first 10 chapters.

The asset portfolio of the firm can be more or less risky depending in part upon the riskiness of the individual assets of which the portfolio is comprised, but also depending upon the intercorrelations of returns among the assets. Financial assets can provide assets whose returns are uncorrelated with the returns of the real assets of the firm.

In addition to providing a means of modifying risk, nonmonetary financial assets can increase the expected return of the firm by serving as substitutes for cash. Some asset portfolios would be unprofitable in the absence of nonmonetary financial assets because the portfolios require large cash balances involving large cash inventory expenses. If nonmonetary financial assets of the appropriate maturity, safety, and return are available as cash substitutes, portfolios may be adopted which otherwise would be rejected because of low profitability.

Viewed as a source of funds, financial claims increase the ability of economic units to raise funds. These funds are attracted by designing financial claims which meet the needs and desires of economic units whose gross savings exceed their own private capital expenditures. With improved ability to attract funds, portfolios can be larger than otherwise might be the case. This is a crucial point when we consider that asset portfolios can be uneconomic until the size of the portfolio exceeds a critical point. For example, an asset portfolio associated with automobile manufacture is not apt to be profitable if the total size of the portfolio is only $100,000.

The issuance of financial claims not only may permit the adoption of larger portfolios than could be accomplished without financial investment, it may allow the adoption of portfolios which would be rejected because of low profitability irrespective of the size of the portfolio. By issuing fixed income claims, such as bonds, the leverage effect of the debt can make portfolios profitable which otherwise would be unattractive. Leverage and risk are associated, but owners and managers may be willing to assume the risk to get the earnings.

It should be noted that the two-sector model described in this section must receive very low grades for facilitating investment. The system has only one negotiable financial asset—money. In fact, the system is only one step away from being a pure barter economy. For financial investment to perform its role of facilitating real investment and economic growth, a much richer variety of financial claims will have to be available.

AN ILLUSTRATION OF FLOW OF FUNDS—TWO-SECTOR, INTERNALLY FINANCED The two-sector internally financed model has been presented primarily to demonstrate the basic equalities of the flow-of-funds system in as simple a form as possible. As indicated before, most of these equalities hold even in more sophisticated systems, but are less easy to grasp in the more complex models. In subsequent models, the entire model will not be presented, just the equalities which have been changed from the basic model.

For similar reasons, the arithmetic example shown in this section in Exhibit 11-2 is more detailed than the examples illustrating the more complex models. Instead of only a flow-of-funds statement, the consolidated income statement and balance sheets for each sector are also shown. These statements generate the data for flow-of-funds, even for the complex models. It is easier, however, to follow the derivation of the flow-of-funds statement in the simple case of two sectors with internal finance than in the more complex models.

Interpreting the example, the household sector generated internal funds in excess of the sector's real investment requirements. The surplus of $5 million was held partially in cash, and the remainder was invested in the ownership shares of the firms. Although the firms generated more internal funds than the households, the business sector's real investments exceeded

Exhibit 11-2(a)

CONSOLIDATED INCOME STATEMENTS
FOR PERIOD, BY SECTORS
(In Millions of Dollars)

HOUSEHOLDS		
Current Receipts		255
Less		
Consumption	240	
Depreciation	10	
Total current charges		250
Net savings		5
FIRMS		
Current receipts		250
Less		
Payments to households for current production	200	
Depreciation	30	
Total current charges		230
Net savings		20

Exhibit 11-2 (b)

CONSOLIDATED BALANCE SHEETS, BEGINNING AND END OF PERIOD, BY SECTORS
(In Millions of Dollars)

	HOUSEHOLDS		
	BEGINNING		END
Cash		70	72
Consumer durables	100		103
Residential housing	300		307
Gross fixed assets	400		410
Less reserve for depreciation	100		110
Net fixed assets		300	300
Ownership of firms		150	153
Total assets		520	525
Retained earnings = Total liabilities and net worth ..		520	525

	FIRMS		
Cash		50	48
Inventory.......................................		70	85
Gross fixed assets	300		340
Less reserve for depreciation	200		230
Net fixed assets		100	110
Total assets..................................		220	243
Ownership shares held by households		150	153
Retained earnings		70	90
Total liabilities and net worth...................		220	243

Exhibit 11-2(c)

FLOW OF FUNDS MATRIX FOR ECONOMY
(In Millions of Dollars)

	HOUSEHOLDS		FIRMS		TOTAL	
	U	S	U	S	U	S
A. Capital consumption allowances	..	10	..	30	..	40
B. Net savings	..	5	..	20	..	25
C = A + B. gross savings	..	15	..	50	..	65
D = E + J. gross investment	15	..	50	..	65	
E = F + G + H + I. capital expenditures ..	10	..	55	..	65	
F. Consumer durable purchases	3	..	..	..	3	
G. Residential housing purchases	7	..	..	..	7	
H. Plant & equipment acquisitions	..	..	40	..	40	
I. Inventory investment	..	..	15	..	15	
J = K − L. net financial investment	5	..	−5	..	0	
K. Net change in financial assets	5	..	−2	..	3	
L. Net change in liabilities	..	0	..	3	..	3
M. Changes in cash	2	..	−2	..	0	
N. Changes in ownership	3	..	..	3	3	3
O. Horizontal Totals....................	15	15	50	50	65	65

their internal funds. The $5 million deficit for the firms was financed by reducing the cash balances of the firms by $2 million and persuading house-hold-owners to invest $3 million in the firms. Financial claims provided the means by which the surplus of one sector was transferred to the deficit sector.

The flow of funds matrix provides a historical record of what occurred in a past period. It just shows what happened, not why it happened. By assuming that the matrix shows changes which reflect simply the desires of the sectors for different kinds of balance sheets, we may miss the mark completely. It is possible that the tastes of firms have simply shifted from financial assets to real assets and that they are willing to accept more lia-bilities as the price for achieving their aims. On the other hand, some elements of the changes may have been unanticipated by the firms. For example, the inventory investment may reflect disappointing sales rather than a deliberate investment decision. Because of poor sales, firms may have received less funds than anticipated, had therefore to reduce cash balances by more than had been planned, and had to go to owners for money because of the combined effect of poor sales and the financial com-mitments to build up plant and equipment. The actual record may represent a complex series of adjustments to some bad surprises rather than the well-planned adjustments of the sectors to a long-run set of goals.

It should also be recognized that what is true for the sector as a whole is not necessarily true for every unit within the sector. Some firms probably increased cash holdings and reduced plant and equipment investment. Some households spent everything on consumption, leaving them with zero net savings. The households that increased cash holdings may not have been the same households that increased equity investment in the firms.

THE TWO-SECTOR FINANCIAL ECONOMY

We retain the same sectors as before. However, firms can now issue a wide variety of financial claims, including long- and short-term debt and ownership shares which are marketable. Households also can issue long- and short-term debt, but not ownership shares.

GLOSSARY

B Short- and long-term debt combined, but not trade credit

E Becomes marketable ownership shares of households in firms

BALANCE SHEET CHANGES—
HOUSEHOLDS

$$(11\text{--}1a) \quad TA_h = {}_hM + {}_hB_f + E_f + CD + RH - RD_h$$

$$(11\text{--}2a) \quad TL_h = B_h + RE_h$$

BALANCE SHEET CHANGES—
FIRMS

$$(11\text{--}4a) \quad TA_f = {}_fM + {}_fB_h + Q + PE - RD_f$$

$$(11\text{--}5a) \quad TL_f = B_f + E_f + RE_f$$

CHANGES IN USES
OF FUNDS—HOUSEHOLDS

$$(11\text{--}10a) \quad d_hFA = d_hM + d_hB_f + dE_f$$

$$(11\text{--}11a) \quad dFL_h = B_h$$

CHANGES IN USES
OF FUNDS—FIRMS

$$(11\text{--}15a) \quad d_fFA = d_fM + d_fB_h$$

$$(11\text{--}16a) \quad dFL_f = dB_f + dE_f$$

SOURCES OF FUNDS

There are no changes in the structure of the equations for the sources of funds. It should be noted, however, that net financial investment for firms, Eq. (11–17), which is subtracted from the current receipts of the firm to arrive at the current receipts of households, is more complex than in the previous model. To the extent that the variety of financial assets is more interesting to the firm, net financial investment will rise, reducing the current receipts of households. A similar effect, running from households to firms, is shown in eq. (11–20).

INTRASECTORAL
EQUALITIES—
HOUSEHOLDS

$$(11\text{--}23a) \quad dTL_h = dB_h + NS_h$$

$$(11\text{--}24a) \quad dTA_h = d_hM + d_hE_f + d_hB_f$$
$$+ (dCD + dRH - D_h)$$

$$(11\text{--}26a) \quad NS_h + D_h = [(d_hM + d_hE_f + d_hB_f)$$
$$- dB_h] + dCD + dRH$$

The left-hand side of Eq. (11–26a) is still gross savings. Net financial investment appears in the large bracket on the right-hand side of Eq. (11–26a), and capital expenditures of the households appear in the last two terms. So, the right-hand side is still gross investment.

INTRASECTORAL
EQUALITIES—FIRMS

$$(11\text{--}28a) \quad dTL_f = dB_f + dE_f + NS_f$$

$$(11\text{--}29a) \quad d_fTA_f = d_fM + dB_h + dQ$$
$$+ dPE - D_f$$

$$(11\text{--}31a) \quad [(d_fM + dB_h) - (dB_f + dE_f)]$$
$$+ dQ + dPE = D_f + NS_f$$

and gross savings for business also equals gross investment.

CHANGES IN
INTERSECTORAL BALANCES

The only change created by a more diversified group of financial claims is to add more claims. However, the claims sold by firms to households must equal the claims on firms purchased by households, and vice versa. Thus, the intersectoral equality of the earlier model Eq. (11–37), still holds, i.e.,

$$NFI_f + NFI_h = 0.$$

AN ILLUSTRATION

The data underlying the flow of funds statement in this and the more complex examples are the income statements and balance sheets for each sector. The relationship among the three kinds of reports was shown in the simple illustration earlier and will not be repeated again. The illustration of the two-sector model with finance in Exhibit 11-3 is very similar to the example shown in Exhibit 11-2.

Exhibit 11-3

FLOW OF FUNDS MATRIX
FOR TWO-SECTOR ECONOMY WITH EXTERNAL FINANCE
(In Millions of Dollars)

	HOUSEHOLDS		FIRMS		TOTALS	
	U	S	U	S	U	S
A. Capital consumption allowances		10	..	30	..	40
B. Net savings		15	..	10	..	25
C = A + B. gross savings		25	..	40	..	65
D = E + J. gross investment	25	..	40	..	65	
E = F + G + H + I. capital expenditures ..	10	..	55	..	65	
F. Consumer durable purchases	3	..	..	..	3	
G. Residential housing	7	..	..	..	7	
H. Plant and equipment	..	..	40	..	40	
I. Inventory changes	..	..	15	..	15	
J = K − L. Net financial investment	15	..	−15	..	0	
K. Net changes in financial assets	17	..	1	..	18	
L. Net changes in liabilities	..	2	..	16	..	18
M. Changes in cash	1	..	− 1	..	0	
N. Changes in consumer finance, B_n	..	2	2	..	2	2
O. Changes in business bonds, B_f	8	..	..	8	8	8
P. Net issues of marketable ownership	8	..	..	8	8	8

Real investment in this illustration is the same as in Exhibit 11-2. In this case, firms have invested $5 million more, and households $5 million less. To finance this greater growth, firms used less internal funds—$40 million as compared to $50 million in the previous example—but relied more on financial sources. The point illustrated is that, in an economy which permits a variety of external financing devices, a greater degree of specialization in capital formation may develop. Households can specialize in saving—as in the current example where households saved $25 million as compared to $15 million in the earlier illustration—, and firms can specialize in real investment. The savings of households are transmitted to firms via financial transactions.

FISCAL AND FINANCIAL GOVERNMENT
AND INTERNATIONAL TRADE

The government sector that will be added here taxes, spends, borrows, and repays debt. It has no monetary power.

There are only two new terms:

GLOSSARY

G Government spending: no differentiation between spending on current account (e.g., civil service salaries) or on capital account (building highways); subscript describes which sector receives spending

T Taxes, with subscript referring to sector source of taxes

g The subscript used to identify the government sector

INCOME STATEMENT
FOR GOVERNMENT

$$(11\text{-}38) \quad NS_g = (T_f + T_h) - (G_f + G_h),$$

which indicates that net savings are zero when the government budget is zero, positive when receipts exceed expenditures, and negative when the government spends more than it receives.

BALANCE SHEET
FOR GOVERNMENT

$$(11\text{-}39) \qquad TA_g = {_g}M$$
$$(11\text{-}40) \qquad TL_g = B_g + RE_g$$

This is a peculiar balance sheet in that there are no real assets. Government accounting is on a cash basis, not an accrual basis. No matter how long a highway may last, it shows up only as a cash disbursement, not as an asset. The retained earnings symbol is merely a balancing figure, much like the retained earnings figure for the household sector. Given the fact the public debt is apt to exceed the money held by government, RE_g is usually negative. This in itself is not disturbing since it reflects the accounting method used rather than financial insolvency.

$$(11\text{-}41) \qquad\qquad TA_g = TL_g.$$

$$(11\text{-}42) \qquad\qquad NFI_g = d_g M - dB_g.$$

GOVERNMENT INVESTMENT
AND SAVINGS

Since the government holds no real assets in an accounting sense, government makes no real asset expenditures, i.e.,

(11–43) $$I_g = 0.$$

Therefore,

(11–44) $$NFI_g = GI_g.$$

Also, with no real assets, there can be no depreciation.

(11–45) $$D_g = 0,$$

and

(11–46) $$GS_g = NS_g.$$

Now, consider Eq. (11–42), which can be restated to say

$$NFI_g = dRE_g, \quad \text{and} \quad dRE_g = NS_g.$$

With these equalities and the equalities shown in Eqs. (11–44) and (11–46), we have

(11–47) $$GS_g = GI_g.$$

CHANGES IN THE BALANCE SHEETS OF HOUSEHOLDS AND FIRMS
Government securities can be held by the other sectors. The only modification that occurs in the balance sheet, then, is the addition to the financial assets of $_fB_g$ for firms and $_hB_g$ for households.

(11–17a) $$CR_h = CR_f - NFI_f - T_f + G_h,$$

CHANGES IN SOURCES OF FUNDS
which indicates that the taxes paid by firms constitute a leakage in terms of reducing household receipts. The leakage may be offset by government spending on households.

(11–18a) $$NS_h = CR_h - (C_h + D_h + T_h).$$

(11–20a) $$CR_f = CR_h - NFI_h - T_h + G_f,$$

which indicates that household spending, hence business receipts, is reduced by the amount of taxes paid, but business receipts are increased by the amount of government expenditures on firms.

(11–21a) $$NS_f = CR_f - (C_f + D_f + T_f).$$

The ability of firms and households to finance internally is offset by taxation.

However, consideration of Eqs. (11–17a) and (11–20a) indicates that net savings may be favorably affected by government spending.

One of the interesting points made here is that government can effect a redistribution of finance through its tax-spending policies, which can operate much like external finance. If government taxes households and spends on firms, the savings of households can be reduced and the savings of firms increased. Unfortunately, there is no guarantee that household tax payments will come out of savings—consumption may be reduced. Also, there is no assurance that added business receipts will increase business savings—payments by firms to households may rise.

NET FINANCIAL INVESTMENT AND GOVERNMENT

If we set Eq. (11–17a) to equal NFI_f, i.e.,

$$NFI_f = CR_f - CR_h - T_f + G_h,$$

and set eq. (11–20a) to equal NFI_h, i.e.,

$$NFI_h = -CR_f + CR_h - T_h + G_f,$$

the following relationship between the net financial investment of the private sectors and the government's fiscal activities emerges when we sum the two revised equations:

(11–48)
$$NFI_f + NFI_h = G_h + G_f - T_h - T_f.$$

The right-hand side of the equation is equal to $-NS_g$, from Eq. (11–38), and also $-NFI_g$, from Eqs. (11–44), (11–46), and (11–47), or

$$NFI_f + NFI_h = -NFI_g,$$

or

$$NFI_f + NFI_h + NFI_g = 0.$$

The most obvious point is that government deficits, which occur when spending exceeds taxes, are financed by other sectors. Instead of receiving a receipted tax bill, the sectors receive a financial claim on the government.

THE FLOW OF FUNDS MATRIX WITH THREE SECTORS

The illustration of the three sectors, shown in Exhibit 11-4, is based on the original illustration of a two sector economy. It is assumed that the impact of government is reflected in the reduction of net savings for households, and the reduction in private capital expenditures for both households and firms. These reductions are reflected in the totals and composition of net financial investment.

The over-all reduction is not intended as a commentary on the impact of government. Good or bad is indistinguishable in the bare bones of a flow

Exhibit 11-4

THE FLOW OF FUNDS MATRIX FOR A THREE-SECTOR ECONOMY
(In Millions of Dollars)

Transactions	HOUSEHOLDS U	S	FIRMS U	S	GOVERNMENT U	S	TOTALS U	S
A. Capital consumption allowances.. ..		10		30		..		40
B. Net savings.....................		3		10		−5		8
C = A + B. Gross savings		13		40		−5		48
D = E + J. Gross investment	13		40		−5		48	
E = F + G + H + I. Private capital expenditures	5		43		..		48	
F. Consumer durable purchases	1		..		..		1	
G. Residential housing	4		..		..		4	
H. Plant and equipment............			30		..		30	
I. Inventory investment			13		..		13	
J = K − L. Net financial investment	8		−3		−5		0	
K. Net changes in financial assets....	9		1		−2		8	
L. Net changes in liabilities		1		4		3		8
M. Changes in cash	3		−1		−2		0	
N. Changes in consumer finance		1	1		..		1	1
O. Changes in business bonds	2			2	..		2	2
P. Changes in business stocks	2			2	..		2	2
Q. Changes in government bonds ..	2		1			3	3	3

of funds matrix. Had the previous levels of capital expenditures been inflationary, the reduction would be good. Also, it is not clear that total spending has been reduced. The observed reductions may be more than offset by current expenditures of government, which include public capital expenditures. The latter may be more or less desirable than the curtailed private expenditures.

FOREIGN TRADE

To this point, we have been dealing with a *closed* economy, i.e., all transactions have taken place between sectors sharing a national identity. The open economy involves transactions with the *rest of the world*, or foreign, sector. All foreign countries will be lumped together to form this sector. However, the only transactions of the foreign sector that are considered in the flow of funds accounts are those involving our domestic economy. Trade between the United Kingdom and France is not recorded. Further, transactions will be recorded as viewed by the domestic economy. If we sell a machine tool to Denmark, the purchase would be viewed as a private capital expenditure by the Danish flow of funds statisticians. We view it as a sale on current account. On the other hand, if we buy an electric generator from West Germany, the West Germans would record this as a sale on current account, but we would record it as an import and as a private capital expenditure on plant and equipment.

GLOSSARY

The subscript indicating the foreign sector is w. Otherwise, the added symbols are

EX Exports, with the subscript indicating who makes the export

IM Imports on current account, which include imports of goods that are intended to be consumed in the current period

IW Imports on capital account which include all imports that effect private capital expenditures

TC Trade credit extended by firms to foreigners, and vice versa, shown consolidated within sectors

$$(11\text{-}49) \quad TA_w = {}_wM + {}_wB_g + {}_wB_f + {}_wB_h$$
$$+ {}_wTC_f + {}_wE_f.$$

BALANCE SHEET FOR FOREIGN SECTOR

Note that the balance sheet assets include only foreign holdings of domestic assets and that trade credit can be extended by foreign sellers to domestic firms. All real assets are excluded.

$$(11\text{-}50) \qquad TL_w = B_w + {}_fTC_w + RE_w + E_w.$$

The liabilities of the foreign sector also exclude purely foreign-held claims. The bonds of the rest of the world refer only to those bonds held by domestic sectors. So, too, the stock issues E_w. The retained earnings shown is simply the summation of past net savings of the foreign sector as defined below.

$$(11\text{-}51) \qquad\qquad TA_w = TL_w,$$

which equality is possible because we have only the transactions between the foreign sector and the domestic economy.

$$(11\text{-}52) \quad NS_w = (IM_h + IM_f + IM_g + IW_h$$
$$+ IW_f) - (EX_h + EX_f + EX_g).$$

INCOME STATEMENT

In other words, net saving for the foreign sector are simply the balance of payments. If they sell more to us than they buy from us, foreign net savings are positive. This is different from the definition of net savings applied to domestic sectors since we do not consider the costs to the foreign sector of physically producing the goods we import or the dividend payments made to foreign owners of the foreign firms.

The exports of households require a word of explanation. These are primarily dividend and interest payments on foreign claims owned by domestic households. The interest and dividend element can exist in the exports of any of the domestic sectors.

$$(11-53) \qquad NS_w = GS_w$$

since real assets owned by the foreign sector in foreign lands are excluded. (Real assets in the United States owned by foreigners are treated as belonging to a domestic sector, i.e., firm or household as appropriate. Foreigners hold financial claims to real assets, which claims appear in the asset portfolio of the foreign sector).

$$(11-54) \qquad NS_w = dRE_w.$$

SOURCES AND USES OF FUNDS

Since all of the balance sheet items for the foreign sector are financial, except for retained earnings, net financial investment can be defined as

$$(11-55) \qquad NFI_w = dTA_w - (dB_w + d_f TC_w + dE_w).$$

The difference between financial assets and financial liabilities is retained earnings, so, using eq. (11–54), we can say

$$(11-56) \qquad NFI_w = NS_w.$$

Real investment is zero for the foreign sector, so that

$$(11-57) \qquad NFI_w = GI_w.$$

And, using the information from Eq. (11–53),

$$(11-58) \qquad GI_w = GS_w.$$

IMPACT ON OTHER SECTORS

$$(11-17b) \qquad CR_h = CR_f - (T_f + NFI_f + IM_f + IW_f) + G_h + EX_h,$$

which indicates that imports of the firms serve to reduce household receipts. In effect, when firms import, they purchase factor services from abroad rather than from domestic households. However, foreign trade adds to household receipts to the extent that households receive payments from abroad, EX_h.

(11–18b) $$NS_h = CR_h - (C_h + IM_h) - D_h - T_h,$$

which indicates that consumption now includes not only domestically produced goods, but consumption goods from abroad. Household net savings would appear to be reduced by the subtraction of the new factor. However, net savings could remain unchanged, and the reduction take place in domestic consumption, as households substitute imported goods for domestic goods.

(11–20b) $$CR_f = CR_h - (NFI_h + T_h + IM_h + IW_h) + G_f + EX_f.$$

Again the circular flow discussed earlier is made more complex by the addition of import leakages and exports as additions to the flow.

(11–21b) $$NS_f = CR_f - (C_f + IM_f) - D_f - T_f,$$

where imports on current account, e.g., raw materials, add to the current expenses of business firms.

(11–38a) $$NS_g = T_f + T_h - (G_f + G_h + IM_g - EX_g).$$

Imports of government include goods and services, e.g., salaries paid to foreign nationals who work for our embassies abroad. Exports of government would include payment of interest to government on loans made to foreign countries, sale of government-owned commodities to foreign countries, etc.

Balance Sheets.

(11–1b) $$TA_h = {}_hM + {}_hB_g + {}_hB_f + {}_hB_w + {}_hE_f + {}_hE_w + CD \\ + RH - RD_h,$$

which expresses the relatively complex structure of the asset portfolio for households. Of course, there is no change in the structure of liabilities and net worth.

(11–4b) $$TA_f = {}_fM + {}_fB_h + {}_fTC_w + {}_fB_g + {}_fB_w + {}_fE_w + Q + PE - RD_f,$$

which indicates the revised asset portfolio for the firm.

(11–5b) $$TL_f = {}_wTC_f + B_f + E_f + RE_f.$$

Exhibit 11-5

ILLUSTRATION OF THE FLOW OF FUNDS MATRIX FOR FOUR SECTORS
(In Millions of Dollars)

Transactions	HOUSEHOLDS U	HOUSEHOLDS S	FIRMS U	FIRMS S	GOVERNMENT U	GOVERNMENT S	FOREIGN U	FOREIGN S	TOTALS U	TOTALS S
A. Capital consumption allowances		10		30						40
B. Net savings		2		8		−6		4		8
C = A + B. Gross savings		12		38		−6		4		48
D = E + J. Gross investment	12		38		−6		4		48	
E = F + G + H + I. Private capital expenditures	5		43						48	
F. Consumer durables	1								1	
G. Residential housing	4								4	
H. Plant and equipment			30						30	
I. Inventory investment			13						13	
J = K − L. Net financial investment	7		−5		−6		4		0	
K. Net changes in financial assets	8		4		−3		10		19	
L. Net changes in liabilities		1		9		3		6		19
M. Changes in cash	2		−3		−3		4		0	
N. Changes in consumer finance		1	1						1	1
O. Changes in business bonds	2			3			1		3	3
P. Changes in trade finance			3	2			1	2	4	4
Q. Changes in business	1			4			3		4	4
R. Changes in government bonds	1		1			3	1		3	3
S. Changes in foreign bonds	1		1					2	3	3
T. Changes in foreign stocks	1		1					2	2	2

THE FOUR-SECTOR MATRIX ILLUSTRATED

Exhibit 11–5 shows the flow of funds matrix for a four-sector economy. The rationale is the same as that used in Exhibit 11-4. Three new financial claims have been added—foreign bonds, trade credit, and foreign stocks. Domestic firms offer trade credit to the foreign sector usually by financing exports to foreign countries. In turn, but not necessarily equal in amount, domestic firms receive trade credit from the foreign sector.

OTHER REAL SECTORS

At this point, the transactions of the major real sectors of the economy have been analyzed, albeit briefly. In the actual flow of funds matrix, the Federal Reserve Board uses a more detailed split of sectors than is found here. The firm sector is divided into three sectors: farm business; nonfarm, nonfinancial unincorporated business; and nonfarm, nonfinancial incorporated business. Government is divided into two sectors: Federal, and state and local. To our household sector, the Federal Reserve adds nonprofit institutions, which include private schools and colleges, private hospitals, etc.

The division into finer groups is desirable because it offers an opportunity to observe differences, as between incorporated and unincorporated business, for example, that would be obliterated otherwise. However, the basic sets of relationships expressed in our system of equations hold regardless of how finely the sectors are subdivided.

SELECTED REFERENCES

Conference on Research in Income and Wealth, *The Flow-of-Funds Approach to Social Accounting*, National Bureau of Economic Research, Inc., New York, 1962.

Copeland, M.: *A Study of Moneyflows in the United States*, National Bureau of Economic Research Inc., New York, 1952.

Federal Reserve Board: *Flow of Funds in the United States*, Washington, D.C., 1955.

———: "A Quarterly Presentation of Flow of Funds, Saving and Investment," *Federal Reserve Bulletin*, Aug., 1959.

Powelson, J.: *National Income and Flow-of-Funds Analysis*, McGraw-Hill, New York, 1960.

The Financial Economy:
A Sectoral Theory of Moneyflows

12

In Chapter 11, the accounting identities and equalities associated with the flow of funds were developed for two-, three-, and four-sector economies. Accounting relationships are correct or incorrect. There is no room for differences of opinion. Given the definitions, accounting relationships specify what must be true. Thus, we know that, for each sector, gross savings must equal gross investment and, for all sectors combined, net financial investment must equal zero. All of these equalities and identities inevitably follow from the definitions.

However, the desires of individuals and firms do not necessarily follow accounting rules. There is no reason for us to expect that the millions of entities that constitute an economic system will plan financial investments and loans so that net financial investment equals zero. Indeed, it is quite improbable that such planning is possible. Yet, despite the conflicts among all of the individual plans, somehow they all mesh to generate the equalities required by the accounting system. It is one of the tasks of economic theory to explain how this meshing occurs.

To do this, it is first necessary to describe how the various entities in the economy behave in terms of the relevant variables of the flow of funds. Such behavioral descriptions, or *functional relationships* as they shall be called in later sections of this chapter, indicate whether economic entities buy more or fewer financial assets when interest rates rise, for example. By combining the behavioral descriptions with the accounting relationships, the meshing of millions of individual plans to generate the required equalities can be analyzed.

Describing the behavior of each entity, when there are millions of entities, is patently impossible. By aggregating entities into groups, or sectors, the number of behavioral descriptions needed are sharply reduced to a manageable system. The sectors dealt with in this chapter will duplicate those used in Chapter 11.

In Chapter 11, aggregation was not only performed for groups of economic entities, but also for types of transactions. For example, all purchases of consumer nondurable goods were grouped together, even though the resulting aggregate consisted of many heterogeneous items. Simplicity is the justification for aggregation, but it can lead to complexities. The complexities consist mainly of index number problems. When we combine all kinds of goods and services into an aggregate, how can we measure the price of the aggregate, since the individual items have different prices and the relation of one item's price to another may change? In the model described in this chapter, a single price index will be used to describe the prices not only of consumer goods, but also of capital goods. Yet, if consumer goods become cheaper than capital goods patterns of demand change and the responses of firms may be different than if capital goods were cheaper than consumer goods.

The problem is even more severe with financial assets. From Parts 1 and 2 of this book, we know that the structure of interest rates for securities of different liquidity, risk, and maturity can change. Such changes can be quite important in explaining things such as the demand for money. In the behavioral descriptions of this chapter, financial assets will be treated as an aggregate. A single interest rate index is used to describe yields of the various kinds of financial claims that can be held. Yet how can such an index be computed? If interest rates fall, investors may switch out of risky and relatively illiquid assets into very safe, liquid securities. The composition of financial assets change, and so should the weights that go into calculating the average interest rate or interest rate index. Such problems as this are solved simply, though not too satisfactorily, by assuming that the structure of interest rates remains unchanged, which implies that the relative distribution of holdings of the various kinds of financial assets is constant.

As will be seen, despite the many efforts at simplification, the resulting model will be quite complex. Complexity makes understanding very difficult. The less simplified the model, the more realistic it is, but, since it is also more complex, the harder it is to understand. Thus, there is a trade-off between realism and comprehensibility, which justifies some degree of simplification.

In the remainder of this chapter, the behavioral descriptions will be combined with the accounting relationships from Chapter 11 in an attempt to explain the workings of the financial economy. The approach will be to start with a two-sector economy, then add the government sector, and finally consider the four-sector economy, which includes the foreign sector.

A functional relationship indicates the effects of changes in one or more independent variables upon another variable. Thus, the quantity demanded of a particular commodity may be stated as being a function of the price of the commodity, the prices of all other goods, income, and tastes. The relationship can be stated more precisely, if we have such precise information, as follows:

$$q_a = 12 - 0.5P_a + 0.3P + 0.1Y,$$

where q_a is the quantity demanded of commodity a, p_a is its price, P is a price index of all other prices, and Y is income. The signs in front of each variable indicate the direction of the relationship. Tastes are not shown separately, since tastes are qualitative, but are reflected in the other variables; e.g., if consumer tastes moved away from the particular commodity, the coefficient preceding income might fall.

The demand equation shown above is very specific and would be estimated by econometric methods. But suppose we have the general idea that demand will fall as the price of the good rises, will rise as the price of other goods rise, and will increase with income. With no knowledge of the values of the coefficients of the variables or even if the functional relationship is linear, the general relationship could be specified as

$$q_a = \alpha(p_a, P, Y).$$

The direction of the relationship between the dependent variable q_a and the independent variables could be given in a table as follows:

	p_a	P	Y
q_a	−	+	+

This will be the form of expression that will be used in the explanations that follow. When using multivariate relationships such as the equation shown, it is possible to discuss the effect of any single variable on the dependent variable by holding all other variables constant. The demand curve, which relates price and quantity, is the most familiar example of this.

An equation similar to the demand equation will be developed for each of the major flows for each of the sectors. Although each equation will be relatively simple, the effect of all of the equations together will be quite complicated despite all of the aggregation used in the model.

The over-all system will be static. Given the data for the balance sheets of the sectors and the functional relationships, we shall be concerned with identifying the changes that will take place to bring the economy to the point where further changes will cease, i.e., to equilibrium. We shall not be concerned with determining the path over time taken to reach the equilibrium. Were we to be concerned with the time path, the model would be dynamic. There are two good reasons for using a static model: First, it is much simpler; second, and more important, too little is known about dynamic processes to permit us to specify a reasonable dynamic model for the financial economy.

On the whole, the same variables will be used as were used in developing the accounting system. The stocks of residential housing and consumer durable goods, net of depreciation allowances, will be combined into a single symbol K_h; and the stocks of business inventories and plant and equipment, net of depreciation allowances, will be represented by K_f. Financial assets will be divided into two kinds: M will represent money and FA' will represent all other financial assets. P will represent the price level, and i will be an index of market interest rates.

As in Chapter 11, the letter d preceding the symbol for a stock variable will make it a flow variable. K_f will represent the stock of business inventories and plant and equipment. dK_f will represent the flow of positive or negative investment which will increase or decrease K_f.

It will be assumed that the economy which is to be described is free of *money illusion*. If the price level doubles and all other asset holdings also double in money value, the members of the economy realize that the increase in the value of asset holdings is nominal and will not change their behavior. A doubling in the value of plant and equipment holdings due only to a doubling of the price level will not lead to any different demand for additions or contractions of the plant and equipment holdings than existed before the price increase. All the nonfinancial variables will be expressed in real terms. The amount of household consumption C_h demanded in the period will be measured in terms of the real quantities of food, clothing, and consumer services demanded and will be, therefore, unaffected by changes in the price level.

Given a price level change, it is reasonable to assume that money values of nonfinancial assets will change proportionately. If the dollar value of a fixed asset is

$$\sum_1^n \frac{1}{(1 + i)^n} S,$$

as was shown in Chapter 2, doubling the price level will double the dollar value of S, thus doubling the dollar value of the fixed asset. But consider the effect of a change in the price level on money holdings. Since the purchasing power of money, i.e., the real value, varies inversely with the price level, we cannot assume that changes in the price level will not affect the real value of the cash held in the various balance sheets. To have the same real value, the cash holdings will have to double when prices double. Thus, the symbol for money holdings M is expressed in nominal terms. Real cash holdings will be M/P.

Financial assets which generate a fixed dollar return, such as bonds, present a problem similar to that of money. The market value of a bond is

$$\sum_1^n \frac{1}{(1+i)^n} I + \frac{1}{(1+i)^n} MV,$$

where i is the interest rate, n is the term of the bond, I is the annual interest payment, and MV is the maturity value of the bond. Unlike nonfinancial assets, I and MV are constant in dollars regardless of changes in the price level. Thus, when prices double, the real value of the bond is halved. For a balance sheet holder to maintain a constant purchasing power value of fixed dollar return financial assets, the nominal dollar value of financial asset holdings must vary with the price level. Thus, FA' will represent the nominal dollar holdings of nonmonetary financial assets and FA'/P will be the real value of these holdings.

Of course, not all nonmonetary financial assets generate a fixed dollar return. The major example is common stock. Financial assets which generate variable returns can be included in FA'/P. If the returns on these financial assets vary directly and proportionately with the price level, both numerator and denominator will increase at equal rates and the real value of the variable return financial assets will be unchanged.

Financial liabilities are affected by price level changes in the same way as are financial assets. To the extent that financial liabilities consist of fixed dollar return obligations, an increase in the price level will reduce the real value of the payments that have to be made. Thus, the real value of financial liabilities will be shown as FL/P, where FL represents the money, or nominal, value of the financial liabilities.

Expectations. What effect will an increase in interest rates have on an economy? The answer depends partly upon what assumption is made about the effect of such a change on expectations. If it is assumed that the effect of the interest rate increase is to create expectations of further interest rate increases in the future, the impact will be quite different than if expectations of increased interest rates are not generated by the initial interest rate change.

Since our interest at this time is not concerned with expectations, we shall assume that expectations play no role in the decisions of the sectors. Technically, this means that the coefficient of elasticity for expectations is zero. The coefficient of elasticity for expectations may be defined as

$$\frac{(x_2 - x_1)/(x_2 + x_1)/2}{(x_1 - x_0)/(x_1 + x_0)/2},$$

where x is any variable such as interest rate, price level, etc., and the subscripts refer to the time period in which the particular value of the variable x exists. Thus, x_2 is the value of x in time period 2, and x_1 is the value of x in time period 1. In this expression, time period 2 may be viewed as the future, time period 1 as the current period, and time period 0 as the past. Given a change in x between period 0 and period 1, the coefficient of elasticity will be zero only if no change is expected between periods 1 and 2.

Balance Sheet Preferences.   We assume balance sheet preferences such that there is a diminishing marginal rate of substitution among asset classes, including consumption, eventually. If firms continue to increase fixed assets, ultimately they will wish to increase holdings of other assets, such as cash. For the firm, the reasons for this may be diversification or the technical requirements that make it inefficient for a firm to operate with enormous quantities of fixed assets and small holdings of cash. For households, diversification is a factor leading toward the balancing of asset holdings, and so are tastes. If nondurable consumption expenditures are high, households may find their tastes are better satisfied by diverting expenditure additions from further expansion of durable goods holding to financial assets.

Among the variables that will determine the expenditures for the sectors will be the level of balance sheet holdings for each asset class. For example, the demand for additions to money holdings will be determined partly by the level of real holdings of fixed assets, nonmonetary financial assets, and money. The demand for additions to money holdings will vary directly with the level of holdings of fixed assets and nonmonetary financial assets, i.e., the larger the holdings of fixed assets, the greater the demand for additions to money holdings. The demand for additions to money holdings will vary inversely with the level of money already held in the balance sheet. The demand equations for each kind of expenditure, or use, of funds will have, as determining or independent variables, the level of holdings for each class of asset. As with the example for money, the demand for expenditures, or uses, of funds for a particular item will be held to increase as the levels of other kinds of assets are large, and to decrease if the stock of the asset which will be increased by the expenditure, or use, is large.

More compactly, the relationship between each demand or use of funds and each asset class can be shown as follows:

	DEPENDENT VARIABLE (DEMAND OR USE)			
Asset Holdings	C	dM	dFA'	dK
M/P	+	−	+	+
FA'/P	+	+	−	+
K	+	+	+	−

Given this, it will not be necessary to present verbal explanations for the direction of the relationship between the dependent variables and asset holdings when they are presented in the separate demand equations.

INTEREST RATE
RELATIONSHIPS

The interest rate is the rate of return on investment in nonmonetary financial assets. The higher the interest rate, the greater the reward for holding nonmonetary financial assets. Therefore, the higher the interest rate, the larger will be *dFA'*. On the other hand, the greater the reward for holding nonmonetary financial assets, the smaller will be the demand for other assets, or consumption, since the interest rate may be viewed as the penalty for purchasing anything else but nonmonetary financial assets.

The demand for financial liabilities, i.e., external sources of funds, will vary inversely with the interest rate. When interest rates are high, sectors will be reluctant to add high cost obligations to the right-hand side of their balance sheets. Conversely, low interest rates will encourage increases in financial obligations.

Compactly, the relationship between the interest rate and the various demands may be shown as

Demands	i
C	−
dM	−
dFA'	+
dK	−
dFL	−

Again, further explanations of the relationship between the interest rate and the various demands will not be given when the separate demand equations are shown.

CURRENT RECEIPTS
RELATIONSHIPS

As used here, current receipts is a measure of each sector's gross income. We assume that the relationship between income and all asset changes, plus consumption, is positive; i.e., the more people make, the more they spend. However, the relationship between current receipts and financial liabilities will be treated as negative, since, all else the same, the larger are current receipts, the less the need to issue financial obligations. Thus, the relationships are

Demands	CR
C	+
dM	+
dFA'	+
dK	+
dFL	−

Households

DEMAND EQUATIONS
(USES AND SOURCES)
FOR THE TWO-SECTOR
ECONOMY

$$(12-1) \qquad C_h = \alpha_1(CR_h, {}_hM/P, {}_hFA'/P, K_h, i).$$

$$(12-2) \quad d_hM = \alpha_2(CR_h, {}_hM/P, {}_hFA'/P, K_h, i).$$

$$(12-3) \quad d_hFA' = \alpha_3(CR_h, {}_hM/P, {}_hFA'/P, K_h, i).$$

$$(12-4) \qquad dK_h = \alpha_4(CR_h, {}_hM/P, {}_hFA'/P, K_h, i).$$

Equations (12–1) through (12–4) indicate the demands for uses of funds. The direction of the relationships between the dependent variables and the independent variables may be shown as

INDEPENDENT	DEPENDENT			
	C_h	d_hM	d_hFA'	dK_h
CR_h	+	+	+	+
${}_hM/P$	+	−	+	+
${}_hFA'/P$	+	+	−	+
K_h	+	+	+	−
i	−	−	+	−

The arguments underlying these relationships have been explained in previous sections.

$$(12-5) \qquad dFL_h = \alpha_5(CR_h, {}_hM/P, {}_hFA'/P, FL_h/P, i),$$

which represents the demand for external financing by the household sector, or the supply of financial claims that the households would like to generate. All else equal, the larger are current receipts, the less the need for external finance because it will be easier to finance needs out of income. Also, the larger the holdings of both money and other financial assets, the more liquid are households, enabling them to finance expenditures by reducing financial asset holdings rather than by issuing obligations. If households already have a large real burden of external obligations outstanding, they are less likely to add to the burden than if the burden of outstanding obligations were small. Finally, the higher the interest rate, the less will be the supply of financial assets provided by households. In summary form, the direction of the relationships are

	dFL_h
CR_h	−
${}_hM/P$	−
${}_hFA'/P$	−
FL_h/P	−
i	−

The remaining functional relationship needed is that for capital consumption allowances. Since this is purely a function of the size and age of the capital stock, it can be shown as

$$(12-6) \qquad\qquad D_h = \alpha_6 K_h,$$

278 · THE FINANCIAL ECONOMY

with a positive relationship between independent and dependent variables.

Other relationships are derived by combining the functional relationships shown above. We know from the accounting Eq. (11–18) that net savings for households is the sum of consumption and capital consumption allowances subtracted from current receipts, or current receipts less the sum of Eqs. (12–1) and (12–6) above. Net financial investment is the difference between the change in financial assets and the change in financial liabilities, or the difference between the sum of Eqs. (12–2) and (12–3) above and Eq. (12–5).

FIRMS The demand equations for the firm sector have the same dependent and independent variables, with the same *direction* of relationship between independent and dependent variables. Note that this is not the same as saying the actual values, or shapes, of the relationships are identical. For these reasons, the equations will be presented without additional commentary.

(12–7) $$C_f = \alpha_7(CR_f, {}_fM/P, {}_fFA'/P, K_f, i).$$

(12–8) $$d_fM = \alpha_8(CR_f, {}_fM/P, {}_fFA'/P, K_f, i).$$

(12–9) $$d_fFA' = \alpha_9(CR_f, {}_fM/P, {}_fFA'/P, K_f, i).$$

(12–10) $$dK_f = \alpha_{10}(CR_f, {}_fM/P, {}_fFA'/P, K_f, i).$$

(12–11) $$dFL_f = \alpha_{11}(CR_f, {}_fM/P, {}_fFA'/P, FL_f/P, i).$$

(12–12) $$D_f = \alpha_{12}K_f.$$

DETERMINATION OF CURRENT RECEIPTS Accounting Eqs. (11–17) and (11–20) showed that, in a two-sector economy, the current receipts of one sector equalled the nonfinancial expenditures of the other. In terms of the functional relationships, this means that

$$CR_h = \alpha_7(\cdot\cdot) + \alpha_{10}(\cdot\cdot),$$

and

$$CR_f = \alpha_1(\cdot\cdot) + \alpha_4(\cdot\cdot),$$

where the bracketed dots represent the independent variables shown in the functional relationships.

The circularity, which was mentioned in the last chapter, is quite important. To show it more clearly, Figure 12–1 has been prepared. To draw this figure, it has been assumed that the relationship between each of the dependent variables and current receipts not only has the direction shown earlier, but that the relationship is also linear.

All the independent variables, except current receipts, have been held constant, just as such variables as income, tastes, and the prices of other goods are held constant in order to draw the demand curve for a single

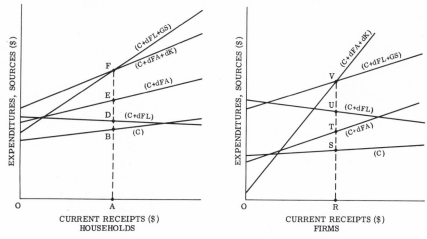

Figure 12-1. Expenditures, sources, and current receipts by sectors.

commodity. If the interest rate index were allowed to rise, C, dK, and dFL would fall for both sectors and dFA would rise. If K were allowed to rise, C and dFA would rise while dK would fall, etc. Note that the demand for money and the demand for other financial assets have been combined into dFA.

For each sector, a perpendicular has been drawn at the point where

$$C + dFA + dK = C + dFL + GS.$$

Subtracting C and dFL from both sides, we have

$$dFA - dFL + dK = GS.$$

The left-hand side is net financial investment plus capital expenditures, or gross investment. Thus, the perpendicular has been drawn at the point where the accounting equalities shown in eqs. (11–27) and (11–32) are satisfied.

Other accounting equalities are also satisfied at this point. Net financial investment for households is the difference between line segments BE and BD, or DE. This is positive net financial investment since dFA_h exceeds dFL_h. For the firms, net financial investment is $ST - SU$, or TU, negative since dFL exceeds dFA. Inspection reveals that $DE + TU = 0$, satisfying eq. (11–37).

$AB + EF$ equal consumption plus investment for households, and measurement reveals that $AB + EF$ equal OR in the firm sector, which satisfies eq. (11–20), while eq. (11–17) is satisfied by

$$RS + TV = OA.$$

Stability and Multipliers. As long as none of the other independent variables change, the level of current receipts will remain at OA for households and OR for firms and all of the dependent variables will be unchanged. This condition may be defined as short-run equilibrium in the sense that desired sources and uses are balanced so that the accounting identities and equalities are satisfied.

Suppose, however, that one of the functional relationships change. Household tastes might shift so that households prefer more consumption and smaller holdings of financial assets at any level of the independent variables. Firms may develop new methods of production which require more spending on nonfinancial assets at any level of the independent variables. In the household case, C_h would shift upward in Figure 12–1. In the second case, dK_f would shift upward. In either case, the sector in which the shift took place would move away from the existing level of current receipts. Since the illustrative shifts increase the sector's expenditures on nonfinancial goods, the receipts of the other sector would also increase, moving it, too, away from the short-run equilibrium.

The purpose of this section is to determine the nonfinancial spending characteristics that are required if the economy is to reach a new short-run equilibrium position once it has been moved from an initial equilibrium point. The key to the answer lies in the way each sector's nonfinancial spending, C and dK, responds to changes in current receipts. Let us define this response as the marginal propensity to spend. If this is represented by the symbol e, then

$$e_h = \frac{d(C_h + dK_h)}{dCR_h},$$

and

$$e_f = \frac{d(C_f + dK_f)}{dCR_h}.$$

Assume that $e_h = e_f = 0.5$, i.e., \$0.50 is spent by each sector on more consumption and more capital goods out of each additional dollar of current receipts. If the capital expenditure function for firms increased so that firms spent \$10 more on capital expenditures, the effect on spending would be

dCR_h	dCR_f
10.00	
	5.00
2.50	
	1.25
0.63	
	0.32
0.16	
.	.
.	.
.	.
13.33	6.67

or a total increase in current receipts of $20 generated by an original increase of $10 in capital expenditures.

The ratio of the ultimate increase in current receipts to the original increase in spending is called the *multiplier*. In the example, its value is 2 and may be derived by

$$\frac{1}{1-e} = \text{multiplier}.$$

Less formally, the multiplier is the ratio of the required change in current receipts to a change in nonfinancial spending needed to bring gross savings into equality with gross investment, and to keep desired net financial investment for the total economy equal to zero. In the example, firms may finance the initial increase in capital expenditures by reducing cash balances, but, at the original level of current receipts, households do not want larger cash balances. As current receipts rise for both sectors, the desired levels of cash, other financial assets, and nonfinancial assets all increase until the new short-run equilibrium is reached.

But if the household demand for financial assets responds weakly to changes in current receipts, total current receipts will have to rise much more than shown in the illustration to bring about short-run equilibrium. On the other hand, if households demand only nonfinancial assets in reponse to an increase in current receipts, equilibrium will never be reached. In this case, $e = 1$, the multiplier has no finite value, and the economy is not stable.

The marginal propensity to spend for households does not have to equal the marginal propensity to spend for firms. For stability, however, $e_h \times e_f < 1$. Suppose $e_h = 2$ and $e_f = 0.5$; if firms increased capital expenditures by $10, the following increases would occur:

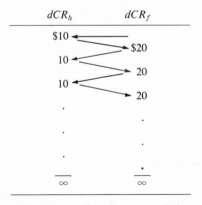

$$
\begin{array}{cc}
dCR_h & dCR_f \\
\end{array}
$$

The unstable process of never-ending increases in current receipts occurs because the product of the two marginal propensities equals 1. Of course, the same process would occur if $e_h = e_f = 1$. If the marginal propensity for households were 1 and for firms 0.5, the pattern would be

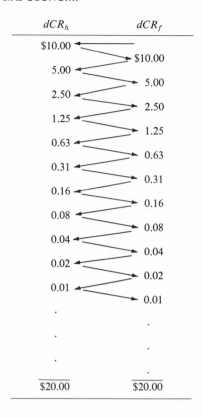

dCR_h	dCR_f
$10.00	
	$10.00
5.00	
	5.00
2.50	
	2.50
1.25	
	1.25
0.63	
	0.63
0.31	
	0.31
0.16	
	0.16
0.08	
	0.08
0.04	
	0.04
0.02	
	0.02
0.01	
	0.01
.	.
.	.
.	.
$20.00	$20.00

where the total increase of $40 is the same as would have occurred if both marginal propensities equaled the product of the two, i.e., 0.5. If the initial increase in expenditures had been generated by the household sector through an increase in consumption expenditures due to a change in tastes, the aggregate increase in total current receipts would have been only $30. When the sectors have different marginal propensities to spend, the effect of a change in spending is greater when it originates in the sector with the lower marginal propensity.

DETERMINATION OF
INTEREST RATES

Demand and supply functions for financial assets and liabilities are shown in Figure 12–2. The dollars demanded and supplied are shown as a function of interest rates, and it is assumed that all other independent variables are held constant. The demand and supply curves for nonmonetary financial assets and liabilities seem to have reversed positions because the vertical axis is not the price of financial claims, but the yield, or interest rate, on financial claims.

Curve DD is the relationship between the interest rate index and the net demand for financial assets. Demand is net in the sense that it represents the difference between the total increases and decreases in holdings of

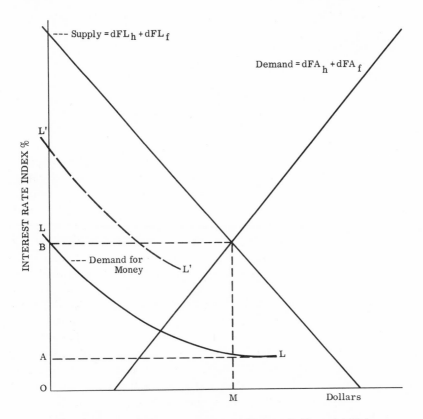

Figure 12-2. The demand and supply of Changes in Financial Claims.

nonmonetary financial assets at the different interest rates. *SS* is the net supply curve of financial claims. *LL* represents the net demand for changes in cash holdings at different interest rates. Since, in this model, there is no money-creating sector, the supply of money is zero at all interest rates.

As indicated in the functional relationships, *dFA'* increases for both sectors as the interest rate rises, *dFL* decreases as interest rates increase, and *dM* decreases as the interest rate rises. The market for nonmonetary financial claims will be cleared, i.e., there will be neither excess demand nor supply, when the interest rate index is that which equates demand and supply, *OB* in the graph. Each different risk and maturity class of financial claim will have its own interest rate, but supply and demand in each of these classes will be equal at some interest rate when the interest rate index is *OB*.

Why is it necessary that the net demand for additions to money holdings also be zero, i.e., equal to supply, at the same interest rate index that brings all other financial supplies and demands into equality? Suppose that the demand for additions to money balances were $L'L'$ instead of LL. At OB, there would be a net positive demand for additions to money holdings. Since the supply of money additions is zero, the demand is an excess demand. Those who wish to add to money holdings have any combination of three means of achieving this end: reduce expenditures on C and I, sell non-monetary financial assets, issue financial liabilities.

Consider first the reduction of nonfinancial expenditures. This will reduce receipts of the other sector, and, through the multiplier, the ultimate decline in total current receipts will be larger than the initial decline in the expenditures of those desiring more cash. At a lower level of current receipts, the demand for financial assets, DD, will shift to the left, raising the interest rate index. Also, as a result of the decline in current receipts, the supply of financial liabilities will increase, shifting SS to the right and, also, raising the interest rate index. However, as the interest rate rises, the demand for additions to money holdings will be reduced because of the higher interest rate, reducing demand along a given LL curve and the downward shift of LL, resulting from the reduction in current receipts. DD will continue to shift to the left, and SS to the right, and $L'L'$ will move down, as long as there is a net positive incremental demand for money. The shifts will stop, and the economy will come to rest, when the demand is zero.

If those who cause the net demand for additional money holdings to exceed zero try to acquire the money by selling nonmonetary financial assets, DD in Figure 12–2 will shift to the left, all else remaining unchanged. This will raise the interest rate. At a higher interest rate, nonfinancial spending will be reduced, reducing current receipts. With a reduction in current receipts, the demand for financial assets, DD, will shift even more to the left. The supply of liabilities will increase, shifting SS to the right. And $L'L'$ will fall. This is very much the same kind of adjustment that occurred when those who had wished to increase money holdings chose to accomplish the increase by directly reducing nonfinancial expenditures. The changes will continue with rising interest rates and declining current receipts until the net demand for additional money holdings is zero.

Finally, if those who wish to add to money holdings do so by issuing additional financial liabilities, SS will shift to the right, raising the interest rate. The higher interest rate will reduce nonfinancial spending and the demand for money. With declining current receipts resulting from the reduction in nonfinancial expenditures, SS will shift more to the right, DD will shift to the left, and $L'L'$ will shift down—much as in the two examples above. Again, interest rates will continue to rise and current receipts to fall until the demand for additional money holdings is zero at the interest rate at which the supply of, and the demand for, financial claims are equal.

Thus, the interest rate index is determined by the level of current receipts and nonfinancial spending (C and dK). The relationship is a complex one involving substantial interactions of current receipts on interest rate and interest rate on nonfinancial spending. To be in short-run equilibrium, it is necessary that current receipts be at such a level that the demand and supply of financial claims of a nonmonetary nature be equal and that the demand for additions to money holdings be equal to the supply of added money, which last is zero in our model. To see this in equations, consider accounting Eq. (11–37),

$$NFI_f + NFI_h = 0.$$

This can be restated as

$$d_f M + d_f FA' - dFL_f + d_h M + d_h FA' - dFL_h = 0,$$

which becomes

$$d_f M + d_h M = 0$$

$$d_f FA' + d_h FA' = dFL_f + dFL_h.$$

In terms of the functional relationships, we are saying

$$\alpha_8(\cdots) + \alpha_2(\cdots) = 0$$

$$+\alpha_9(\cdots) + \alpha_3(\cdots) = \alpha_{11}(\cdots) + \alpha_5(\cdots).$$

The parentheses contain the independent variables, and indicate that all of the variables are important in the determination of the interest rate.

THE PRICE LEVEL

Given the economy's productive capacity, the price level will be determined by desired nonfinancial spending, i.e., by

$$(12–13) \qquad P = \alpha_{13}(C_h, dK_h, C_f, dK_f),$$

with the price level rising as desired nonfinancial expenditures rise. Thus,

	P
C_h	$+$
dK_h	$+$
C_f	$+$
dK_f	$+$

Although the price level is determined by desired nonfinancial expenditures, the volume of nonfinancial expenditures will not be directly affected by the price level. The reason for this is that the nonfinancial variables were defined in real terms. If prices double, the dollars spent on nonfinancial goods and services will double but the real quantities of these goods and services are assumed to remain unchanged.

In fact, the dollars spent on nonfinancial goods and services will not double when the price level doubles because the price level has indirect effects on the demands for nonfinancial items. As the price level increases, the real value of FA' and M will fall. The real value of M will vary inversely and proportionately with changes in P. To the extent that FA' consists of variable-return financial assets, such as common stock, FA' and P will move in the same direction leaving the real value of nonmonetary financial assets unchanged. However, the portion of FA' consisting of fixed-return assets will vary inversely with P, with the real value of holdings of fixed-return financial assets falling when the price level rises. Thus, if there are any fixed-return assets included in FA', the real value of financial assets will vary inversely with the price level.

Financial liabilities also include both fixed- and variable-return claims. As the price level rises, the real burden represented by variable-return claims does not change. If the price level doubles, the dollars paid out as dividends also double. But the real burden of fixed- return claims falls as prices increase because the dollars paid as interest and for redemption of debt are fixed. Thus, the real burden of financial liabilities varies directly with the price level if there are any fixed-return claims outstanding.

An increase in current receipts is caused by an increase in nonfinancial expenditures, which in turn will increase prices. As the price level rises, the real value of financial asset holdings will fall, assuming some fixed-return assets in FA', and the real burden of liabilities outstanding will fall. There will be an increase in the demand for additions to financial asset holdings, resulting in a shift to the right of the demand curves for both nonmonetary financial assets and money (Figure 12-2). There will also be a greater tendency to issue debt, resulting in a rightward shift in the supply curve of financial claims. If the increase in dFA exceeds the increase in dFL, the difference between the two will have to be financed by increased savings, which implies a decrease in nonfinancial expenditures. The decrease in nonfinancial expenditures will serve as a brake to the growth of current receipts.

It is also possible, however, that the increase in dFL will exceed the increase in dFA. In this event, savings will not have to rise to finance the increase in the demand for financial assets. Indeed, savings can decline, allowing expenditures on current account to rise, with no change in capital expenditures. Under these conditions, the price increase serves to spur on the growth of current receipts.

Interest Rate-Price Interactions. Regardless of whether the change in dFA is greater or less than the change in dFL, the shifting demand curve for money combined with the shifting demand and supply curves for nonmonetary claims will raise the interest rate. The increased interest rate will shift expenditures from nonfinancial to financial assets and serve to brake the growth in current receipts. It should be noted that the interest rate effect can be relied upon only if the money supply is constant. If there were a monetary authority which could increase the supply of money, the interest rate effect could be eliminated or, at least, reduced.

Just the reverse occurs when current receipts fall. Declining expenditures result in a reduced price level, which increases the real value of financial assets and the real burden of financial claims. As a result, the demand for money shifts downward, the demand for nonmonetary financial assets shifts to the left, as does the supply of financial claims. If the decrease in dFA exceeds the decrease in dFL, nonfinancial expenditures will be encouraged and the price level will have worked as a brake on the decline of current receipts. However, if the change in dFL exceeds the change in dFA, the declining price level will encourage further declines in current receipts as the economy seeks to redeem debt by more than its reduction in financial asset holdings. The latter can be accomplished only by reducing nonfinancial spending. Nonetheless, the downward shift in the demand for money will result in a fall in interest rates, which will encourage nonfinancial spending.

To sum up, changes in the price level may or may not serve directly to stabilize the economy. Indirectly, changes in the price level will serve as a stabilizer through the interest rate. Price increases result in an increased demand for money additions which raises the interest rate, reducing nonfinancial expenditures. Price decreases set off a downward shift in the demand for money, which reduces the interest rate, increasing nonfinancial expenditures.

Long-run Equilibrium. The accounting equalities in Chapter 11 will always hold. Short-run equilibrium exists when the desired values generated by the functional relationships developed in this chapter coincide with the actual values for the different variables. But it is not necessary that this coincidence be anything more than fleeting.

As the real value of the holdings of any asset increases, the demand for increases in that asset declines. In terms of Figure 12–1, this means that the appropriate curve shifts downward. For example, dK will fall as K increases. Or, dFA' will fall as FA/P increases. The same is true for liabilities. These shifts will change current receipts, the interest rate, and the price level and move the economy in the direction of a new short-run equilibrium, which will be maintained only until the real value of some balance sheet item is altered.

For long-run equilibrium, it is necessary not only that the desired flows equal the actual flows, but that the components of the balance sheet remain unchanged. This means that

$$dK = D$$

for both sectors. With capital expenditures equal to depreciation allowances, K will remain unchanged and will not cause changes in the desired level of capital expenditures.

For financial assets, it is necessary that $dFA' = 0$. This does not mean that there will be no demand for nonmonetary financial assets. As assets, such as bonds, mature and are redeemed, the holder will replace the redeemed financial asset with a like one. But dFA' is the net demand for nonmonetary financial asset increases, i.e., net of maturing financial assets. Even in short-run equilibrium, $dM = 0$.

With respect to liabilities,

$$dFL = 0$$

in long-run equilibrium. As with financial assets, liabilities will be issued to replace those that have matured and have been redeemed.

There will still have to be an interest rate high enough to make people willing to buy replacements for redeemed financial assets and so high that issuers are unwilling to replace redeemed liabilities.

When these conditions are realized, the economy has achieved a long-run static, i.e., unchanging, equilibrium.

THE THREE-SECTOR ECONOMY

The third sector is government. Governmental functions include taxation, nonfinancial expenditure, management of the public debt, and management of the government's cash position.

As before, the government does not have the power to change the total money supply.

FISCAL POLICY

We assume tax receipts to be a function of economic activity. Specifically,

$$(12\text{–}14) \qquad T = \alpha_{14}(CR_f, CR_h).$$

This can include both sales and income taxes. Tax receipts will rise with current receipts. The government can change the tax schedule, which means that the quantitative relationship between tax receipts and the independent variables is altered.

Government expenditure on nonfinancial items is set by government. However, certain elements such as agricultural subsidies and relief payments will be sensitive to current receipts, varying inversely with current receipts.

$$(12\text{–}15) \qquad G = \alpha_{15}(CR_f, CR_h).$$

The portion of government expenditures that is set without regard to current receipts will not affect the inverse relationship but simply increase or decrease the level of government expenditures at any level of current receipts.

With both taxes and government expenditures, the composition of current receipts for each of the private sectors is different than in an economy without government. Current receipts for households are defined as

$$CR_h = C_f + I_f + G_h + T_h,$$

and for firms,

$$CR_f = C_h + I_h + G_f - T_f.$$

Either or both private sectors may experience an increase in current receipts through government expenditures' exceeding taxes, even though the expenditures of the other private sector have not changed. Of course, current receipts fall for a sector if taxes exceed government expenditures. Thus, government can induce changes in the level of total current receipts, and the total change will reflect the multiplier.

If the government operates a balanced budget, i.e., $G = T$, it is still possible that current receipts will change if the budget is not balanced for each sector and if $e_h \neq e_f$. Suppose that the government spends more on households than it receives in tax revenues from households, and taxes firms more than it spends on firms. Households experience an increase in current receipts, which increases household expenditures and could set off a multiplier effect. Firms experience a decrease in current receipts and decrease expenditures, which could set off a negative multiplier effect. If the increase in household expenditures exactly equals the decrease in firm expenditures, i.e., if $e_h = e_f$, the two actions will nullify each other and total current receipts will remain unchanged. But if $e_h > e_f$, the increase in household expenditures will exceed the decline in firm expenditures and total current receipts will rise. Just the reverse would occur if $e_h < e_f$. Thus, if fiscal policy is to have neutral effects on current receipts, it is necessary that tax revenues equal government expenditures for each sector as well as for the economy as a whole.

Given the functional relationships shown for taxes and government expenditures, government fiscal policy will be a stabilizing factor. If one of the sectors increases nonfinancial expenditures to set off a multiplied effect on current receipts, tax payments will rise and government expenditures will fall as current receipts increase. As the definitions of current receipts for the private sectors show, this will tend to reduce current receipts for each sector. Initially, the effect of government may not be enough to stop the increase caused by the expansion of private sector expenditures. However, as current receipts continue to rise, the increments to current receipts will get smaller and the government surplus, $G - T$, will get larger, so that, even if the impact of government does not stop the increase in current receipts, the increase will be moderated. Just the opposite occurs if spending and current receipts decline. The government moves to a deficit position, $G > T$, which tends to offset the decline in current receipts.

The government can choose to take more active steps to affect current receipts by shifting tax and expenditure functions. These can be contra-cyclical. When current receipts rise, the government would raise the tax schedule and decrease government expenditures. The tax schedule would be lowered, and expenditures increased in the face of declines in total current receipts. Contracyclical policies are not necessary. The government, for example, could have the policy of maintaining some rate of increase in total current receipts and would then adjust taxes and government expenditures to mantain the target rate of increase.

Financial and Monetary Policy. As indicated in Chapter 11, the government balance sheet contains one asset, money, and one financial liability, the public debt. It is possible to present functional relationships determining the desired changes in these two variables on the basis of the interest rate. But this would miss the point of government. While government may not be happy about issuing debt when interest rates are high, the debt may be issued anyhow if the government needs the money for urgent purposes. The government may not want to hold large cash balances when interest rates are high, either, but if the effect of reducing governmental cash balances would be to cause inflation of prices, government may hold the cash for policy reasons. Thus, the government's demand for increments to governmental cash holdings and the government's desired supply of net additions to the public debt will be treated as variables which are determined by government policy and not necessarily as functions of other variables in the model.

As an example, suppose that government policy is to maintain a stable price level. Assume that the government prefers not to change tax schedules or the expenditure system, but will rely on fiscal policy to the extent that taxes and expenditures work toward stabilization automatically. Instead of manipulating taxes and expenditures, the government chooses to maintain stable prices by varying government cash holdings and the size of the public debt.

In this model, the price level varies directly with the desired level of nonfinancial spending. Given the output of which the economy is capable, desired increases in nonfinancial spending will raise prices. At the higher level of prices, the real value of financial assets declines and the desired increases in nonfinancial spending are reduced so people accumulate more financial assets. Conversely, if the desired level of nonfinancial spending falls, prices will fall, increasing the real value of financial asset holdings. In effect, the economy holds excess financial assets. The excess is removed by selling nonmonetary financial assets and using the proceeds and excess cash holdings to buy nonfinancial goods and services, which pushes the economy in the direction of the original price level. However, the automatic stabilizing features of the economy may be insufficient to restore the economy to the original price level. Even if the economy will return to the original price level, the process may take a long time.

The government can hasten the restoration of the original price level by the way in which it manages the public debt and its cash holdings. When dollar current receipts rise, government revenues tend to exceed government expenditures. The surplus can be held in the form of cash or used to reduce the public debt. If held as cash, the net additions to the supply of money available to the private sectors moves from zero to a negative supply. In Figure 12–2, the supply of additional money shifts from the vertical axis to a point to the left of the vertical axis. This will hasten and enlarge the interest rate increase, which would result from the increase in current receipts anyhow. And the result of a sharp increase in interest rates will be a reduction both in desired cash holdings and in nonfinancial expenditures. The reduction in desired expenditures will tend to reduce prices.

If the government should use the surplus generated by the increase in aggregate dollar current receipts to reduce the public debt, the supply of financial liabilities shifts to the left, reducing interest rates and encouraging nonfinancial spending. As a result, prices will tend to rise. It follows that price stability policy is better achieved if surpluses generated by rising current receipts are held as cash rather than used to reduce debt. Indeed, it would be better not only to hold the surplus as additions to government cash, but to add even more to cash by increasing the public debt. An increase in public debt will shift the supply of financial claims to the right, increasing interest rates still more.

When current receipts fall, government deficits are apt to occur. Should the deficits be financed by reducing government cash or by increasing the public debt? If financed by reducing government cash balances, the supply of money additions available to the private sectors shifts to the right of the vertical axis in Figure 12–2, which increases the downward movement of the interest rate that would occur with declining aggregate current receipts. The interest rate fall stimulates both additions to private cash holdings and nonfinancial expenditures. The latter will increase current receipts and raise the price level back toward the point which it held prior to the decline in current receipts.

Financing the deficit by increasing the public debt results in an increase in interest rates since the supply of financial claims is increased. The higher interest rate tends to depress current receipts and the price level even more. If the government financed deficits out of cash and *decreased* the public debt, using its cash balances for debt redemption as well as to finance operating deficits, the supply of financial claims would shift to the left, forcing interest rates even lower and encouraging nonfinancial expenditures which would raise the price level.

When the government sector manipulates its cash balances and the public debt in order to achieve policy aims, it is using tools of monetary policy. In the example, its financing decisions—i.e., whether to accumulate surpluses as cash and finance deficits with cash—resulted in a variation in the money supply available to private sectors, even though the total money supply was constant. The decision to increase the public debt in order to reduce prices and decrease the debt to increase prices is the equivalent of what is referred to in the United States economy as *open market operations*. In the real world, the Federal Reserve buys and sells government debt in order to increase money available to private sectors or decrease the private money supply. The institutional framework in the United States economy will be discussed later, but the effect of these operations is just the same as the effect of the government in our model when it expands and contracts the public debt. In other words, the ability to create new money is not necessary for a government which wishes to use the tools of monetary policy.

Equilibrium. To be in long-run equilibrium, the same equalities hold for the private sectors as held in the two-sector model. In addition, the government must operate at a balanced budget, i.e., $G = T$. Otherwise, the government will have to vary the public debt or the money supply available to the private sectors in order to finance deficits and absorb surpluses, which will result in interest rate variations and lead to disequilibrium.

It follows that the public debt will be constant, i.e.,

$$dFL_g = 0,$$

with the government issuing debt only to replace maturing debt. Also,

$$d_g M = 0.$$

THE FOUR-SECTOR ECONOMY

The fourth sector is the rest of the world, or foreign sector. Discussion will be divided into two parts: First, we shall consider the determinants of the balance of trade; then, the balance of payments will be analyzed.

The Balance of Trade Imports of nonfinancial goods and services, whether on capital or current account, will be referred to as IM'. The balance of trade is the difference between exports and imports. It is favorable when exports exceed imports, and unfavorable when imports are larger than exports.

Given the relative production advantages of the domestic economy as compared with the rest of the world, both exports and imports will be determined by the relationship of the domestic price level P to foreign prices P_w. Exports will rise when the ratio of domestic prices to foreign prices, P/P_w, falls. Imports will vary directly with changes in P/P_w. Thus,

$$(12\text{-}16) \qquad\qquad EX = \alpha_{16}(P/P_w);$$
$$(12\text{-}17) \qquad\qquad IM' = \alpha_{17}(P/P_w).$$

As shown in eqs. (11–17b) and (16–20b), imports tend to decrease aggregate current receipts and exports to increase current receipts. Thus, if exports exceed imports, i.e., the balance of trade is favorable, current receipts can rise by a multiple of the balance of trade. An unfavorable balance of trade can induce negative multiplier effects. Even if exports equal imports for the entire economy, multiplier effects can occur if $e_h \neq e_f$ and exports do not equal imports for each sector. If the sector with the higher propensity to spend also has more exports than imports, the economy as a whole will have rising current receipts, at least in money terms. Current receipts would fall if the sector with the higher e had an unfavorable balance of trade. However, we shall ignore this complexity by assuming that $e_h = e_f$.

Suppose that imports rise, causing a decline in current receipts. Desired expenditures will also decline, forcing prices down. As domestic prices decline, the demand for imports will fall and exports will increase according to the behavioral equations. This assumes that foreign prices are constant. With this assumption, it is seen that the current receipts–price level relationship tends to stabilize and correct imbalances in the balance of trade. The correction is helped by what happens in foreign countries when our imports increase. To foreign countries, this is an increase in exports, which increases their current receipts, raising their desired expenditures and increasing foreign prices. Thus, not only does the domestic price level fall, but the foreign price level will rise. Combined, desired imports will decline and exports will increase until a balance is reached.

Just the reverse occurs when our exports increase. Our current receipts, desired nonfinancial expenditures, and price level rise, while foreign prices fall. These combine to increase our imports and reduce exports until equilibrium is regained.

Government Policy and Equilibrium. For the automatic adjustment of the balance of trade to occur, it is necessary that the price level and the money value of current receipts be allowed to fluctuate. However, this may be in opposition to government policy. The government may prefer stable prices and shift taxation and expenditures schedules, as well as manipulate government cash balances and the public debt, to achieve stability. Such actions would thwart the automatic balance of trade adjustments.

Even if the domestic government is unwilling to accept unstable prices, the automatic adjustment can occur through variations in foreign prices. As pointed out earlier, foreign prices will move inversely to domestic prices, given a trade imbalance. But, if foreign governments are also unwilling to accept price instability, neither domestic prices nor foreign prices will be free to adjust.

The consequences of this is the persistence of trade imbalance. If the domestic economy has an adverse balance of trade, domestic prices will be stabilized by continuing injections of government cash into the private sectors and by a reduction in public debt. Should these actions cease, prices will fall. However, at some point, the public debt reaches zero and the government runs out of money. When this happens, the government can no longer support the price level and prices will fall. If, however, foreign trade is a small part of the total economy, it is conceivable that the government will be able to stabilize prices virtually forever. The result of this is a permanent trade disequilibrium.

The Balance of Payments. As the domestic economy exports goods and services to the rest of the world, domestic sectors are paid in cash, or in claims on foreigners. To the extent that the claims are marketable, they may be converted into money, or into other claims which the domestic sector prefers holding. When the domestic economy imports goods, the imports are paid in cash or claims, and foreigners may convert these claims into money or other claims. In the model developed here, money is really similar to gold if there were no way to augment the world supply of gold. Thus, if domestic imports exceed exports and foreigners prefer money to holding domestic claims, there is a money drain out of the domestic economy. On the other hand, if the domestic economy has a favorable balance of trade and prefers money to foreign claims, foreigners face a money drain and the domestic economy has a net inflow of money.

The balance of payments refers to the international flow of money payments. When money paid to foreigners equals money paid to the domestic economy by foreigners, the balance of payments are—balanced. The balance of payments is related to the balance of trade, but they are not the same. Given an unfavorable balance of trade for the domestic economy, an unfavorable balance of payments is not a necessary result. Suppose foreigners prefer holding domestic financial assets rather than money. In this event, the balance of payments could be favorable if foreigners were not only willing to hold financial claims against the domestic economy as payment for the domestic economy's excess imports, but were willing to convert foreign money into claims on domestic sectors. Similarly, a favorable balance of trade for the domestic economy could occur with an unfavorable balance of payments if the domestic sectors prefer holding financial claims on foreigners to holding cash.

From the point of view of the domestic economy, the balance sheet for the rest of the world consists of money, nonmonetary financial assets, and financial liabilities, i.e., claims on foreigners held by the domestic economy. The functional relationships are

$$(12\text{–}18) \qquad d_w M = \alpha_{18}(EX, IM', {_w}FA'\, FL_w, i/i_w);$$

$$(12\text{–}19) \qquad d_w FA' = \alpha_{19}(EX, IM', {_w}FA', FL_w, i/i_w);$$

$$(12\text{–}20) \qquad dFL_w = \alpha_{20}(EX, IM', {_w}FA', FL_w, i/i_w).$$

The symbol i_w represents interest rates in the rest of the world. The direction of the relationship between each independent variable and each dependent variable is

	$d_w M$	$d_w FA'$	dFL_w
EX	−	−	+
IM'	+	+	−
$_w FA'$	+	−	+
FL_w	−	−	−
i/i_w	−	+	−

When exports are large, foreigners pay by reducing their holdings of cash, selling claims on the domestic economy, or by issuing foreign claims to the domestic economy. Conversely, when imports are high, foreigners can increase cash holdings and holding of claims on the domestic economy and can reduce foreign debt.

If foreigners already hold a large amount of domestic claims, they are less likely to add to these claims than if the holdings are small. So, they will either increase cash holdings or reduce their liabilities. If foreign debt is high, foreigners are apt to want to reduce the debt and will reduce their cash holdings and financial asset holdings to achieve the debt reduction.

When domestic interest rates are high relative to foreign rates, foreigners will reduce money holdings and increase holdings of financial claims on the domestic economy. Foreigners will also be reluctant to issue financial claims in high-interest-rate domestic financial markets.

THE BALANCE OF PAYMENTS AND THE BALANCE OF TRADE

We have already seen that the balance of trade has an effect on the interest rate through changes in the price level. With a favorable balance of trade, domestic prices rise, increasing the demand for additions to money holdings and raising the interest rate. Interest rates will fall because of the price decline associated with an unfavorable balance of trade.

The functional relationships for foreign balance sheets indicate that there will be effects on the interest rate caused by the balance of trade other than those that result from price changes. With a favorable balance of trade, foreigners will reduce money holdings and holdings of nonmonetary financial assets. The reduction in money holdings effectively increases the supply of money available to the domestic sectors. This is similar to what happens when the government reduces its cash holdings. Interest rates will have to fall to absorb the additional domestic cash available.

The change in demand for increments to nonmonetary financial asset holdings by foreigners as a result of the balance of trade will move in the opposite direction from the demand for cash increments by the rest of the world. With a favorable balance of trade from the domestic economy's point of view, foreigners will reduce holdings of nonmonetary financial assets. This will shift the demand curve for nonmonetary financial assets to the left, tending to increase interest rates. Foreigners will also supply additional claims, again tending to move interest rates up.

From our model, it is impossible to say which way interest rates will move in fact. With a favorable balance of trade and upward price movements, the domestic sectors will be adding to financial assets, including money. If the demand for money is strong, the added money supplied by the foreign sectors may be absorbed without lowering interest rates. In that event, the effect of the reduced demand for financial assets by the rest of the world and the increased supply of foreign claims will raise interest rates. On the other hand, the domestic economy may be more interested in buying nonmonetary claims, so that the increased domestic demand for nonmonetary financial assets, induced by the price increase, will more than offset the reduced demand of the foreign sector. If domestic sectors are also willing to expand the supply of claims issued by domestic economic units, again because of the price increase, interest rates may fall in order to bring the demand for cash increments into equality with supply.

Suppose that there is an unfavorable balance of trade. If the domestic sectors reduce their demand for financial assets, because of the associated price decline, by more than the increased demand of the foreign sector, interest rates will tend to rise. The foreign demand for nonmonetary financial assets will rise sharply if the domestic interest rate exceeds the foreign interest rate. Foreign demand for money will fall, and the balance of payments will be favorable even though the balance of trade is unfavorable. The same contrast can obtain with a favorable balance of trade, when the balance of payments could be unfavorable if the supply and demand for financial claims shift so as to reduce domestic interest rates below foreign rates.

LONG-RUN
EQUILIBRIUM

For long-run equilibrium to obtain in the four-sector economy, the equalities described for the domestic sectors still hold. In addition, the level of exports must equal imports, and desired balance sheet changes for the foreign sector must equal zero. The latter means that the balance of payments must also equal zero, since $d_w M = 0$, under long-run static equilibrium.

SUMMATION

General equilibrium models of the type developed here start out with almost simpleminded building blocks. Despite this, they rapidly become complicated. Part of the reason for this is that each sector of the economy potentially interacts with every other sector. Once we move beyond two sectors, it is very difficult to predict what will happen, given a change in the system, unless we know the specific quantitative weights assigned to each variable. Of course, all that was specified here was the direction of change between dependent and independent variables.

The complications become almost impossible in a multisectoral model if variables such as expectations are included or if the number of sectors is expanded. Therefore, the theoretical model of this chapter will not be formally expanded to include the various sectors for financial institutions. Instead, the next chapter will include a general discussion of the impact of financial institutions on the nonfinancial economy. Later chapters will describe the impact of specific financial institutions on nonfinancial sectors but without a formal theoretical model.

SELECTED REFERENCES

Gurley, V., and E. Shaw: *Money in a Theory of Finance*, Brookings, Washington, D.C., 1960.

Patinkin, D.: "Financial Intermediaries and Monetary Theory," *American Economic Review*, Mar., 1961.

————: *Money, Interest, and Prices*, Row Peterson, 1956.

Vandermeulen, D., and A. Vandermeulen: *National Income Analysis by Sector Accounts*, Prentice-Hall, Englewood Cliffs, N.J., 1956.

APPENDIX

Gross National Product and the Aggregate of Current Receipts

Throughout this chapter, the money value of aggregate current receipts for the private sectors was used as an indicator of economic activity, much as GNP is used ordinarily. Current receipts were used that we might remain within the framework of the flow of funds. Generally, it is more convenient to use GNP if only because GNP estimates are available in a regular series and GNP is a better-known measure. What are the differences between aggregate current receipts and GNP?

Considering an economy of firms and households, the aggregate of current receipts is

$$CR_h + CR_f = C_h + C_f + dCD + dRH + dQ + dPE.$$

The goods and services produced by firms are either sold to households or held as increments to the firms' assets. Thus, the value of goods and services, produced by firms, i.e., *GNP*, is

$$GNP = C_h + dCD + dRH + dQ + dPE.$$

The actual estimate of GNP prepared by the Department of Commerce includes some different definitions than those above. We shall consider only the more important of these differences.

GNP consumption estimates include purchases of consumer durable goods, i.e., these goods are treated as if they are used up within the year. Thus,

$$C_{gnp} = C_h + dCD.$$

Household changes in residential housing and business changes in inventories and plant and equipment are included as investment.

$$I_{gnp} = dRH + dQ + dPE.$$

Thus,

$$GNP = C_{gnp} + I_{gnp}.$$

As a result of treating consumer durable goods as current consumption, capital consumption charges in GNP accounts are smaller than capital consumption in the flow of funds.

Those interested in other differences in treatment can find a more complete analysis in the publications of the Federal Reserve Board listed in the bibliography at the end of Chapter 11.

Introduction to Financial Sectors and Commercial Banking

13

So far, emphasis has been placed on the real sectors of the economy. In this and the succeeding chapters, we shall treat the financial sectors. But, what is the difference between a real sector and a financial sector?

Some very important differences are shown in Table 13-1. The two major private nonfinancial sectors are compared with the various financial sectors. The last two rows of the table emphasize the differences. For each dollar spent on real assets, capital expenditures, the nonfinancial sectors spend considerably less than a dollar on financial assets; whereas the financial sectors spend several dollars on financial assets for each dollar expended on real assets. Two of the financial sectors had virtually no capital expenditures. Thus, one difference between financial and real sectors is that the asset portfolio of financial institutions contains primarily financial assets, while real assets predominate for the real sectors.

A similar difference is shown on the other side of the balance sheet. For each dollar of internal funds used to finance the acquisition of assets, nonfinancial businesses issued only $0.39 of financial claims and the consumer nonprofit sector issued $0.25. In contrast, the banking sector issued $80.75 in financial claims for each dollar of internal financing, and the miscellaneous financial sector actually had a negative flow for internal financing. Thus another difference between financial and real sectors is that real sectors rely mainly on internal financing, while the financial sectors predominantly use external financing.

Table 13-1

SELECTED BALANCE SHEET AND INCOME STATEMENT CHANGES
FOR REAL AND FINANCIAL SECTORS, 1962
(In Billions of Dollars)

	Nonfinancial Business*	Consumers and Nonprofit Institutions	Banking	Savings Institutions	Insurance	Other Financial Institutions
Change in financial assets	10.1	43.6	19.9	15.3	11.9	5.1
Change in financial liabilities	19.3	21.9	19.4	14.1	9.8	5.5
Capital expenditures	56.2	69.5	0.3	...	0.4	
Gross savings	49.8	86.6	1.2	1.2	0.7	−0.8
Ratio of change in financial assets to capital expenditures	0.18	0.63	66.33	...	29.75	
Ratio of change in financial liabilities to gross savings	0.39	0.25	80.75	12.75	14.00	−6.88

*Nonfinancial business includes farms, unincorporated nonfinancial business, and incorporated nonfinancial business.
Source: Federal Reserve Bulletin, August, 1963, p. 1153.

Still another very important difference between financial institutions and most nonfinancial institutions is that the balance sheets of financial institutions are generally subject to direct governmental regulation. To some extent this is also true of a few nonfinancial institutions, such as public utility holding companies. On the whole, however, the balance sheets of the real sectors are not subject to direct supervision by government.

The reasons for regulating financial institutions provide additional clues as to differences between financial and nonfinancial sectors. For example, the most important financial claim issued by the largest financial sector, the banking sector, is money. Other financial institutions issue claims which are peculiarly related to the economic security of the citizenry. Such claims include life insurance and personal savings.

The nature of financial claims provides only part of the justification for regulating financial institutions. Most of their assets are financial claims, i.e., intangibles. As a result, it is very difficult for purchasers of the financial sectors' claims to evaluate the asset portfolio of which they are purchasing a share. Further, the intangible nature of financial assets makes it easier for the firm selling claims on itself to misrepresent the value of its assets.

In this and the next chapter, we shall concentrate on the banking sector, which includes commercial banks, the Federal Reserve System, and the monetary operations of the United States Treasury. Chapter 15 will consist of an analysis of the major thrift and insurance institutions.

The material in Chapters 11 and 12 were necessarily abstract because we were discussing economic systems with no real counterpart. As the financial sectors are added, the structure becomes increasingly realistic. This will make it possible to use the actual data of the United States economy for examples and illustrations.

In one respect, the discussion of the financial sectors will be simplified, resulting in less realism. The simplification consists of ignoring the direct real effects of the financial sectors. Although the financial sectors use labor and capital goods, thus buying the output of households and firms and affecting the receipts of these real sectors, this relationship will be ignored. Instead, we shall discuss only the financial effects of the operations of the financial sectors. The loss of realism is only slight, since capital expenditures of the financial sectors are relatively insignificant. Even employment is not important for the financial sectors. In 1962, there were 55.3 million workers employed outside agriculture. Of these, about 5 per cent, less than 3 million, were employed in the financial sectors.

THE DEMAND FOR CLAIMS ON FINANCIAL INSTITUTIONS

Financial institutions issue liabilities which they sell to the real sectors. The proceeds of the sales are then used mainly to purchase liabilities issued by real sectors. This is a somewhat roundabout method of moving savings from surplus sectors to deficit sectors as compared with the more direct method of having surplus sectors buy the liabilities of deficit real sectors themselves. Nonetheless, the use of financial institutions has become highly characteristic of the process by which we finance capital expenditures in the United States. This section is aimed at answering the questions: Why are savers willing to purchase the liabilities of real sectors indirectly through the purchase of the liabilities of financial sectors? What effect do financial institutions have on the level and rate of growth of GNP?

As a rough generalization, it appears fair to say that nonfinancial firms are primarily interested in their asset portfolios, choosing a capital structure that fits the asset portfolio in terms of the resultant size and variance of expected net worth, subject to the acceptance of stockholders and creditors. In short, the asset portfolio is an important determinant of the capital structure. A firm requiring a preponderance of long-lived assets will be reluctant to issue a preponderance of short-term claims. If the maturity yield structure favors short-term claims, the firm will adjust its asset portfolio toward shorter-lived assets as much as technology permits. If the high cost of long-term claims still reduces the expected value of net worth below some minimally acceptable level, and if short-term claims increase risk above an acceptable level, the firm may be forced out of business.

In contrast, financial institutions may be thought of as choosing capital structures containing liabilities for which there is strong demand, and adjusting asset portfolios so that the balance sheet generates sufficiently high values of net worth with low risk. Nonfinancial firms prefer safe capital structures because they have risky asset portfolios. Financial firms prefer safe asset portfolios because they have risky capital structures.

In many instances, it turns out that the individual financial firm cannot, or will not, voluntarily adjust its asset portfolio to insure a stable supply of its claims. If the claims issued by the institution are believed to be imbued with the public interest, two avenues are open. First, public or quasi-public institutions can be created to protect the claim. Thus, the Federal Reserve was created largely to protect the liquidity of commercial banks in order to protect the stability of the supply of the primary financial liability of commercial banks—demand deposits. The Federal Deposit Insurance Corporation was also created to protect demand deposits by insurance.

This kind of solution, the creation of auxiliary institutions, is necessary when the individual financial firm is unable to adjust its asset portfolio in a manner appropriate to the claims it issues. Often, however, the problem may be that the firm is unwilling to make the appropriate adjustment. The financial firm may be anxious to take on the added risks of investing in speculative common stocks, even though such investments are not appropriate to the nature of its financial liabilities. In these cases, the public policy answer is regulation of the asset portfolio.

Through management of asset portfolios and with the assistance of auxiliary institutions and regulation, financial institutions are able to issue liabilities with features quite unlike those that can be issued by nonfinancial firms. A prime example is money. Time deposits and savings shares provide a degree of safety which cannot be matched by the claims of nonfinancial firms, although United States government securities are at least equally safe. Life insurance policies offer features that nonfinancial firms cannot add to their liabilities.

Savers usually cannot duplicate the nature of the liabilities of financial institutions by direct investment. The household which, instead of paying life insurance premiums, invests the funds in the liabilities of real sectors duplicating the relative asset holdings of life insurance companies, would not have a life insurance policy. Withdrawing a bank deposit and reinvesting the funds by duplicating the investments made by commercial banks would not provide the household with a new set of claims that have the feature of money.

One of the factors that makes the difference between buying claims of financial firms and buying claims directly from the real sectors is that certain financial institutions can rely upon a *large number principle.* A life insurance company can bet that all of its policyholders will not die at once and can manage its asset portfolio on that assumption. The individual who invests an amount equal to the life insurance premium on his own has no such assurance. In fact, in his private life insurance operation, everyone will die at once. So too, a commercial bank can bet that all of its depositors will not withdraw their funds at once, and, as a result, the bank needs less than 100 per cent liquidity. The individual who withdraws his bank deposit and uses it to duplicate the bank's asset portfolio cannot count on this. He may need his entire investment in liquid form at once. Savings and loan associations invest most of the funds received as savings shares in long-term mortgages, but can meet the withdrawal demands of savers because all savers do not withdraw funds at once. An individual who invests his funds directly in mortgages has, as a result, considerably less liquid investments than if he made the investment indirectly by buying savings and loan shares.

The large number principle enunciated above is one of several *advantages of scale* available to financial institutions. It is the major one which would not be available to any individual. Other advantages are more like economies of scale, concerning diversification and the spreading of fixed costs. Effective diversification, for example, requires a large asset portfolio. The relatively small investor may be willing to accept a lower yield from a mutual fund than could be realized if he invested directly in the stocks of business corporations. However, the portion of the fund's asset portfolio he purchases is safer than he could achieve independently, because of diversification. Diversification works for almost all financial institutions. An investor could not achieve the safety of a savings and loan share if the investor placed his funds directly in mortgages unless his savings were large enough to permit the purchase of many mortgages. Commercial banks make a large number of risky business loans which are less risky in aggregate than they are individually.

Investment knowledge and administrative costs are other examples of economies of scale. Financial institutions can spread the costs of acquiring information and portfolio administration over a large portfolio. Large individual investors can do much the same. For small and medium sized investors, however, the costs would represent a very large share of investment income. Thus, even though the liabilities of financial institutions may yield less than a portfolio of liabilities of the real sectors, the small and medium-sized investor may actually realize a larger net yield on the indirect claims, after deducting the costs of administration and gathering information.

To sum up, the claims issued by financial firms find a market because these claims are different in nature than those that can be issued by nonfinancial firms or that can be created through individual portfolios. For investors of limited means, the net yield from investing in claims on financial institutions may exceed the net yield from investing directly in the claims on real sectors because the financial firms enjoy economies of scale with respect to diversification and portfolio management. In part of this chapter and the following two chapters, the nature of these advantages will be examined with respect to specific institutions.

ECONOMIC GROWTH
AND FINANCIAL
INSTITUTIONS

The primary role of the financial institution is that of a middleman between savers with inadequate capital expenditure opportunities and spenders with inadequate savings. As already indicated, financial institutions make negligible capital expenditures, have low gross savings, and are not important as employers or purchasers of other services or goods. Thus, the effect of financial institutions on GNP will take place primarily as a result of their function as allocators of savings.

To illustrate the impact of financial institutions, we shall consider a two-sector economy in which one sector specializes in saving and the other in making capital expenditures. As a first step, financial institutions will be ignored.

Figure 13–1 shows the two sectors without financial institutions. Sector 1's demand for capital expenditures is expressed by line *BN*, and 2's larger demand for capital expenditures is shown by line *DQ*. Both curves assume a given state of risks and preferences, and merely show that, as yields fall, an increasing quantity of capital expenditures will be undertaken. *MS*, for sector 1, shows gross savings and sector 2's gross savings are shown by *PS′*. For simplicity, it has been assumed that gross savings are perfectly inelastic to the rate of return.

For the moment, let us concentrate on the demand and gross savings functions. Assume that there are no financial markets, i.e., no means exist

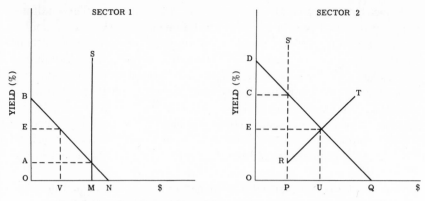

Figure 13-1. The effect of financial markets on a two sector economy.

for transferring savings from one sector to another. Each sector will then invest all of its gross savings in capital expenditures since financial assets do not exist. Gross savings will equal capital expenditures not only for the entire economy but for each sector individually. Sector 1 will make capital expenditures equal to *OM*, which equals gross savings, and sector 2 will make capital expenditures of *OP*. The results are clearly not consistent with a rapidly growing economy. Sector 1 has made capital expenditures yielding as low a rate as *OA*, even though sector 2 has had to forego investing in many expenditures which yield a higher rate of return. The average yield of all capital expenditures would be raised if a way were devised for sector 2 to acquire some of the savings of sector 1.

This is precisely the purpose of a financial market. Assume now that financial instruments exist. Again for simplicity, assume that the risk and return features of these instruments are identical to those of capital expenditures, so that the only reason to prefer a financial instrument to a capital good is yield. Now, sector 2 can offer financial instruments to sector 1 in order to attract funds. Sector 1 will be willing to accept these instruments as long as the yield exceeds the yield on available capital expenditures. Sector 2 will be willing to issue the instruments as long as it can invest the proceeds in capital goods with a higher yield. As sector 1 foregoes capital expenditures in order to acquire financial assets, it moves back up line *BN*. The funds made available to sector 2 may be viewed as the difference between capital expenditures and gross savings for sector 1. When financial assets yield *OB*, sector 1 will be willing to supply all of its savings to sector 2. At a yield of *OA*, it will supply none and will invest all savings in its own capital expenditures. The funds made available are also shown by the line *RT* in sector 2's graph. By adding it to sector 2's gross savings, starting at a yield of *OA*, for no funds will be transferred at a yield below OA, the supply curve of funds to sector 2 can be described by *PRT*.

With the financial market, sector 2 will issue financial claims so that it can finance capital expenditures equal to OU, increasing capital expenditures from what they had been in the absence of a financial market by an amount PU. Sector 1 will decrease capital expenditures to a level of OV, a decline of VM. VM equals PU necessarily. The total level of capital expenditures has not changed since gross savings have not changed either in total or for each sector. Gross savings for the economy equal capital expenditures. For sector 1, gross investment is, as it was without financial markets, OM, but now consists of capital expenditures of OV plus net financial investment of VM. For sector 2, gross investment also has not changed. Its composition now consists of capital expenditures OU plus negative net financial investment of UP.

What effect has the financial market had on GNP? It has had no effect on the level of investment, because this can only be changed by. changing the level of savings. It has had an effect on the productivity of investment. The least productive capital expenditure made in the economy now yields OE, and the average yield on capital expenditures has also risen over the average in the absence of financial markets. If the yields expected on investment are realized, the productive capacity of the economy and, assuming no increase in unemployment, GNP will both grow more rapidly as a result of the superior allocation of funds with financial markets.

If we assume no direct effects on GNP by financial institutions, i.e., assume negligible capital expenditures, savings, and employment by financial institutions, the two indirect effects of financial institutions will concern the level of saving by the real sectors and the allocation of saving among the real sectors. Turning first to the level of saving, if financial institutions operate to increase gross saving in the economy, total capital expenditures will also increase. Households must be willing to exchange nondurable consumer goods and services for bank deposits, savings accounts, life insurance policies, and pension claims. Firms must be willing to reduce dividend payments and current production expenditures (to the extent that such reductions will not also reduce sales revenues). In the short-run such exchanges may not seem reasonable. However, over a longer period of time, they may occur. Given a rising GNP, the share of incremental income going to buy claims on financial institutions may rise. Thus, savings can increase over time, while the absolute level of current expenditures also grows.

It is also possible that financial institutions may decrease savings. To some extent, financial claims, such as mutual fund shares, make it possible to achieve portfolio characteristics, such as diversification, with a smaller financial asset portfolio than would be needed in the absence of financial institutions. The security provided by a life insurance policy involves a much smaller asset portfolio than if the insured tried to achieve a similar level of protection using only claims on real sectors. Probably the existence of financial institutions increases saving for some economic entities and decreases saving for others. My guess is that on the whole, financial institutions increase saving, but the data do not exist for a convincing proof of this proposition.

Turning now to the effect of financial institutions on a more efficient allocation of savings, the problem is more complex than that of the aggregate level of saving. Figure 13–2 provides some illustrations of the possibilities. In this figure, we deal again with two real sectors and have duplicated the demand and supply functions from Figure 1. The dashed line *BN* is the same demand for capital expenditures for sector 1 as shown in the previous figure. The dashed line *PRT* is the same supply curve for sector 2 as in Figure 1, and the dashed line *DQ* is the demand for capital expenditures. The level of savings for each sector is identical with that of Figure 1.

The new solid lines illustrate some of the possibilities resulting from the introduction of financial institutions. *B'N'* is the demand for capital expenditures by sector 1, given the existence of financial institutions. It is lower than *BN* because we have assumed a substitution of financial assets for real assets. Parenthetically, such a shift could take place without the existence of financial institutions, providing deficit sectors can differentiate their liabilities so that surplus sectors will be attracted to them not only because of yield, but also because the financial asset has characteristics not possessed by real assets available to the surplus sector. For example, fixed claim bonds have a more stable nominal dollar return than do real assets. To the extent that deficit sectors can issue such claims, they function as financial institutions.

Sector 1 has a lower demand for capital expenditures because it now has financial asset alternatives which are attractive because of nonyield characteristics, such as liquidity, marketability, safety, etc. The effect of this may be seen in the new supply curve of funds to sector 2, *PT'*, which lies to the right of the old supply curve. The horizontal difference between the two supply curves reflects the reallocation impact of financial institutions. Where in Figure 13–1, sector 1 would have been willing to forego all capital expenditures with a yield *OB*, it now requires only *OB'* to turn all of its savings over to sector 2. Note that the additional funds do not go directly to sector 2, but move through financial institutions.

The two lines *D'Q'* and *D''Q''* show two possible effects of financial institutions on sector 2's demand for capital goods. *D'Q'* will prevail if sector 2 reacts to the availability of the new kinds of financial assets in the same way as sector 1, i.e., by substituting financial assets for real assets. The result of this is that sector 1 has capital expenditures of *OV'* and net financial investment of *V'N'*, while sector 2 makes capital expenditures of *OU'* and negative net financial investment of *U'P*. Net financial investment is less than it was in Figure 13–1, and sector 1 has larger capital expenditures, while sector 2 has smaller expenditures. The effect of financial institutions in this case has been to reduce the reallocation of funds between sectors. Since the lowest yielding capital expenditure yields *E'*, less than *E*, the productivity of investment and, probably, the growth of GNP, are also reduced.

Equally reasonable is the alternative shown by $D''Q''$. Without financial institutions, deficit sectors have to design financial instruments which may not be optimal in terms of their asset portfolios, but are necessary if funds are to be attracted. As a result, some capital expenditures may be rejected because the effect of raising funds to finance them may either reduce expected net worth or increase risk beyond an acceptable level. If financial institutions make funds available on more favorable terms, not necessarily in yield, but maturity terms, etc., than can be had from surplus sectors directly, the rejected expenditures may become acceptable. Further, the deficit sector may also become a customer for the liabilities of financial institutions. If these financial assets permit more effective diversification of the asset portfolio, i.e., reduce the variance of the asset portfolio, the deficit sector may be willing to undertake capital expenditures which otherwise would be too risky. In other words, financial assets are not only competitive with other assets, they are complementary in their effect on total asset portfolio risk.

With the demand curve $D''Q''$, sector 1 spends less on capital expenditures and sector 2 spends more. Net financial investment increases for sector 1 and the sector 2 counterpart, negative net financial investment, becomes more negative. The yield on the last accepted dollar spent on capital goods is E'', higher than the yield without financial investments, so that capital expenditures are more productive and the growth rate of GNP rises.

Figure 13–2 does not exhaust the possibilities. For example, just as financial institutions may increase the demand for capital expenditures of the deficit sector, it may do the same for the surplus sector. In that event, the supply curve of funds to sector 2 would shift to the left above PRT. Given any of the demand curves shown for sector 2, the higher supply curve

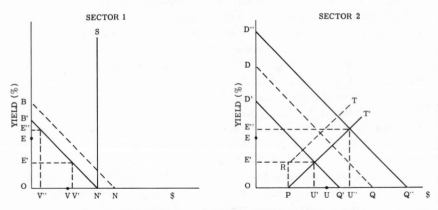

Figure 13-2. Illustrations of the Effect of Financial Institutions on the Allocation of funds between two real sectors.

would result in a reduction of capital expenditures by sector 2, but also an increase in the average yield on all capital expenditures.

Thus, the effect of financial institutions on the productivity of capital expenditures will depend on the direction and degree of shifting of both sectors' demand curves. If demand curves of both are shifted upward, the productivity of capital expenditures will rise. If both demand curves fall, the productivity of capital expenditures will fall. If one sector's demand curve falls and the other sector's rises, the productivity of capital expenditures will rise providing the upward shifting demand curve shifts by more than the decreased demand sector's curve falls. Otherwise, the productivity will remain constant or decline.

Underlying the shifts in the demand for capital goods is the nature of the relationship between the demands for financial assets and real assets. To the extent that financial assets are substitutes for real assets, demand for real assets will fall with the introduction of a more varied and numerous group of financial assets. If the demands are complementary, the demand for capital expenditures will increase as a result of the introduction of more varied financial assets by financial institutions. Both relationships probably hold.

As pointed out in the chapter on cash management, the availability of demand deposits is an essential part of business operations. The complementarity is enhanced by the availability of cash substitutes such as time deposits which reduce the cost of holding cash. Further, financial assets can be used to moderate the risk inherent in certain kinds of asset portfolios. However, the competitive relationship can become effective when yields on real assets fall. Yield is the major advantage of real assets over financial assets, since the latter tend to have safety, liquidity, or other desirable characteristics not possessed to the same degree by real assets. When the yield on real assets falls, the difference in yield between financial and real assets may not be sufficiently great to overcome the other advantages of financial assets and financial assets can then be substituted for real assets.

Following this reasoning, we can argue that in periods of slack activity, when expected yields on real assets are low, the demand for financial assets will increase and the competitive relationship between financial and real assets will predominate. The role of financial institutions will actually depress the productivity of capital expenditures by increasing the supply of funds and decreasing demand for capital expenditures. On the upswing, however, demand for capital expenditures will rise, decreasing the supply of funds to other sectors and raising the productivity of investment. From the point of view of cyclical stability, financial institutions serve to counter cycles. In periods of low business activity, the cutoff rate, i.e., minimally acceptable yield, on real assets is reduced, which tends to increase the level of capital expenditures. In times of high expected yields, when the economy is near full employment, financial institutions tend to raise the cutoff point for investment in real assets, tending to reduce the level of capital formation and, thus, reduce inflationary tendencies.

In the remainder of this chapter and the next two chapters, we shall be concerned with the nature of the reallocation process generated by financial institutions. We cannot directly measure the impact of these institutions on either the productivity of capital expenditures or on the level of savings. We can determine, however, the sectors which provide funds for financial institutions and the sectors to which the institutions make funds available.

COMMERCIAL BANKING

As noted above, the banking sector consists of commercial banking, Treasury monetary operations, and the Federal Reserve. The Treasury and Federal Reserve are governmental agencies. However, the commercial banking subsector consisted of 13,558 separate private corporations as of November, 1963.

INDUSTRIAL COMPOSITION

Sources of Charter. Commercial banks may apply for a corporate charter from any one of the 50 states, or from the Federal government. State banks are those which have received charters from state governments and are subject to regulation by the appropriate state authority. National banks are those which have received charters from the Federal government and are subject to regulation by the Comptroller of the Currency, an official of the United States Treasury Department.

Member Banks. National banks must be members of the Federal Reserve System. State banks have the option of not joining. Later on, a more complete study of the Federal Reserve will be undertaken. For now, we can say that the Federal Reserve is a "banker's bank." Member banks may borrow from the Federal Reserve and can draw coin and currency out of the Federal Reserve. In addition, the Federal Reserve operates a check clearing system to which members have access. However, membership entails costs, and member banks are subject to regulation by the Federal Reserve. The majority of commercial banks are not members.

Insured Banks. All member banks are required to have deposit liabilities insured by the Federal Deposit Insurance Corporation. The FDIC insures depositors against losses up to $10,000 in deposits, because of bank failure. As with most insurance companies, the FDIC tries to reduce loss payments by correcting situations that are apt to lead to losses. Thus, insured banks are also subject to regulation by FDIC.

The Over-all Pattern of Commercial Banking. Table 13–2 provides a picture of commercial banking. As stated above, the majority of commercial banks are not members of the Federal Reserve, but the nonmember banks are quite small, holding only 16 per cent of total commercial banking assets. Fewer than 300 banks are not insured by the FDIC, but the uninsured banks hold less than 1 per cent of total assets.

Table 13-2

COMMERCIAL BANKS CLASSIFIED BY SOURCE OF CHARTER, FEDERAL RESERVE MEMBERSHIP, AND FDIC MEMBERSHIP, BY NUMBER AND PERCENTAGE OF TOTAL COMMERCIAL BANK ASSETS, JUNE, 1963

	Number of Banks	*Percentage of Total Bank Assets,*
All commercial banks	13,482	100
National banks.................	4,537	54
State banks	8,945	46
Member banks.................	6,058	84
Insured banks	13,191	99

Source: *Federal Reserve Bulletin*, December, 1963, pp. 1674 and 1676.

CAPITAL STRUCTURE
OF COMMERCIAL BANKS

Commercial banks have a higher degree of financial leverage built into their capital structures than virtually any other privately owned enterprise. Typically, a manufacturing corporation will use about $0.50 of debt, including short-term and accruals, for each dollar of equity. Banks typically have about $10 of debt for each dollar of equity.

Demand Deposits. These constitute the largest single item in the capital structure of commercial banks. As of the end of November, 1963, commercial bank demand deposits exceeded $158 billion, 51 per cent of total liabilities and net worth. Almost $15 billion were so-called "interbank" deposits, i.e., deposits of one commercial bank with another. Deposits of the United States government came to $4.4 billion. The remainder, almost $139 billion, were held by all other sectors.

The interbank deposits reflect correspondent banking relationships. Banks perform a wide variety of services, such as providing foreign exchange and foreign credit. Most banks have an insufficient number of requests for such services to warrant maintaining the staff necessary to offer them. Instead, they can develop a correspondent relationship with a large bank that has the necessary staff and provide the service indirectly to their customers. There are many other advantages to correspondent banking. Small banks may ask large correspondents to participate in large investment ventures, and vice versa. Credit information, investment advice, etc., are circulated within the network of correspondent banks. Banks in the network, particularly the smaller ones, are often required to hold demand deposits in the other correspondents. In the flow of funds system, interbank deposits are netted out of the commercial banking subsector.

The commercial bank deposits of the United States government are called *tax and loan accounts*. When the government disburses cash, it does not usually draw checks on tax and loan accounts. Instead, the funds are transferred from the commercial bank to the Federal Reserve, and the disbursement is drawn on the government's account with the Federal Reserve.

The rationale behind the use of tax and loan accounts provides some insights into the nature of commercial banking. The accounts are created by government as a result of tax collections made in the area in which the bank is located or because the government has sold securities to the particular bank or to the customers of the bank. If the government immediately withdrew the proceeds of tax collections or bond sales from the commercial banks on which the tax payers or bond buyers had drawn their checks, the banks would be in the same position as a firm faced with the problem of a large loan coming due. All would be well if another lender could be found so that a new claim could be substituted for the old. Failing this, the firm would have to liquidate assets in order to pay the due debt.

When the government sets up a tax and loan account deposit, the government deposit substitutes for the now extinguished claim that had been held by the tax payer or bond buyer. If the government did not do this, the bank would have to liquidate assets. Most of these assets are securities and loans extended by the banks. Tax payments and bond purchases affect a large number of banks at the same time. The result would be that large numbers of securities would be dumped on the markets, forcing down securities prices and raising interest rates. Business loans would be canceled, causing considerable disruption in normal economic activity. In the jargon of the finance trade, money would be tight, with the tightness having no necessary relationship to the degree of inflation or unemployment in the economy. Thus, government deposits operate to smooth out what would otherwise be an erratic fluctuation in the flow of funds.

The remaining demand deposits are held by households, firms, state and local governments, foreigners, and financial institutions other than banks. These demand deposits are treated usually as part of the money supply, even though they are the obligations of private corporations and are not legal tender. Demand deposits constitute the largest part of the total United States money supply.

Time Deposits. These are also claims of commercial banks. There are three important differences between demand deposits and time deposits: Funds deposited in a demand deposit, or checking account, can be transferred from one owner to another simply by writing an order to do this (a check) to the bank of deposit, whereas time deposits must be withdrawn by mail or in person; interest is paid on time deposits, but interest payments are forbidden on demand deposits; demand deposits can be withdrawn immediately on demand of the depositor, whereas the bank can make the holder of the most liquid form of savings account wait for 30 days before withdrawing funds, though this is normally not enforced.

The maximum interest rate which can be paid on the various classes of time deposits is set by the Federal Reserve for member banks, and by the Federal Deposit Insurance Corporation for nonmember insured banks. The maxima used by both agencies are the same. As of November 1964, the interest rate was 4.0 per cent maximum on savings accounts. In addition to savings accounts that are held by individuals and households, but not by business firms, commercial banks issue savings certificates. These are of large denomination, negotiable, and carry interest. The maximum rate on these time deposits as of November 1964, was 4 per cent for notes maturing in less than 90 days 4.5 per cent for notes maturing in more than 90 days.

Maximum rates on time deposits were unchanged from 1936 to 1957. During this period, the rates were 2.5 per cent on all classes of time deposits except for short-term time deposits of businesses on which the rate was 2 per cent for deposits maturing in 90 days to 6 months and 1 per cent for deposits maturing in less than 90 days. Following the increases of January 1, 1957, further increases came in January, 1962, on July 17, 1963, and on November 24, 1964. From the end of 1949 to the end of 1956, just before the rates were first changed in the postwar period, time deposits rose from $33.9 billions to $46.8 billion, about $1.8 billion average annual increase. Between 1956 and the end of 1961, time deposits rose to $70.7, an average annual increase of $4.8. During 1962, time deposits rose by $11.5 billion, to a total of $82.2 billion. By the end of November, 1964, time deposits at commercial banks had risen to $124.1 billion, an increase of $49.1 billion in less than two years. The rate changes noted above were at least partially responsible for the enormous increase in time deposits.

The large increase in time deposits is important both in absolute terms and relative to the growth of demand deposits. At the end of 1950, commercial banks held approximately $2.90 in demand deposits for each dollar of time deposits. In 1964, the ratio was about $1.01 of demand deposits per dollar of time deposits. Funds made available through demand deposits are usually on deposit for a relatively short period of time. In 1964, demand deposits had a turnover rate of more than 30 times a year. Since the funds provided by demand deposits are likely to be drawn out of the individual bank, the bank is likely to invest such funds in highly marketable and/or short-term assets. Time deposits, on the other hand, are a somewhat longer-term source of funds and can be invested in less liquid and longer-lived assets.

Borrowings. In addition to time deposits, demand deposits, and net worth, commercial banks may borrow from the Federal Reserve Banks. Such borrowing is not viewed as a permanent means of commercial bank financing and is discouraged except for temporary purposes. Normally, borrowing is accomplished by discounting the commercial bank's promissory note with the Federal Reserve. The note must have collateral. Eligible collateral is defined by the Federal Reserve to include short-term, high quality securities, and promissory notes owned by the commercial bank. Short-term treasury bills are often used as eligible collateral. The borrowing bank may also use other collateral, should it lack sufficient eligible paper. However, a penalty rate of 1/2 per cent is added to the discount rate for commercial bank borrowings supported by ineligible paper.

The discount rate charged on these borrowings is set by the Federal Reserve Banks. Since there are 12 Federal Reserve Banks, occasionally and for a short period of time, there may be more than one discount rate prevailing. As of December, 1964, the rate was 4.5 per cent. Previously, the rate had been 4.0 per cent. The rate change occurred in the period November 24–30, 1964. Five of the banks had raised the rate on the 24th, and by the 30th only two banks had failed to raise the rate.

In addition to raising the discount rate so that it exceeds the rate on very high quality short-term paper, the Federal Reserve Banks can discourage commercial banks from borrowing simply by refusing credit to the commercial banks. Membership in the Federal Reserve gives a commercial bank the privilege of borrowing from the Federal Reserve, not the unconditional right to do so. Unless the Federal Reserve were to set the discount rate much higher than it is, it must have the power to refuse discount facilities. For example, short-term unsecured business loans were yielding in excess of 5 per cent throughout 1963, above the discount rate which would make borrowing from the Federal Reserve profitable. As a result, banks borrow from the Federal Reserve to finance temporary needs for cash reserves resulting, e.g., from a withdrawal of currency such as occurs during vacation periods. Borrowings from the Federal Reserve tend to fluctuate sharply from day to day and even over the year. For example, borrowings averaged $906 million in December, 1959, but were only $87 million in December, 1960.

Commercial banks had outstanding borrowings totaling about $4,500 million on November 25, 1964. Discounts constituted $430 million. The bulk of commercial bank borrowings came from other banks. These interbank loans constitute the Federal funds market, a market in which banks make loans to other banks for one day. The purpose of these loans will be discussed later. Since banks can make short-term loans from the Federal Reserve banks, the rate on Federal funds normally will not exceed the discount rate.

Liabilities and Net Worth. Table 13-3 presents the actual data for the right-hand side of the commercial banking balance sheet.

Table 13-3

SELECTED LIABILITIES AND NET WORTH ITEMS
FOR COMMERCIAL BANKS, DECEMBER, 31, 1945, 1960, 1961, 1962
(In Millions of Dollars)

	1945	1960	1961	1962
Interbank demand deposits ⎱ 14,065		17,080	17,914	16,008
Interbank time deposits ⎰		1,800	481	535
Demand deposits 105,921		139,324	147,866	147,870
U.S. government ⎱ 105,921		5,945	5,946	6,829
Other ⎰		133,379	141,920	141,041
Time deposits.................... 30,241		71,641	82,429	97,709
Borrowings...................... 219		163	471	3,627
Capital accounts 8,950		20,986	22,459	24,094

Source: Federal Reserve Bulletin, November, 1962, p. 1464 and December, 1963, p. 1674.

The equation for the commercial banking sector's liabilities and net worth can be stated

(13–1)

$$TL_c = {}_hDD_c + {}_fDD_c + {}_wDD_c + {}_gDD_c + {}_iDD_c + TD_c + {}_rB_c + E_c + RE_c.$$

The subscript c refers to the commercial banking sector; the subscript r indicates the Federal Reserve, and i stands for nonbank financial institutions, such as life insurance companies and savings banks. DD are demand deposits and TD are time deposits. Interbank deposits and borrowing have been consolidated out of the equation. Despite the fact that most of the liabilities are deposits, these operate in much the same way as short-term debt works for the real sectors.

THE ASSET PORTFOLIO
FOR COMMERCIAL BANKS

The asset portfolio for commercial banking can be divided into cash assets and earning assets. The cash assets consist of currency and coin held by banks, of deposits in other banks including the Federal Reserve banks, and of cash items in process of collection, which are checks that are in process of being cleared. The largest portion of the cash assets are deposits in Federal Reserve banks.

Earning assets in turn are divided into two main groups—loans and investments. The difference between the two has little analytic significance. Investments are evidenced by promissory notes for which there is some established market where the investments can be sold. Loans are also evidenced by promissory notes for which, however, there is no established market. Investments can be longer-term than loans because of marketability. However, loans that are eligible collateral for discounting can be liquidated at least as easily as can investments. What is more, the mere existence of a market is no guarantee that the sale of a security will occur with no loss.

Though we shall discuss loans and investments separately, the difference between the two groups is no greater than the difference between two types of inventory in a manufacturer's balance sheet.

As shown earlier, banks have a high-leverage capital structure. The risk associated with leverage can be offset partly by maintaining a very safe asset portfolio. And this is precisely the way banks and most financial institutions operate. In contrast, most nonfinancial corporations have a relatively safe capital structure but a risky asset portfolio. The safety of the asset portfolio is indicated partly by the ratio of earning assets to cash assets. This ratio is shown in Table 13–4. As a reference point, the ratio of earning assets to cash for manufacturing was $13.50 in 1958 when the commercial banking ratio was about $3.79.

Table 13-4

CASH ASSETS AND EARNING ASSETS
FOR COMMERCIAL BANKS, DECEMBER, 1957–DECEMBER, 1962

Date	Cash Assets ($ Millions)	Earning Assets ($ Millions)	Earning Assets/ Cash Assets (Dollars)
1957	48,428	170,068	3.52
1958	48,990	185,165	3.79
1959	49,467	190,270	3.85
1960	52,150	199,509	3.83
1961	56,432	215,441	3.82
1962	54,079	235,839	4.36

Source: *Federal Reserve Bulletin*, December, 1963, p. 1674 and November, 1960, p. 1247.

The ratio is affected by factors similar to those affecting any business—expectations as to return, and risk and preferences between return and risk. In addition to stockholders' operating as a veto group via the cost of capital, commercial banks also have the regulatory authorities who constitute a veto group. Despite this, there is considerable variation in the importance of earning assets. Within the limited time range of Table 13-4, the ratio has fallen as low as $3.52 of earning assets for each dollar of cash assets to a high of $4.36. In periods of uncertainty and weak demand for loans by business, we should expect the ratio to be low, and the reverse.

Cash Assets. The cash assets of commercial banks consist primarily of currency and coin, known as *vault cash*, and demand deposits of the commercial banks which are held by the Federal Reserve banks. In addition, there are the interbank demand deposits, which were discussed earlier, but which are consolidated out for the entire commercial banking sector.

One reason for holding cash assets is liquidity. As with other businesses, banks must have enough cash to finance disbursements, i.e., transactions and precautionary balances. The ability to borrow very rapidly from the Federal Reserve reduces the required size of precautionary balances, but some cash is needed to pay withdrawals of demand and time deposits and to cash checks presented at the teller's window.

If all demand depositors wished to convert checking accounts into currency, even the high level of cash assets held by commercial banks would be insufficient. To protect against a "run" of creditors' demands for currency, banks would have to forego holding earning assets, except for an amount equal to net worth. This is similar to the problem that would be faced by nonfinancial businesses if virtually all their liabilities could mature any time creditors wished to liquidate their claims. Despite the fact that most commercial banks' liabilities could mature suddenly, such a situation has not occurred since the early 1930's when many banks had to close because they had insufficient currency and coin to meet all depositors' demands. Normally, withdrawals of deposits do not require the high level of cash assets maintained by commercial banks.

Cash assets are maintained at a relatively high level because banks which are members of the Federal Reserve System are required to hold a percentage of demand and time deposits as coin and currency in the vaults of the commercial bank and/or as a deposit with the Federal Reserve bank. The percentage is known as the *reserve ratio* and is higher for demand deposits than for time deposits. The difference in the treatment of the reserves for the different deposit classes exists because demand deposits are more volatile than time deposits.

The volatility of demand deposits varies depending on the nature of the deposit. Large corporate balances and the speculative balances of individuals may be withdrawn suddenly when attractive investment opportunities arise. Family deposits are much more stable. Volatile deposits are more apt to be found in larger cities than in small towns. The Federal Reserve recognizes this by distinguishing between reserve city banks and country banks. Reserve city banks usually have a higher reserve ratio on demand deposits than is required of country banks. As of the end of 1964, there were 210 reserve city banks. At that time, the reserve ratio for demand deposits in reserve city banks was $16\frac{1}{2}$ per cent, and 12 per cent for country banks. The reserve ratio for time deposits was 4 per cent for all classes of commercial banks.

Banks which fail to maintain legal reserves are subject to a penalty. However, it is relatively easy to fulfill the reserve requirement. Required reserves are averaged weekly for reserve city banks and semimonthly for country banks. A short-term loan, either from the Federal Reserve or from a commercial bank with excess reserves, can be used to pull the average up to the required level. This is the origin of much of the borrowing discussed in the section on commercial bank liabilities. Analytically, it is useful to distinguish between three classes of reserves. First are the required reserves, which have been discussed already. Second are excess reserves. Usually, but not always, total reserves will exceed required reserves to meet the need for coin and currency as a result of checking account withdrawals. The funds needed for legal reserves cannot be paid out to demand depositors who wish to withdraw currency. The difference between total reserves and required reserves is called *excess reserves*. Third are free reserves. Excess reserves may either result from bank borrowings or truly represent free cash assets which banks have preferred to hold regardless of reserve requirements. Thus, borrowings from the Federal Reserve are subtracted from excess reserves to show the amount of free reserves, i.e., reserves which neither are required by law nor are temporary reflections of short-term borrowing. The free reserves are not completely free, since short-term borrowing from other commercial banks are not deducted. Data on reserves are shown in Table 13-5.

Table 13-5

RESERVES OF MEMBER BANKS, 1955–1962
(Averages of Daily Figures for December, in Millions of Dollars)

Year	Total	Required	Excess	Borrowings from F.R.	Free Reserves
1955	19,240	18,646	594	839	−245
1956	19,535	18,883	652	688	− 36
1957	19,420	18,843	577	710	−133
1958	18,899	18,383	516	557	− 41
1959	18,932	18,450	482	906	−424
1960	19,283	18,514	769	87	682
1961	20,118	19,550	568	149	419
1962	20,040	19,468	572	304	268

Source: *Federal Reserve Bulletin*, February, 1964, p. 180.

From the point of view of the individual bank, the existence of free reserves means that earning assets are less than is legally possible, since banks could use the free funds to acquire earning assets. As with any firm, banks may find earning asset opportunities unattractive because of yield and/or risk, so that excess cash assets are held. This appears to be a good explanation for the fact that free reserves equaled about 44 per cent of total reserves in December, 1939.

From the point of view of the economy, the existence of free reserves means that the money supply is less than it would be if free reserves were reduced. The relationship between the level of demand deposits (part of the money supply) and the level of required reserves was discussed earlier. What we are interested in now is the relationship between the level of free reserves and the level of demand deposits.

When a commercial bank makes a loan, it provides the borrower with a demand deposit. On the bank's balance sheet, the asset *loans* increases and the liability *demand deposits* also increases. However, the composition of reserves also changes even though total reserves may be unchanged. Required reserves increase because demand deposits have grown, and, assuming bank borrowings from the Federal Reserve or from other banks have remained unchanged, free reserves decline.

Should the bank buy a security rather than make a loan, a similar result occurs. The seller of the financial asset receives a check from the buying bank, which the seller can deposit in his own bank. The seller's bank of deposit can collect the proceeds of the check by sending the check to the Federal Reserve, which reduces the reserve deposits of the buying bank and increases the reserve deposits of the bank depositing the check. Demand deposits of commercial banks rise. Total reserves of commercial banks remain the same, although the distribution of reserves among commercial banks is altered. Free reserves are reduced, since the second bank has increased both required and free reserves while the first bank has reduced free reserves only.

When we discuss the Federal Reserve System, a somewhat more complex relationship between commercial bank reserves and demand deposits will be shown. For now, some useful generalizations can be drawn about the interrelationships among earning assets, cash assets, and that part of the money supply made up of demand deposits. When commercial banks increase earning assets, free reserves decline. Usually demand deposits will also increase, as was pointed out above. When won't demand deposits increase? First, if the borrower or seller of financial assets prefers currency or a time deposit rather than a demand deposit. Second, if the seller of the financial asset is a foreigner who moves the proceeds of the loan or sale outside of the United States by converting the demand deposit into foreign exchange. Third, if the seller is the Federal Reserve, since the Federal Reserve collects the proceeds by reducing the buying bank's reserve deposit. Finally, if the seller is the United States Treasury when the Treasury does not keep the proceeds of the sale on deposit in a tax and loan deposit. Normally, then, an increase in the volume of earning assets held by commercial banks results not only in a decline in free reserves, but in an increase in demand deposits.

It follows that the reverse is also true. When commercial banks sell earning assets, free reserves increase. Demand deposits will fall except when the sale is paid for in currency; by the proceeds of a time deposit; by a foreigner who pays by converting foreign exchange; by the Federal Reserve, which pays by increasing the reserve deposit of the selling bank; or by the Treasury, which pays with a check drawn on the Federal Reserve.

Investments. Investments consist primarily of United States government securities. Next in importance are the tax-free issues of state and local governments. Commercial banks purchase tax-exempt securities because the banks do not have the various tax shields available to other financial institutions. Commercial banks pay normal corporate income taxes. Finally, banks own some corporate securities, mainly very high grade bonds and some railroad equipment certificates. Regulatory authorities frown on risky investments and may require that the bank anticipate losses on such investments by substantially reducing the value of these investments shown on the balance sheet. Table 13-6 shows the breakdown of investments for commercial banking.

Table 13-6

INVESTMENTS OF COMMERCIAL BANKS,
AS OF DECEMBER 1947, 1958, 1960, AND 1962
(In Millions of Dollars)

Date	Totals	UNITED STATES GOVERNMENT SECURITIES				STATES & LOCALS	OTHERS
		Bills	Certificates	Notes	Bonds		
1947	69,221	2,193	7,789	6,034	53,205	5,276	3,729
1958	66,376	6,294	7,399	13,396	39,287	16,505	4,070
1960	61,003	8,072	2,920	19,013	30,998	17,570	3,294
1962	66,434	11,674	3,932	23,841	26,987	24,755	4,543

Source: *Federal Reserve Bulletin*, November, 1960, p. 1250; November, 1962, p. 1462; December, 1963, p. 1678.

The relatively low interest rates prevailing on government securities explains much of the shift out of government securities shown in the table between 1947 and 1960. Most of the shifts occurred in bonds and certificates, with holdings of the very liquid bills rising. Notes are shorter term than bonds, but provide higher yields than either bills or certificates. The tax-exempt obligations of state and local governments provided a more attractive alternative than did the United States bonds, and the tax exempts absorbed over $19.5 billion of the $26.3 billion reduction in United States bond holdings. The shifts in portfolios for commercial banks have the same general determinants as would be used in explaining the shifts in the portfolios of nonfinancial corporations.

The importance of commercial banks as suppliers of funds to Federal and state and local governments is of interest. On December 31, 1962, the United States securities held by the public totaled $255.6 billion. Commercial banks held approximately 26 per cent of this total, a larger amount than held by any other sector except consumer and nonprofit. Commercial banks also held over 32 per cent of the $76.7 billion debt outstanding in state and local securities, again second in size of holdings only to the consumer and nonprofit sector.

Loans. The primary difference between loans and investments is that loans are private placements of funds, whereas investments involve the purchase of securities which are available in a securities market. In effect, the bank has to wait for someone to apply for a loan, but can take the initiative in making an investment. The levels of the two classes of earning assets and their relative importance are shown in Table 13-7.

Table 13-7

LOANS AND INVESTMENTS FOR COMMERCIAL BANKS,
AS OF DECEMBER 31, 1947, 1955–1962
(In Billions of Dollars)

Date	Loans	Investments	Loans/Investments	Index of Industrial Production
1947	38.1	78.2	0.49	
1955	82.6	78.3	1.06	96.6
1956	90.3	74.8	1.21	99.9
1957	93.9	76.2	1.23	100.7
1958	98.2	87.0	1.13	93.7
1959	110.8	78.5	1.41	105.6
1960	117.6	81.9	1.44	108.7
1961	124.9	90.5	1.38	109.8
1962	140.1	95.7	1.47	118.3

Source: *Federal Reserve Bulletin*, Loans and Investments of Commercial Banks by Classes. Industrial Production Index from Selected Business Indexes on Annual basis.

The most obvious point in the table is that loans have been far more dynamic than have investments. Loans increased by over $100 billion from 1947 through 1962, whereas investments rose only by about $17.5 billion. The ratio *loans/investments* varies with the level and rate of change of industrial production. Though the relationship is rough, the ratio *loans/ investments* changed in the same direction as industrial production in six of the seven year-to-year changes shown in the table. In 1961, industrial production rose very slightly, while the loans/investments ratio declined. A reasonable explanation of the coincidence of movements of the production index and the loans/investment ratio is that businessmen make more bank loans when business activity is increasing and fewer loans when business activity slackens. This illustrates the passive role of commercial banks in the loan market.

Table 13-8 shows the distribution of commercial bank loans among the various sectors of the economy. Nonfinancial businesses represent what is often thought of as the traditional area of commercial bank lending. The traditional business loan was supposed to have been a short-term loan, of sufficient maturity that the businessmen would have time to convert raw materials to finished goods or that the farmer could harvest and ship his crops. Modern bank loans tend to be somewhat longer-term than the traditional loans. However, the difference can be overstated. The traditional short-term bank loan could be and often was renewed so that it became effectively long-term. Further, banks make industrial loans on a revolving credit basis, with inventory as the initial security; when sale of inventory occurs, the inventory is replaced by accounts receivable, the loan is paid off, or new inventory becomes the security. The relative importance of agricultural loans had not changed between 1947 and 1962. Commercial and industrial loans, which constituted almost half of all loans in 1947, made up about one-

Table 13-8

CLASSIFIED LOANS OF COMMERCIAL BANKS, 1947 AND 1962

Classification	1947		1962	
	$ Billions	%	$ Billions	%
Total loans	38.1	100	140.1	100
Commercial and industrial........	18.2	48	48.7	34
Agricultural	1.7	6	7.1	5
For purchasing or				
carrying securities	2.0	5	7.2	5
To brokers and dealers	0.8	2	5.1	4
To others	1.2	3	2.1	1
To financial institutions	0.1	*	11.1	8
To other banks..............	0.1	*	2.6	2
To nonbanks	...	...	8.5	6
Real estate	9.4	25	34.3	24
Others to individuals	5.7	15	30.6	21
Other loans	0.9	2	3.9	3

*less than 1%.
Source: "Loans and Investments by Class of Banks," *Federal Reserve Bulletin*, December, 1963.

third the bank loans in 1962. Despite this, the commercial and industrial loan classification remains the largest single classification group.

The rates charged on industrial and commercial loans vary depending on the alternative yields available to banks, the risk of the borrower, and the cost associated with making the loans. Table 13-9 shows the rates charged by banks in 19 large cities on short-term business loans. The year-to-year changes in the over-all rates reflect movements in the general structure of interest rates, i.e., they reflect the alternative yields available to banks.

Table 13-9

BANK RATES ON SHORT-TERM BUSINESS LOANS
IN 19 LARGE CITIES, 1954–1962
(Per Cent per Annum)

Date	All	SIZE OF LOAN (IN THOUSANDS OF DOLLARS)			
		1–10	10–100	100–200	200 and up
1954...........	3.6	5.0	4.3	3.9	3.4
1955...........	3.7	5.0	4.4	4.0	3.5
1956...........	4.2	5.2	4.8	4.4	4.0
1957...........	4.6	5.5	5.1	4.8	4.5
1958...........	4.3	5.5	5.0	4.6	4.1
1959...........	5.0	5.8	5.5	5.2	4.9
1960...........	5.2	6.0	5.7	5.4	5.0
1961...........	5.0	5.9	5.5	5.2	4.8
1962...........	5.0	5.9	5.5	5.2	4.8

Source: *Federal Reserve Bulletin*, December, 1963, p. 1683.

The inverse relationship between size of loan and rate reflects both risk and costs. Small loans tend to be made by small firms, and large loans, by large firms. Small firms are much more prone to failure than are large businesses. For example, R. Sanzo presented a study on business failure in the December, 1957, issue of *Dun's Review and Modern Industry*, which showed that over 75 per cent of the business failures had liabilities of less than $100,000, with less than 1 per cent having liabilities in excess of $1 million. In their study *Federal Lending and Loan Insurance**, R. Saulnier, T. Halcrow, and N. Jacoby showed that the loss rate on direct business loans made by the Reconstruction Finance Corporation (a federal lending agency now defunct, from which has come the current Small Business Administration) was substantially greater for loans made to small firms than on loans made to large firms. More relevant to the explanation of the inverse relationship between size of loan and rate is the study by G. Moore and others entitled "Risks and Returns in Small Business Financing," which appeared in *Financing Small Business***. This essay showed that the loss rate experienced by commercial banks on loans varied directly with the proportion of small business loans made.

Risk of loss is only part of the explanation for the data shown in Table 13-9. Many of the costs incurred by a bank in processing a loan application do not vary with the size of loan. These fixed costs represent a higher proportion of a small loan than of a large loan. In order to net the same profit from the small loan, the bank must charge the small borrower a higher interest rate.

Loans for carrying or purchasing securities may be made by members of any sector. These loans have been the subject of special regulation. During the 1920's, stock purchases were financed extensively by bank credit. A purchaser could purchase stock using his own money for as little as 10 per cent of the stock price. As long as the price of stock rose, or at least did not fall, all was well. However, when stock prices declined as they did in 1929, banks required that borrowers reduce their indebtedness. In the terms of the trade, this was a request for more margin.

Banks were motivated to call for more margin because, with a margin of, say, 10 per cent, a decline in stock price of more than 10 per cent would leave the bank holding collateral of less value than the loan. In a declining stock market, the request for more margin usually was not met, and the stock was therefore sold. This added to the supply of stock and increased the downward price movement. On the other hand, when stock prices were moving up, purchasers would borrow in order to acquire more shares than their own capital would permit, forcing stock prices up even more rapidly. Thus, loans to carry or purchase securities tended to destabilize the stock market as long as banks were willing to lend a large portion of the stock's value.

*Princeton, N.J., 1958.
**United States Gov. Printing Office, Washington, D.C., 1958.

The Securities Exchange Act of 1934 empowered the Federal Reserve Board to set the margin requirements, i.e., to set the minimally acceptable portion of the security price which the securities buyer must invest with his own funds. The margin requirement applies to all lenders, not just commercial banks. The Board tends to vary the margin requirement on stock with the general price movements of the stock market. For example, the Board set a stock margin requirement of 70 per cent in July, 1960. At this time, the Standard and Poor's common stock price index was 55.84. The price index rose to a peak of 71.74 in December, 1961, and then fell slowly to March, 1962, when the index was 70.29. By June, the index had slipped to 55.63, and the Board lowered the margin requirement to 50 per cent on July 10, 1962. For the week ending November 2, 1963, the index had reached 74.12, and the Board raised the margin requirement to 70 per cent on November 6, 1963. The changes in margin also reflect the total amount of borrowing for carrying and purchasing securities. In July, 1962, when the margin requirement was lowered, total borrowing on securities, except United States governments, from all lenders totaled $3.4 billion. By November, 1963, the borrowing had almost doubled, rising to $6.2 billion.

The most dramatic change in the loan portfolios of commercial banks between 1947 and 1962 was in loans made to other financial institutions. Ignoring loans made to other banks, which reflect the lending of federal funds discussed earlier, loans to nonbanking financial institutions rose from nothing to 6 per cent of total loans between 1947 and 1962. The financial institutions that borrow from banks include those that lend to business on accounts receivable and/or inventory collateral, among which are sales finance companies, commercial finance companies and factors; those that lend to households, such as personal finance companies; and a miscellaneous group of short-term lenders and mortgage companies. In addition, savings and loan associations borrow from commercial banks.

The role of the commercial bank in financing what are essentially its own competitiors—for commercial banks make all kinds of short-term business and consumer loans and even buy mortgages—is quite interesting. The small specialized lender, such as the factor, takes over the entire credits and collections function of a firm making credit sales, i.e., manages accounts receivable and pays the firm immediately upon the credit sale. Without bank funds to finance the factor's operations, the factor would be in grave trouble. Although banks lend on accounts receivable also, the banks do this on a *recourse* basis; i.e., if the credit sale is not collected, the borrowing firm has to make the loan good. The factor usually lends on a nonrecourse basis; i.e., if the receivable is not collected, the factor bears the loss. In this case, the competitive relationship is not strong. The bank specializes in supplying funds. The factor specializes in the development and implementation of credits and collections policies. Both institutions do compete in the area of recourse accounts receivable financing, but even here, the bank apparently finds it more profitable to finance a factor than to hire more loan officers specializing in accounts receivable loans.

Commercial and sales finance companies are much stronger competitors for commercial banks than are factors. The competition extends to inventory financing as well as accounts receivable. In addition, commercial and sales finance companies do finance some plant and equipment with mortgages, which compete with commercial bank term loans and mortgages. Unlike factors, commercial and sales finance companies have two significant alternative sources of funds. These companies issue commercial, or open market, paper as short-term sources and subordinated debentures as long-term sources. But even these sources of funds are not completely separated from bank financing. Commercial and sales finance companies had $6 billion of commercial paper outstanding at the end of 1962. Commercial banks were the second largest holder of such paper, holding some $3.1 billion.

Competition between the commercial banks and the finance companies is not restricted to purchasing financial assets. The finance companies place over two-thirds of their short-term notes directly and the remainder through commercial paper dealers. Direct placements are made to business corporations usually. The corporations are attracted to the commercial paper investment as an alternative to holding demand deposits. Thus, the competition between the two kinds of financial institutions extends to sources of funds as well as to uses.

In times of "tight" money, finance companies have argued that commercial banks have been reluctant to supply them with short-term loans. As a result, efforts at direct placement of commercial paper and the sale of subordinated debentures have been increased. The subordinated debentures are long-term instruments which are subordinate to the claims of short-term creditors. This subordination is necessary in order to keep the buyers of short-term commercial paper satisfied that their claims on the finance companies involve relatively little risk.

Mortgage companies also utilize bank credit as part of mortgage warehousing. The function of mortgage companies is to prepare and assemble real estate mortgages for eventual purchase by large mortgage lenders such as insurance companies. The mortgage company handles the problem of assessment of the value of the property and the fulfillment of necessary legal aspects, such as verifying the soundness of title to the property. It assembles individual mortgages into packages and holds these until the ultimate lender, usually an insurance company, is ready to buy the package. Frequently, the mortgage company also services the mortgages after the package has been placed with the ultimate lender. Banks enter the picture by financing the mortgages between the time that funds have to be made available to the builder or buyer of the real estate and when the mortgages are sold to the insurance company.

All this indicates the dual role of commercial banks. On the one hand, banks are department stores of credit. They make virtually every kind of loan to businesses and households, and they invest in government securities, Federal, state and local. But the commercial banks also are wholesalers of credit. They supply funds to other financial institutions, who then retail the funds to businesses and households.

Commercial banks are not viewed ordinarily as being important mortgage lenders. Nonetheless, mortgages loans are the second most important loan category and have tended to be larger than the personal loan classification. About one-forth of commercial bank loans are in mortgages. Table 13-10 classifies the mortgages held by banks. Residential mortgages are divided

Table 13-10

MORTGAGE LOANS HELD BY COMMERCIAL BANKS, 1956–1962
(In Billions of Dollars)

| End of year | Total | RESIDENTIAL | | | | OTHER | |
		Total	FHA	VA	Con-ventional	Nonfarm	Farm
1956	22.7	17.0	4.8	3.9	8.3	4.4	1.3
1957	23.3	17.2	4.8	3.6	8.7	4.8	1.4
1958	25.5	18.6	5.5	3.3	9.8	5.5	1.5
1959	28.2	20.3	6.1	3.2	11.0	6.2	1.6
1960	28.8	20.4	5.9	2.9	11.7	6.8	1.7
1961	30.4	21.2	6.0	2.6	12.6	7.5	1.8
1962	34.5	23.5	6.5	2.7	14.3	9.0	2.0

Source: Federal Reserve Bulletin, February, 1964, p. 215.

into those that are underwritten or insured by the United States government, i.e., loans underwritten by the Federal Housing Administration or insured by the Veterans Administration, and those that are normal, or conventional, residential housing mortgages. In the case of the former, the mortgage lender is protected against loss in the event that the borrower defaults on his loan agreement. In addition to residential mortgages, banks lend on industrial and commercial buildings and, to some extent, on farm buildings.

Almost $252 billion of mortgage debt was outstanding at the end of 1962. Financial institutions, including banks, held about three-fourths of this. Ranked in order of importance, the significant institutions and their mortgage holdings at the end of 1962 were

Savings and loan associations .... $78.8 billion
Life insurance companies .... 46.9 "
Commercial banks .... 34.5 "
Mutual savings banks .... 32.3 "

There are differences in the part of the mortgage market in which each of these institutions operated. Savings and loan associations held 86 per cent of nonfarm mortgages in conventional mortgages; 72 per cent of nonfarm commercial bank mortgages were conventional; 62 per cent of nonfarm life insurance mortgages were conventional; while mutual savings banks held only 41 per cent.

Rarely are particular loan classifications singled out for regulation. However, national banks, which had been forbidden any real estate loan prior to 1913, may not lend a total amount of mortgage money exceeding 100 per cent of net worth or 60 per cent of time deposits, whichever is greater. Amortized mortgages, i.e., mortgages in which principal is repaid over the life of the mortgage, as are sinking fund bonds, may be made by national banks for periods of up to 20 years, and the mortgage may not be more than 75 per cent of the appraised value of the property. Unamortized mortgage loans must mature within 5 years, and may not exceed 50 per cent of the appraised value of the property. This reflects the past when commercial banks have suffered because of investing large amounts in long-term unamortized mortgages only to have to foreclose mortgages during a depression when property values declined.

The final important classification of loans are those to individuals. This classification and the loans made to financial institutions were the only groups of loans which showed a relative increase in the period 1947–1962. Most of the loans to individuals are what is called *consumer credit*. Table 13-11 shows the distribution of all consumer credit by nature of loan, i.e., installment and noninstallment, or single, payment, and by type of security.

Table 13-11

CONSUMER CREDIT, 1939, 1956, AND 1963

	1939		1956		1963	
	$ *Billions*	%	$ *Billions*	%	$ *Billions*	%
Total all consumer credit	7.2	100	42.3	100	69.9	100
Total installment credit	4.5	62	31.7	75	53.8	77
Automobile paper	1.5	21	14.4	34	22.2	32
Other consumer goods	1.6	22	8.6	21	13.8	20
Repair and modernization loans ..	0.3	4	1.9	5	3.4	5
Personal loans	1.1	15	6.8	16	14.4	21
Noninstallment credit	2.7	28	10.6	25	16.2	23

Source: Federal Reserve Bulletin, February, 1964, p. 218.

The table indicates the shift from noninstallment to installment consumer credit, accounted for mainly by the 50 per cent increase in relative importance of automobile loans. Most of the other categories remained surprisingly stable in relative terms over the 24-year period. Of course, the most striking thing is the enormous growth in consumer credit—a 970 per cent increase as compared to an increase in GNP of less than 650 per cent.

Table 13-12 shows some of the shifts that have occurred in the sources

Table 13-12

CONSUMER INSTALLMENT CREDIT, BY HOLDER, 1939, 1956, AND 1963.

Holder	1939 $ Billions	%	1956 $ Billions	%	1963 $ Billions	%
Total installment credit	4.5	100	31.7	100	53.8	100
Financial institutions	3.1	69	27.0	85	47.0	87
Commercial banks	1.1	24	11.8	37	21.6	40
Sales finance companies	1.2	27	9.1	29	13.5	25
Credit unions	0.1	2	2.0	6	5.6	10
Personal finance companies	*		2.9	9	4.6	9
Other financial institutions........	0.7*	16	1.1	3	1.7	3
Retail outlets	1.4	31	4.7	15	6.8	13

*Personal finance companies included with other financial institutions for 1939.
Source: Federal Reserve Bulletin, February, 1964, p. 218.

of consumer credit. Financial institutions have participated much more heavily in supplying installment consumer finance since 1939 than have retailers, although there has been a substantial dollar increase from both groups. Among the financial institutions, commercial banks and credit unions are the only institutions which have shown a growth of relative importance. The combined *personal finance companies* and *other financial institutions* supplied a smaller share of installment money in 1963 than they had in 1939. The relative share of sales finance companies remained approximately constant over the period. By 1956, the importance of commercial banking in installment finance for consumers had grown to the point where the banks were the single largest supplier.

The Regulation of Earning Assets. Commercial banks are regulated in virtually every aspect of their operations. They come into being only with the specific permission of a governmental authority. They may create branch offices only if the state laws allow, and, even then, the branch permit may not be granted if it is believed by the regulatory authorities that there is no need for a branch. Mergers of banks also have to be approved. Regulations and regulatory authority extend potentially to all balance sheet items. The regulations on the ratio cash assets/deposits have been noted earlier. So too have the restrictions on mortgage lending for national banks. State laws vary, but a number of states have similar restrictions on mortgage lending.

National banks may not lend to a single borrower an amount in excess of 10 per cent of the bank's unimpaired capital and surplus, i.e., roughly of its net worth. State banks have similar restrictions, although the percentage may be higher. Loans may not be made to the bank examiners or officers of the bank.

All member banks are forbidden to hold securities of one issue in excess of 10 per cent of unimpaired capital and surplus, except for issues guaranteed or issued by Federal, state, or local governments. Further, member banks are generally forbidden to purchase common stocks. Also, commercial banks may not engage in the investment banking business by underwriting or selling securities. These various restrictions are statutory.

In addition, there are a group of restrictions which are administrative in nature and are implemented by the examination process. State banks are examined by state authorities and, if they are also members of the Federal Reserve, by the Federal Reserve. Usually both agencies examine at the same time. National banks are examined by the Comptroller of Currency whose reports are accepted by the Federal Reserve. The Federal Deposit Insurance Corporation reviews reports on member bank examinations and makes its own examination of nonmember insured banks. The bank examiners enforce statutory regulations and try to determine whether banking assets are of sound quality. Quality is by nature subjective, and examiners must use good judgment, particularly in evaluating loans.

Reasonably objective standards have been set with regard to investments, and these standards have been agreed to by the Federal Reserve, the Comptroller of the Currency, the FDIC, and the National Association of Supervisors of State Banks. Investments are divided into four groups. The first group includes high-grade securities, such as governments. Nongovernmental securities included in this category must be rated in one of the top four bond classifications by two of the three recognized rating agencies. These investments are carried at the lower of book value or cost, and price rises or declines are not recorded.

Group 2 investments are more speculative than those in group 1. They are valued at market price, and the bank's net worth can be reduced by 50 per cent of the net decline in market price. Compare this treatment to that of group 1 securities for which market-price declines do not have to be recognized at all. Banks along with other financial institutions are reluctant to show losses. Thus, the treatment of valuation for group 2 securities is a powerful deterrent to acquiring them. Most investments are in the group 1 category.

Group 3 securities are those which have been defaulted, and group 4 securities are common stock. The latter may be all a bank can acquire from a borrower when it forecloses a loan. Both groups are valued at market price, with the complete amount of price decline charged against the bank's net worth.

Loans too may be classified. In 1938, federal regulatory authorities agreed to a set of classifications and valuation practices for loans. Many states have adopted the same procedures. Loans are divided into four groups. The first are *unclassified*, when repayment appears certain. *Substandard* loans are those having more than a normal risk for reasons such as the financial condition of the debtor or insufficient security. The latter loans are so classified to bring them to the attention of the bank management.

Doubtful loans are those on which ultimate collection is doubtful, but the full amount of loss is not yet certain. Fifty per cent of the maturity value of doubtful loans are deducted from net worth. *Loss* loans are those which are viewed as uncollectible, and the full amount of the loan is charged off as a loss against net worth.

The Asset Equation. As with the liabilities and net worth equation, inter-bank loans are consolidated out of the commercial banking asset equation. The new subscript introduced is *t* and refers to the monetary functions of the United States government not included in the activities of the government discussed in the previous chapter. These will be discussed in detail in chapter 14. In addition, two new symbols are introduced: RD represents reserve deposits of the commercial banks held by the Federal Reserve and is shown as a liability of the Federal Reserve; CC represents coin and currency and is a liability either of the Treasury or of the Federal Reserve. Coin and currency will be discussed in more detail in the next chapter.

(13–2)

$$TA_c = {}_cRD_r + {}_cCC_r + {}_cCC_t + {}_cB_g + {}_cB_f + {}_cB_h + {}_cB_w + {}_cB_i + {}_cE_r.$$

Note that all of the assets shown are financial. As discussed earlier, the amount of real assets is negligible for financial institutions and will be ignored in our presentation.

Although commercial banks may end up holding equity claims as a result of a loan foreclosure, the amount of such claims is extremely small and has not been shown. The only equity instrument shown in the asset portfolio is the stock of the Federal Reserve banks. Member banks are required to subscribe for the stock of the Federal Reserve banks in an amount equal to 6 per cent of the commercial bank's net worth. Only half this is actually paid in, with the remainder on call. In return, the commercial banks receive a 6 per cent cumulative dividend on the amount of paid-in capital. At the end of January, 1964, the paid-in capital of the Federal Reserve banks was $501 million.

Flow concepts, such as net financial investment, will not be shown at this point. The commercial banks represent a subsector of the banking sector, and the flow concepts will be presented when we discuss the entire banking sector.

SELECTED REFERENCES

Alhadeff, D.: "Recent Bank Mergers," *Quarterly Journal of Economics*, Nov., 1955.
———: "A Reconsideration of Restrictions on Bank Entry," *Quarterly Journal of Economics*, May, 1962.

————: "The Struggle for Commercial Bank Savings," *Quarterly Journal of Economics*, Feb., 1958.

Commission on Money and Credit, *Industry Study of Commercial Banking*, Prentice-Hall, Englewood Cliffs, N. J., 1963.

Kreps, C., and D. Lapkin: "Public Regulation and Operating Conventions Affecting Sources of Funds of Commercial Banks and Thrift Institutions," *Journal of Finance*, May, 1962.

Rozen, M.: "Competition Among Financial Institutions for Demand and Thrift Deposits," *Journal of Finance*, May, 1962.

Wicker, E.: "Some Loanable Fund Concepts and Banking Theory," *Journal of Finance*, Sept., 1960.

The Consolidated
Banking Sector

14

Commercial banking is one of the three subsectors which together comprise the consolidated banking sector. The other two sectors are the Treasury and the Federal Reserve. In this chapter, each of the last two subsectors will be discussed separately. Then, the operations of all three subsectors will be consolidated into a single sector.

THE TREASURY

The United States Treasury is part of the organization of the federal government. In Chapter 12, we discussed the fiscal and financial functions of the federal government, i.e., the functions connected with taxation, expenditure, and the management of the public debt. In this section, the monetary functions of the Treasury will be discussed.

The monetary functions of the Treasury can be separated from the fiscal and financial operations and be treated as a separate balance sheet. The liabilities are the various forms of currency and coin issued by the Treasury. The assets are the gold and silver stocks held by the Treasury.

CURRENCY AND COIN

Currency includes all kinds of paper money except checks. The Treasury and the Federal Reserve are the two sole sources of currency in the United States. Federal Reserve currency will be discussed later. Silver coins include silver dollars, half-dollars, quarters, and dimes. Minor coins include pennies and nickels. Table 14-1 shows the quantities of Treasury coin and currency outstanding and in circulation as of December, 1963.

Table 14-1

TREASURY CURRENCY AND COINS OUTSTANDING
AND IN CIRCULATION, DECEMBER, 1963
(In Millions of Dollars)

Type	Outstanding	Treasury Cash	In Federal Reserve	In Circulation
Silver dollars	485*	11	5	452
Silver certificates	1,999	..	136	1,863
Subsidiary silver coin	1,891	4	15	1,872
Minor coin	709	1	1	706
U.S. notes	347	1	25	321
In process of retirement	166	**	**	165

*Includes $17 million of silver coin held as reserve against silver certificates.
**Less than $50,000.
Source: *Federal Reserve Bulletin*, February, 1964, p. 187.

Silver Certificates. Silver certificates and standard silver dollars represent a legislative attempt to maintain the bimetallic monetary system, based on both gold and silver, which prevailed during most of the nineteenth century. The Treasury purchased silver at a price of not less than $0.905 an ounce, which generally was above the market price. The payment for the silver came in the form of a check drawn on the government's checking account held by the Federal Reserve. The government account was returned to its original balance when the Treasury issued silver certificates and coins of an amount equal to the silver purchase. The newly issued currency was deposited with the Federal Reserve, which credited the government's account and used the currency and coins to meet the demands of commercial banks. Although the value of silver was assigned a monetary value of $1.29 an ounce, the Treasury issued currency and coin based not on the monetary value of the silver purchased, but on the actual purchase price.

As of June, 1963, the Treasury's tie to silver was officially cut. The Treasury will gradually retire silver certificates. The retired certificates will be replaced by currency of the Federal Reserve banks. Between December, 1962, and December, 1963, silver certificates in circulation had declined by $123 million.

United States Notes. These are also Treasury obligations. These notes are what is left of the paper money issue used to finance the Civil War and are often called "greenbacks." The amount outstanding has been fixed at $347 million, against which the Treasury holds a reserve of $156 million in metallic gold. The remaining Treasury currency includes the odds and ends of our monetary history and is generally in process of being retired.

GOLD

The monetary system of the United States is based on gold. Practically, this means that the Treasury stands ready to buy and sell gold at a fixed price, $35.00 a fine ounce, to all legitimate holders. Except for licensed domestic users such as dentists and jewelers, gold may not be held by anyone in the United States but the Treasury. As of December, 1963, the Treasury held $15,513 million of gold valued at the $35.00 price. The gold holdings of the United States Treasury have been declining since 1957, when Treasury holdings were $22,781 million.

Gold and the Money Supply. When a gold seller completes a sale to the Treasury, he receives a check drawn on the Treasury's account with the Federal Reserve for the value of the gold. The seller either cashes the check or, more likely, deposits it in his bank. The money holdings of the gold seller have risen by the amount of the sale.

The Treasury's checking account with the Federal Reserve has fallen by the amount of the gold sale. However, the Treasury can issue gold certificates, which are legal money only for transactions between the Treasury and the Federal Reserve, for the amount of the gold sale. The new gold certificates are deposited with the Federal Reserve, which credits the Treasury account for the deposit, returning government deposits to the level that they were prior to the purchase of gold. The immediate impact of the gold purchase is to increase the total money supply of the United States by an amount equal to the value of the gold purchased.

Just the reverse occurs when the Treasury sells gold. Such sales are made to foreign governments or to their financial agents. In terms of the flow of funds, this indicates that the foreign countries prefer to hold gold rather than to hold United States money or other financial claims on the United States. To pay for the gold, the purchaser presents a check drawn on a domestic bank, reducing total checking accounts. The Treasury releases the gold, deposits the check in its account with the Federal Reserve. Finally, the Treasury withdraws the gold certificates from the Federal Reserve in an amount equal to the gold sale. The Federal Reserve reduces the Treasury's deposits by the amount of gold certificates withdrawn. The result is that the total money supply falls by the amount of gold sold.

Two facts may be interesting. When gold is sold by the Treasury, the purchaser usually does not physically remove the gold from the Treasury vaults. Instead of incurring the expense and risk of a physical removal, the gold is merely tagged as belonging to the foreign government Second, gold certificates are not actually issued or canceled between the Federal Reserve and the Treasury. Rather than go to the expense of engraving and moving such certificates, bookkeeping memoranda are exchanged between the two parties concerned in the gold certificate transactions.

Gold and Commercial Bank Reserves. In addition to increasing the money supply, a gold purchase by the Treasury has the effect of increasing commercial bank reserves. When the gold seller's bank of deposit receives the check drawn on the Treasury, the bank sends the check to the Federal Reserve for collection. The Federal Reserve clears the check simply by reducing the Treasury's account and increasing the reserve deposit of the commercial bank.

The total reserves of the commercial bank are not affected if the gold seller simply cashed the check rather than depositing it. In that event, the commercial bank merely switched reserves from vault cash to reserve deposits. However, let us assume that the check was deposited, as is the case with most substantial transactions.

With an increase in reserves, the commercial bank can increase its earning assets if it wishes. If it increases earning assets by lending, not only do earning assets increase, demand deposits also increase. If it increases earning assets by purchasing an investment, the seller of the investment can deposit the check drawn on the buying bank with the seller's bank of deposit. Demand deposits go up as with loans and, when the check is cleared through the Federal Reserve, the bank of deposit is credited with reserves equal to the amount of the check. Total reserves have not changed because of the investment purchase—just the title to the reserves.

Thus, the gold purchase by the Treasury can result in an increase in the money supply not only equal to the value of the gold purchased, but by a multiple of the purchase. This assumes that people are willing to hold the money supply in the form of demand deposits and not in currency nor as time deposits, and that commercial banks want to acquire earning assets. Under these assumptions, what is the ultimate value of the ratio *increased demand deposits/increased reserves?*

Assume a $10,000 gold purchase by the Treasury, and that the reserve ratio set by the Federal Reserve is 20 per cent, i.e., commercial banks must hold at least 20 per cent of demand deposits on reserve. The initial bank of deposit receives the $10,000, increasing both reserves and deposits. Required reserves rise by 20 per cent of $10,000, or $2,000. The bank lends the $8,000 excess, and the borrower of the $8,000 spends the proceeds of the loan. Since the borrower spends the money, someone must have received it. Maintaining the assumptions above, the recipient deposits the $8,000 in his bank which now has an increase of $8,000 in both deposits and reserves. Excess reserves are $6,400 ($8,000 − $1,600), which are loaned out. The second borrower spends the money, and the recipient deposits the $6,400 in another bank, or the same one, for it makes no difference. This bank can lend $5,120, etc. The progression is shown in Exhibit 14-1.

Exhibit 14-1

EXPANSION OF $10,000 NEW RESERVES,
ASSUMING ALL ADDED MONEY IS HELD AS DEMAND DEPOSITS
AND BANKS DO NOT WANT EXCESS RESERVES

Bank	New Deposit	Added Required Reserves	Added Earning Assets
A	$10,000.00	$2,000.00	$8,000.00
B	8,000.00	1,600.00	6,400.00
C	6,400.00	1,280.00	5,120.00
D	5,120.00	1,024.00	4,096.00
E	4,096.00	819.20	3,276.80
F	3,276.80	655.36	2,621.44
G	2,621.44	524.29	2,097.15
H	2,097.15	419.43	1,677.72
I	1,677.72	335.54	1,342.28
J	1,342.28	268.46	1,073.82
K	1,073.82	214.76	859.06
L	859.06	171.81	687.25
M	687.25	137.45	549.80
N	549.80	109.96	439.84
O	439.84	87.97	351.87
P	351.87	70.37	281.50
Q	281.50	56.30	225.20
R	225.20	45.04	180.16
S	180.16	36.03	144.13
T	144.13	28.83	115.30
U	115.30	23.06	92.24
V	92.24	18.45	73.79
W	73.79	14.76	59.03
X	59.03	11.81	47.23
Y	47.23	9.45	37.78
Z	37.78	7.56	30.22
.	.	.	.
.	.	.	.
.	.	.	.
Totals	$50,000.00	$10,000.00	$40,000.00

Under the stated assumptions, the process can be reasoned as follows: Each bank holds only required reserves and lends out the rest. The reserve ratio is 20 per cent, and the addition to reserves from the gold purchases is $10,000. When, for the banking system as a whole, the addition to required reserves is equal to the added reserves, the expansion process stops. In other words, if R represents the added reserves and r is the reserve ratio, growth in the money supply, M, will continue until $rM = R$, or the limit to the added money supply is $M = R/r$. Substituting the numbers from the example, $R = \$10,000$, $r = 0.2$, so $M = \$50,000$.

The assumptions underlying the expansion are crucial and deserve repetition. Should any recipient in the chain desire currency instead of a bank deposit, the expansion stops at that point. If some holder prefers time deposits, the expansion continues, but, because of the lower reserve ratio in time deposits, the total expansion will exceed the value shown. Should any bank be content to hold excess reserves, the expansion stops. Although most of the money supply is held as demand deposits, currency and coin are also held. And, as was pointed out earlier, banks often do hold excess reserves. Thus, the five-fold expansion shown in Exhibit 14-1 is a theoretical limit. Ordinarily, the expansion will not be five-fold, but some multiple expansion is likely.

If, as has been shown, expansion of Treasury gold holdings are likely to lead to a multiple expansion of the money supply, it follows that a reduction in gold holdings, such as has been the experience of the United States for the last several years, will lead to a multiple reduction in the money supply, all else unchanged. From the discussion in Chapter 12, the following consequences of a decline in the money supply are possible: (1) If for some reason the desired domestic cash balances fall by the amount of the decline in the money supply, there will be no effects on interest rates or GNP; (2) however, if the desired domestic cash balances do not fall by this amount automatically, spending may be reduced and/or firms and households will sell nonmonetary financial assets in order to expand cash holdings.

A reduction in spending will have the direct effect of reducing GNP. At a lower GNP, transactions balances will be reduced, though probably not proportionately, but the inverse movement in speculative and precautionary demand for cash may more than offset the decline in transactions demand. Should this occur, GNP will continue to fall sharply.

A reduction in holdings of nonmonetary financial assets will reduce the prices of these assets, raising interest rates. The increase in interest rates will ultimately reach a point at which the demand for the financial assets will equal the supply. In effect, nonmonetary financial assets will substitute for cash. If real investment and consumption are insensitive to interest rate movements, GNP will be unaffected. However, should either of these demands be interest-elastic, GNP will fall as firms and households shift from real assets to financial assets.

Of course, neither of these unhappy consequences has really occurred in our economy despite the decline in gold holdings. The reason for this is that all else has not remained unchanged. A major factor has been that, through discretionary monetary policy, the money supply has not been allowed to shrink. Discretionary monetary policy will be discussed in the next section.

A final note on the multiple expansion of the money supply. In the illustration, the factor that set off the expansion was an increase in the excess reserves of commercial banks resulting from a gold purchase by the Treasury. The important factor, however, was that excess reserves were increased. There are other ways of increasing excess reserves besides buying gold. For example, the reserve ratio could be reduced. As a result, a multiple expansion of the money supply could be set off. In the section concerning the Federal Reserve, we shall consider other ways in which the volume of excess reserves can be manipulated. It should be remembered that the multiple expansion or contraction is possible whenever excess reserves are increased or decreased.

THE TREASURY'S
BALANCE SHEET

The assets of the monetary segment of the Treasury's balance sheet consist of gold and silver. With these represented by MM (monetary metals), we have

$$(14\text{--}1) \qquad TA_t = MM.$$

The other assets of government, such as deposits with the Federal Reserve, are shown in the balance sheet for fiscal and financial segments of government.

The monetary liabilities of the Treasury are gold certificates, currency, and coin. Using GC as the symbol for gold certificates, the right-hand side of the Treasury's monetary balance sheet is

$(14\text{--}2)$

$$TL_t = {_r}GC_t + {_c}CC_t + {_r}CC_t + {_f}CC_t + {_h}CC_t + {_w}CC_t + {_i}CC_t.$$

Since the Treasury issues coin and currency equal in value to the price it has paid for the monetary metals,

$$(14\text{--}3) \qquad TA_t = TL_t.$$

THE FEDERAL RESERVE BANKS

Many of the functions of the Federal Reserve banks have been covered already. The Federal Reserve collects checks for commercial banks by reducing the reserve deposits of the commercial bank on which the check is drawn and increasing the deposits of the commercial bank which submits the check to the Federal Reserve. Commercial banks may call on the Federal Reserve to supply coin and currency requirements. The Federal Reserve collects for the coin and currency by reducing the commercial bank's reserve deposit. Temporary reserve needs of commercial banks can be met by borrowing from the Federal Reserve. The Federal Reserve also has certain powers over the commercial banks. It supervises and examines the banking activities of member banks. It sets reserve ratios for member banks. It sets the discount rate, i.e., the rate of interest which commercial banks pay in order to borrow from the Federal Reserve, and decides which banks will be refused access to the discount privilege.

The Federal Reserve also performs functions for the United States government. The government maintains checking accounts with the Federal Reserve. All cash disbursements of the Treasury are made by checks drawn on the Federal Reserve. The Federal Reserve is the conduit through which Treasury coin and currency are distributed to the economy. By holding gold certificates, the Federal Reserve is an important cog in the gold system of the United States.

STRUCTURE
OF THE FEDERAL RESERVE

The Federal Reserve System came into being by act of Congress in 1913, following an extensive investigation of the weaknesses of the commercial banking system prior to that time. In its original form, it was inadequate, as was proven by the continuation of a high rate of bank failure. For the period 1906–1910, the annual average of bank failures was 84. It was 123 for 1911–1915, 75 for 1916–1920, 520 for 1921–1925, and even higher for 1926–1930. Over 4,000 banks failed in 1933. Reforms were embodied in the Glass-Steagall Act of 1932, which gave the Federal Reserve more flexibility, and the Federal Deposit Insurance Corporation was formed in 1933. In 1934, only 57 banks failed. Since 1940, the failure rate has been less than 10 banks annually, with most of these failures being nonmember banks.

The Federal Reserve consists of 12 regional banks, each of which is a separate corporation. Six of the nine directors of each of the regional banks are chosen locally, and three are appointed by the Board of Governors. Bank examination, lending to commercial banks, supplying currency needs —these are functions of the regional bank. Since the regions have grown in population since 1913, branches have been established. As of 1963, there were 24 branches.

Coordination, control, and much policy making for the regional banks is the role of the Board of Governors of the Federal Reserve, which consists of seven Governors appointed by the President of the United States. Each appointment is made for 14 years, so that every 2 years the President must make a new appointment. The purpose of this is to provide the System, which is referred to as a "central bank," independence from political pressures. The Board of Governors determines reserve ratios, sets the margin requirements for security loans, and reviews the discount rates set by the regional banks, in addition to general supervision of the regional Federal Reserve banks.

The Open Market Committee, consisting of the Board of Governors and five representatives elected by the Federal Reserve banks, determines the policy of the central banking system with respect to the government securities portion of the Federal Reserve banks' asset portfolios. The Reserve banks are required to buy and sell government securities in accordance with the instructions of the Open Market Committee.

There is also a Federal Advisory Council, which consists of a representative of each of the geographic Federal Reserve districts selected by the board of directors of the particular Federal Reserve bank. It meets in Washington four times a year at least. Its functions are to advise the Board of Governors on the affairs of the Federal Reserve System.

Underneath the regulatory apparatus are the 6,000 commercial banks which are members of the System. The practice followed so far and to be continued in this chapter is to refer to the Federal Reserve banks, the Board of Governors, and the Open Market Committee by the term Federal Reserve. The member banks will be referred to as member banks or commercial banks.

LIABILITIES
AND NET WORTH

Table 14-2 lists the types and quantities of liabilities and net worth for the 12 regional Federal Reserve banks, including branches, as of the end of December, 1956, 1960, and 1963. The Board has no balance sheet so that all discussion of the balance sheet of the Federal Reserve really concerns the regional banks.

Table 14-2

LIABILITIES* AND NET WORTH FOR ALL FEDERAL RESERVE BANKS,
END OF DECEMBER, 1956, 1960, AND 1963
(In Millions of Dollars)

Item	1956	1960	1963
Federal Reserve notes**	27,125	27,924	32,381
Deposits total	20,249	18,336	18,391
Member bank reserves	19,059	17,081	17,049
U.S. Treasurer-General account	441	485	880
Foreign	322	217	171
Other	426	554	291
Other liabilities	17	31	82
Total liabilities	47,742	46,817	50,854
Paid-in capital	326	409	497
Surplus	884	817	990
Total liabilities and net worth	48,600	47,518	52,341

*Excludes deferred availability cash items (see discussion of float in text).
**Net of holdings of other Federal Reserve banks.
Source: *Federal Reserve Bulletin*, January, 1957, 1961, and 1964.

Federal Reserve Notes. These are part of the total currency supply. Until mid-1963, these included bills in denominations of $5 or more. Since then, $1 denomination bills are included also. Comparison with Table 14-1 indicates that Federal Reserve notes outstanding are approximately six times the size of total Treasury currency and coin.

Deposits. The first two deposit items in Table 14-2—member bank reserves and the Treasurer's account—have already been discussed. The apparent decline in reserve deposits is a result of a change in regulations. As of November 23, 1960, commercial banks were allowed to count vault cash as reserves. Prior to December 1, 1959, no vault cash was counted as reserves for purposes of calculating the reserve ratio. In between December, 1959, and November, 1960, part of the vault cash was permitted to be counted in. As shown in Table 13-4, the cash assets of commercial banks, all of which are now counted as reserves, have risen over the period. Only the amount held as reserve deposits has fallen.

Foreign deposits include balances of foreign central banks. (i.e., foreign counterparts of the Federal Reserve), foreign governments, and international agencies, such as the United Nations. Most of the foreign deposits are held for balance of payments clearings. A simple example may help. If a merchant in the United Kingdom wishes to buy United States goods, he may bring pounds sterling to his English bank. The English bank can buy a claim to United States dollars through the Bank of England, which is the United Kingdom central bank. The Bank of England accepts the pounds and makes dollar claims available through its account with the Federal Reserve Bank of New York, which deals with most of the foreign accounts. There are a number of other ways in which such a transaction could be handled, but the foreign payments mechanism is beyond the scope of this book.

The other deposits are mainly accounts maintained by nonmember banks. Such accounts entitle the nonmembers access to the check clearing and collection facilities of the Federal Reserve.

Other Liabilities.   These consist primarily of accounts payable, such as wages payable, and unearned discounts on notes. The latter occur when the Federal Reserve banks discount a note which will not mature until after the date of the balance sheet. The Federal Reserve collects the discount when the note is offered to the bank, but will not earn it all until the maturity date of the note.

Paid-in Capital.   This consists of the stock owned by member banks.

Surplus.   Surplus represents primarily that part of earnings of the Federal Reserve banks which has not been distributed. The Federal Reserve pays a statutory 6 per cent dividend on its stock. Ninety per cent of earnings after the dividend are turned over to the United States Treasury. The remainder goes to surplus. However, additions have not been made to surplus in recent years since the Board believes the surplus account is large enough.

ASSETS   As with commercial banks, the assets of the Federal Reserve banks can be divided between cash assets and earning assets. When the system of commercial banks acquires earning assets, either total demand deposits or currency outside commercial banks will rise, usually the former. When Federal Reserve banks acquire earning assets, demand deposits or currency may rise, commercial bank reserves may rise, or Treasury deposits at the Federal Reserve may rise depending on who sells the asset to the Federal Reserve. In the last instance, the increase will usually be spent by the Treasury, resulting in an increase in commercial bank demand deposits or currency, and, if demand deposits rise an increase in commercial bank reserves.

First, assume the Federal Reserve buys an asset from an individual or firm. The seller receives a check drawn on the Federal Reserve bank making the purchase. The seller may deposit the check at a commercial bank, in which case demand deposits rise. The commercial bank sends the check to the Federal Reserve, which honors the check by increasing the commercial bank's reserve deposits. Thus, both commercial bank demand deposits and total reserves increase. If the seller of the earning asset prefers currency to a demand deposit, currency outside commercial banks increases. The bank sends the check to the Federal Reserve, so that the bank's reserve deposit rises. But commercial bank reserves have not increased because the increase in reserve deposits is matched by the decrease in commercial bank vault cash.

Next, assume the Federal Reserve buys an earning asset from a commercial bank. In this case, the earning asset could be a government security, but it also may be a promissory note discounted by the commercial bank with the Federal Reserve. The selling bank receives payment when its reserve deposit at the Federal Reserve is increased. There is no immediate increase in demand deposits.

Finally, the Federal Reserve may purchase government securities directly from the Treasury. The Treasury's demand deposit with the Federal Reserve is increased. When the Treasury spends the borrowed money, individuals and firms will receive Treasury checks which they can either deposit in commercial banks or cash and hold as currency. In the former case, demand deposits and reserves both rise, since commercial banks will collect the checks by sending them to the Federal Reserve, which will increase the commercial bank's reserve deposit and decrease the Treasury's deposit.

In each case, except where currency is preferred to demand deposits, an increase in the earning assets of the Federal Reserve results in an increase of commercial bank reserves. You will recall that an increase in commercial bank reserves caused by a Treasury gold purchase allowed a multiple expansion of the money supply in the form of demand deposits. The multiple expansion is not restricted simply to reserve increases caused by gold purchases. Any increase in commercial bank reserves can result in multiple expansion of demand deposits. For this reason, the level and composition of Federal Reserve assets is very important. In fact, the Federal Reserve, which has the responsibility of setting the monetary policy for the nation, implements much of its monetary policy by manipulating the levels of Federal Reserve earning assets.

Gold Certificate Reserves. These are a result of gold transactions of the Treasury. The diminution in gold certificates represents the gold drain of recent years.

Table 14-3

ASSETS FOR ALL FEDERAL RESERVE BANKS
END OF DECEMBER, 1956, 1960, AND 1963
(In Millions of Dollars)

Item	1956	1960	1963
Total gold certificate reserves	21,269	16,414	15,237
Cash	306	363	182
Member bank borrowing	25	25	31
Other borrowing	26	8	32
Acceptances	69	74	162
Bought outright	34	53	70
Held under repurchase agreement	35	20	92
U.S. government securities	24,915	27,384	33,593
Bought outright	24,610	26,984	33,582
Bills	1,721	2,900	4,142
Certificates	10,933	9,060	7,066
Notes	9,154	12,481	17,729
Bonds	2,802	2,543	4,645
Held under repurchase agreement	305	400	11
Total loans and securities	25,034	27,491	33,818
Float	1,665	1,868	2,600
Bank premises	73	108	104
Other assets	252	209	400
Total assets	48,600	47,518	52,341

Source: *Federal Reserve Bulletin*, January, 1957, 1961, and 1964.

Prior to March, 1965, gold certificates had a very important legal role in the balance sheet of the Federal Reserve. Gold certificates were required to be held in an amount equal to at least 25 per cent of deposit and currency liabilities of the Federal Reserve. Thus, gold certificate reserves as of the end of 1963 were sufficient to support about $61 billion of deposit and currency liabilities, which actually were $51 billion. Though this $10 billion margin may seem substantial, the difference between the maximum currency and deposit level permitted and the actual level had been $38 billion at the end of 1956. By the end of January, 1965, the margin between maximum deposits and notes and actual levels had fallen to less than $7 billion.

From the point of view of monetary policy, the gold outflow of recent years threatens the ability of the Federal Reserve to increase its holdings of earning assets which provide banks with sufficient reserves so that the banks can meet the demand for loan and investment funds necessary to maintain a reasonable degree of prosperity. There are two solutions to this possible dilemma. The first is to reduce the reserve ratio applied to commercial banks. With a reduced reserve ratio, reserve deposits at the Federal Reserve would fall below what they would be otherwise, thus freeing gold certificates. In addition, existing commercial bank reserves could cover larger amounts of deposits. The second solution would be to reduce the ratio of gold certificates to deposit and note liabilities, thus allowing a smaller gold cover for Federal Reserve obligations. Both solutions have been adopted.

In December, 1951, commercial bank deposits were $130 billion against which were held reserves of $20 billion. Deposits had increased to almost $250 billion in December, 1964, but total reserves were less than $22 billion. Reserves accounted for 17.5 per cent of total deposits in 1951 but less than 9 per cent in 1964. Part of this decline was due to a reclassification of commercial banks and part was due to a decrease in reserve requirements.

Prior to December 1, 1960, the Federal Reserve had three classifications of commercial banks for purposes of setting reserve ratios. In addition to the reserve city and country classifications, large banks in New York and Chicago were classified as central reserve city banks. As of December 1, 1960, the central reserve city classification was dropped which, in effect, reduced the reserve ratio for the many large banks located in Chicago and New York.

In addition, the reserve ratio applied to reserve city banks' demand deposits was reduced from 20 per cent to 16.5 per cent in stages since July 1953. The reserve requirements on the demand deposits of country banks were increased from 11 per cent to 12 per cent in November, 1960, which increase partially offset the reduction in reserve requirements applied to reserve city banks. The increase in country bank reserve requirements was due to the fact that country banks have had large amounts of free reserves during the post-World War II period, as contrasted to reserve city banks, which have typically held negative free reserves. The country banks were lending their reserves to reserve city banks via the Federal Funds market, which action moderated the effectiveness of the Federal Reserve when it wished to tighten bank credit. The net effect of the two changes in reserve ratios was to reduce reserve requirements. The reduction in reserve ratio for reserve city banks was larger than the increase for country banks; and the reduction applied to a larger volume of demand deposits (reserve city banks held about $83 billion in demand deposits in January, 1965 compared to less than $43 billion for country banks) than did the country bank increase.

Both the net reduction in reserve ratios and the reclassification of commercial banks served to reduce the reserve requirements for the commercial banking system. In 1960, the Federal Reserve permitted vault cash (cash on hand in the commercial bank) to be counted as reserves. Since vault cash is not a liability of the Federal Reserve, and so would not require gold certificates as a legal cover, the effect of this ruling was to free gold certificates from covering a portion of commercial bank reserves. As of December, 1964, about $3.7 billion of reserves, almost 17 per cent of total commercial bank reserves, were held as vault cash.

Despite these efforts, it has already been noted that the difference between actual and required gold certificate holdings was less than $7 billion at the end of January, 1965. A similar decline in the difference between actual and required gold holdings had occurred during World War II. At that time, the Federal Reserve was required to hold gold certificates in an amount equal to 40 per cent of Federal Reserve note issue and 35 per cent of Federal Reserve deposit liabilities. Had this law remained unchanged, the difference between actual and required gold holdings would have shrunk to less than $4 billion by December, 1945. However, Congress changed the gold cover law in 1945, reducing required gold holdings to 25 per cent of note and deposit liabilities. Similarly, in 1965, Congress again changed the gold cover requirement. The gold cover for note issues of the Federal Reserve remain unchanged; but the gold cover requirement for deposit liabilities has been eliminated. Had the new law been in effect in January, 1965, $4.8 billion would have been added to the difference between actual and required gold certificate holdings.

It should be noted, finally, that the Federal Reserve does have some flexibility in meeting the gold cover requirement. If the gold cover falls below 25 per cent of note issue but not below 20 per cent, the Board of Governors imposes a nominal tax on the Federal Reserve Banks. If the cover falls below 20 per cent, the tax becomes progressively steeper. The tax is required to be added to the discount rate charged commercial banks for borrowing from the Federal Reserve.

Cash.   Cash holdings of the Federal Reserve consist of Treasury coin and currency which is distributed through the Federal Reserve banks.

Member Bank Borrowings.   These result from discounting operations of the Federal Reserve. All such notes are due within 90 days. Almost 80 per cent of member bank borrowing was from reserve city banks during December, 1963, which is consistent with the observation made earlier that country banks, unlike reserve city banks, have typically not needed additional reserves.

Other Borrowing.   This consists partially of loans made to foreign central banks which are secured by gold. In addition, there are discounts made to nonmember banks and other financial institutions, for which the security behind the borrower's note consists of United States Treasury securities. These discounts usually are charged a higher rate than applies to member bank borrowing.

Finally, the Federal Reserve is authorized to make industrial loans to businesses directly when normal borrowing facilities are unavailable. Usually, member banks or nonmember banks make the direct loan and the Federal Reserve agrees to purchase or discount the loan from the bank on demand. The financial institution making the loan must agree to bear one-fifth of any loss sustained by the Federal Reserve, with the Federal Resrve bearing the remainder. The agreement to purchase or discount the paper is known as a commitment, and the Federal Reserve charges a commitment fee for making it. The rate at which such paper is discounted by the Federal Reserve is above the discount rate charged to member banks.

Acceptances. These are similar to promissory notes, except that the maker of the acceptance orders someone else to pay the payee. With promissory notes, the maker promises to pay the payee.

The acceptances held by the Federal Reserve are bankers' acceptances, i.e., acceptances for which a commercial bank has agreed to make payment. Instead of advancing funds to a borrower, the commercial bank agrees to accept the order to pay the bearer of a banker's acceptance. The maker of the acceptance agrees to pay the bank the face value of the acceptance by the time the acceptance comes due, and the bank uses the funds received from the maker to pay the payee. Since the bank has accepted payment, it in effect guarantees the acceptance which, since the creditworthiness of a commercial bank is usually superior to that of an individual or firm, makes the acceptance highly negotiable. For years, the Federal Reserve has attempted to stimulate the use of banker's acceptances by standing ready to buy prime banker's acceptances at the market rate. However, except for international trade, acceptances have not been widely used.

Sometimes the holder of securities has a temporary need for funds, but does not want to alter his investment portfolio permanently by selling securities to acquire the needed money. The Federal Reserve will buy banker's acceptances from those who have invested in them, but need funds temporarily, subject to an agreement wherein the seller of the acceptance agrees to repurchase it from the Federal Reserve at a later date. A similar arrangement is available to commercial banks with United States government securities.

United States government securities. These constitute the bulk of Federal Reserve earning assets. Changes' in these assets represent the day-to-day implementation of monetary policy. As the Federal Reserve purchases government securities, it increases the money supply and, to the extent that commercial bank reserves also rise as a result of Federal Reserve purchases, the increase in money supply can be a multiple of the securities purchases. Just the reverse occurs when the Federal Reserve sells government securities. The purchases and sales of government securities comprise what is called *open market operations.*

The Federal Reserve is charged with managing the money supply in a manner consistent with the aims of economic growth and stable prices. The reserve ratio, the discount rate, and open market operations are all tools to accomplish these ends. The reserve ratio tool is very powerful in that it affects all banks in the reserve ratio classification. If the Federal Reserve wishes to contract the flow of credit and thus raises reserve requirements, some banks may be forced to contract loans so sharply that the economy may be pushed into a recession. On the other hand, the discount rate may be too weak. Raising the discount rate as a means of restricting credit may have little effect on banks with profitable lending and investment opportunities. Such banks can find other sources of reserves, such as the Federal funds market, or may be willing to pay a higher discount rate because of the high yield on loans and investments.

Open market operations provide a relatively sensitive, yet reasonably powerful tool. If the Federal Reserve sells securities in order to contract credit, reliance is not placed on any action of the commercial banks, as with discount rates. The customers of the commercial banks can purchase these securities, reducing both demand deposits and commercial bank reserves. The Federal Reserve can increase or decrease the tempo of security sales almost instantaneously so that an overcontraction of credit can be corrected much more easily that if the reserve ratio had been used as the tool of contraction. The same arguments apply when the Federal Reserve wishes to expand credit and buy securities.

In addition to the achievement of broad goals of monetary policy, open market operations are used to smooth the flow of credit seasonally. At various times of the year, such as during the Christmas shopping season and the vacation period, the economy prefers a higher proportion of currency and coin than ordinarily. Demand deposits fall as withdrawals are made. With the decline in demand deposits, commercial bank reserves fall and this can affect the lending and investment policies of commercial banks. The situation is temporary, since most of the currency will be redeposited in the banks after the season. However, the short-run affects of a curtailment of bank credit could have serious effects on the stability of the economy. To smooth out the temporary decline in reserves, the Federal Reserve uses two tools. Discounts tend to increase and the Federal Reserve also buys government securities. After the temporary reserve drain is over, the Federal Reserve sells government securities, sopping up the reserves created by the original purchases.

At the end of December, 1963, the Federal Reserve banks held 11 per cent of the gross public debt. Though this is small relative to the holdings of commercial banks, the Federal Reserve holdings are subject to a centralized management, the Open Market Committee, whereas commercial bank holdings are subject to over 6,000 uncoordinated managers. As a result, Federal Reserve open market operations have an important effect on the yields of government securities. During World War II and more or less to 1951, the Federal Reserve "pegged" the yield structure of government debt by standing ready to buy all government securities at the pegged rate appropriate to the particular security's maturity class. The yield structure which was supported had low rates for securities maturing in a short time and higher rates for longer term instruments.

Initially, the price support activities of the Federal Reserve were aimed at facilitating the financing of the war. However, there was pressure to maintain Federal Reserve support afterwards. Among reasons for this was that the Treasury wanted to keep yields on government securities low so as to have a low service charge on the public debt. This fear of a sharp rise in interest rates if the Federal Reserve discontinued its support was based on: (1) a growing demand for funds by businesses and households, putting upward pressure on interest rates; and (2) the increased risk of capital loss to holders of government securities without pegged rates.

But it was for precisely these reasons that the Federal Reserve wanted to stop support activities. In effect, the Federal Reserve had given up its powers to shape monetary policy. Commercial banks could simply sell government securities to the Federal Reserve at a fixed price any time that the banks needed more reserves. Should there have developed an inflationary expansion of bank credit, the Federal Reserve was powerless to stop it.

Friction between the Treasury and the Federal Reserve increased during 1950. Finally, in March, 1951, the so-called "Accord" was reached between the Treasury and the Federal Reserve. Support of the existing structure of yields was to be abandoned. The Federal Reserve would limit its support activities simply to the maintenance of orderly market conditions.

Float.   This is actually the difference between a Federal Reserve asset *cash items in process of collection* and the liability *deferred availability cash items.* Both of these items arise from Federal Reserve bank check clearing. If a commercial bank has received a check drawn on an out-of-town bank, it deposits the check with its Federal Reserve bank. When the Federal Reserve receives the check, it debits the asset account *cash items in process of collections,* and credits the liability *deferred availability cash items.* The check then is sent to the bank on which it is drawn. If the Federal Reserve bank waited until the payer bank honored the check before it credited the depositing bank's reserve deposit with the proceeds, both the asset and the liability would be reduced at the same time. No float would arise.

In fact, however, the Federal Reserve will reduce the liability *deferred availability* and increase the depositing bank's reserve account, not when the check is honored, but according to a time schedule. Currently, no more than two days elapse before the depositing bank's reserve account is increased. Since it often takes more than two days before the check is honored, the asset *cash items in process of collection* will not be reduced at the same time that the schedule calls for the reduction of the liability item. Thus, the asset account will exceed the liability account, and the difference is referred to as *float*.

The significance of float is that the depositing bank has the use of reserves before the payer bank has lost the use of reserves. In effect, commercial bank reserves have been increased. The volume of float is a function of the volume of business activity. Although float results from a mechanical procedure, it is very important. Note that the only assets which are larger than float in the Federal Reserve asset portfolio are gold certificates and United States securities.

Should the collection procedures of the Federal Reserve be modified to eliminate float, it is likely that other changes would occur. Banks would lose over $1 billion in reserves. This could be met by a reduction in the reserve ratio, an increase in discounts, or an increase in Federal Reserve open market purchases. However, float has advantages over these alternatives as a means of supplying additional reserves when needed, since float automatically varies with business activity.

Other Assets. These consist of accrued interest on investments, accounts receivable, and convertible foreign currencies held as a result of *swap agreements* between the Federal Reserve and foreign monetary authorities, as well as some other minor asset items.

THE BALANCE SHEET EQUATIONS

The asset portfolio can be presented conveniently if the asset classifications are altered so that all the financial claims of the Federal Reserve on a particular sector are included in one symbol. The only exception to this will be for the Treasury, where gold certificates and government securities will be shown separately since we have separated the monetary functions of government (gold certificates) from the fiscal and financial.

$$(14\text{--}4) \qquad TA_r = GC_t + {}_rCC_t + {}_rB_c + {}_rB_g + {}_rB_f + {}_rB_w.$$

In the liabilities equation, member banks are grouped with nonmember banks, and it is assumed that all the small amount of other liabilities is owed to the business sector.

$$(14\text{--}5) \qquad TL_r = {}_cCC_r + {}_fCC_r + {}_hCC_r + {}_wCC_r + {}_iCC_r + {}_cRD_r$$
$$+ {}_gDD_r + {}_wDD_r + {}_fB_r + {}_cE_r + RE_r.$$

$$(14\text{--}6) \qquad TA_r = TL_r.$$

At this point, flow considerations will be ignored.

THE CONSOLIDATED BANKING SECTOR

The banking sector consists of the three subsectors which have been described separately in this and the previous chapter —commercial banking, the Treasury, and the Federal Reserve. To consolidate the subsectors, we follow the normal accounting rules of consolidation, which is that claims of one subsector on another are removed both as asset and liability. To follow this process, the three asset and three liability equations are repeated below, omitting real assets so that total assets become total financial assets.

$$(13\text{–}2) \quad FA_c = {}_cRD_r + {}_cCC_r + {}_cCC_t + {}_cB_g + {}_cB_f + {}_cB_h + {}_cB_w$$
$$+ {}_cB_i + {}_cE_r$$

$$(13\text{–}1) \quad TL_c = {}_hDD_c + {}_fDD_c + {}_wDD_c + {}_gDD_c + TD_c + {}_rB_c + E_c$$
$$+ RE_c + {}_iDD_c$$

$$(14\text{–}1) \quad FA_t = MM$$

$$(14\text{–}2) \quad TL_t = {}_rGC_t + {}_cCC_t + {}_rCC_t + {}_fCC_t + {}_hCC_t + {}_wCC_t + {}_iCC_t$$

$$(14\text{–}4) \quad FA_r = GC_t + {}_rCC_t + {}_rB_c + {}_rB_g + {}_rB_f + {}_rB_w$$

$$(14\text{–}5) \quad TL_r = {}_cCC_r + {}_fCC_r + {}_hCC_r + {}_wCC_r + {}_iCC_r + {}_cRD_r$$
$$+ {}_gDD_r + {}_wDD_r + {}_fB_r + {}_cE_r + RE_r.$$

Consolidating out all intrasectoral claims leaves the following for the asset equation:

$$(14\text{–}7) \quad FA_b = MM + {}_cB_g + {}_rB_g + {}_cB_f + {}_rB_f + {}_cB_h + {}_cB_w + {}_rB_w + {}_cB_i.$$

By combining claims on a given sector, we simplify the above to

$$(14\text{–}7a) \quad FA_b = MM + {}_bB_g + {}_bB_f + {}_bB_h + {}_bB_w + {}_bB_i.$$

Using the same approach for the liabilities of the consolidated banking sectors, we have

$$(14\text{–}8) \quad TL_b = {}_hDD_b + {}_fDD_b + {}_wDD_b + {}_gDD_b + {}_iDD_b + {}_hCC_b$$
$$+ {}_fCC_b + {}_wCC_b + {}_iCC_b + TD_b + {}_fB_b + E_b + RE_b.$$

Table 14-4 presents estimates of the actual values for the balance sheet items shown in Eqs. (14–7) and (14–8).

Financial assets do not equal liabilities because of the omission of items including real assets and net worth. The particular groupings shown in the table are not exactly like the items shown in the equations. Partly, it is a matter of detail, such as grouping businesses and households into a single group for reporting deposits and currency holdings. This will be remedied when we consider the listings of financial assets and liabilities for the real sectors. In other cases, the data are in greater detail than shown in the equations. Thus, crop loans to farmers under the Federal programs of agricultural price supports (Commodity Credit Corporation guaranteed) are reported separately, not included as part of business loans as shown in the equation. These differences result from the fact that our system of equations, cumbersome as it is, is supposed to simplify reality. The Federal Reserve

Table 14-4

FINANCIAL ASSETS AND LIABILITIES OF THE CONSOLIDATED BANKING SYSTEM, DECEMBER 31, 1952, 1957 AND 1962
(In Billions of Dollars)

Financial Assets	1952	1957	1962
Holdings of gold, silver, and foreign exchange.	28.0	27.9	21.6
Short-term government securities	34.0	40.1	40.8
Other government securities	55.6	47.4	58.9
Total government securities	89.6	87.5	99.7
State and local obligations	10.2	13.9	24.8
Corporate and foreign bonds...............	2.1	1.4	0.8
1–4 Family mortgages.....................	11.1	16.2	22.0
Other mortgages	4.6	6.9	12.3
Consumer credit	9.4	15.8	23.6
Bank loans not elsewhere shown	35.0	50.3	70.8
to nonfinancial business	28.7	40.2	55.7
to nonbank financial institutions	4.9	6.3	7.6
to nonprofit organizations and foreign......	1.4	3.8	7.5
Other loans, secured or guaranteed	1.8	2.0	5.0
Commodity Credit Corp. guaranteed	0.7	0.5	1.1
Open market paper collateral	0.1	0.2	0.4
Secured by deposits	0.4	0.6	0.8
Security loans	3.2	4.2	7.3
Miscellaneous	1.5	2.9	5.3
Total financial assets	196.2	226.1	293.3
Financial Liabilities			
Net demand deposits and currency	138.8	147.1	163.8
Due to U.S. government.................	8.8	6.7	9.2
Due to foreigners......................	3.6	3.9	3.7
Due to others	126.4	136.5	150.8
Net demand deposits	100.2	109.0	120.3
Currency	27.7	28.5	31.3
Time Deposits	41.7	57.8	98.0
Due to U.S. government.................	0.3	0.3	0.3
Due to foreigners......................	0.7	1.6	2.7
Due to state and local governments	1.6	2.8	6.5
Due to all others	39.1	53.1	82.2
Other liabilities.........................	3.5	4.7	10.1
Total liabilities.......................	184.0	209.6	271.8

Source: *Federal Reserve Bulletin*, August, 1963, Table 8g.

has prepared technical notes for those who wish to probe further into the system of accounts. These notes may be found as footnotes to the tables in the *Federal Reserve Bulletin* and in other publications of the Federal Reserve listed in the selected references at the end of Chapter 11.

THE MONEY SUPPLY

The primary financial asset acquired by the rest of the economy from the banking sector is money. Which of the liabilities shown in Table 14-4 or in Eq. (14–8) should be included in the money supply? Custom and law dictate that the money supply consists of demand deposit liabilities, coin, and currency. As of December 31, 1962, these liabilities totaled $163.8 billion.

The statistic defined by the Federal Reserve as the money supply averaged $158 billion over the second half of December. Part of the difference between that and the monetary liabilities of the consolidated banking sector is accounted for by the difference in timing of the estimates, the Federal Reserve estimate being a two-week average and the consolidated banking sector being the figure at the end of one day. Most of the difference arises from a difference in definition, viz., the Federal Reserve estimate omits demand deposits due the United States government. Since the two estimates can be reconciled, either estimate may be used. A major advantage of the Federal Reserve estimate is that it is available more frequently than are the quarterly estimates of the Flow of Funds.

We have already indicated that the fact that money can be defined does not mean that there is no substitutability of money for other financial assets. At various points in the text, we have emphasized that time deposits, Treasury bills, and open market paper may serve as substitutes for cash holdings. An entire section of Chapter 5 was devoted to the development of decision rules concerning the substitution of interest-bearing financial assets for cash.

Varying the Money Supply. In the last chapter, the stock of domestic money could only be increased if foreign net financial investment was positive, i.e., when exports exceeded imports. With a consolidated banking sector, the money supply can be changed in a variety of ways. The balance sheet provides a handy way of describing the factors which change the money supply. If we revise Eq. (14–8) so that

$$M_b = {}_hDD_b + {}_fDD_b + {}_wDD_b + {}_iDD_b + {}_hCC_b + {}_fCC_b + {}_wCC_b + {}_iCC_b,$$

we have

(14–8a) $$TL_b = M_b + TD_b + {}_fB_b + E_b + RE_b.$$

Since total assets equal total liabilities, Eqs. (14–8a) and (14–7a) can be combined to show that

$$M_b = (MM + {}_bB_g + {}_bB_f + {}_bB_h + {}_bB_w + {}_bB_i)$$
$$- (TD_b + {}_fB_b + E_b + RE_b),$$

which says that the money supply may be defined as the difference between financial assets and liabilities, except monetary liabilities, plus net worth. If the assets of the consolidated banking sector increase, with time deposits, other nonmonetary liabilities, and net worth remaining constant or increasing by less than the asset increase, the money supply will rise. And the money supply will fall if assets decline and nonmonetary liabilities plus net worth fall by less than the asset decline. This can be put as follows:

(14–9) $\qquad dM_b = dFA - d(TD_b + {}_fB_b + E_b + RE_b).$

Reviewing the data in Table 14-4, monetary claims owed by the consolidated banking sector rose by \$8.3 billion between 1952 and 1957. All the assets of the sector increased, except for monetary metals and corporate and foreign bonds. Loans to nonfinancial businesses, consumer credit, and mortgages showed the largest increases. Time deposits due to all others showed the greatest increase of the nonmonetary liabilities, the increase in time deposits being larger than the increase in monetary liabilities.

Between 1957 and 1962, the pattern of change was somewhat different. Monetary liabilities rose by \$16.7 billion, double the amount of increase in the preceding five years. Monetary metals diminished over \$8 billion, and holdings of corporate and foreign bonds fell by about the same amount as between 1952 and 1957. Bank loans to nonfinancial businesses once again showed the largest increase. Holdings of United States government securities rose sharply between 1957 and 1962. Consumer credit and mortgages also increased substantially. Though not large in volume, the increase in holdings of security loans was about three times as great during 1957–1962 as it had been during 1952–1957. Part of this was due to the rise in common stock prices during the later period. Much of the growth in financial assets was offset by a very large increase in time deposits, particularly time deposits due all others. Nonetheless, the net result was a much larger increase in monetary liabilities than had been the case during 1952–1957.

SECTORAL INVESTMENT AND SAVINGS

Net financial investment for the consolidated banking sector is defined exactly as it was for the real sectors.

(14–10) $\qquad NFI_b = dFA_b - dFL_b.$

Financial assets were defined in Eq. (14–7).

(14–11) $\qquad dFL_b = dM_b + dTD_b + d_fB_b + dE_b.$

As was shown in Table 13-1, net financial investment for the consolidated banking sector is very small, \$0.5 billion in 1962. However, capital expenditures consist of expenditures on bank premises and totaled \$0.8 billion in 1962.

$$(14\text{–}12) \qquad\qquad I_b = dPE_b;$$

$$(14\text{–}13) \qquad\qquad GI_b = I_b + NFI_b.$$

On the savings side, the banking sector retains earnings and depreciates plant and equipment, so that

$$(14\text{–}14) \qquad\qquad GS_b = dRE_b + D_b.$$

Since total assets equal total liabilities,

$$(14\text{–}15) \qquad\qquad dPE_b + dFA_b = dFL_b,$$

and

$$(14\text{–}16) \qquad\qquad dPE_b - D_b + dFA_b = dTA_b,$$

$$(14\text{–}17) \qquad\qquad dFL_b + dRE_b = dTL_b.$$

Since total assets equal total liabilities,

$$(14\text{–}18) \qquad\qquad dPE_b - D_b + dFA_b = dFL_b + dRE_b.$$

Adding depreciation to both sides and subtracting the change in financial liabilities from both sides, we have

$$(14\text{–}18a) \qquad\qquad dPE_b + dFA_b - dFL_b = dRE_b + D_b.$$

Equations (14–12) and (14–13) indicate that the left-hand side of Eq. (14–18a) is gross investment, and Eq. (14–14) indicates that the right-hand side is gross savings, so that

$$(14\text{–}19) \qquad\qquad GI_b = GS_b.$$

Table 14-5 shows the annual flows of gross investment and gross savings for 1952, 1957, and 1962. These should not be confused with the balance sheet data of Table 14-4. The annual flows show the changes that have occurred during the year, not the total value of holdings and claims at the end of the year.

It will be noted that gross savings do not equal gross investment in the table. Nonetheless, the equality developed above is a true equality. However, the data represent estimates drawn from many sources, some of which

Table 14-5

**ANNUAL SOURCES AND USES OF FUNDS
FOR THE CONSOLIDATED BANKING SECTOR, 1952, 1957, AND 1962**
(In Billions of Dollars)

Item	1952	1957	1962
1. Net operating surplus, including depreciation ..	2.1	3.3	4.0
2. Profits, taxes, and net dividend payments	1.4	2.2	2.8
3. Gross savings = 1 − 2	0.7	1.1	1.2
4. Gross investment = 5 + 6	0.8	1.3	0.8
5. Capital expenditures	0.1	0.2	0.3
6. Net financial investment = 7 − 18	0.7	1.1	0.5
7. Net acquisition of financial assets	10.5	6.2	19.3
8. Monetary metals and foreign exchange	0.4	1.2	− 1.5
9. Credit market instruments................	10.2	4.4	19.3
10. Government securities	2.6	− 0.6	2.2
11. State and local obligations	1.0	1.0	4.5
12. Corporate and foreign bonds	− 0.1	0.1	− 0.1
13. Mortgages	1.1	0.6	4.0
14. Consumer credit.....................	1.9	1.2	2.2
15. Bank loans not elsewhere shown	3.1	2.3	6.0
16. Guaranteed bank loans	0.5	− 0.2	0.5
17. Security loans	0.6	− 0.1	1.1
18. Miscellaneous	− 0.8	0.6	0.4
19. Net increase in liabilities	9.8	5.1	18.8
20. Demand deposits and net currency	6.2	− 0.1	3.5
21. Due to U.S. government	1.8	0.2	1.0
22. Due to foreigners	0.2	0.2	0.1
23. Due to others	4.2	− 1.4	2.4
24. Time deposits	3.1	5.5	15.3
25. Due to consumers	2.7	5.2	11.5
26. Due to others	0.4	0.3	3.8
27. Other liabilities	0.3	0.3	− 0.1
28. Discrepancy = 3 − 4.....................	− 0.2	− 0.2	0.4

Source: *Flow of Funds Accounts*, 1945–1962, Board of Governors of the Federal Reserve System, Table 4A, pp. 60–61.

are either incomplete or inaccurate. The data must be treated as rough estimates of the relationships shown in the equation. Those interested in a detailed discussion of the techniques of statistical estimation used in developing the flow-of-funds data may refer to the selected readings shown at the end of Chapter 11.

INTERSECTORAL
IMPACT

The activities of the consolidated banking sector serve to provide the other sectors with a greater variety of financial assets than were shown in Chapters 11 and 12. Instead of holding one kind of money or gold, the real sectors can hold currency and coin, demand deposits, and/or time deposits. In terms of convenience, safety from thieves, and yield, these financial assets differ and are different from other financial assets available in a bankless economy. It is likely that the quantity of financial assets held by the real sectors will be larger with a banking sector than without one. It is not unreasonable to expect that households and firms will substitute the new assets not only for other financial assets, but, to some extent, will substitute financial assets for real assets and, perhaps, even for nondurable consumer goods. The rate of substitution of claims on the banking sector for other financial claims depends upon: relative yields; expectations as to business conditions, with unfavorable expectations leading to a substitution of monetary claims and time deposits for other financial assets; expectations as to price movements, with inflationary expectations leading to a substitution of time deposits, other interest-bearing claims, and stocks for monetary liabilities; and the preferences of economic units between risk and return.

The degree of substitutability between real assets and financial assets is probably much less than among financial assets. A bank deposit is not a good substitute for an automobile. Nonetheless, some substitution will take place depending upon: the quantity of real assets relative to the quantity of financial assets held by the various economic units, with a high ratio of real assets leading to more substitution by financial assets; price expectations, with inflationary expectations favoring the holding of real assets as compared to fixed-return financial assets (this excludes stock); the yields on financial assets; the risk features of financial assets; and the preferences between consuming and saving of the various economic units, with high savings favoring financial assets.

The banking sector not only provides a greater variety of financial assets, it also serves as an addition to the demand for the claims issued by the real sectors. As a result, the real sectors may be able to sell claims at lower interest rate than otherwise. Competition among buyers of claims is not limited to yield. In order to persuade the real sectors to sell their financial claims to the banking sector, bargaining will occur not only on yield, but on other conditions surrounding the claim, such as maturity, the quality, quantity, and closeness of control of collateral, and flotation costs. The result is likely to be that the real sectors will be more willing to issue claims.

What effect will all of this have on the rate of economic growth? On the one hand, the greater willingness of the real sectors to hold financial claims will be a deterrent to growth by reducing the demand for real assets. It will also serve as a brake on inflation. On the other hand, the ease and low cost of issuing financial claims will tend to encourage the accumulation of real assets and, perhaps, consumption. This will increase growth and, depending upon the level of employment and productivity of factors of production, lead to the possibility of price rise.

To the extent that the banking sector is a more efficient allocator of investment funds than are individuals and firms, the existence of the banking sector should serve both to foster economic growth and to reduce risk. This is quite likely since the banks are specialists in the allocation of funds.

Offsetting this is the instability of the banking system itself. During most of the nineteenth century, commercial bank failures resulting from inadequate liquidity of the banking system and poor judgment by bankers added to the instability of the country. However, much of this has been corrected through regulation and supervision by the operations of the Federal Reserve Banks and through the insurance of commercial bank deposits. On the whole, most economists would agree that the banking sector is a vital part of our economic system and its net contribution to economic progress is positive.

SELECTED REFERENCES

Brunner, K., and A. Meltzer: "Predicting Velocity: Implications for Theory and Policy," *Journal of Finance*, May, 1963.

Federal Reserve Board, *The Federal Reserve System: Purposes and Functions*, Washington, D.C., 1963.

Friedman, M., and A. Schwartz: *A Monetary History of the United States*, Princeton, N.J., 1963.

———: "Money and Business Cycles," *Review of Economics and Statistics*, Special Supplement, Feb., 1963.

Goldenweiser, R.: *American Monetary Policy*, Committee for Economic Development, New York, 1950.

Johnson, H.: "Monetary Theory and Policy," *American Economic Review*, June, 1962.

Meigs, A.: *Free Reserves and the Money Supply*, Chicago, 1962.

Minsky, H.: "Central Banking and Money Market Changes," *Quarterly Journal of Economics*, May, 1957.

Modigliani, F.: "The Monetary Mechanism and Its Interaction with Real Phenomena," *Review of Economics and Statistics*, Special Supplement, Feb., 1963.

Selden, R. :*The Postwar Rise in the Velocity of Money*, National Bureau of Economic Research, New York, 1962.

Nonbank
Financial Institutions

15 In this chapter, we shall examine some of the more important types of nonbank financial institutions. The significant questions are: What sectors have found the claims of these institutions attractive? To which sectors have the funds raised by financial institutions been reallocated? Actually, we have already asked these questions with respect to the best known financial institution, the commercial bank. The answers for that institution are found in the balance sheet. Commercial banks raise money by selling claims, i.e., demand and time deposits, to just about every sector in the economy. Similarly, the funds raised were reallocated to about every sector in the economy. Most other financial institutions are considerably more specialized both with respect to the market for their claims and the sources of their earning assets. The institutions that will be considered in some detail are savings and loan associations, mutual savings banks, and life insurance companies. More briefly, we shall note the balance sheets of noninsured pension plans, non-life insurance companies, finance companies, security brokers and dealers, and open-end investment companies.

SAVINGS AND LOANS ASSOCIATIONS

Savings and loan associations are part of the major flow of funds sector called *Savings Institutions*. The associations are specialized mortgage lenders with over 86 per cent of financial assets held in mortgages. The primary source of funds for the associations is the sale of savings accounts and shares. These are mainly dividend bearing shares with these dividends treated as interest for tax purposes. The savings accounts, or shares, comprised over 95 per cent of liabilities and net worth in 1962.

There were 6,277 associations at the end of 1962; 1,941 were chartered federally and the remainder by the state. The federal associations, holding 53 per cent of total savings and loan association assets, were larger on the average than state-chartered associations. Most of the associations are organized on a mutual basis, with no distinction made between savings shares and common stock, but 11 states allow stock corporations.

In 1901, savings and loan associations held $565 million in assets. Over the next 29 years, assets grew until, in 1930, they were $8,829 million. Throughout the depressed '30's, savings and loan assets fell, reaching a low of $5,597 million in 1939. During the war years, growth in assets was positive, but slight, as there was little residential construction. By 1950, savings and loan assets stood at $16,893 million. By 1962, savings and loan assets were $93,816 million.

The number of associations did not grow with assets. In 1901, there were 5,302 associations. The number of associations increased, reaching a peak of 12,804 in 1927. At the peak year in assets, 1930, there were only 11,777 associations. The number fell even when assets began to rise, reaching a low in 1949, when there were 5,983 associations. Despite a more than six-fold increase in assets between 1949 and 1962, the number of associations increased only by about 5 per cent. The slow growth in numbers reflects mergers, which diminish numbers, and the establishment of branches, particularly in California.

Although all the states have savings and loan associations, the distribution is far from equal. Eighteen per cent of the assets of insured savings and loan associations are in California. The next largest savings and loan state, Illinois, holds less than 10 per cent. New York and Florida are the third and fourth largest savings and loan states, holding about 7 and 5 per cent of total assets, respectively. Even within states, there is considerable concentration. The savings and loan associations in the greater Los Angeles area hold over two-thirds of total California insured savings and loan assets, while Chicago holds almost 80 per cent of assets in Illinois.

THE SAVINGS
AND LOAN SYSTEM

The savings and loan system consists of a central bank for the associations, an organization for the insurance of savings deposits, and the individual savings and loan associations. The functions and structure of the system are somewhat similar to that of the Federal Reserve System. For the savings and loan industry, the system is called the *Federal Home Loan System.*

Federal Home Loan Banks. The depression of the early '30's brought forth a number of policies aimed at restoring prosperity. One of these was an attempt to increase residential construction by creating a large and accessible reservoir of credit for home financing. To accomplish this, Congress established the Federal Home Loan Bank Board in 1932, which was empowered to create regional Federal Home Loan banks. These banks, of which there are now 11, were to supply credit facilities to, and supervise the operations of, local thrift and home financing institutions.

In 1933, Congress gave the Home Loan Bank Board authority to issue federal charters and to supervise local mutual corporations, known as *Federal Savings and Loan Associations.* In 1934, as part of the National Housing Act, the Home Loan Bank Board was authorized to direct and manage the Federal Savings and Loan Insurance Corporation. The FSLIC has purposes similar to the Federal Deposit Insurance Corporation. The latter insures commercial bank deposits up to $10,000, and the former does the same for savings and loan association shares, or deposits.

All federal savings and loan associations must be both insured and members of the Federal Home Loan Bank System. State savings and loan associations, savings banks, and insurance companies may join the System and/or be insured. No insurance companies and only 33 savings banks are members. Unlike the situation in commercial banking, more associations are members of the System than are insured. Table 15-1 shows the division

Table 15-1

SAVINGS AND LOAN ASSOCIATIONS CLASSIFIED
BY SYSTEM AFFILIATION AND INSURANCE COVERAGE, DECEMBER, 1962

		ASSETS	
	Number	*$ millions*	*Per cent*
Total	6,277	93,816	100
Federal Home Loan Bank members	4,888	91,895	98
Insured by FSLIC	4,332	89,545	95

Source: *Savings and Home Finance Source Book, Home Loan Bank Board, USGPO 1963.*

of savings and loan associations by system affiliation and insurance coverage. Over two-thirds of all associations, controlling almost all the assets of the industry, are members of the system and/or insured. All member associations are subject to examination and regulation by the Board.

The seasonal variations of the level of savings, caused by withdrawals for tax payments, vacation and Christmas spending, etc., and advance lending committments made to builders by the associations, combine to create seasonal shortages of mortgage funds. Normally, the associations can secure relatively short-term advances from the Home Loan banks to offset these variations. The advances may be secured by mortgage collateral. The rates charged on advances varies among the banks, reflecting the regional nature of the market for mortgages. As of the end of 1962, the range was from 3.5 to 4 per cent. Advances for a single association may not exceed half the association's net assets or half its liabilities for sharesa nd deposits. Further, a member association may not borrow more than 17.5 per cent of its withdrawable savings accounts for purposes of *expanding* the association's mortgage holdings.

ADVANCES TO MEMBER ASSOCIATIONS is the most important single asset classification, or use of funds, of the Home Loan banks. Next is investment in United States Treasury securities. The two classifications account for over 96 per cent of total assets of the Home Loan banks.

As of December, 1962, the largest source of funds was the liability *Consolidated Obligations*. These are usually 6- to 11-month maturities, but may extend to 3 years. The obligations are the joint obligations of all the Home Loan banks and represent a means of raising funds from capital markets which savings and loan associations normally cannot tap directly. The breadth of the market for consolidated obligations is somewhat imperfectly indicated by Table 15-2. Among the 'all other investors' categories are business corporations and miscellaneous financial institutions.

Table 15-2

TYPES OF PURCHASERS AND RELATIVE HOLDINGS
OF FEDERAL HOME LOAN BANK CONSOLIDATED OBLIGATIONS
DECEMBER, 1952 AND 1962

| | PERCENTAGE HOLDINGS | |
Purchasers	1952	1962
Commercial banks......................	57	32
Mutual savings banks	2	5
Insurance companies...................	4	3
All other investors.....................	37	60
Total	100	100

Source: *Annual Report of the Federal Home Loan Bank Board, 1962, p. 19.*

As a digression, it is worth noting that the Federal Home Loan banks are included in the United States government sector of the Flow of Funds. The consolidated obligations are not guaranteed by the United States and are therefore not part of the public debt. The Home Loan banks are treated as one of the federally sponsored credit agencies set up to attract funds from capital markets, which are then made available to parts of the economy which otherwise would be unable to acquire funds directly. The part of the economy to which the Home Loan banks divert funds is home construction. The Federal National Mortgage Association is another federally sponsored credit agency which uses capital market funds to maintain a secondary market for home mortgages. A secondary market is one in which exchange of financial assets takes place after initial issuance. Thus, the secondary market in mortgages is similar in function to the organized securities exchanges. The other major federally sponsored credit agencies are mainly aimed at making capital market funds available to farmers and farm cooperatives. These include banks for cooperatives, Federal Intermediate Credit Banks, and Federal Land banks. The Home Loan banks are larger than any of the other federally sponsored credit agencies.

Turning back to the sources of funds available to the Home Loan banks, the second largest source consists of the demand and time deposits of member associations. Interest is paid on time deposits up to a maximum of 3.5 per cent for funds on deposit for more than 30 days. The deposits provide a means of making mortgage funds more mobile than otherwise would be the case. The mortgage market is notoriously regional, not national. There can be a strong demand for funds in one part of the nation where construction activity is at a high level and a very weak demand for mortgage money in another part. Associations with a weak demand for mortgage money can deposit excess funds with their Home Loan bank, which then can, sometimes by lending the funds to another Home Loan bank, make the funds available to far-distant mortgage markets where demand is strong.

Capital stock in the Home Loan banks is now owned completely by member associations, although, until 1951, the United States Treasury held stock also. Prior to 1962, member associations were required to subscribe to stock in their regional Home Loan bank in an amount equal to 2 per cent of the association's unpaid mortgage assets or $500, whichever was greater. The percentage requirement was reduced to 1 per cent for new members beginning in 1962. Member associations are required to hold stock equal to 8.5 per cent of the individual association's indebtedness to its Home Loan bank. Thus, the capital stock account grows with the size of the mortgage asets of the associations and with the total amount of advances made to associations.

Table 15-3 lists the major assets and liabilities of the Federal Home Loan banks for 1952, 1957, and 1962.

Regulation of Member Associations. Members of the Federal Home Loan Bank System are primarily long-term home mortgage lenders. In addition to mortgages, they are allowed to hold cash, Treasury securities, and obligations of the Federal National Mortgage Association and the Federal Home Loan banks.

Mortgages are primarily single-family, first mortgages on homes located within 50 miles of the particular savings and loan association's home office. Mortgage loans on any single piece of property usually may not exceed $35,000. To a limited extent, loans may be made on multi-unit residences. Also, associations are allowed to invest not more than 20 per cent of assets

Table 15-3

**MAJOR ASSETS AND LIABILITIES
OF FEDERAL HOME LOAN BANKS, 1952, 1957, 1962**
(In Millions of Dollars)

	1952	*1957*	*1962*
MAJOR ASSETS			
Advances to members......................	846	1,265	3,479
U.S. securities	311	908	1,531
Cash	43	63	173
MAJOR LIABILITIES			
Member deposits..........................	420	653	1,213
Consolidated obligations	449	826	2,707
Paid-in on capital stock	316	685	1,127

Sources: *Federal Reserve Bulletin, August, 1963, p. 1118; and Savings and Home Financing Source Book, Home Loan Bank Board, USGPO, 1963, p. 6.*

in mortgage loans beyond the 50-mile limit, but not beyond a 100-mile limit. Other regulations are applied to the term of mortgage and the ratio of mortgage loan to value of mortgaged property. As of May 1964, associations were allowed to invest up to 5 per cent of assets in conventional mortgages in any of the 216 densely populated urban areas classified as standard metropolitan areas.

The Balance Sheet of Savings and Loan Associations. Table 15-4 shows the financial assets and liabilities of the consolidated savings and loan association subsector. The only significant asset that has been omitted is real estate, which had been $21 million in 1952 and gradually rose to $450 million in 1962. Part of the real estate account is the value of the association office building. However, it also includes foreclosed mortgages. In 1935 the real estate account rose to $1,163 million, mainly due to foreclosures.

The only significant liability omitted is net worth. For mutual savings and loan associations, net worth consists solely of retained earnings. Some states, however, allow stock associations. In 1962, net worth was $6,539 million, a more than four-fold increase over the 1952 level.

The most striking aspect of Table 15-4 is the growth over the 10-year period. Two assets—demand deposits and currency, and securities—failed to grow as rapidly as total assets. On the other hand, other mortgages increased by over 900 per cent in the face of a total asset increase of about 400 per cent.

The relatively low level of cash assets has been commented on unfavorably as providing insufficient liquidity. The comparison is usually made with commercial banks, which, you will recall, are very liquid. However, savings and loan associations are not commercial banks. Savings accounts have a

Table 15-4

FINANCIAL ASSETS AND LIABILITIES
FOR THE CONSOLIDATED SAVINGS AND LOAN ASSOCIATION
SUBSECTOR, DECEMBER, 31, 1952, 1957, AND 1962
(In Billions of Dollars)

Item	1952	1957	1962
Total financial assets......................	22.2	47.1	91.4
Demand deposits and currency	0.9	1.5	2.7
Treasury securities......................	1.9	3.6	6.1
1- to 4-family mortgages	17.6	38.0	71.6
Other mortgages	0.8	2.0	7.4
Consumer credit*	0.3	0.6	1.2
Deposits and stock FHLB	0.7	1.3	2.3
Total liabilities	20.1	43.3	84.1
Savings accounts	19.2	41.9	80.4
Bank loans	0.1	0.1	0.2
FHLB advances........................	0.9	1.3	3.5

*Mainly short-term loans to savers on passbook collateral.
Source: *Flow of Funds Accounts, 1945–1962, 1963 Supplement*, Board of Governors
of the Federal Reserve System, pp. 15–16.

much lower turnover than do demand deposits. Further, the Home Loan banks provide a source of liquidity. The Home Loan banks, however, will not lend an association more than 50 per cent of its savings accounts under current regulations, so, even if the Home Loan banks could raise this much money without Treasury assistance, savings and loan associations were qualified to borrow a total of $40.2 billion as of the end of 1962. As with commercial banks, a run of shareholders attempting to withdraw their funds would lead to chaos. Under normal conditions, the savings and loan associations can rely on savings inflows, mortgage repayments, and Home Loan bank facilities to provide liquidity.

Much more serious is the possibility that savings and loan associations may be forced to invest in increasingly risky mortgages. In recent years, the rates paid by associations on savings shares have spiraled upward. Partly, this has been in response to rate increases on time deposits by commercial banks. Partly, this is due to the tax law, which allows associations to deduct reserves as a ratio of deposits so that the tax deduction is a function of the rate of growth of deposits. Mortgage rates have not risen as rapidly. To some extent, associations have taken on riskier mortgages in order to maintain the spread between the dividend rate on savings shares and the rate of return on assets. In 1952, for example, the ratio of mortgage loans to real estate purchase prices was 57.8 per cent. In 1962, the associations were lending an average of almost 73 per cent of the purchase price of real estate. In 1958, the ratio of delinquent mortgage loans to total mortgage loans was 1.3 per cent, but crept up to 1.7 per cent in 1962. The ultimate health of the industry depends on a depression-resistant economy and, ideally, a high level of home construction.

MUTUAL SAVINGS BANKS

Mutual savings banks are mutual corporations formed under state charter to provide a safe place for individual savings, with investment in long-term claims. Only 18 states provide for mutual savings banks. Eighty-five per cent of the banks are found in Massachusetts, New York, Connecticut, New Hampshire, and Maine. Fifty-eight per cent of mutual savings bank assets are in New York banks with Massachusetts, Connecticut, Pennsylvania and New Jersey accounting for most of the remainder of the industry's assets. In the last few years, attempts have been made to permit national chartering of mutual savings banks, which would allow a broader geographic distribution and more growth, but attempts have so far been unsuccessful.

There is no equivalent to the Home Loan banks for mutual savings banks, although they may join the Home Loan Bank System. The major source of funds are various kinds of savings deposits. Savings include regular savings accounts, Christmas and other club deposits, school savings deposits, and payroll savings accounts. Total savings deposits were 11 times greater than net worth in 1962. Savings deposits are insured by state funds and/or by the Federal Deposit Insurance Corporation. Regulation thus comes from states and the FDIC.

Mutual savings banks provide an interesting example of how financial institutions compete with each other in terms of increasing the variety of their financial claims. Massachusetts, Connecticut, and New York permit mutual savings banks to sell life insurance policies, presumably at low cost since agents' commissions are avoided. The total amount of such insurance is not large. In 1962, some $1.5 billion of life insurance policies were in force, a small amount compared to total liabilities and net worth of $46 billion.

Financial assets and liabilities for the mutual savings bank subsector are shown in Table 15-5. Financial assets comprised over 99 per cent of total assets in 1962. Financial assets have grown more rapidly for mutual savings banks between 1952 and 1962 than for commercial banks. However, savings and loan associations have shown far greater growth than either commercial banks or mutual savings banks. Of the $20.6 billion growth in financial assets over the decade, mutual savings banks have placed $16

Table 15-5

FINANCIAL ASSETS AND LIABILITIES FOR MUTUAL
SAVINGS BANKS, 1952, 1957, AND 1962 END OF YEAR
(In Billions of Dollars)

Item	1952	1957	1962
Total financial assets......................	25.1	34.9	45.7
Demand deposits and currency	0.7	0.8	0.7
Time deposits	0.2	0.1	0.2
U.S. treasury securities	9.5	7.9	6.7
State and local obligations	0.3	0.7	0.5
Corporate bonds	2.5	3.2	3.5
1- to 4-family mortgages	6.2	14.1	22.2
Other mortgages.......................	5.2	7.1	10.1
Consumer credit.......................	0.1	0.1	0.3
Other loans and corporate stock..........	0.4	0.9	1.5
Total liabilities = savings accounts	22.6	31.7	41.6

Source: *Flow of Funds Accounts, 1945–1962, 1963 Supplement* Board of Governors of the Federal Reserve System, pp. 15–16.

billion in 1- to 4-family mortgages. The total mortgage increase exceeded the growth in financial assets slightly. The increase in mortgages as well as almost all the other assets was financed partly by growth in savings accounts and partly by a decline in holdings of Treasury securities.

Although the changes that took place between 1952 and 1957 resulted in a less diversified list of financial assets, the aggregate portfolio is still considerably more diversified than it is for savings and loan associations. Even within the mortgage portfolio, mutual savings banks are more conservative than savings and loan associations. About two-thirds of residential mortgage loans held by mutual savings banks at the end of 1962 were either insured by the Federal Housing Administration or guaranteed by the Veteran's Administration. The comparable ratio for savings and loan associations was less than 15 per cent and, even for commercial banks, guaranteed and insured residential mortgages were only 39 per cent of total residential mortgages. Only life insurance companies hold a larger total of insured and guaranteed mortgage loans than do mutual savings banks.

The cash position of mutual savings banks is quite low, slightly more than 1.5 per cent of financial assets in 1962, whereas savings and loan associations held almost 3 per cent of their financial assets in cash. Given the fact that savings and loan associations have access to liquidity via the Home Loan banks whereas the mutual savings banks, for the most part, have no such standby, it is not clear that savings and loan asset portfolios are substantially more risky than mutual savings banks' portfolios.

SAVINGS INSTITUTIONS SECTOR

Mutual savings banks, savings and loan associations, and credit unions comprise the savings institutions sector. Credit unions have not been discussed separately. They are quite small, however, holding an aggregate of $2.1 billion in financial assets, mostly consumer credit loans, in 1962. The major source of funds is savings shares of individuals.

There is little point in presenting the financial assets and liabilities for the savings institutions sector, since the major subsector balance sheets have already been presented. Virtually all the funds are made available to the sector through savings shares and accounts and come almost exclusively from households. Almost three-fourths of the asset portfolio of the sector goes directly back to the household sector in the form of 1- to 4-family mortgages and consumer credit. Treating other mortgages as loans to business, slightly more than 15 per cent of the portfolio is invested in business mortgages, other debt instruments of businesses, and corporate stock. The remainder is invested in demand deposits, time deposits, currency, Treasury securities, and state and local obligations.

THE INSURANCE SECTOR

The insurance sector consists of three subsectors: life insurance companies; noninsured pension plans; and other insurance companies (fire and casualty companies, fraternal orders, and nonprofit medical plans). Over 60 per cent of total financial assets of the sector are in the life insurance subsector. The remaining financial assets are divided quite closely between noninsured pension plans and other insurance companies, with the former somewhat larger.

LIFE INSURANCE COMPANIES

At the end of 1962, there were 1,479 life insurance companies in the United States, 80 per cent organized as stock corporations and the remainder as mutual corporations. In 1950, there were only 649 life insurance companies.

The primary sources of life insurance funds result from the sale of insurance and annuity policies. A policyholder agrees to pay a series of premiums to the life insurance company, which, in turn, agrees to pay the policyholder, or someone named by the policyholder, either a fixed lump sum or periodic benefit payments. The premium payments stop and the benefit payments begin at a previously agreed upon time or when a given event occurs. With life insurance, the event at which benefit payments commence is the death of the policyholder. The amount of benefits may be predetermined, for example, as a lump-sum payment to the beneficiary or a series of payments for as long as the beneficiary lives.

There is enormous variety in the kinds of claims sold by life insurance companies, as the companies design new claims in order to increase demand. The major classifications are life insurance policies; annuities, including pension plans; and health insurance policies. Almost all the claims include both insurance and savings features. The savings aspects of insurance policy claims will be less attractive in periods of inflation than when prices are stable or declining, as with any fixed-value claim such as savings deposits.

Life Insurance. Life insurance may be divided into two main types— permanent and temporary. Permanent life insurance policies are those in which the holder agrees to a series of level premium payments for as long as he lives or for a set period of time. The life insurance company agrees to pay benefits *whenever* the holder dies. Temporary life insurance is usually referred to as *term insurance*. The holder makes a payment or series of payments and the insurance company agrees to pay benefits *if* the holder dies within a specified period of time. Savings features are almost nonexistent in very short term life insurance, but are quite important in permanent life insurance.

Pure life insurance, i.e., with no savings feature at all, is almost nonexistent. However, an example is useful. Life insurance companies use, as one of the determinants of the premium payment, what are called *mortality tables*. These are estimates of the probability of death for the population, classified in various ways, as by age, sex, and occupation. The tables are based on the actual death patterns found in the population. In effect, the mortality tables are similar to the probability tables used earlier in this book, but are not subjective.

Suppose a 20-year-old wants to be insured for $1,000 for one year, and the mortality tables indicate that the probability of death for 20-year-olds within a year is 0.00179. The expected value, or cost, of the life insurance benefit to the company is the conditional benefit payment, $1,000, times the probability that the benefit will be paid, 0.00179, or $1.79. To this, of course, must be added the costs of running the insurance company, but we shall ignore such costs. If the life insurance company has enough policyholders so that probabilities are meaningful, it will charge $1.79 as the premium for the one-year term insurance policy. Note that if it has only one policyholder of this age, the actual benefit payments made by the life insurance company will be either $1,000 or nothing, depending on whether or not the holder dies. With a large number of holders, the company expects to pay benefits for the 1.79/1,000 holders who will die in the year. The benefits will be $1,790/1,000 holders and the premium income, exclusive of costs, will be $1,790/1,000 holders.

Even in this case, some savings are possible. Not everyone will die at once. In fact, the odds are that most of those who die will die in the second half of the year because the probability of death increases with age. To be conservative, the life insurance company might assume equal deaths, hence benefit payments, each month. It could then invest the premiums in short-term highly marketable safe securities. Suppose the average annual rate of interest is 4 per cent. Over the year, half the premiums would be invested on the average, i.e., $895/1,000 policyholders, and interest income would be $35.80/1,000 policyholders over the year.

The policyholder may not receive the interest. Whether or not he does will depend on the state of competition among insurance companies and, perhaps, between insurance companies and other financial institutions. If competition is sufficiently keen, the insurance company will reduce the premiums. The minimum premium for the policy is equal to the present value of the expected value of benefit payments. In the illustration above, the premium could be as low as

$$0.00179(\$1,000)\frac{1}{1.04^{0.5}} = \$1.75 \quad \text{approximately,}$$

a savings of about $0.04 from what would have been the premium, had the premium receipts not been invested. Still ignoring administrative costs, the actual premium will range between $1.75 and $1.79 depending on competition.

Two factors emerge as important in determining premium. The first is the probability of paying benefits which is determined from the mortality table. The second is the interest rate which can be earned on the invested premiums.

Next, suppose the 20-year-old wanted to buy a term policy for two years. Assume that the probability of dying the second year of the policy is 0.00183. A single premium could be charged of

$$0.00179(\$1,000)\frac{1}{1.04^{0.5}} + 0.00183(\$1,000)\frac{1}{1.04^{1.5}} =$$
$$\$1.75 \quad + \quad \$1.73 \quad = \$3.48.$$

Note that the premium for the second year's coverage is increased by the mortality table, but sharply decreased by the additional year's interest. If the customer wanted to make two annual payments for the policy, the formulation would be

$$0.00179(\$1,000)\frac{1}{1.04^{0.5}} + 0.00183(\$1,000)\frac{1}{1.04^{0.5}} =$$

$$\$1.75 \qquad + \qquad \$1.79 \qquad = \$3.54.$$

The $0.06 difference between that portion of the two-year single premium to cover the second year's insurance of $1.73 and the second year's premium in the two-payment policy of $1.79 reflects the fact that, with the two-year premium, the insurance company has an additional year during which it can earn interest on the second year's premium.

If the policyholder preferred two annual payments of equal amount, called *level payments*, the life insurance company would determine this as follows: The single-premium two-year contract is $3.48, payable at the beginning of the contract period. Two payments, one coming at the beginning and the other after a year passes, must have the same present value as the single payment. Using x to stand for the level payment and 4 per cent as the discount factor, we have

$$\$3.48 = x + x\left(\frac{1}{1+i}\right)$$

$$= x\left(1 + \frac{1}{1+i}\right)$$

$$= x\left(1 + \frac{1}{1.04}\right),$$

$$\frac{\$3.48}{1.962} = x,$$

$$\$1.77 = x.$$

Since the company only needs $1.75 plus the interest earned on this amount to cover the first year's insurance, but will need $1.79 to cover the second year's insurance, the $0.02 extra on the first year's premium becomes a *liability reserve*, representing a prepayment of insurance premium. With a single payment for the two-year policy, the prepayment factor was even larger. However, most life insurance involves level premium payments. The reserves, or prepayments, generate the major share of the investment funds available to life insurance companies.

The longer the term of the insurance policy, the greater are the reserves. For example, assuming the probabilities of death during the 22, 23, and 24 years to be respectively 0.00186, 0.00189, and 0.00191, the lump sum premium for a five-year term policy taken out at age 20 with an interest rate of 4 per cent would be $8.41. The level premium would be almost $1.82, a larger prepayment than for the two-year policy.

Permanent life insurance premiums are determined in much the same way as are the premiums for term insurance. In effect permanent life insurance is a permanent term policy. Mortality tables are still important because, although it is certain that the benefits will ultimately be paid, the question of when benefits are likely to be paid is a partial determinant of the premium. Savings aspects are far more important than in short-term insurance simply because of the longer term of the contract. The savings feature is recognized more explicitly in permanent insurance than in term, with the recognition taking the form of a cash value. The cash value is the sum of the prepayments of premium resulting from level premiums plus the interest earned on the prepayments less administrative costs. This value may be realized by the policyholder either by *cashing in* his policy or by borrowing up to the cash value from the life insurance company.

Premium calculations are sharply affected by the estimated interest rate. However, the insurance company often must project expected interest rates over several decades. If the expected value of the benefit payments for each year are discounted by an interest rate above what the insurance companies can actually earn, the premiums will be too low to generate the necessary reserves. Ultimately, such insurance companies will be unable to honor their insurance contracts. If the interest rate used for discounting is below what actually can be earned, premiums will be too high. In the latter instance, demand for policies with important savings features will fall off. Instead, insurance will be switched to term policies as policyholders prefer to invest savings themselves at yields above what the insurance company uses for calculation.

Over the life of a permanent policy, interest rates can be expected to vary substantially. Since the policy is a firm commitment to pay benefits ultimately, insurance companies will tend to invest in safe financial assets and to be conservative in choosing the expected interest rate. Thus, during periods when interest rates are high, policyholders are apt to prefer term insurance with minimal savings aspects to low-yielding insurance savings. The reverse will be true when interest rates are low. To some extent, mutual life insurance companies offer an advantage in this respect over stock companies. The policyholders in mutual companies are effectively stockholders. When interest rates are high and insurance companies earn at a rate above the expected interest rate, policyholders in mutual companies receive dividends, which are really a reduction in premiums.

Life insurance policies can be subdivided beyond the classifications of term and permanent. Ordinary insurance includes policies to individuals in denominations of $1,000 or more. Group life insurance, which is mainly term, is sold to employee and other groups with the rate determined by group ages and occupations. Industrial life insurance is usually permanent, but in less than $1,000 denominations, with premium payments weekly, semimonthly, or monthly. Credit life insurance is decreasing term insurance, with the decrease set to match the declining indebtedness of the policyholder as he reduces his indebtedness on a home or consumer durable good.

About three-fourths of ordinary life insurance policies are permanent policies. The total split, however, between term and permanent insurance is almost equal, mainly because of the importance of group insurance, which, in 1962, accounted for about 31 per cent of all life insurance in force in the United States. Group life insurance has grown more rapidly than ordinary insurance. In 1952, group life accounted for only 23 per cent of all life insurance. The growth in group insurance, which, as has been said, is mainly term insurance, accounts for the decline in the relative importance of insurance reserves. Although policy reserves increased over the decade by more than $15.3 billion, reserves as a percentage of the total obligations and surplus fell from about 86 per cent in 1952 to 82 per cent in 1962.

Annuities.   These are policies on which the benefits are paid when an event other than death occurs. The bulk of annuity policies are designed to provide retirement income. Often, there is a death benefit feature, i.e., life insurance, if the beneficiary dies before retirement.

The determinants are much the same as with life insurance. Mortality tables are used to determine the length of time after retirement that the insurance company will have to pay benefits. The interest rate determines the earnings that will be generated by the reserves accumulated through the prepayment of premiums.

Annuities fall into three groups: individual annuities; group annuities, also called *insurance pension plans;* and supplementary contracts, which are part of a life insurance policy providing not only insurance but retirement income. Group annuities constituted over 72 per cent of the total annual income promised under all annuities in force with life insurance companies in 1962. In 1952, group annuities were only 52 per cent of total promised annuity income.

It has already been pointed out that insurance reserves have declined slightly relative to the total obligations and surplus of life insurance companies. This was attributed to the relative growth in importance of term insurance. The decline in reserves would have been even greater had it not been for the growth in annuities, particularly group pension plans. Reserves generated by insured pension plans rose from $7.7 billion in 1952 to $21.6 billion in 1962. In 1952, the pension plan reserves were about 12.3 per cent of total insurance company reserves. By 1962, they were almost 20 per cent. Subtracting pension reserves from total reserves, the remaining reserves would have fallen from 74.8 per cent of obligations and surplus in 1952 to 65.2 per cent in 1962. Insured pension funds have generated reserves which have, in effect, replaced the reserves of permanent life insurance policies. The substitution may be compared to that made by a merchant who finds demand waning for a product and so offers a new product in order to maintain sales.

Health Insurance.   This provides small reserves. Health policies are essentially term contracts. Most of these are group policies, as shown by the pattern of benefit payments. In 1962, group health benefit payments made by life insurance companies were over four times larger for group policies than for individuals.

GROSS SAVINGS

The primary source of funds for life insurance companies is premium income. For short-term policies, such as term life insurance and health insurance, premium income for a given year approximates the amount paid in benefits plus the costs of administration and, for stock companies, some profit. Although premiums from short-term policies do not generate substantial savings, because they are paid out rapidly, the funds can be invested in long-term assets as long as the volume of these premium payments does not decline. With a constant or growing level of short-term premium receipts, renewal premiums plus additions to premium payments year by year generate the funds needed to pay benefits, and the premiums can be invested in long-term assets. This is analagous to a business firm which, by renewing short-term loans, can use the short-term funds as if they were long-term. The flow of short-term premiums, thus, is permanent, even though the individual policies are not.

Table 15-6 presents the annual flows, which generate gross savings, and the changes in the levels of life insurance company liabilities for 1952, 1957, and 1962.

Table 15-6

ANNUAL GROSS SAVINGS AND LIABILITY RESERVE FLOWS AND BALANCE SHEET LEVELS FOR LIFE INSURANCE COMPANIES, 1952, 1957, AND 1962
(In Billions of Dollars)

	1952	1957	1962
FLOWS			
Investment income less operating exp.	0.1	0.1	0.1
Plus premiums received....................	8.4	11.6	14.7
Less benefits paid	4.1	6.7	9.3
Less credits imputed to consumers..........	4.2	4.2	5.3
Equals gross savings	0.1	1.0	0.3
Net increase in liabilities	4.2	4.2	5.3
Life insurance reserves	3.0	2.6	4.0
Pension fund reserves	1.1	1.6	1.3
BALANCE SHEET ITEMS			
Life insurance reserves	56.2	71.9	89.9
Pension fund reserves	7.7	14.1	21.6
Surplus and stock (net worth)*	9.5	15.3	21.8

Source: *Flow of Funds Accounts, 1945–1962, 1963 Supplement*, Board of Governors of the Federal Reserve System, pp. 68–69 and pp. 18–19.

*Net worth item derived by subtracting life insurance reserves and pension fund reserves from total obligations and surplus funds presented on p. 60 of the *1963 Life Insurance Fact Book*, Institute of Life Insurance, N.Y.

The credits to consumers consist of the prepayments of premiums via level payments and the interest credited as earnings of past accumulations on prepaid premiums. It will be noted that the increase in credits imputed to consumers equals the increase in life insurance and pension fund reserves. The latter reflect the savings of policyholders as they buy life insurance and pension fund claims. As with all financial institutions, gross savings are quite small, and the debt to equity ratio, using surplus and stock as net worth, is quite high.

EARNING ASSETS

Insurance companies are, on the whole, long-term investors. This results from the long-term commitment embodied in permanent life insurance policies and annuities. Even though term insurance has become relatively more important in recent years, the growth in premium income, shown in Table 15-6, has allowed the insurance companies to invest these short-term commitments in long-term assets. Should the rate of growth level off or decline in the future, with no relative decline in the importance of term insurance, short-term investments would become more important.

Table 15-7 indicates the financial assets held by life insurance companies at the end of 1952, 1957, and 1962.

Table 15-7

FINANCIAL ASSETS OF LIFE INSURANCE COMPANIES,
1952, 1957, AND 1962
(In Billions of Dollars)

	1952	1957	1962
Demand deposits and currency	1.1	1.3	1.5
U.S. government securities	10.3	7.1	6.3
State and local obligations	1.2	2.4	4.0
Corporate bonds	30.6	41.7	53.1
Corporate stock.........................	2.4	3.4	6.7
1- to 4-family mortgages	11.8	21.4	27.0
Other mortgages	9.5	13.8	20.0
Multifamily and commercial	7.8	11.2	16.6
Farm	1.7	2.6	3.4
Other loans.............................	2.7	4.1	6.6
Total financial assets................	69.6	95.2	125.0

Source: *Flow of Funds Accounts, 1945–1962, 1963 Supplement,* Board of Governors of the Federal Reserve System, pp. 18–19.

The asset portfolios of life insurance companies are determined partly by the long-term nature of life insurance obligations, i.e., policies. Since these obligations usually involve fixed-dollar sums, safety is an important feature. In addition, life insurance companies are regulated by the states in which the companies are domiciled.

State regulations vary among the states, but general patterns can be described. The generality of regulation is a result of the regional concentration of life insurance companies. As of 1960, 58 per cent of life insurance company assets belonged to companies domiciled in New York. Six states —New York, New Jersey, Massachusetts, Connecticut, Wisconsin, and Pennsylvania—contained companies owning almost 94 per cent of total life insurance company assets.

Regulations are aimed at safety of the individual investment as well as achieving diversification of the portfolio. Examples of the first point include the setting of maximum loan to value ratios on real estate mortgages, requiring that preferred and common stock investments have a history of earnings and dividend payments, and stipulating the nature and quantity of collateral for corporate bonds. As examples of restrictions aimed at achieving diversification, New York State limits bondholdings of one issuer to no more than 5 per cent of total assets, limits mortgage loans to a total not to exceed 40 per cent of total assets, and sets limitations of 2 per cent of total assets on preferred stock and 5 per cent on common stock.

As with all economic units, taxation plays a role in determining the asset portfolio. Life insurance companies are taxed differently than most corporations. Prior to 1959, life insurance companies paid ordinary corporate income taxes on only 15 per cent of investment income. Since 1959, this proportion has been raised to 21 or 22 per cent, depending on recent losses. In addition, the 1959 Act taxes half of operating income, i.e., gains beyond those needed for policy reserves, at normal corporate rates immediately and the remainder when and if distributed to stockholders. Prior to 1959, operating income was not taxed. Federal income taxes, as a percentage of total income, were 16 per cent in 1958 and rose to almost 21 per cent in 1960. Although there is no evidence to support the notion that the tax increase has been responsible for a shift in portfolio policies, the movement toward high-yielding corporate securities and tax-exempt state and local obligations, which movement is shown in Table 15-7, is consistent with the tax increase. Since the shift was obvious before the tax increase, it cannot be considered causal.

The major difference between the portfolios of thrift institutions and the portfolios of life insurance companies is the greater share of the portfolio invested in the business sector by life insurance companies. Corporate bonds and stock accounted for almost half of all financial assets over the decade. Almost 60 per cent of the corporate bonds and stock are issued by industrial corporations, and about 35 per cent are in public utilities. The remainder are railroad securities, mainly bonds. About two-thirds of the stockholdings are in common stock. In addition to the securities, the commercial mortgages go to the business sector. Finally, the other loans include finance company paper and loans made by policyholders on the cash value of policies. The sales finance paper provides indirect business financing, and some share of the policy loans are made for business purposes. Thus, life insurance companies may be viewed primarily, but not exclusively, as buyers of business claims.

Life insurance companies are dominant in the corporate bond market. In 1962, life insurance companies held over two-thirds of the $83 billion of corporate nonfinancial bonds outstanding. In 1952, the percentage was 58 per cent, and in 1945, only 48 per cent.

NONINSURED PENSION PLANS

We have already indicated the growing importance of insured pension plans to life insurance companies for which pension fund reserves were almost 20 per cent of total reserves in 1962. Total private pension fund reserves amounted to $78.8 billion in 1962. Excluded from this figure are the large state and local pension funds as well as the Federal plans, including Old Age Security Insurance (OASI). Governmental plans are included in the government sectors.

Contributions to noninsured pension plans are usually placed in a trust fund and administered by a commercial bank or by a union and/or management committee. The contributions depend on the amount of benefits to be paid, which is partly determined by mortality tables and partly by the investment yield. The contributions plus earnings on past contributions constitute the source of benefit payments. If the contributions and earnings are larger than benefit payments, noninsured pension plan reserves grow. In 1952, reserves were $8.8 billion, and they increased almost five times by 1962 to reach $42.2 billion. Since 1955, noninsured pension plan reserves have risen by over 250 per cent, from $16.7 billion to $42.2 billion, whereas insured pension fund reserves rose by about 190 per cent.

The growth differential is caused by the greater investment freedom of the noninsured funds. Even when administered by banks, pension fund assets are segregated from bank assets and are not subject to commercial bank portfolio regulations. Insurance companies are not allowed to invest pension fund reserves any differently than nonpension fund reserves. Despite the movement, noted earlier, of insurance company investment policies toward higher yields, the noninsured funds have considerably greater freedom. With higher yields, the noninsured funds can compete with lower premiums than life insurance companies for a given level of benefits.

As shown in Table 15-8, noninsured pension funds held almost three times as much common stock as did life insurance companies in 1962, despite the fact that total financial assets of the noninsured funds were about one-third those of life insurance companies. Over 87 per cent of noninsured pension fund financial assets were in corporate bonds and stocks in 1962, as com-

Table 15-8

**FINANCIAL ASSETS AND RESERVES OF NONINSURED
PENSION FUNDS, 1952, 1955, 1957, AND 1962**
(In Billions of Dollars)

Asset	1952	1955	1957	1962
Total financial assets..................	8.8	16.7	21.2	42.2
Demand deposits and currency	0.3	0.4	0.5	0.7
U.S. government securities	2.3	2.8	2.4	3.0
Corporate bonds	4.4	7.6	10.9	17.0
Corporate stock....................	1.7	5.6	6.9	19.9
1- to 4-family mortgages	0.1	0.3	0.5	1.5
Reserves	8.8	16.7	21.2	42.2

*As of 1955, includes multi-employer and union-administered plans.
Source: *Flow Funds Accounts, 1945–1962, 1963 Supplement*, Board of Governors of the Federal Reserve System. pp. 18–19.

pared with 38 per cent in 1955. Almost all the growth in noninsured pension funds between 1955 and 1962 was invested in corporate securities, more in stock than in bonds. Most of the stock investment has been in common stocks.

There are no state and local obligations included in the portfolios of the noninsured plans, because the tax-exempt features of these securities are of little value to the plans, which are not taxed. Beneficiaries pay personal taxes on benefits when received.

Stockholdings of the noninsured pension plans place these institutions as the largest stockholder group among financial institutions. As of the end of 1962, institutional stockholdings were

Noninsured pension funds ....$19.9 billion;
Other insurance companies .... 11.3 billion;
Life insurance companies .... 6.7 billion;
Open-end investment companies ...... 18.1 billion.

The largest stockholding sector was *households and nonprofit institutions* with $436.6 billion in corporate stockholdings at the end of 1962.

OTHER INSURANCE
COMPANIES

The final subsector in the insurance sector consists of fire and casualty companies, fraternal orders which offer life insurance, and nonprofit medical plans such as Blue Cross. Fire and casualty companies dominate the subsector, and most of the discussion will be cast in terms of their actions.

Premiums on fire, casualty, and health policies are set in much the same way as life insurance premiums. Instead of mortality tables, fire, casualty, and health experience tables are used, although these are not as accurate as mortality tables. The premium equals the expected value of the loss, plus what is called an *underwriting factor*, which includes administrative and other expenses plus profit. Interest is less important because the policies are term insurance. However, interest earnings are usually recognized in that the premium for, say, a three-year policy is less than three times as large as three annual premiums. Virtually all insurance is prepaid, and the prepayments are significant as a source of funds, as is shown in the $17.2 billion for prepaid premiums and benefit claims payable for 1962 in Table 15-9. As with term life insurance, the prepayments become virtually a permanent source of funds as long as insurance sales do not decline. The *benefit claims payable* account reflects the time gap, often substantial, between when the company estimates that it may have to pay a claim and when the payment is actually made.

Table 15-9

FINANCIAL ASSETS AND LIABILITIES OF "OTHER
INSURANCE COMPANIES," 1952, 1957, AND 1962
(In Billions of Dollars)

Item	1952	1957	1962
Total financial assets........................	18.1	25.3	37.0
Demand deposits and currency	1.5	1.5	1.6
U.S. government securities	6.5	6.4	6.8
State and local obligations	2.2	5.9	10.6
Corporate bonds	1.9	2.4	3.4
Corporate stock	4.4	6.8	11.3
Multifamily and commercial mortgages........	0.6	0.8	1.0
Policy loans...............................	0.1	0.1	0.1
Trade credit = receivables from agents	0.9	1.5	2.4
Total liabilities	10.4	14.7	19.6
Prepaid premiums & benefit claims payable....	8.9	12.8	17.2
Life insurance reserves	1.5	1.9	2.4

Source: *Flow of Funds Accounts, 1945–1962, 1963 Supplement*, Board of Governors of the Federal Reserve System, pp. 18–19.

Net worth is far more important for casualty and fire insurance companies than for almost any other kind of financial institution. In 1962, the ratio of financial liabilities to financial assets was 0.53 for the other insurance companies, indicating that 0.47 of financial assets were financed by net worth. The liabilities to financial assets ratio was 0.92 for life insurance companies in 1962, 1 for noninsured pension funds, 0.91 for mutual savings banks, 0.92 for savings and loan associations, and 0.92 for commercial banks.

The relative importance of net worth explains much of the nature of the asset portfolios of these companies. With mainly term insurance, even with growing insurance sales, we should expect a higher proportion of short-term investments than is found. We should also expect that long-term investments would be in safe securities. Actually, corporate stock is the single largest financial asset. The next largest, state and local obligations, are safe, but are probably important in the portfolio more because fire and casualty companies are taxed as ordinary corporations than because of safety. With a relatively high proportion of net worth, however, these companies have a safer capital structure than most financial institutions and so can afford to have a relatively risky asset portfolio.

The structure of the balance sheet for fire and casualty companies suggests that these firms perform two related but different kinds of functions. First, they sell insurance and acquire most funds this way. Creditors of fire and casualty companies are thus interested in the financial claims sold by the companies for purposes of protection against various kinds of calamities. Second, they sell stock. Stockholders are interested in the profits generated by insurance underwriting and are also interested in the returns generated by the asset portfolios of the fire and casualty companies. In this sense, the insurance companies act as do investment companies, selling expert investment knowledge and diversification. Common stockholders prefer holding the indirect claims issued by the fire and casualty companies rather than buying the same assets as are bought by the insurance firms.

SUMMARY OF INSURANCE SECTOR ACTIVITY

The insurance sector provides a sharp contrast to thrift institutions. The latter sell their claims almost exclusively to the household sector. Most of the financing for the insurance sector is also derived from households, although some life insurance savings and a substantial share of fire and casualty insurance prepaid premiums and benefit claims payable come from firms.

Sharper differences appear when we compare the asset portfolios of the two sectors. First, let us reclassify the financial asset categories in terms of which sector issued the claims. Demand deposits, currency, and time deposits are issued by financial institutions. Both United States Treasury securities and state and local obligations will be treated as being issued by a single government sector. Consumer credit is obviously issued by households. A problem is raised by mortgages, which are issued by several sectors. 1- to 4-family mortgages outstanding at the end of 1962 totaled $168.4 billion. Of this, almost 96 per cent represented claims on households. The remainder was divided between claims on unincorporated business and nonfinancial corporations. Given this division, 1- to 4-family mortgages can reasonably be treated as claims on households. Other mortgages include farm mortgages, commercial mortgages, and multi-unit residential mortgages. At the end of 1962, $82.1 billion of these were outstanding, with households having issued less than 4 per cent. The remainder were claims on farm business, nonfarm unincorporated firms, and nonfinancial business corporations. It appears reasonable to classify other mortgages with corporate stock and corporate bonds as obligations of business. Insurance policy loans will be handled as obligations of households. Table 15-10 shows the absolute and relative distributions of the asset portfolios of the two sectors at the end of 1962.

The percentage columns tell a simple story. These sectors have an almost identical distribution of assets with one important difference. Savings institutions invest almost the same proportion of their portfolios in the household sector as insurance companies invest in the business sector.

Insurance companies can be viewed roughly as institutions which take the surplus of households, i.e., the difference between gross savings and capital expenditures for households, and serve as a means of moving the surplus to businesses. Savings institutions work to move funds from surplus households to households whose capital expenditures exceed their gross savings.

Table 15-10

**FINANCIAL ASSET PORTFOLIOS FOR SAVINGS
AND INSURANCE SECTORS, DECEMBER, 31, 1962**

Sector Issuing Claim	SAVINGS SECTOR		INSURANCE SECTOR**	
	$ Billions	%	$ Billions	%
Other financial institutions	5.1	3.6	3.8	1.9
Government	15.8*	11.0	30.6	15.2
Business	22.0	15.4	132.2	65.4
Households	100.7	70.0	35.3	17.5
Totals	143.6	100.0	201.9	100.0

*Includes savings and loan deposits with Federal Home Loan Banks.
**Excludes trade credit of insurance companies to agents.
Source: *Flow of Funds Accounts, 1945–1962, 1963 Supplement,* Board of Governors of the Federal Reserve System, Tables 9 and 11.

The differences between the two sectors reflect differences in the nature of the institutions, in the kind of claims issued, and the regulations and laws under which they operate. Savings institutions are small relative to insurance companies and operate primarily in regional markets. In regional markets and particularly in the mortgage market, being close to the scene offers advantages. Claims on insurance companies are considerably less volatile than on savings accounts, which permits insurance companies to invest in relatively illiquid assets. Further, an important subsector of the insurance sector, noninsured pension funds, is subject to almost no portfolio regulations, and another subsector, fire and casualty companies, issues substantial amounts of stock.

FINANCE N.E.C.

The final financial sector contains the institutions not included elsewhere, i.e., *not elsewhere classified*. It contains five subsectors. In order of size, as of 1962, they are: finance companies, including sales finance companies, consumer finance companies, factors and other commercial lenders, mortgage companies, and miscellaneous short-term lenders; open-end investment companies; security brokers and dealers; agencies of foreign banks; and banks in United States possessions. We shall consider, briefly, only the largest three which, as of 1962, held 93 per cent of the total financial assets of the entire sector.

FINANCE COMPANIES

This subsector consists of short-term lenders to households and, to a lesser degree, firms. Business lending is on inventory and accounts receivable collateral. Household lending is primarily on a conditional sales contract basis, with the purchase of consumer durables as the basis of the financing.

Loans to households include indirect financing of business. Sellers of consumer goods sell the resulting account receivables to finance companies. In the absence of this financing, sellers would have to find other means of finance or, possibly, shift the burden of financing to the customer with the possibility of loss of sale.

Some of the short-term lenders perform services in addition to financing. Factors, for example, not only buy accounts receivable, but actually assume the entire credit-management function for the firm, because the factor takes the risk of noncollection unlike most sales finance companies. Customer and credit limits must be approved by the factor prior to sale.

Mortgage companies are somewhat different than most of the institutions in this subsector. As described earlier, mortgage companies perform the functions of a middleman in the process of mortgage placements. They are particularly important to national lenders, such as insurance companies, which are not in a position to evaluate, prepare, and service local mortgages. For the national lenders, the mortgage companies not only evaluate the mortgage risk and finally service the mortgage, i.e., collect mortgage payments and check on fulfillment of other mortgage terms, they also group the mortgages so that the insurance firms can make a single large placement of mortgage funds in an area rather than many small placements. The mortgage companies maintain a smooth flow of mortgage funds to the building industry by acquiring mortgages for inventory and holding them until ultimate lenders are ready to take over the financial assets. This is particularly important, for insurance companies often make *forward commitments* of loans and investments for periods of six months or even a year in advance of the actual placement. Forward commitments are made to large borrowers, such as those who build large apartment houses or residential tracts. The residential mortgages shown in Table 15-11 reflect the role of the mortgage companies.

Table 15-11

FINANCIAL ASSETS AND LIABILITIES
OF THE SUBSECTOR "FINANCE COMPANIES," 1952, 1957, AND 1962
(In Billions of Dollars)

Item	1952	1957	1962
Demand deposits and currency	1.2	1.6	2.3
1- to 4-family mortgages	0.5	0.8	2.6
Consumer credit.........................	7.1	13.5	17.2
Loans to business	2.6	4.8	9.8
Total financial assets....................	11.3	20.8	31.9
Corporate bonds	2.3	7.1	11.2
Bank loans not elsewhere classified..........	4.8	6.2	7.5
Other loans, commercial paper	1.4	2.3	4.7
Total liabilities	8.5	15.6	23.4

Source: *Flow of Funds Accounts, 1945–1962, 1963 Supplement*, Board of Governors of the Federal Reserve System, pp. 21 and 22.

Note in the table that finance companies have considerably less leverage in their balance sheets than do banks, thrift institutions, or life insurance companies. However, the finance companies have more leverage than non-life insurance companies, mainly because of the importance of fire and casualty companies.

Mortgage investments are not large in aggregate, partly because mortgage companies are relatively small and because the mortgage inventory of these companies are really short-term investments from the point of view of the mortgage companies, although they are long-term to the ultimate lender. As a result, mortgages have a higher turnover rate than would be suspected from their maturity dates. Nonetheless, mortgages grew more rapidly between 1952 and 1962 than did the total financial assets of the entire industry. Mainly, this reflects greater mortgage company activity, which reflects, in turn, the increased importance of life insurance companies in the mortgage market.

Both commercial paper and corporate bonds became relatively more important over the decade. Bonds were 27 per cent of liabilities in 1952 and almost 48 per cent in 1962. These represent primarily subordinated debentures issued by sales finance companies. The debentures were discussed earlier in relation to bank credit. To repeat what was said there, the increased importance of corporate bonds and open market, or commercial, paper represents attempts of the finance companies to reduce their reliance on bank credit.

Commercial paper was 16 per cent of total liabilities in 1952, but rose to 20 per cent by 1962. As noted earlier, commercial paper can be placed directly with investors or sold on the market. Direct placements have varied in importance since 1952. About 68 per cent of commercial paper was directly placed in 1952. The percentage was almost 80 per cent at the end of 1957. It was about 65 per cent at the end of 1962. There is a rough inverse relationship between the importance of direct placements and the willingness of banks to buy commercial paper. The latter depends on the degree of tightness of the money supply.

Regulation of finance companies is relatively slight. Various licensing fees are set by the states, and, particularly for personal finance companies, some states limit the size of a single office. Loan rates for consumer finance are subject to usury laws of the various states. Some states have minimum net worth requirements for personal loan companies. On the whole, however, finance companies are not subject to the relatively close regulation of banks, savings institutions, and life insurance companies.

OPEN-END INVESTMENT COMPANIES Open-end investment companies are mutual investment funds. Organized usually as corporations, but sometimes as trusts, these companies issue common stock claims, the proceeds of which are invested in purchasing financial assets, mainly corporate securities and, of these, mainly common stocks. The dividends, interest, and capital gains generated by the asset portfolios are used to cover the costs of administering the fund and to pay the stockholders. Virtually no earnings are retained in the investment company.

Holders of mutual fund shares, as the stockholders of investment companies are called, prefer holding claims on the investment companies rather than investing directly in business corporations because the funds offer diversification and investment knowledge, features which are either very expensive or impossible for a small investor to achieve independently. The mutual fund shares are redeemable at the request of the holder, with value determined by the net asset value, i.e., assets less liabilities, of the mutual fund's portfolio at the time of redemption. New issues of mutual fund shares are marketed in the same way as are stock issues of business corporations.

Open-end investment companies usually have a management contract with an investment adviser. The adviser may also act as a broker in executing securities orders for the company and may float the stock issues of the investment company. Adviser fees vary, with 1/4–1/2 per cent of average assets not uncommon. Often the investment company is started by someone who is interested in becoming the manager.

Regulations of investment companies are aimed at protecting the stockholders from fraud and are embodied in the Securities Act of 1933, the Securities Exchange Act of 1934, and the Investment Company Act of 1940. The first two laws apply to open-end investment companies in the same way that they apply to business corporations.

The Investment Company Act of 1940 is also aimed at protecting investors. To protect investors against funds which are too small to offer diversification, investment companies must have net worth of at least $100,000 before publicly issuing stock. Also, there must be at least 25 stockholders. No long-terms claims may be issued which are senior to common stock with respect to either income or assets. Bank loans are permitted if assets are three times the size of the bank loan.

The Act reflects the concern of Congress with mutual funds that have been set up by investment counselors or securities brokers and dealers as a means of increasing counseling, purchases and sales, or underwriting business. At least 40 per cent of the board of directors of the mutual fund must not be involved in management of the fund, i.e., have no pecuniary interest in the management contract. No more than half the board may be in the securities brokerage business. Management contracts and underwriting agreements are subject to majority approval of the stockholders and may not be in effect for more than two years without receiving annual approval of the majority of stockholders or directors.

Investment counselors are subject to regulation by the Securities and Exchange Commission through the Investment Adviser's Act of 1940. Primarily, this is aimed at preventing fraudulent, deceptive, or manipulative acts by investment advisers. Until 1960, the Act simply required registration and provision of information by investment advisers, excluding certain kinds of advisers who either provide advice at cost or advise small numbers of clients or financial institutions. In 1960, the Act was amended to permit the SEC to develop rules which would actively prevent fraud and other illegal acts.

Open-end investment companies usually pay no taxes. To qualify for this treatment, the company must receive 90 per cent of its income from security interest, dividends, or capital gains; income from the sale of securities held for three months or less must constitute no more than 30 per cent of income; 90 per cent or more of income must be paid out as dividends; and 50 per cent of total assets must be financial assets. The stockholders are, of course, taxed on their dividends. Investment companies are viewed essentially as conduits of income from securities issuers to the stockholders of the investment companies.

Financial assets for open-end investment companies are shown in Table

15-12. The most striking point is the very rapid growth shown by these institutions. No other financial institution has shown a more rapid growth rate between 1957 and 1962. The portfolio is primarily common stock, as is the capital structure. It should be noted again that, at the end of 1962, open-end investment companies were second only to noninsured pension funds in institutional holdings of common stocks.

Table 15-12

FINANCIAL ASSETS OF OPEN-END INVESTMENT COMPANIES, 1952, 1957, AND 1962
(In Billions of Dollars)

Asset	1952	1957	1962
Total financial assets.........................	3.9	8.7	21.3
Demand deposits and currency	0.1	0.2	0.6
U.S. government securities	0.1	0.3	0.7
Corporate bonds	0.3	0.8	1.8
Corporate stocks	3.3	7.4	18.1

Source: *Flow of Funds Accounts, 1945–1962, 1963 Supplement,* Board of Governors of the Federal Reserve System, pp. 21–22.

According to the *Study of Mutual Funds*, a report of the Committee on Interstate and Foreign Commerce of the House of Representatives*, almost 59 per cent of open-end investment company assets were in mutual funds investing solely in common stocks as of 1958. Balanced funds, investing in a combination of debt and equity securities, held 31 per cent of the industry's assets. The remaining 11 per cent was held by funds specializing in foreign securities, debt and preferred stocks, and special industry funds, e.g., uranium mining companies.

Excluded from the data shown in Table 15-12 are closed-end investment funds. These are funds which do not rely on common stock issues as a major source of funds. Instead of redeeming stock, holders sell the stock, usually over the counter. The balance sheet data for closed-end investment companies, which are quite small relative to the open-end companies, are included in the nonfinancial business sector.

BROKERS AND DEALERS

Brokers and dealers are not really financial institutions, but operate to facilitate financial activities by distributing securities and acting as middlemen in securities transactions. In process of fulfilling these functions, the dealers purchase securities on their own account both from customers who wish to alter their portfolios and from firms—as part of investment banking and underwriting. These securities

*United States Gov. Printing Office, Washington, D.C., 1962.

constitute an inventory. To finance the inventory, security loans are made, usually from banks.

Brokerage transactions also generate accounts receivable and accounts payable. The accounts payable occur when a customer orders the broker to sell securities, but leaves the proceeds from the sale on deposit with the broker, anticipating a purchase of securities in the future. Such balances may be required before the broker is willing to execute a large purchase order.

Accounts receivable are generated primarily by the execution of purchase orders by the broker before the broker receives payment. If the broker knows the customer, he will be willing to extend this kind of credit, much as a business firm will ship goods before receiving payment.

The broker-dealer group includes not only general securities operations but also a number of specialized dealer firms in United States government securities, state and local securities, etc. Specialists in government securities are exempt from regulation. Most brokers and dealers in interstate commerce are regulated by state and Federal law. The Federal law is part of the Securities Exchange Act of 1934, administered by the SEC. Mainly, it permits the SEC to refuse or suspend licenses for brokers and dealers who violate the provisions of the Securities Exchange Act on fraud, deception, manipulation, etc. The only capital structure requirement is that net capital be at least 5 per cent of indebtedness. In addition to the SEC regulations, brokers and dealers who are members of organized securities exchanges, such as the New York Stock Exchange, are subject to inspection and regulation by the particular exchange. Over-the-counter dealers and brokers are subject to regulation and examination by the National Association of

Table 15-13

FINANCIAL ASSETS AND LIABILITIES OF SECURITIES BROKERS AND DEALERS, 1952, 1957, AND 1962
(In Billions of Dollars)

Item	1952	1957	1962
Total financial assets	5.1	6.3	9.2
Demand deposits and currency	0.5	0.5	0.6
U.S. gov. securities	0.8	0.7	1.8
Other securities*	2.2	2.2	2.1
Customer debit balances	1.5	2.8	4.6
Total liabilities	3.1	4.3	7.2
Security loans from banks	2.1	2.6	5.1
Security loans from agencies of foreign banks	0.2	0.7	0.7
Customer credit balances	0.8	1.0	1.3

*Includes state and local obligations and corporate bonds and stocks.

Source: *Flow of Funds Accounts, 1945–1962, 1963 Supplement,* Board of Governors of the Federal Reserve System, pp. 21–22.

Securities Dealers. The SEC coordinates its examinations with both the exchanges and the NASD.

Financial assets and liabilities of brokers and dealers are shown in Table 15-13. It should be noted that virtually all debt is short-term. Currently, those broker-dealers who are incorporated are not permitted to make public issues of their own stock, but this may be changed in the future. The result of such a change could be not only a transformation of the capital structure of broker-dealers, but some movement in the direction of acquiring longer-term financial assets, i.e., becoming an investment company.

FINANCIAL INSTITUTIONS
AND REDISTRIBUTION OF SAVINGS

It was argued earlier that financial institutions could affect GNP and the rate of growth of GNP either by changing the level of savings, thus increasing investment, or by changing the productivity of investment. On theoretical grounds it was not possible to predict what the effect would be, and a reduction in the growth rate of GNP is as much a possibility as is an increase. An attempt to test the effect of financial institutions on the growth and level of GNP is beyond the scope of this book and, in any event, would be quite difficult. A simpler and cruder question, however, may be asked: Do financial institutions redistribute savings among sectors? The answer to this question does not really answer whether financial institutions redistribute savings so as to increase the productivity of investment. It is possible to have redistribution take place within sectors and increase investment productivity. It is also possible to have redistribution among sectors, but have no change in investment productivity. Nonetheless, if a redistribution does take place among sectors, it suggests that the savings-investment process has been affected by financial institutions and, therefore, that the study of financial institutions has economic relevance.

The test that will be applied to answer the question of whether financial institutions redistribute savings among sectors is quite simple in concept. The percentage of outstanding financial claims on financial institutions held by the household and nonprofit sectors, the nonfinancial business sector (including corporations, unincorporated businesses and farms), federal government, and the state and local government sectors will be compared with the percentage of total financial assets representing claims on the same real sectors held by financial institutions. The financial institutions whose balance sheets will be examined are commercial banks, savings institutions, life insurance companies, pension funds, mutual funds, and sales finance companies.

Table 15-14(a) shows the real sectors' holdings of claims on financial

Table 15-14(a)

HOLDINGS OF CLAIMS ON FINANCIAL INSTITUTIONS BY THE HOUSEHOLD AND NONPROFIT, BUSINESS, FEDERAL GOVERNMENT, AND STATE AND LOCAL GOVERNMENT SECTORS, 1952, 1957, AND 1962

	1952		1957		1962	
Sector and Item	*$ Billions*	%	*$ Billions*	%	*$ Billions*	%
Households total	229.5	77	307.6	74	459.1	76
Demand dep. & currency	57.8	19	60.8	15	71.2	12
Time dep. & savings acct.	93.6	31	129.0	31	210.5	35
Life ins. & pens. reserve.	74.2	25	109.1	26	156.1	26
Mutual fund shares.	3.9	1	8.7	2	21.3	4
Firms total	46.4	15	51.4	12	56.0	9
Demand dep. & currency	45.5	15	50.4	12	49.8	8
Time dep. & savings acct.	0.9	*	1.0	*	6.2	1
Fed. government total.	5.4	2	4.0	1	7.3	1
Demand dep. & currency	5.1	2	3.7	1	7.0	1
Time dep. & savings acct.	0.3	*	0.3	*	0.3	*
State & local governments	10.6	4	13.6	3	18.7	3
Demand dep. & currency	9.0	3	10.8	3	12.3	2
Time dep. & savings acct.	1.6	1	2.8	1	6.4	1
Total real sectors	229.5	98	376.6	90	541.1	89
Total Liabilities of						
Financial Institutions ·	299.3	100	412.6	100	603.5	100
Commercial banks	154.7	50	180.4	44	241.9	40
Savings institutions	44.1	15	78.4	19	131.9	22
Insurance	83.1	28	121.8	30	173.3	29
Finance n.e.c.	17.4	6	32.0	8	56.4	9

*Less than 1 per cent.
Items do not necessarily add to totals because of rounding.
Source: *Flow of Funds Account, 1945–1962, 1963 Supplement*, Board of Governors of the Federal Reserve System, pp. 4–12.

sectors. It is assumed that all insurance and pension fund reserves are held by households, even though firms may hold life insurance policies on important executives. However, this is the assumption made by the Federal Reserve. Holdings of stocks and bonds issued by commercial banks, and other incorporated financial institutions are omitted because the flow of funds accounts do not differentiate between the stock and bond issues of nonfinancial business corporations and those of financial corporations. Nonetheless, the most important financial claims are shown.

The holdings shown as a percentage of the total liabilities of financial institutions reveal some interesting phenomena. Most striking is the relative decline in the importance of holdings of demand deposits and currency. Except for the federal government, all sectors held relatively less money in 1962 than was held in 1952. This is reflected also in the fact that the importance of financial claims issued by commercial banks fell relative to the total financial liabilities of all financial institutions. Savings institutions and financial institutions N.E.C. had a relative growth between 1952 and 1962 equal to the decline in the relative importance of commercial banking.

It will be noted that real sectors do not hold all the liabilities issued by financial institutions. Part of the remainder is held by the one real sector omitted from the table, the rest of the world. The foreign sector, however, held about 1 per cent of the total liabilities of the financial sectors for the three observations. The difference is caused primarily because the financial sector statements are not completely consolidated, i.e., claims of sales finance companies on banks, and vice versa, are not consolidated. Thus, an increasing percentage of the liabilities of financial institutions are held by other financial institutions.

Table 15-14(b) shows the holdings by financial institutions of claims issued by households, firms, and governments. The relatively small amount of bank loans to nonprofit institutions have been omitted. Bonds and mortgages issued by nonfinancial businesses are lumped with all bonds and other mortgages in the flow of funds. The bond and other mortgage holdings of financial institutions issued by nonfinancial business was estimated by assuming that institutional holdings of nonfinancial bonds and mortgages

Table 15-14(b)

HOLDINGS OF CLAIMS ON REAL SECTORS BY FINANCIAL SECTORS, 1952, 1957, AND 1962

Sector and Item	1952 $ Billions	1952 %	1957 $ Billions	1957 %	1962 $ Billions	1962 %
Households total	65.2	20	123.9	27	242.4	36
Consumer credit	17.6	5	32.4	7	47.5	7
1- to 4-family mortgages	47.6	15	91.5	20	194.9	29
Firms total	99.0	30	148.2	33	228.2	34
Bonds*	37.2	11	52.2	11	65.9	10
Stocks	13.2	4	26.2	6	57.8	9
Other mortgages**	19.9	6	29.6	6	48.8	7
Bank loans, n.e.c.	28.7	9	40.2	10	55.7	8
Federal gov. total	97.3	29	89.9	19	102.4	15
State & local gov. total	14.1	4	23.1	5	40.4	6
Total real sectors' claims Held by financial institutions	275.6	83	385.1	84	613.4	91
Total financial assets of financial sectors	333.9	100	462.9	100	677.9	100

*Bonds of nonfinancial corporations as a percentage of total corporate bonds were 87% in 1952, 85% in 1957, and 82% in 1962.

**Other mortages issued by firms as a percentage of total other mortgages were 97% in 1952, 96% in 1957, and 96% in 1962.

Source: *Flow of Funds Accounts, 1945–1962, 1963 Supplement*, Board of Governors of the Federal Reserve System, pp. 21–22.

were relatively the same as the holdings of the entire economy. For example, 85 per cent of all coprporate bonds outstanding in 1957 were issued by nonfinancial business. It was therefore assumed that 85 per cent of bond-holdings by financial institutions were also bonds issued by nonfinancial corporations.

Stocks present a more difficult problem. The flow of funds data show stocks at market value held by the various sectors. However, stock is not shown as a liability of any sector. Since many financial institutions are stock-issuing corporations, there is no way of separating nonfinancial corporate stock from total stockholdings. Stockholdings of financial institutions have all been treated as if the stock had been issued by nonfinancial corporations, which biases the stock estimate upward. The same treatment was applied in Table 15-14(a) where stockholdings by real sectors were treated as if the stock had all been issued by nonfinancial corporations despite the fact that some of the stock was in fact issued by banks, fire and casualty insurance companies, and other financial institutions.

Institutional holdings show a sharp relative increase for 1- to 4-family mortgages and a sharp decline in holdings of United States government securities. The increase in stock reflects both an increase in number of shares and the effects of stock prices. The remainder of the claims on real sectors held by financial institutions has been surprisingly stable in relative terms.

Table 15-14(c) summarizes the two previous tables. The first pair of columns for each year indicates the absolute and relative amounts of funds supplied to financial institutions by the real sectors. The second pair of columns indicates the absolute and relative amounts of funds supplied to the real sectors by the financial sectors. When the first pair of columns is larger than the second for a given sector, that sector may be viewed as a net supplier of funds, i.e., it provides more funds to financial institutions than it receives from them. The only net supplier is the household sector. Even here, the percentages indicate that households have become less of a net supplier over the period studied.

Firms have been net demanders of funds over the entire period since they receive more funds from financial institutions than the firms supply to the institutions. Between 1952 and 1962, the percentage of financial institutions' liabilities held by firms fell from 15 to 9 per cent, while the percentage of financial institutions' assets which were obligations of firms rose from 30 to 34 per cent. In effect, the relative demand position has become larger over the period.

The United States government had the strongest net demand position of all the real sectors. In 1952, financial institutions held about $18 of Treasury securities for each dollar of claims on financial institutions held by the Treasury. By 1957, the ratio had risen to $22.50 of Treasury securities held by institutions for each dollar of claims on institutions held by the Treasury. The ratio was about $14 in 1962, when, in contrast, the ratio for firms was only $4.08.

Table 15-14(c)

SUMMARY OF ASSETS OF FINANCIAL INSTITUTIONS ISSUED
BY REAL SECTORS, AND FINANCIAL INSTITUTIONS' LIABILITIES
HELD BY REAL SECTORS, 1952, 1957, AND 1962

| | 1952 | | | |
Sector	$ Billions	% of Liabilities	$ Billions	% of Assets
Households	229.5	77	65.2	20
Firms	46.4	15	99.0	30
U.S. gov.	5.4	2	97.3	29
State & local gov.	10.6	4	14.1	4
Totals	229.5	98	275.6	83
	1957			
Sector	$ Billions	% of Liabilities	$ Billions	% of Assets
Households	307.6	74	123.9	27
Firms	51.4	12	148.2	33
U.S. gov.	4.0	1	89.9	19
State & local gov.	13.6	3	23.1	5
Totals	376.6	90	385.1	84
	1962			
Sector	$ Billions	% of Liabilities	$ Billions	% of Assets
Households	459.1	76	242.4	36
Firms	56.0	9	228.2	34
U.S. gov.	7.3	1	102.4	15
State & local gov.	18.7	3	40.4	6
Totals	541.1	89	613.4	91

Source: *Flow of Funds Accounts, 1945–1962, 1963 Supplement*, Board of Governors of the Federal Reserve System, pp. 21–22.

State and local governments also had net demand positions with respect to financial institutions. Unlike the federal government, the relative net demand position rose over the period 1952–1962 from a ratio of $1.33 of claims on state and local government held by financial institutions for each dollar of claims on financial institutions held by state and local governments to a ratio of $2.16 by 1962.

In order of strength of net demand position, the federal government was first of the real sectors, followed by firms, and finally by state and local governments. By 1962, however, financial institutions held over $2 of claims on firms for each dollar of claims on the Treasury.

To sum up, financial institutions do distribute savings among sectors. As would be guessed, households are suppliers of funds. The allocation of household savings via financial institutions goes to the United States government, business firms, and state and local governments. This, however, does not imply either that household savings are necessarily increased because of financial institutions or that the productivity of real investments are increased.

SELECTED REFERENCES

Alhadeff, D.: "Credit Controls and Financial Intermediaries," *American Economic Review*, Sept., 1960.

Andrews, U.: "The Supply of Loanable Funds from Non-Insured . . . Pension Trusts," *Journal of Finance*, May, 1961.

Brimmer, A.: *Life Insurance Companies in the Capital Market*, U. of Mich., 1962.

Brunner, K., and A. Meltzer: "The Place of Financial Intermediaries in the Transmission of Monetary Policies," *American Economic Review*, May, 1963.

Clarkson, J.: *Portfolio Selection: A Simulation of Trust Investment*, Prentice-Hall, Englewood Cliffs, N.J., 1962.

Commission on Money and Credit, *Industry Report on Life Insurance Companies*, Prentice-Hall, Englewood Cliffs, N.J., 1963.

————: *Industry Report on Mutual Savings Banks*, Prentice-Hall, Englewood Cliffs, N.J., 1963.

————: *Industry Report on Property and Casualty Insurance Companies*, Prentice-Hall, Englewood Cliffs, N.J., 1963.

————: *Industry Report on Savings and Loan Associations*, Prentice-Hall, Englewood Cliffs, N.J., 1963.

Committee of Interstate and Foreign Commerce, *A Study of Mutual Funds*, Washington, D.C., 1962.

Culbertson, J., J. Gurley, and, E. Shaw: "Intermediaries and Monetary Theory," *American Economic Review*, Mar., 1958.

Freedman, R.: "Federal Credit Agencies and the Structure of Money Markets, Interest Rates, and the Availability of Capital," *Quarterly Journal of Economics*, Aug., 1955.

Garvy, G.: "Structural Aspects of Money Velocity," *Quarterly Journal of Economics*, Aug., 1959. Also see "Comments" by T. Miller and Garvy's "Reply" in the *Journal*, Nov., 1960.

Gurley, J., and E. Shaw: "Financial Aspects of Economic Development," *American Economic Review*, Sept., 1955.

————: "Financial Institutions and Interrelationships," *Journal of Finance*, May, 1956.

Klaman, S.: *The Post-War Residential Mortgage Market*, National Bureau of Economic Research, New York, 1961.

Life Insurance Association of America, *Life Insurance Fact Book*, Washington, D.C., 1963.

Miller, N.: "Trends in Private Pension Funds," *Journal of Finance*, May 1961.

Securities and Exchange Commission, *Report of Special Study of Securities Markets*, Parts, 1–5, Washington, D.C., 1963–'64.

Smith, P.: "Cost of Providing Consumer Credit," *Journal of Finance*, Sept., 1962.

————: "Financial Intermediaries and Monetary Controls," *Quarterly Journal of Economics*, Nov., 1959.

Tobin, J., and E. Brainard: "Financial Intermediaries and the Effectiveness of Monetary Controls," *American Economic Review*, May, 1963.

Wright, K., C. Torrance, and S. Mills: "Gross Flows of Funds through Savings Institutions," *Journal of Finance*, May, 1960.

The Flow of Funds
and Corporate Finance

16

In this, the final chapter, we shall discuss three matters: First, the actual financial assets and liabilities for the real sectors will be presented. You will recall that, in Chapters 10 and 11, the conceptual balance sheets for the real sectors were presented, excluding the role of financial institutions. Financial institutions will be included in the data shown here, but real assets will be excluded. Second, the actual flow of funds matrix published by the Federal Reserve will be presented and discussed. Here, particular concern will be shown for the differences between the conceptual equalities developed in Chapters 10 and 11 and the actual data published. Finally, we shall consider the relationships among growth of the corporate sector, aggregate savings in the economy, and securities prices.

FINANCIAL ASSETS AND LIABILITIES
FOR THE REAL SECTORS

Financial assets are usually larger than liabilities for financial institutions. This is because the institutions typically invest most of their assets in financial claims. The same is not usually true for the real sectors. For households and firms, real asset investment is a significant share, often a predominant share, of total assets, and financial assets tend to be relatively small. This is not always apparent in the data, particularly

394

for households. In the data to be examined, household financial assets will exceed liabilities. Household net worth is not included in the data and a substantial part of this is used to finance financial assets. Further, the liability structure of households tends to be small, including primarily mortgage indebtedness and consumer credit. And, of course, the household sector includes nonprofit institutions, which have little debt but may hold substantial quantities of financial assets.

Table 16-1 shows the absolute and relative holdings of financial assets for real sectors. In effect, the data show the extent to which each real sector supplies funds to other sectors. One important financial asset is omitted— the proprietary interest of the household sector in unincorporated business.

Table 16-1

FINANCIAL ASSETS HELD BY REAL SECTORS
1952, 1957, AND 1962

	1952		1957		1962	
Sector	$ Billion	%	$ Billion	%	$ Billion	%
Households and nonprofit ..	515.1	68.4	728.3	70.2	1074.2	71.4
Farms	7.5	1.0	7.2	0.7	7.0	0.5
Unincorporated nonfarm business	16.2	2.2	19.8	1.9	21.8	1.5
Corporate nonfinancial business	122.1	16.2	158.1	15.2	211.7	14.1
U.S. government	33.3	4.4	38.9	3.8	56.2	3.7
State and local governments	28.1	3.7	43.0	4.1	61.9	4.1
Rest of world	30.6	4.1	42.8	4.1	69.0	4.6
Totals.............	752.9	100.0	1038.1	100.0	1501.8	100.0

Source: *Flow of Funds Accounts, 1945–62, 1963 Supplement,* Board of Governors of the Federal Reserve System, pp. 4–12.

The real sectors have held a fairly constant percentage of all financial assets, about 67 per cent, over the 10-year period. On the whole, the relative distribution of financial asset holdings among the real sectors has also been nearly constant. Households show a slight relative increase, and corporations show a slight decline. No other sector has had a relative change of as much as 1 percentage point. Dollar holdings approximately doubled over the 10-year period.

In Table 16-2, liabilities are shown in absolute and relative terms for the real sectors. Data for corporations have been altered to include an estimate of stock issues. The Federal Reserve Board shows stockholdings at market value as an asset of the holding sector, but not as a liability of the issuing sector. Since stock is issued by banks, insurance companies, finance companies, and the rest of the world, as well as by nonfinancial corporations,

Table 16-2

FINANCIAL CLAIMS ON REAL SECTOR,
BY ISSUING SECTOR 1952, 1957, 1962

Sector	1952		1957		1962	
	$ Billion	%	$ Billion	%	$ Billion	%
Households and nonprofit institutions	88.7	12.6	160.7	17.1	247.6	18.5
Farms	13.6	1.9	17.8	1.9	27.2	2.0
Unincorporated, nonfarm business..................	25.6	3.6	37.6	4.0	55.3	4.1
Nonfinancial business corporations*	232.6	33.0	352.9	37.5	542.9	40.5
U.S. government	255.5	36.3	251.6	26.8	289.0	21.6
State and local governments ..	55.1	7.8	71.6	7.6	110.9	8.3
Rest of world	32.9	4.7	47.9	5.1	68.0	5.1
Totals...............	704.0	100.0	940.1	100.0	1340.9	100.0

*Stock estimate for 1952 was $117 billion; for 1957, $188.1 billion; and for 1962, $317.9 billion.

Source: *Flow of Funds Accounts, 1945–1962, 1963 Supplement*, Board of Governors of the Federal Reserve System, pp. 4–12.

the liability is difficult to estimate. The Federal Reserve, however, does provide data on net stock issues at market value by issuing sector. Nonfinancial corporations issued 63 per cent of the net stock issues over the period 1946–1962. It has therefore been assumed that 63 per cent of total stockholdings are claims on the nonfinancial corporate sector. Two possible sources of error exist: If nonfinancial corporations issued more than 63 per cent of net stock prior to 1946, the estimate is lower than it should be, and vice versa; if stock prices of nonfinancial business corporations have risen more rapidly than prices of all stocks, the estimate is again too low, and the reverse is also true.

All but three of the sectors have shown little relative change over the period. The relative shares of the household and corporate business sectors increased substantially over the decade. Federal government was the only sector that declined, falling from the largest real-sector issuer of claims to second largest, with business corporations taking the lead among the real sectors. Over-all, real sector liabilities grew by a little less than 100 per cent.

As indicated earlier, the real sectors tend to issue more claims than they hold financial assets. The only sectors for which this is not true are households, where the net worth account is very large and not shown, and the foreign sector. The foreign sector, however, has no real assets attributed to it. We measure only the financial assets which have been purchased from domestic sectors, and the financial claims which have been sold to domestic sectors. All the transactions in real assets by the foreign sector are treated as transactions on current account, leaving the rest of the world balance sheet composed solely of financial items and net worth, i.e., the balance of trade on current account.

THE MATRIX OF FINANCIAL ASSETS AND LIABILITIES   The Federal Reserve prepares an annual table of the financial assets and liabilities for all sectors. Since it is presented in matrix form, we can observe not only the claims issued by each sector, but also the sectors which hold these claims as financial assets. The matrix as of December, 1963, is reproduced as Table 16-3.

The matrix provides an interesting contrast of two approaches to the financial process. By considering the sectors and moving vertically down the page, finance is treated on a sectoral basis, which is the primary approach used in this book. Alternatively, we can move across the page horizontally, by row, and study finance in terms of markets for particular instruments, such as corporate stocks, mortgages, or consumer credit. The difference between the two approaches is a matter of emphasis, and both are equally valid.

The data shown in the table are consistent with the data shown earlier in this chapter and Chapter 15. The household sector is the major source of finance for the entire economy. All the other real sectors, except the foreign sector, are net demanders of finance. All the financial sectors are net suppliers.

FINANCIAL ASSETS AND LIABILITIES OF NONFINANCIAL CORPORATIONS   Of all the real sectors, we are particularly concerned with the corporate nonfinancial sector. Table 16-4 contains the financial assets and liabilities for nonfinancial business corporations for 1952, 1957, and 1962. The following assets increased over the decade at a more rapid rate than total corporate financial assets: time deposits; state and local obligations; holdings of finance company paper, direct placements mainly; trade credit; and holdings of foreign exchange and investments in foreign countries. The last category moved up in relative position from fourth largest financial asset in 1952 to second largest in 1962. Trade credit was the largest financial asset category in all three observations. Cash holdings declined relatively from about 24 per cent of total assets in 1952 to 15 per cent in 1962, which is consistent with the observations made in the previous chapter about the diminishing importance of commercial banking deposit liabilities. United States government securities were the only financial asset showing an absolute decline over the decade, although holdings increased between 1957 and 1962.

Over the decade, liabilities rose by about 96 per cent of the 1952 level, i.e., roughly doubled. Mortgage financing, bank loans, loans from finance

Table 16-3

FINANCIAL ASSETS AND LIABILITIES, DECEMBER 31, 1963
(Amounts Outstanding in Billions of Dollars)

Code	Transaction Category	Consumer and nonprofit Org. A	L	Farm A	L	Non-corporate A	L	Corporate A	L	U.S. Gov. A	L	State and Local A	L	Banking System A	L	Savings Institutions A	L	Insurance A	L	Finance n.e.c. A	L	Rest of the World A	L	All Sectors A	L
K	Total assets	1,208.0		7.1		22.2		226.7		59.1		67.7		317.5		161.8		220.7		75.8		73.0		2,439.6	
L	Total liabilities		274.7		30.3		62.4		243.7		294.9		120.7		294.3		148.5		187.3		40.2		73.5		1,770.5
M	Gold and U.S. official fgn. exchange													16.8									26.7	43.5	1.2
N	Treasury currency										2.8			5.4										5.4	2.8
O	Demand deposits and currency	77.0						30.8		*					170.4					4.5				163.8	170.4
P	Private domestic			5.5		12.5						13.2			157.6	4.0		3.9						151.5	157.6
Q	U.S. gov.									7.9					8.4									7.9	8.4
R	Foreign														4.4							4.4		4.4	4.4
S	Time and savings accounts	232.1													112.4	1.4	143.5							255.9	255.9
T	At commercial banks	89.8										8.1			112.4	0.2								112.4	112.4
U	At savings institutions	142.3								0.3						1.2	143.5							143.5	143.5
V	Life insurance reserves	102.9									6.7								96.2					102.9	102.9
W	Pension reserves	117.8									17.2		27.2						73.4					117.8	117.8
X	Credit market instruments	670.2	264.0	26.6		6.2	64.5	37.7	177.4	43.3	261.8	46.4	90.8	281.9	100.1	154.1	5.0	214.3		64.1	27.6	25.9	29.7	1,544.1	947.3
Y	U.S. gov. securities[1]	74.0						19.9			261.0	21.7		100.1		13.7		16.1		12.9				261.4	261.0
Z	State and local govt. securities	32.2						2.4				7.0	88.0	29.9		0.4		15.6		0.5		0.7		88.0	88.0
AA	Corporate and foreign bonds	6.5							86.9			15.7		1.0		3.3		77.9		2.8		7.9	11.2	107.8	107.8
AB	Corporate stocks[2]	516.3						n.a.	37.8					n.a.		1.1		44.3		23.2		n.a.		561.1	n.a.
AC	1- to 4-family mortgages	11.8	178.2			5.8		2.1		5.9				25.0		107.7		30.1		3.5				186.0	186.0
AD	Other mortgages	29.4	3.2		17.1		34.5		10.9	5.2		2.0		14.5		20.2		23.3		3.5			4.7	92.6	92.6
AE	Consumer credit		70.2					4.4		5.9				26.6		7.4				19.1				70.2	70.2
AF	Bank loans n.e.c.		3.6		6.7		10.7		42.3					79.9		0.2							1.1	80.0	80.0
AG	Other loans		8.8		2.8		0.3	4.4	4.4				2.8	4.8		0.3		7.2	0.5	11.9	0.3	1.1	17.1	61.5	61.5
AH	Open market paper								0.3					3.3								1.1	2.2	9.6	9.6
AI	Federal loans		0.6		2.8		4.5		1.5	31.6					3.3		4.8				0.3	2.2	14.9	31.6	31.6
AJ	Security credit	1.5												7.9						7.2		0.1	0.1	16.7	16.7
AK	To brokers and dealers	1.5												5.4						1.1		0.1		8.1	8.1
AL	To others		8.5											2.5						6.1				8.6	8.6
AM	Trade credit							103.6	58.8	2.5				7.9						1.1		0.1		108.6	80.7
AN	Misc. financial instruments	6.4	2.2	1.6	3.5	3.5	-2.1	3.5		3.5	2.9	2.7		5.4	11.5		2.3	2.5			4.5	12.2	42.5	68.9	86.6

[1] Includes savings bonds and postal savings system deposits.

[2] Assets shown at market value; no specific liability attributed to issuers of stocks for amounts outstanding.

[3] Net of trade credit assets.

[4] Prepaid premiums and benefits payable. Distributed as assets to consumer and business sectors. For description see Nov. 1962 BULL., p. 1406.

[5] Not elsewhere classified.

NOTE.—For description of sectors and transaction categories, see Aug. 1959 BULL., pp. 846–57.

These asset and liability levels are consistent with those shown in the 1963 Supplement to the flow of funds accounts and the net changes over 1963; they do not incorporate revisions in underlying data made since last August, most notably in consumer credit and mortgages.

Source: *Federal Reserve Bulletin*, Apr., 1964, p. 517.

Table 16-4

FINANCIAL ASSETS AND LIABILITIES
FOR NONFINANCIAL BUSINESS CORPORATIONS, 1952, 1957, AND 1962
(In Billions of Dollars)

Item	1952	1957	1962
Total financial assets	122.1	158.1	211.7
Demand deposits and currency	28.7	32.1	31.8
Time deposits	0.9	1.0	6.2
U.S. gov. securities	19.8	18.4	19.4
State and local obligations............	0.7	1.5	2.4
Consumer credit	5.9	7.6	10.3
Finance company paper.............	1.2	1.8	3.7
Trade credit	47.0	66.5	95.6
Foreign exchange and investments	17.9	29.3	42.3
Total liabilities, except Stock			
and Tax Accruals..................	115.6	164.8	225.0
Corporate bonds	43.4	62.7	83.2
Other mortgages	14.0	20.6	35.2
Bank loans, n.e.c....................	16.4	26.0	38.0
Loans from finance companies,			
commercial paper and gov. loans	2.4	3.8	7.8
Trade debt	35.8	46.8	53.4
Direct foreign investment	3.5	4.8	7.5

Source: *Flow of Funds Accounts, 1945–1962, 1963 Supplement*, Board of Governors of the Federal Reserve System, pp. 5–6.

companies, sales of commercial paper and government loans, and direct foreign investment all rose at a more rapid rate than total liabilities. Bonds rose by about the same rate as the total, while trade debt increased at a lesser rate. Corporate bonds remained the largest nonstock liability over the decade, and trade debt also held second position during the period.

Common stocks are not shown in the table because the estimates of corporate stock prepared for Table 16-2 include not only the effect of increased issues, but of increased prices. The importance of stock as a source of funds to corporations in recent years will be considered later when we treat the financial flows. It is of some interest, now, to note that the stock estimate of $117 billion for 1952 would place stock as the most important liability. However, the market value of stock includes a valuation for retained earnings as well as anticipated earnings, so that such a conclusion would be misleading. As we shall see later, common stock has changed at a very low rate over the decade 1952–1962.

THE FLOW OF FUNDS

Equations and illustrations were used in Chapters 11 and 12 to indicate the nature of the funds flows for the entire economy and the individual sectors. Actual flow matrices are prepared on a quarterly basis, in both raw and seasonally adjusted versions, and on an annual basis by the Federal Reserve. These data appear regularly in the

Table 16-5

SUMMARY OF FLOW OF FUNDS ACCOUNTS FOR FOURTH QUARTER, 1963—NOT SEASONALLY ADJUSTED
(In Billions of Dollars)

	Sector / Transaction Category	Consumer and Nonprofit Org. U	S	Farm U	S	Non-corporate U	S	Corporate U	S	U.S. Gov. U	S	State and Local U	S	Banking System U	S	Savings Institutions U	S	Insurance U	S	Finance n.e.c.** U	S	Rest of the World U	S	All Sectors U	S	Discrepancy	Natl. Saving and Investment
A	Gross saving		22.7		2.1		3.5		11.6		-5.4		-1.1		-0.2		-0.7		-0.7		0.4		-1.4		31.6	-5.7	33.0
B	Capital consumption		12.6		1.1		2.3		8.2																24.2		24.2
C	Net saving A – B		10.0						3.4																7.4		8.7
D	Gross investment, E + J	27.2		2.1		3.5		10.2		-6.0		0.5		0.6		-0.7		0.7		-0.4		-1.1		36.7		0.7	38.4
E	Private capital expenditures, net	22.0		1.2		3.4		10.5																37.3			37.3
F	Consumer durables	15.9																						15.9			15.9
G	Residential construction	5.2				0.7		0.7																6.6			6.6
H	Plant and equipment	1.0		1.2		2.8		9.3																14.5			14.5
I	Inventory change			0.1		-0.2		0.5																0.4			0.4
J	Net financial investments, K – L	5.1		0.9		0.1		-0.3		-6.0		0.5		0.5		-0.7		0.6		-0.4		-1.1		0.7		0.7	1.1
K	Financial uses, net	13.8		-0.9		0.6		7.2		-1.2		2.7		12.1		4.8		3.2		2.2		0.5		45.9			1.6
L	Financial sources		8.7		0.5				7.5		4.8		2.3		11.6		5.4		3.2		2.6		1.6		46.6		0.5
M	Gold and official U.S. foreign exchange										*				*								*		*		
N	Treasury currency									*					*										*		
O	Demand deposits and curr.	3.5						2.5				1.7			7.8			0.1		0.1		0.1		6.2	7.8		
P	Private domestic														10.2		0.5				0.1			8.4	10.2		
Q	U.S. gov.									-2.4					-2.5									-2.4	-2.5		
R	Foreign														0.1							0.1		0.1	0.1		
S	Time and svgs. accounts	5.3											0.7		3.3		0.1							7.9	7.9		
T	At coml. banks	0.8													3.3									3.3	3.3		
U	At svgs. institutions	4.5															4.6							4.6	4.6		
V	Life insurance reserves	1.0																1.0						1.0			
W	Pension fund reserves	2.4									*		0.8					1.5						2.4			
X	Credit market instr	2.3	8.5	-0.1	0.6	0.6	3.2	2.4	5.2	1.2		1.4	1.4	11.1	0.2	4.0	0.8	3.1		2.0	2.2	0.9	-0.2	26.8	26.8	0.9	
Y	U.S. gov. securities	1.6						1.1		4.3	3.9		-0.1	2.1		-0.1		0.1		-0.6		-0.1	-0.1	3.9	3.9	*	
Z	State and local oblig	0.7									1.4		1.4	0.4		-0.1		0.3						1.4	1.4		
AA	Corp. and foreign bonds	0.2							1.2							0.5		1.0		0.5		0.1	-0.1	2.2	2.2		
AB	Corp. stocks	0.1							-0.1									0.5	1.0	*		0.1	0.1	0.1	0.1		
AC	1- to 4-family mtgs	0.1	4.8				1.2		-0.1	0.1				0.7		3.3	0.8	0.5		0.4	1.0			4.6	4.6		
AD	Other mortgages	0.6		0.3		0.6	1.2	1.4	1.4					0.5	0.5	0.8	0.8	1.0		*				3.0	3.0		
AE	Consumer credit		3.4					1.4						0.7		0.2				0.7				3.4	3.4		
AF	Bank loans n.e.c.	0.1	0.1		-0.1	-0.1	1.4		3.0		1.1		0.1	6.0		*					1.1		0.5	6.0	6.0		
AG	Other loans	0.1	0.2	-0.3		0.7	-0.1		-0.1	1.1	0.5		0.1	0.7		0.8	0.2	-0.1	-0.1	0.8	-0.3	0.2	0.4	2.3	2.2		
AH	Open market paper			-0.3			*	*	*					0.7			*				-0.3	-0.1		-0.2	-0.2		
AI	Federal loans		*	-0.3		0.3		*		1.1		0.1		0.2		0.8	-0.2				-0.2	0.2		1.1	1.1		
AJ	Security credit	0.2	0.2					0.1						0.1				0.1		0.1	0.1			0.5	0.5		
AK	To brokers and dealers	0.2	0.2											0.1							-0.1			0.3	0.3		
AL	To other		0.2					0.1						*						0.2		*			0.2		
AM	Trade credit	-0.8		-0.4		-2.3	-0.4	0.1	2.2	0.1		*						-0.1			0.1			-0.3	-0.3	-0.3	
AN	Equity in noncorp. business	-0.8		-0.4						0.2												0.3	0.6		2.1	-0.8	
AO	Misc. financial trans.	0.6	0.2	*		*	*	0.6	*	0.1	0.2	0.1		0.8	0.3	0.2	*		0.1	0.1	0.1	0.3	0.6	2.1	1.4	1.4	
AP	Sector discrepancies, A – D	-4.5		*		*		1.3		0.6		-1.6		-0.4		*		-0.2				-0.3		-5.0		-5.1	-5.5

* Less than $50 million.
**Not elsewhere classified.
Source: *Federal Reserve Bulletin*, Apr., 1964, p. 508.

Federal Reserve Bulletin. The matrix for the fourth quarter, 1963, is reproduced as Table 16-5.

Examination of the table and comparison with the simpler illustrations of Chapter 11 reveal an immediate difference—the actual flows do not show the equalities of the illustrations or of the equations in Chapters 11 and 12. The fault lies not in the equations, but in the data. The flow-of-funds estimators do not have access to sets of accounts for each sector of the economy. Estimates come from a variety of independent sources, which are not all consistent or complete. The result is that the estimates do not always, not even usually, show the equalities that a perfect picture of reality would reveal.

Data discrepancies can be estimated only where the estimates fail to show an equality that should exist. Thus, the next to last vertical column corrects, for total economy, errors in gross savings and gross investment, which should be equal, and net financial investment, which should be zero for the entire economy. Corrections are also made for individual transaction categories, such as trade credit, where independent estimates are available separately for sources and uses of funds. The latter is not always the case; e.g., both sources and uses of mortgages come from the regulatory authorities concerned with the institutions issuing mortgages. However, where separate estimates are available, a discrepancy exists when sources do not equal uses for a particular transaction category. All the discrepancies shown in the vertical column should be treated as corrections in the "Use" column for "All Sectors."

Row AP indicates sector discrepancies. These are only correct for the equality of gross savings and gross investment by sector. It should be noted that sector discrepancies are always treated as corrections to the Use column, although gross savings and/or gross investment could be incorrect.

Discrepancies aside, it is probably worth repeating that the equalities shown in the flow table are no indication of equilibrium. On an *ex post* basis, the equalities will always hold because of the underlying accounting rationale. We have no comparable *ex ante* data, and it is these data on plans and expectations which determine whether or not equilibrium has been achieved. When *ex ante* data are not in balance, GNP, interest rates, and securities yield change until, finally, the actual equalities emerge. But in this process, the various sectors encounter surprises to which they must adjust. Thus, the flow table cannot be viewed as a statement of the desires or plans of any sector. It is purely a historical record of the results of the interaction of millions of plans in the economy.

CORPORATE FLOWS The procedure used to examine sectoral balance sheets, looking at three observations, will not be followed in considering corporate flows. Flows are net, i.e., they show change in the balance sheet item, and are therefore relatively unstable. Viewing the flow for a given year can lead to very erroneous conclusions. For example, between 1956 and 1957, the corporate bond flow rose from $3.7 billion to $6.3 billion. By 1959, the corporate bond flow had fallen to $3 billion. Capital expenditures also provide an interesting illustration of how variable flows are from year to year. In 1957, capital expenditures were $33.1 billion, but fell to $23.9 billion in the following year.

As an alternative, we shall consider cumulated flows for the more important flow items. Flows will be cumulated, e.g., from 1946 through 1962, and we shall show the cumulated totals as of 1952, 1957, and 1962. The major advantages of cumulating flows include: Changes which have occurred over a slice of time can be considered without direct reference to earlier events; an estimate can be derived of the real asset components of the balance sheet which can be compared with the methods of financing the real asset acquisitions; and we have a measure of the importance of stock financing without having to include the effects of price changes on stocks that were issued in a prior period.

Looking first at aggregate uses, there was a tendency over the period for capital expenditures to increase at a slightly more rapid rate than financial asset expenditures. Over the 1946–'52 period, $0.31 was spent on financial assets for every dollar spent on real assets. The cumulated flow for 1946–'62 shows that slightly more than $0.28 was spent on financial assets per dollar expenditure on real assets.

As indicated in the first chapter, internal sources of funds predominate in the financing picture for business corporations. Indeed, internal sources became more important over the period of 1946–'62. For the six-year cumulated total during 1946–'52, external funds provided about 36 per cent of total sources. For the 16-year total, 1946–'62, external funds were only 33 per cent of the total sources.

The composition of internal funds changed radically over the period of 1946–'62. The cumulated total for retained earnings roughly doubled between 1946 and 1962, while cumulated capital consumption allowances increased almost 4.7 times.

The meaning of this change becomes clear if we adopt the general assumption that capital consumption allowances are a reasonable estimate of capital expenditures made to replace worn-out real assets. Between 1946 and 1952, about 59 per cent of capital expenditures were net additions to the capital stock, i.e., not replacements of worn-out assets. Between 1946 and 1957, the ratio of new capital expenditures total dropped to 48.2 per cent, and the ratio declined to 38.3 per cent for 1946–'62.

Another way of viewing the same phenomenon is to calculate the annual growth rate in cumulated net capital expenditures (total capital expenditures less capital consumption allowances) for 1952–'57 and 1957–'63. The rate of growth for 1952–'57 was about 33 per cent, but it was only 25 per cent for 1957–'62. To the extent that prices for capital goods have risen, depreciation allowances understate actual replacement needs, and the growth rate of additions to the capital stock will be less than shown.

Turning to the specific financial assets, trade credit is the largest investment. Its twin on the liabilities side, trade debt, is substantially smaller, indicating that the corporate sector is a net trade creditor. The importance of the trade credit item is clearer if a set of adjustments are made. If trade credit is subtracted from financial assets in Table 16-6 and trade debt is

Table 16-6

CUMULATED ANNUAL FLOWS FOR NONFINANCIAL BUSINESS CORPORATIONS FROM 1946–1952, 1946–1957, AND 1946–1962
(In Billions of Dollars)

Item	1946–'52	1946–'57	1946–'62
Uses			
Total capital expenditures	140.6	281.0	441.2
Total financial assets	43.8	75.2	125.2
Total uses	184.4	356.2	566.4
Plus cumulated discrepancy*	4.3	11.0	27.9
Total uses plus discrepancy	188.7	367.2	594.3
Sources			
Retained earnings	61.9	94.5	126.7
Capital consumption	58.3	145.3	272.0
Total internal funds.................	120.2	239.8	398.7
Total external liabilities	68.5	127.4	195.6
Total sources	188.7	367.2	594.3
Detail on Selected Financial Assets			
Demand deposits and currency	9.7	13.1	10.2
Time deposits	—	1.0	5.3
U.S. government securities.............	−2.3	−3.7	−2.9
Trade credit	28.1	47.6	76.8
Foreign exchange and investments	5.7	12.7	22.2
Detail on External Liabilities			
Corporate bonds	20.4	40.1	61.1
Corporate stock	10.4	20.5	30.1
Mortages	7.7	14.4	29.0
Bank loans, n.e.c.	10.6	20.2	31.1
Other loans	1.5	2.6	6.8
Trade debt.........................	17.8	28.8	36.3

Source: *Flow of Funds Accounts*, 1945–1962, 1963 Supplement, Board of Governors of the Federal Reserve System, pp. 5–6.
*Discrepancy includes a very small rounding error.

subtracted from external sources, the difference between the two items, net trade credit, can be added back into financial assets. We can then see the amount of trade credit that had to be financed by means other than trade debt. The cumulated net trade credit total between 1946 and 1962 was $40.5 billion, over 45 per cent of financial assets. Another way of looking at the importance of trade credit is as follows:

Billions

1946–'62 Cumulated capital expenditures	$441.2
Less 1946–'62 cumulated internal funds	398.7
To be financed externally, capital expenditures......................	$ 42.5
1946–'62 Cumulated financial assets, net of trade credit	48.4
1946–'62 Cumulated net trade credit	40.5
Total cumulated uses..	$131.4
Plus cumulated discrepancy	27.9
Total cumulated uses + discrepancy	$159.3
Total cumulated external funds, except trade debt	$159.3

In words, cumulated net trade credit absorbed about as much external funds as capital expenditures, about 25 per cent of external sources, over the period 1946–'62. Even when trade debt is subtracted, no other financial asset flow was as large as the investment in trade credit.

Next in importance as a financial use of funds were foreign investments and holdings of foreign currency. The cumulated total grew at an annually compounded rate of about 15 per cent between 1952 and 1962 as compared with capital expenditures of the sector, which grew at a rate of 12 per cent over the decade. Though the difference between the two rates is not great, it provides some indication that foreign investments were more attractive to the corporate sector than domestic investments. Although not as convincing as the capital expenditures data, this is an additional indication of slow corporate growth.

Holdings of cash increased between 1952 and 1957, but declined between 1957 and 1962. Government security holdings declined net over the decade, but there was a rise between 1957 and 1962. Time deposits, though not large even in 1962, cumulated rapidly between 1957 and 1962. Considering cash, government securities, and time deposits together, the 1957–'62 period may be described as a period during which near-cash earning assets were substituted for cash.

The external liabilities are conveniently divided into three groups: corporate stock or equity; long-term debt consisting of corporate bonds and mortgages; and other debt, including bank loans not elsewhere classified, other loans which are mainly from finance companies, and trade debt. Other loans are primarily short-term. However, some of the bank loans may extend for more than one year. Grouped this way, the cumulative flows for the dates indicated are in billion of dollars:

	1946–'52	*1952–'57*	*1957–'62*
Common corporate stock..........	10.4	12.4	12.0
Long-term debt	28.1	33.0	43.3
Other debt	29.9	25.0	24.2

Debt issues, both long- and short-term, were far more important than stock issues. Long-term debt exceeded other debt in significance from 1952 on, and in the period 1957–'62, long-term debt flows exceeded the total of all other external sources.

Another interesting way of viewing sources is to consider the ratio of cumulated debt flows to cumulated equity flows, which is similar to the debt/equity ratio used to analyze balance sheets. Retained earnings flows are included with corporate stock. The ratios of cumulated debt flows/cumulated equity flows are

	1946–'52	1952–'57	1957–'62
Total debt/equity...................	0.8	1.2	1.4
Long-term debt/equity	0.4	0.7	0.9

One explanation, offered by David Durand, for the increased use of debt financing in the postwar period is that debt funds have been relatively cheap because of the growth of financial institutions, the largest of which are restricted in their ability to purchase equity claims. The inability of these institutions to shift from purchasing debt claims to equity creates a market biased in favor of debt, holding interest rates down, and generally making it easier and cheaper for firms to issue debt. Another argument is that stockholders oppose additional stock issues. They are willing to absorb the added risks of negative leverage and rigidities of cash outflows in order to increase the probability of earning long-term capital gains, which are taxed more favorably than ordinary income. It also can be argued that the postwar period has been one of substantial stability, so that the probability of adverse leverage effects resulting from debt has been assessed as low.

An additional factor may be found in the declining rate both of expenditures on new capital goods and of net savings. If capital expenditures had risen at a more rapid rate, firms would have been forced to use new stock issues more than was the case in order to avoid unacceptably high debt/equity ratios. Had the growth of retained earnings been larger, the use of debt would have been less necessary. The combination of a low level of capital expenditures and a low level of net savings resulted in the financing patterns observed above.

SECTORS SUPPLYING
EXTERNAL SOURCES

Aside from the obvious sectors supplying funds, such as the commercial banks supplying bank loans, it is not easy to identify the supplying sectors. The main reason for the difficulty is that corporations issue no unique claim. Banks, insurance companies, and finance companies, to name a few, also issue corporate stock. Corporate bonds are issued by finance companies as well as by nonfinancial corporations. And, of course, many sectors issue nonresidential mortgages, trade debt, and other loans. The best that can be done is to concentrate on the two claims in which business corporations predominate: corporate bonds, of which nonfinancial corporations issued about 73 per cent of the total claims cumulated during 1946–'62; and corporate stock, of which nonfinancial corporations had issued almost 62 per cent of total stock cumulated over the same period.

The cumulated stock and bond flows of the important supplying sectors are shown in Table 16-7. It should be noted again that we have no good way of determining which of these sectors bought issues of nonfinancial corporations predominantly.

Table 16-7

CUMULATED STOCK AND CORPORATE
BOND PURCHASES FROM 1946–1962, BY SECTOR
(In Billions of Dollars)

Instrument and Sector	1946–'52	1952–'57	1957–'62
CORPORATE BONDS			
Total	23.2	48.1	76.6
Insurance sector	23.4	41.6	59.7
State and local governments	1.6	5.2	13.2
Other sectors	−1.8	1.3	3.5
CORPORATE STOCK			
Total	13.2	28.9	48.8
Households and nonprofit sector	8.2	15.1	18.5
Insurance sector	3.4	8.5	19.6
Finance, n.e.c.	1.5	4.1	8.7
Other sectors	0.1	1.2	42.0

Source: *Flow of Funds Accounts, 1945–1962, 1963 Supplement*, Board of Directors of Federal Reserve System, pp. 4–12.

Much of what is shown in the table is quite familiar from earlier chapters, except that, in this comparison, the real sectors have been included. The picture for corporate bonds is that life insurance companies have clearly taken over the role of predominant supplier of funds. The state and local government holdings reflect the growth in pension funds for civil servants and public school systems.

The pattern for stock indicates also the tendency toward institutionalization of the holdings of claims on real sectors. Up to 1957, households had been the predominant supplier of funds in the stock markets. However, between 1957 and 1962, all but $3 billion of the approximately $20 billion of stock issued were by financial institutions, specifically noninsured pension funds, mutual funds, and fire and casualty insurance companies. This does not mean that households no longer invested funds; households apparently have found the indirect claims issued by financial institutions more attractive than the direct stock issues of business.

STOCK PRICES
AND GROWTH
Over the postwar period, stock prices have moved up dramatically. Standard and Poors' price index of 500 stocks moved from an annual average of 15.17 in 1947 to a high of 79.21 for the week ending March 21, 1964. The movement was somewhat discontinuous, with the annual average moving up by 11 points in 1955 (from 29.69 to 40.49), by 11 points in 1959 (from 46.24 to 57.38), by 11 points in 1961 (from 55.85 to 66.27), and the most recent jump in 1964 from the 1963 average of 69.87. How can these sensational price increase, over 500 per cent in an 18-year period, be reconciled with the evidence that the corporate sector, the primary issuer of these securities, has been in a period of slow growth? Particularly, how can the price increase be explained when most of it has occurred in the latter half of the period, while corporate growth was considerably slower than in the immediate period after the war?

Many explanations have been offered for increased demand for stock. The tax factor has been cited as a cause for increasing stock demand. Stock price gains on securities held for more than six months are taxed at half the rate at which ordinary income is taxed. Convincing data to demonstrate the tax effect are not yet available but, if it is an important factor, the evidence in 1965 and 1966 should indicate a weakening of demand for stock as a result of the newly passed reduction in the personal income tax rates.

Another factor that can be considered is the speculative fever caused by price increases. The argument is that demand increases because investors believe that future price movements will at least equal those of the past. This argument cannot be easily denied, given the financial history of the United States. However, it is hard to credit it as being as important in the period since World War II as it was, say, in the 1920's. Regulations on margin buying and short sales as well as the truth laws applied to registered corporations work against speculation. Further, most of the stock purchases have been made by professional investors, who, presumably, are less prone to speculative excesses and wishful thinking.

Supply factors may also have played a role in the stock price rise. To see this, we shall consider the relevant periods as 1947–'54 and 1955–'62. Although stock prices moved up in the earlier period, the large increases took place in the latter period. The major source of funds for stock investment comes, directly or via financial institutions, from households. Household savings available for investment in financial assets, i.e., gross household savings less household capital expenditures, totaled $48.1 billion over the years 1947–'54. Net stock issues by nonfinancial corporations totaled $12.8 billion during the same period. From 1955 to 1962, household savings available for investment in financial assets totaled $85.3 billion, whereas net stock issues totaled $16.3 billion.

If the funds available for financial investment are treated as a rough index of the supply of funds, part of which would be invested in stock, and the stock issues are treated as part of the demand for funds, it seems clear that supply increased substantially more rapidly than demand over the entire 16-year period. Between 1947 and 1954, about 26.6 per cent of household savings, less capital expenditures, were required to absorb nonfinancial corporate stock issues. Had the same share of savings been used to buy corporate stock from 1955 to 1962, almost $22.7 billion of stock would have had to be issued, about $6.4 billion more than were actually issued.

It is one of the most elementary facts of economic life that when supply is less than demand, assuming flexible prices, price rises. The irony of this analysis is that the relatively small supply of stock which contributed to the sharp increase in stock prices was caused by a decline in the rate of growth of the nonfinancial corporate sector.

THE FINANCIAL ECONOMY:
A SUMMARY

In the first 10 chapters of this book, we concentrated on the internal problems of the firm: the variables determining its choice of assets and capital structure. But the decisions made by the firm are shaped in large degree by the condition of its environment, by the extent or lack of prosperity, by the stability of the economy, and by the willingness of the economy to provide funds. The actions of the individual firm have little impact on the total economy. However, the aggregate actions of all firms, as measured by the business corporate sector, have considerable impact on the rest of the economy.

This complex set of interlocking relationships is what is portrayed by the flow of funds. If the sectors of the flow of funds were unchanging in their various roles, full understanding would be quite difficult. As we have shown, the sectors change. In the brief period since 1952, for example, commercial banks became less important relative to other financial institutions, while noninsured pension funds moved to the position of a major financial institution. And the use of financial institutions as intermediaries in the saving-investing process increased substantially. It would take a braver man than I to forecast what the flow of funds will look like in 1972. Certainly, it is likely that the changes will be as great as were observed between 1952 and 1962.

This book has concentrated on a particular sector—the business corporation. In a sense, the concentration makes the study somewhat narrow. It is believed, however, that the method of analysis used, the study of balance sheets, has some general applicability. If households, government, and the various financial institutions can be profitably studied by considering the determinants of their balance sheets, the reader has received not only a technique which is applicable to the study of the firm, but a general set of tools that will enhance the study of any sector.

Index

2